Praise for *Free Speech in Its Forgotten Years*

"Rabban's book offers a valuable historical perspective on free speech in general, and speech about sex in particular."
  – Marjorie Heins, *New York Law Journal*

"Rabban shows that, contrary to popular and current scholarly belief, federal and state courts regularly decided free speech issues during the approximate half century between the end of the Civil War and the end of the First World War.... Rabban rescues from neglect the small and brave group of libertarians who stood up for individual autonomy against the power of both state and church.... Rabban interestingly and compellingly makes his case that there was, during the 'forgotten years' from about 1870 to about 1920, a substantial body of free speech law rarely mentioning the First Amendment and almost invariably repressive."
  – Jeremiah S. Gutman, *The Federal Lawyer*

"... he has unearthed a lost world of legal thought. By bringing the First Amendment's 'forgotten years' back to light, he has done all of us a great service."
  – Daniel A. Farber, *Constitutional Commentary*

"In this meticulously researched book, he seamlessly knits together his earlier essays and expands upon them, achieving an unusually successful blend of historical research and legal analysis. It will be indispensible reading, not only for legal historians, but for anyone who wants to understand liberalism and its curiously convoluted history over the last century and a half."
  – Thomas L. Haskell, *Texas Law Review*

"What a wonderful piece of research. Professor of Law David M. Rabban has exposed, for the first time, the meaning, suppression, debate, and judicial attention given to free speech between the Civil War and World War I.... The epilogue, one of the best chapters in the book, draws current parallels to prewar progressive thought. This is an enormously important book for attorneys, historians, and librarians. The author presents a fascinating story and challenges much that we thought we knew about the First Amendment and offers new perspectives on the history of American speech reform during a period in our history which previously had been ignored. Everyone, especially those devoted to civil liberties, will want to read this exceptional book."
  – Gene D. Lanier, *Newsletter on Intellectual Freedom*

"The gulf that separates contemporary understanding of the First Amendment from that which prevailed in earlier years emerges with striking clarity in this absorbing book.... Rabban's examination...of the place of freedom of speech in the thought of social progressives like John Dewey and Herbert Croly opens an important and heretofore neglected chapter in American intellectual history."
– Terrance Sandalow, *Academe*

"This enlightening work fills a void in First Amendment civil liberties studies. Deserving careful scrutiny by scholars and others alike, it is highly recommended for all libraries."
– Stephen Kent Shaw, *Library Journal* (starred review)

"... the book makes a compelling case that commentators have wrongly ignored the rich history of free speech between the Alien and Sedition Acts of 1798 and the Espionage Act of 1917...his work is a valuable contribution to the study of free speech as a historical idea. Although Rabban accounts for notable decisions often ignored by commentators, this book is more than a legal history of the most precious of our civil liberties.... By considering the interplay between these decisions and legal doctrine, Rabban enriches our appreciation of the complex relationship between social forces and legal doctrine. David Rabban's *Free Speech in Its Forgotten Years* belongs in the library of anyone with a genuine interest in freedom of expression."
– Dale A. Herbeck, *Journal of Communication*

"It would be hard to overestimate the value of *Free Speech in Its Forgotten Years* as we reshape First Amendment theory and doctrine in the next century."
– Paul Finkelman, *Boston University Law Review*

"*Free Speech in Its Forgotten Years* fundamentally revises our understanding of the history of free speech in America between the 1870s and World War I. Rabban skillfully recovers libertarian and antilibertarian attitudes toward speech that a long tradition of twentieth-century commentary has ignored."
– Edward White, *University Professor and John B. Minor Professor of Law and History, University of Virginia*

"Future scholarship on the First Amendment will henceforth begin with this exceptional book. Rabban wholly reorients free speech history with newly mined facts and sharp insights about two lost generations of scholars, activists, and their fierce struggles."
– Norman Dorsen, *Stokes Professor of Law, New York University, and President, ACLU, 1976–91*

Free Speech
in Its Forgotten Years

Most American historians and legal scholars assume that controversies and litigation about free speech began abruptly during World War I. Rabban's book reveals that this conventional view is incorrect. There was substantial popular, legal, and intellectual debate about free speech issues between the Civil War and World War I. Important free speech controversies, which often involved the activities of sex reformers and labor unions, preceded the Espionage Act of 1917. Scores of legal cases presented free speech issues before the famous postwar opinions of Justices Holmes and Brandeis. A significant organization, the Free Speech League, became a principled defender of free expression two decades before the establishment of the ACLU in 1920.

Knowledge of this prewar period demonstrates that World War I produced a major transformation in American liberalism. Progressives who had viewed constitutional rights as barriers to needed social reforms came to appreciate the value of political dissent during its wartime repression. They subsequently misrepresented the prewar judicial hostility to free speech claims and obscured prior libertarian defenses of free speech based on commitments to individual autonomy.

The history recounted in this book sheds light on important current debates about "rights talk" and about the complicated historical enterprise of studying ideas over time. It also compels significant reevaluations of familiar figures, such as Justices Holmes and Brandeis, and important organizations, such as the ACLU.

CAMBRIDGE HISTORICAL STUDIES IN AMERICAN LAW AND SOCIETY

Editors

Arthur McEvoy   *University of Wisconsin Law School*
Christopher Tomlins   *American Bar Foundation*

Previously published in the series:
Michael Grossberg: *A Judgment for Solomon:
The d'Hauteville Case and Legal Experience in Antebellum America*

Free Speech
in Its Forgotten Years

David M. Rabban
University of Texas at Austin

CAMBRIDGE
UNIVERSITY PRESS

PUBLISHED BY THE PRESS SYNDICATE OF THE UNIVERSITY OF CAMBRIDGE
The Pitt Building, Trumpington Street, Cambridge CB2 1RP, United Kingdom

CAMBRIDGE UNIVERSITY PRESS
The Edinburgh Building, Cambridge CB2 2RU, UK   http://www.cup.cam.ac.uk
40 West 20th Street, New York, NY 10011-4211, USA   http://www.cup.org
10 Stamford Road, Oakleigh, Melbourne 3166, Australia

First published 1997
First paperback editon 1998

Printed in the United States of America

Typeset in Baskerville

A catalogue record for this book is available from the British Library

Library of Congress Cataloguing-in-Publication Data is available

ISBN 0-521-62013-9 hardback

To My Parents
Elana and Meyer Rabban

Contents

Acknowledgments

My interest in the history of free speech in the United States developed while I was a student at Stanford Law School between 1971 and 1974. During my three years at Stanford, I took general survey courses in constitutional law and American legal history, advanced courses in constitutional law, and seminars in constitutional history and free speech. As I completed these classes, I increasingly was struck by the common, though largely unarticulated, assumption that no significant legal interpretation of free speech had occurred between 1801, when the Sedition Act of 1798 expired, and 1917, when Congress passed the Espionage Act soon after the United States entered World War I. By the end of my third year of law school, I questioned this assumption. Drawing on my rudimentary knowledge of American history, I thought of numerous social and political controversies during the nineteenth and early twentieth centuries that seemed likely to have generated free speech activities. Just in the decades immediately before 1917, I suspected, agitation by workers, anarchists, and advocates of birth control tested the meaning of free speech.

Classes taught by two of my law professors, Yosal Rogat and Gerald Gunther, reinforced my interest in searching for a possibly forgotten history of free speech before World War I. Professors Rogat and Gunther challenged the prevailing view that the famous opinion by Justice Oliver Wendell Holmes, Jr., in *Schenck v. United States*[1] (1919) marked the beginning of significant First Amendment adjudication in the United States. They both emphasized that Judge Learned Hand's decision in an earlier Espionage Act case, *Masses Publishing Co. v. Patten*[2] (1917), provided an attractive doctrinal alternative to the "clear and present danger" test Holmes announced in *Schenck*. Yosal Rogat had uncovered a few other lower court decisions in Espionage Act cases and pointed out similarities between several prewar opinions by Justice Holmes and his later Espionage Act opinions.[3] Perhaps, I thought, additional free speech cases preceded *Schenck*.

---

[1] 249 U.S. 47 (1919).
[2] 244 F. 535 (S.D.N.Y.), rev'd, 246 F. 24 (2d Cir. 1917).
[3] See Gerald Gunther, Learned Hand and the Origins of Modern First Amendment Doctrine: Some Fragments of History, 27 Stan. L. Rev. 719 (1975); Yosal Rogat and James M. O'Fallon, Mr. Justice Holmes: A Dissenting Opinion – The Speech Cases, 36 Stan. L. Rev. 1349 (1984).

x Acknowledgments

Gerald Gunther encouraged my interest in writing a seminar paper about the history of free speech before World War I even though neither of us knew what, if anything, I might find. For many years and in countless ways, he has supported my efforts to develop my seminar paper into what has now become this book.

A fellowship awarded in 1979 by Project '87, jointly sponsored by the American Historical Association and the American Political Science Association, allowed me to spend four months at the Brookings Institution, where I did much of the work on the long manuscript that preceded my first published articles on the forgotten history of free speech. I appreciate the personal interest James MacGregor Burns and Richard B. Morris, the cochairs of Project '87, took in my work. Paul L. Murphy, a member of the Project '87 board and a pioneering scholar of the history of free speech in the twentieth century, provided expert advice as well as encouragement during my fellowship. Andrew Lipps read every draft of my original manuscript and had many useful suggestions throughout. He provided invaluable intellectual companionship and reassurance during the lonely process of writing. After I completed the manuscript, Jamie Kalven and Jonathan Knight made exceptionally detailed and helpful written criticisms.

I am grateful for the subsequent institutional and personal support I have received. Grants from the American Bar Foundation in 1981–82 and from the National Endowment for the Humanities in 1987–88 assisted the completion of two articles. During a fellowship in 1994–95 at the Woodrow Wilson International Center for Scholars, I finished the first draft of this book. I have received generous research support from the University of Texas School of Law since I joined the faculty in 1983, but the stimulating intellectual life at the law school has made an even greater contribution.

In each of the five law review articles on which this book is based,[4] I have thanked the many people who read and commented on my work. I want to reiterate my thanks here to those who have contributed to several of these articles: Jerold Auerbach, Daniel Ernst, Mark Graber, Stanley Katz, Michael Klarman, Douglas Laycock, Sanford Levinson, Staughton Lynd, Robert Post, Scot

---

[4] David M. Rabban, The First Amendment in Its Forgotten Years, 90 Yale L. J. 514 (1981); David M. Rabban, The Emergence of Modern First Amendment Doctrine, 50 U. Chi. L. Rev. 1205 (1983); David M. Rabban, The Free Speech League, the ACLU, and Changing Conceptions of Free Speech in American History, 45 Stan. L. Rev. 47 (1992); David M. Rabban, The IWW Free Speech Fights and Popular Conceptions of Free Expression Before World War I, 80 Va. L. Rev. 1055 (1994); and David M. Rabban, Free Speech in Progressive Social Thought, 74 Texas L. Rev. 951 (1996).

Powe, Frederick Schauer, Jordan Steiker, Mark Tushnet, William Van Alstyne, Samuel Walker, and G. Edward White.

Willy Forbath and Laura Kalman read a late draft of this book with extraordinary care and thoughtfulness. Willy wrote a lengthy, chapter-by-chapter critique. Laura provided a running commentary on the manuscript; page after page contained detailed reactions, questions, and suggestions.

Arthur McEvoy and Christopher Tomlins, the editors of this series for Cambridge University Press, cared enough about my project to make me think hard about the many thematic, stylistic, and organizational issues presented by my effort to transform many related articles into a cohesive book. I especially thank Chris Tomlins, the primary editor of this book, for believing that it deserved the substantial time he devoted to making it better. Chris challenged me throughout the editorial process while always making clear that the book should be the one I wanted to write.

Elana and Meyer Rabban have followed my work on the history of free speech both as loving parents and as interested readers. Their own lives have demonstrated their respect for intellectual integrity and freedom of expression. I dedicate this book to them.

Introduction

Most scholars divide the history of free speech in the United States into three major periods: (1) from the framing of the Constitution through the prosecutions under the Alien and Sedition Acts of 1798; (2) from roughly 1800 until World War I; and (3) from the passage of the Espionage Act of 1917 until the present. They assume intense debate and activity over the meaning of free speech during the first period, negligible judicial and rare general attention to free speech issues during the second period, and the creation of the modern First Amendment during the third period. They typically view Justice Holmes's 1919 decision in *Schenck v. United States*[1] as the Supreme Court's initial confrontation with the meaning of free speech, and "Freedom of Speech in War Time,"[2] published three months later by Professor Zechariah Chafee, Jr., as the earliest major law review article dealing with the subject. They similarly regard the American Civil Liberties Union (ACLU), founded in 1920, as the first significant organization devoted to defending freedom of expression. Many perceive the legal history of free speech since World War I primarily as the development of a "worthy tradition"[3] of protection for unpopular speech, begun by the famous, mostly dissenting, opinions of Justices Holmes and Brandeis from 1919 through the 1920s, and reaching fruition in a series of landmark decisions by the liberal Supreme Court in the 1960s and early 1970s.

When I graduated from law school in 1974, I already doubted the assumed absence of legal disputes over free speech during the long period between 1800 and 1917. The social unrest of the late nineteenth and early twentieth centuries – the years immediately before the supposed beginning of First Amendment jurisprudence – seemed especially likely to have produced debate and litigation about free speech. My hunch proved correct, and this book is the result. It uncovers the extensive and diverse history of free speech

---

[1] Schenck v. United States, 249 U.S. 47 (1919).
[2] Zechariah Chafee, Jr., Freedom of Speech in War Time, 32 Harv. L. Rev. 932 (1919).
[3] See Harry Kalven, Jr., A Worthy Tradition: Freedom of Speech in America (Jamie Kalven, ed., 1988).

1

between 1870 and 1920, reveals a key transformation in American liberalism, and suggests the advisability of further research into the still largely unknown years between 1800 and the Civil War. This book also sheds light on key current debates about the nature of historical understanding and about the limits of "rights talk" in interpreting the First Amendment.

THE FORGOTTEN YEARS

The free speech controversies during and after World War I did not spring from a void. Disputes over free speech had previously arisen in an enormous variety of contexts, ranging from political, labor, and sexual radicalism to commercial advertising and election reform. Judges, law professors, officials at all levels of government, activists, social thinkers, and diverse members of the general public addressed free speech issues throughout the decades before the war. Legislation affecting speech preceded the Espionage Act, legal decisions preceded *Schenck,* scholarship preceded Chafee, and defense organizations preceded the ACLU.

Within the wide range of views about free speech articulated before the war, two traditions stand out. A pervasive judicial hostility to virtually all free speech claims contrasted sharply with a comprehensive defense by libertarian radicals of broad protection for almost every expression. Judges in both federal and state courts overwhelmingly invoked the alleged "bad tendency" of speech to deny claims of abridgment in numerous doctrinal settings, such as libel, contempt of court, obscenity, and breach of the peace. Many judges relied on William Blackstone's eighteenth-century commentaries on the English common law of free speech. Some, including Justice Holmes in an important 1907 decision for the Supreme Court,[4] limited the First Amendment and analogous provisions of state constitutions to the English prohibition against prior restraints on speech. The criticism of these decisions by eminent legal scholars had no apparent impact on the courts. At the opposite end of the ideological spectrum from the judiciary was the long American tradition of libertarian radicalism that originated before the Civil War in individualist anarchism, radical abolitionism, freethought, and free love. Prompted by their underlying commitment to the right of individual autonomy in all aspects of life, libertarian radicals maintained that speech on virtually any subject should be protected from legal regulation by the state.

My investigation of the prewar period made me realize that

---

[4] Patterson v. Colorado, 205 U.S. 454 (1907).

developments during and immediately after World War I did not spontaneously create the modern era of free speech. Instead, these developments rapidly obscured the libertarian radical tradition and transformed judicial interpretation of the First Amendment. The impact of the war and its aftermath on progressives lies at the core of this process and reveals a decisive turning point in the history of American liberalism. In brief, World War I transformed many progressives into civil libertarians.

Before World War I, most progressives challenged traditional conceptions of individual rights protected by the Constitution. They identified constitutional rights with the excessive individualism to which they attributed the destructive inequality and division they saw throughout American society. Judicial recognition of these rights, they pointed out, blocked necessary social reform through positive state action. Property and liberty of contract – individual constitutional rights that the Supreme Court increasingly invoked to invalidate reform legislation – dominated the progressive attack on rights. But progressives were not sympathetic to other assertions of individual constitutional rights, including claims based on the First Amendment.

The emphasis by progressives on social harmony similarly limited their conception of free speech. Progressives often appreciated free speech, and even dissent, as qualities that a democratic society should nurture. But many reacted against dissent that was not directed toward positive social reconstruction. Progressives often saw no value in speech that expressed the structural inevitability of class conflict or that denied the feasibility of ultimate social unity.

World War I brought to the surface these latent but important views about free speech that had been embedded in the prior scholarship of progressive intellectuals. Most progressives supported the war. They often treated pacifists with impatience or even hostility, a reaction most dramatically illustrated by a series of essays John Dewey published in *The New Republic* soon after the United States entered the war in 1917. Dewey, who was the leading public intellectual in the country, emphasized the social importance of widespread critical inquiry more than most progressives. Yet he criticized pacifist opposition to the war as a failure to seize its democratic possibilities and ridiculed dissenters for invoking "early Victorian platitudes" about "the sanctity of individual rights."[5]

The failure of World War I "to make the world safe for democracy," combined with the widespread repression of speech during

---

[5] John Dewey, Conscription of Thought (1917), reprinted in 10 John Dewey, The Middle Works 1899–1924, at 276, 279 (Jo Ann Boydston ed., 1980).

and after the war, forced many progressives, including Dewey, to reconsider both their prewar faith in a benevolent state and their corresponding aversion to constitutional rights. They retained their belief that property and liberty rights should not block progressive social and economic legislation. They also came to recognize, however, the state as a constant threat to civil liberties, and they emphasized the centrality of constitutional free speech to the democratic themes that they had elaborated before the war. This combination of views became the core of New Deal constitutional ideology in the 1930s.

The progressives who became postwar civil libertarians developed a conception of free speech that differed significantly from defenses that prevailed before the war. Reflecting the lingering impact of their earlier views, the postwar civil libertarians based their emerging concern about free speech on its contribution to democracy rather than on its status as a natural right of autonomous individuals. They stressed the social benefits derived from freedom of political expression and essentially ignored the many other free speech issues that libertarian radicals, legal scholars, and other commentators addressed before the war. The actual circumstances that transformed progressives into civil libertarians, especially the severe repression of antiwar and postwar radical speech, reinforced their intellectual predisposition to focus on the protection of political expression.

In a pragmatic and largely successful effort to advance their new commitment to freedom of political speech, the postwar civil libertarians obscured both the more restrictive judicial tradition and the more protective libertarian radical tradition. Chafee's 1919 article in the *Harvard Law Review* was the key document in this effort. Like many progressives, Chafee had been uninterested in free speech issues before World War I. He began his study of free speech cases when he became an assistant professor at Harvard Law School in 1916. His reading soon led him to decisions holding that antiwar speech violated the Espionage Act, results that horrified Chafee. By the time he wrote "Freedom of Speech in War Time," Chafee had come to share the widespread disappointment among progressives with the outcome of the war. The failure to achieve the idealistic goals underlying American intervention, Chafee suggested, could be attributed to the repression of dissenting speech that had precluded honest debate during the war. Like most progressives who became civil libertarians, Chafee stressed social interests rather than individual rights in free speech. He especially emphasized that the emergence of truth about matters of public concern requires broad safeguards for political expression.

Chafee's article and subsequent 1920 book, *Freedom of Speech*,[6] soon became the starting point for analyzing the meaning and history of the First Amendment. Yet Chafee's own account of that history was seriously misleading. He essentially ignored prewar discussion of free speech that differed from his own focus on the protection of political dissent in a democracy. Chafee did not fairly portray the prewar cases. Moreover, despite the urgings of other scholars he conspicuously ignored the extensive publications of Theodore Schroeder, the leading prewar commentator on free speech who wrote from the perspective of libertarian radicalism. The contrast between their scholarship is telling. For example, Schroeder emphasized that the use of antiobscenity legislation to censor publications about contraception and other sexual topics violated the First Amendment, whereas Chafee claimed that laws prohibiting obscenity did not raise constitutional issues.

To support his interpretation of the First Amendment, Chafee made related historical and legal arguments. He maintained that the framers of the Constitution, in order to secure the popular sovereignty won by the American Revolution, intended the First Amendment to overthrow the English common law on free speech as formulated by Blackstone earlier in the eighteenth century. Blackstone interpreted the common law to preclude prior restraints on speech, but to allow subsequent punishment of expression for its tendency to disrupt peace and good order. Until Congress passed the Espionage Act in 1917, Chafee asserted, American federal and state courts rarely decided cases involving free speech claims. He added that the few prewar cases had not indicated the boundaries between protected and unprotected speech. As a result, he lamented, federal judges lacked sufficient guidance when suddenly confronted with an avalanche of prosecutions against antiwar speech under the Espionage Act.

Chafee complained that most of these judges applied the ancient English common-law test of bad tendency, which allowed the state to punish speech that had any tendency, however remote, to bring about violations of law. According to Chafee, prosecutors and judges previously relied on the bad tendency test only once in American history – under the Alien and Sedition laws passed by the Federalist Congress in 1798. The repressive results, Chafee stressed, enraged the American people and destroyed the Federalist party. Chafee was incredulous that American judges more than one hundred years later had revived this discredited approach.

---

[6] Zechariah Chafee, Jr., Freedom of Speech (1920).

Among the many judicial interpretations of the Espionage Act, Chafee found a few hopeful signs. He praised at length a decision by federal district judge Learned Hand, which overturned the refusal of the New York Postmaster to mail *The Masses,* a radical journal that contained articles and cartoons opposing the war.[7] Hand had rejected the bad tendency test while construing the Espionage Act to require a direct incitement to unlawful activity before speech could be punished. Chafee found further encouragement in the opinion by Justice Holmes in *Schenck v. United States,* one of the initial group of Espionage Act cases decided by a unanimous Supreme Court in March 1919. Although all four of these cases had upheld convictions for antiwar speech, Chafee maintained that Holmes's opinion in *Schenck* – particularly a sentence containing the phrase, *clear and present danger* – closely resembled Hand's incitement standard and clearly rejected the bad tendency test.

For decades, scholars accepted uncritically Chafee's major conclusions. Many of his contemporaries in the law schools shared his revulsion at the repression of antiwar speech and had little incentive to question his welcome analysis. Subsequent scholars, who generally agreed with Chafee's defense of broad protection for political speech, did not reexamine the underlying research of what had become a classic article by an eminent professor. In 1960, however, Leonard Levy's *Legacy of Suppression*[8] vigorously attacked Chafee's interpretation of the original meaning of the First Amendment. Based on extensive historical investigation that Chafee himself never undertook, Levy "reluctantly" concluded that the framers of the First Amendment had not intended to abolish either the English common-law crime of seditious libel or the bad tendency test. Both before and after Levy's book, other major scholars criticized Chafee's claim that Holmes intended the phrase *clear and present danger* in *Schenck* as a protective standard of First Amendment interpretation. Still, when I was a law student in the early 1970s, Chafee's historical assertion that no significant judicial encounters with free speech occurred between 1800 and 1917 remained unchallenged.

My research in Chafee's private papers and published reminiscences revealed that he was familiar with many of the prewar free speech cases when he wrote "Freedom of Speech in War Time." I

---

[7] Masses Publishing Co. v. Patten, 244 F. 535 (S.D.N.Y.), rev'd, 246 F. 24 (2d Cir. 1917).

[8] Leonard W. Levy, Legacy of Suppression: Freedom of Speech and Press in Early American History (1960).

realized that this seminal article had obscured the earlier cases both by minimizing their extent and significance and, more importantly, by refusing to disclose their heavy reliance on the alleged bad tendency of speech to deny free speech claims. An accurate presentation of the judicial tradition would have undermined Chafee's historically incorrect assertion that judges construing the Espionage Act of 1917 had revived that bad tendency test for the first time since the disastrous Sedition Act prosecutions at the close of the eighteenth century. Instead of criticizing the prewar cases directly, as had many previous scholars, Chafee tried to hide them as part of a disingenuous attempt to create a protective interpretation of the First Amendment out of a restrictive past. Chafee's accounts of the framers' original intent and of clear and present danger, which both ascribed more protection to speech than the evidence permitted, supported my conclusion that he was writing more as an advocate than as a scholar.

Chafee had a receptive audience for his legal and historical misconstructions as the wartime and postwar repression of speech transformed a growing number of Americans into civil libertarians. Most significantly, Chafee's article provided intellectual cover for Justices Holmes and Brandeis when they began to dissent in First Amendment cases in the fall of 1919. Holmes had written three of the four Espionage Act decisions for the unanimous Supreme Court the previous March.[9] Justice Brandeis wrote the fourth, which avoided addressing the underlying First Amendment issues by dismissing the case on technical grounds. The Supreme Court decided its next Espionage Act case, *Abrams v. United States*,[10] in November 1919. During the intervening months, when the hysteria of the postwar "Red Scare" and the disillusionment with the Versailles Peace Treaty peaked, Holmes and Brandeis entered the ranks of the postwar civil libertarians. Although the Supreme Court majority in *Abrams* closely followed Holmes's March opinions while again rejecting First Amendment attacks on Espionage Act convictions, Holmes, joined by Brandeis, dissented.

In writing his dissent in *Abrams*, Holmes faced a major problem. Shackled by the heavy weight of restrictive precedents, including his own earlier Espionage Act opinions, Holmes had to find legal doctrines to support his changed views. Chafee's article, published in June 1919 between the original March decisions and *Abrams*, provided a brilliant and convenient solution. The myth Chafee

---

[9] Schenck v. United States, 249 U.S. 47 (1919); Frohwerk v. United States, 249 U.S. 204 (1919); Debs v. United States, 249 U.S. 211 (1919).
[10] 250 U.S. 616 (1919).

created about the original appearance of clear and present danger in *Schenck* allowed Holmes in *Abrams* to reject the bad tendency test without repudiating his own prior decisions that had relied so heavily upon it. Holmes actually developed the concept of clear and present danger from a theory of judicial deference to majority will and used the phrase as a variant of the bad tendency test. Yet clear and present danger became, through Chafee's mediation, a protective standard of constitutional adjudication in the *Abrams* dissent. In a remarkable series of opinions from 1920 through 1927, Brandeis, relying heavily and often explicitly on Chafee's scholarship, elaborated and expanded the protection for speech introduced by Holmes in *Abrams*. Like other postwar civil libertarians, Holmes, and especially Brandeis, emphasized the importance of political speech in a democracy.

Just as Holmes and Brandeis, with the substantial assistance of Chafee, transformed and obscured the restrictive prewar judicial tradition, the ACLU, with which Chafee maintained a close affiliation, overshadowed and superseded the libertarian radicals who had led the defense of free speech since the Civil War. Like other progressives who became postwar civil libertarians, many of the people who founded the ACLU in 1920 had little interest in the subject of free speech before the war. Aroused by the Espionage Act prosecutions and the ensuing Red Scare, they conceived of free speech almost exclusively in political terms. The early organizational work of the ACLU reflected this ideological orientation. Concentrating on the protection of political speech, the ACLU ignored many issues that had preoccupied prewar defenders of free speech and that would become part of its own agenda in subsequent decades. It is revealing that in 1923 the ACLU rejected pleas from Schroeder and other libertarian radicals to defend a serious play about prostitution closed under a New York obscenity law. Although opposition to obscenity prosecutions had dominated the defense of speech by libertarian radicals before the war, the ACLU, reflecting Chafee's scholarly views, denied that the suppression of allegedly obscene material posed any significant threats to free expression.

In Chafee, Holmes, Brandeis, and the many eminent people who joined the ACLU, World War I created a larger and more influential group than ever before committed to the defense of free speech. Themes that Justices Holmes and Brandeis borrowed from Chafee and developed in opinions throughout the 1920s became accepted by the Supreme Court majority in the 1930s. Many Supreme Court cases since the 1930s have reversed or implicitly overruled restrictive precedents decided before World

War I. Yet the same postwar civil libertarians who ultimately helped transform judicial interpretation of the First Amendment viewed it more narrowly than had libertarian radicals and many other prewar commentators whose conception of free speech extended beyond political expression.

FREE SPEECH AND THE HISTORY OF IDEAS

By uncovering the forgotten history of free speech between 1870 and 1920, and by exploring the transformation of progressives into civil libertarians, this book illuminates some key historiographical themes. At its most fundamental level, the topic of free speech in American history raises the complicated issues posed by any attempt to study ideas over time. Debate over these issues, and over the very feasibility of the enterprise, has been a central concern of twentieth-century historiography.[11] Many scholars warn that an idea can have such radically different meanings for different people that any attempt to analyze it as a coherent subject is doomed to failure. Even people living in the same country at the same time can have incompatible understandings of a particular idea. This problem is often exacerbated by comparing conceptions of an idea in different historical periods. Moreover, it is likely or perhaps inevitable that historians will search the past for origins or illustrations of their own conceptions of an idea. As a result, historians may be unable even to recognize the ways in which prior generations understood the idea differently.

Some scholars, without denying these difficulties, do not find them insurmountable. While acknowledging that the multiple meanings of an idea may make it impervious to coherent analysis,

---

[11] See, e.g., David A. Hollinger, In the American Province: Studies in the History and Historiography of Ideas (1985); J.G.A. Pocock, Politics, Language, and Time: Essays on Political Thought and History (1971); Michel Foucault, Nietzsche, Genealogy, History, in The Foucault Reader (Paul Rabinow ed. 1984); David Harlan, Intellectual History and the Return of Literature, 94 Am. Hist. Rev. 581 (1989); Martin Jay, Should Intellectual History Take a Linguistic Turn? Reflections on the Habermas-Gadamer Debate, in Modern European Intellectual History: Reappraisals and New Perspectives (Dominick LaCapra and Steven L. Kaplan eds. 1982); Donald R. Kelley, Horizons of Intellectual History: Retrospect, Circumspect, Prospect, 48 J. Hist. Ideas 143 (1987); Leonard Krieger, The Autonomy of Intellectual History, 34 J. Hist. of Ideas 499 (1973); Dominick LaCapra, Rethinking Intellectual History and Reading Texts, in Modern European Intellectual History, supra at 47; Maurice Mandelbaum, The History of Ideas, Intellectual History, and the History of Philosophy, History and Theory, Beiheft 5, at 33 (1965); Quentin Skinner, Meaning and Understanding in the History of Ideas, 8 History and Theory 3 (1969).

they believe that at least some conceptions of some ideas have sufficient similarities, "family resemblances," or other relationships to justify treating an idea as a topic of study. And while agreeing that one can only approach the past from the perspective of the present, they are confident that a sensitive historian can be open to the possibility of difference in the past. Such a historian should be able to avoid reducing the unfamiliar past to the categories of the familiar present. Historical exploration may disclose meaningful origins and illustrations of a current conception of an idea, but it may also uncover lost versions that are better as well as different. Through what the German philosopher, Hans-Georg Gadamer, calls a "fusion of horizons" between the present and the past,[12] we can interrogate our own assumptions and liberate ourselves from their constraints.

Among scholars who study the history of ideas, the relationships between continuity and change in ideas over time and between specialized and general ideas have attracted substantial attention. Some historians detect lengthy continuities in the history of ideas, punctuated by "ruptures" during which ideas are rapidly, and often inexplicably, transformed. Others perceive more gradual changes over time and provide explanations for them. Whereas some historians portray individuals as representatives of a general intellectual tradition or "discourse," others emphasize how exceptionally creative thinkers manipulate and even revolutionize ideas. Sophisticated historians point out that similarities in ideas at very different times may reflect the continuing influence of earlier thinkers or may reveal nothing more than structural parallels and recurrences.

The history of ideas, many scholars add, must be sensitive to the possible interactions between ideas in a specialized field of inquiry – such as religion, science, art, philosophy, or law – and broader intellectual trends. Ideas in a particular field may change only in reference to that speciality. At other times, however, broader intellectual trends influence, or are influenced by, ideas within a speciality. Yet thinkers may derive similar or even identical ideas on a specialized subject from very different general traditions. Moreover, relationships between specialized fields and more general structures of thought may be clearer in retrospect to the historian than they were to the past thinkers themselves.

For some scholars, relationships among ideas are much less significant than are relationships between ideas and society. At one extreme, scholars maintain that ideas are essentially autonomous. At the opposite extreme, scholars view ideas as epiphenomenal-

---

[12] See Jay, supra note 11, at 95; Kelley, supra note 11, at 156.

dependent variables determined by social forces. Rejecting both extremes, others assert that ideas can neither be reduced to nor divorced from social context. They deny dichotomies between idealism and materialism, and they search instead for the complex interactions between thought and environment. Ideas, they believe, can influence as well as reflect society. Scholars who recognize the "relative autonomy" of ideas stress that ideas can be traced to social forces that they may later transcend and sometimes limit or alter. Even when external events prompt people to revise their ideas, the events may not determine the content of the changed ideas. And scholars who are skeptical about the influence of events on ideas often recognize that social context may help explain the meaning of social thought.

Legal historians have addressed many of these general historiographical themes.[13] They frequently identify three successive, but partially overlapping, periods in the study of American legal history. During the first long period, legal historians viewed law as autonomous from society and focused on the internal history of legal doctrine. These specialized histories typically traced the origins and evolution of current legal doctrine without connecting law either to its social context or to broader ideas. Beginning with the pioneering work of J. Willard Hurst in the 1940s and peaking in the 1960s and 1970s, many of the most important legal historians rejected this internal, doctrinal approach. They focused instead on law as an instrument of external social forces and examined the functions law performed in society. They often ignored entirely the content of legal ideas, which they tended to treat with disdain as uninteresting and unimportant reflections of the independent, mostly economic, forces that provided the basis for historical explanation. More recently, legal historians have avoided the internalist and externalist extremes. Influenced by the concept of relative autonomy, they have observed that legal doctrine, which initially may have served the purposes of dominant social interests, became an independent force that constrained those same interests and even assisted weaker members of society while simultaneously limiting their vision of more radical alternatives. They have

---

[13] See, e.g., Lawrence M. Friedman, American Legal History: Past and Present, 34 J. Legal Ed. 563 (1984); Robert W. Gordon, Critical Legal Histories, 36 Stan. L. Rev. 57 (1984); Robert W. Gordon, Historicism in Legal Scholarship, 90 Yale L.J. 1017 (1981); Michael Grossberg, Social History Update: "Fighting Faiths" and the Challenges of Legal History, 25 J. Soc. Hist. 191 (1991); Hendrik Hartog, The Constitution of Aspiration and "The Rights That Belong to Us All," 74 J. Am. Hist. 661 (1987); Christopher Tomlins, How who rides whom. Recent 'new' histories of American labour law and what they may signify, 20 Soc. Hist. 1 (1995).

also stressed that changes in the social structure have not necessarily produced corresponding changes in legal doctrine.

Many legal historians agree that constitutional history has remained a historiographical backwater, still mired in the internal study of legal doctrine, and even more narrowly in the decisions of the United States Supreme Court.[14] Particularly within the past decade, however, some scholars have tried to reinvigorate constitutional history by examining the "rights consciousness" of Americans who were not official interpreters of the Constitution.[15] Virtually all of these scholars have focused on groups that challenged prevailing official interpretations, such as blacks, women, and labor unions. Their work typically portrays an interpretative contest, often embedded in concrete social struggles, between an elite of legal insiders and subordinated outsiders advocating alternative constructions of constitutional rights.

Specific evidence provided by the history of free speech both illustrates and demonstrates the limitations of many of these historiographical theories. In fact, the history of free speech indicates that historiographical theories frequently regarded as in competition with each other may actually be consistent and complementary. For example, there may be consensus as well as contest about the meaning of a constitutional right, gradual as well as rapid changes in consciousness, and external influences on ideas that also develop internally.

I obviously would not have written a book about the history of free speech without becoming convinced that this subject constitutes a coherent field of study. Although there have been many conceptions of free speech over the course of American history, the kinds of free speech issues and the range of ideological and doctrinal responses to them have remained remarkably similar over time. The identity of individuals and groups holding various positions about free speech has changed much more than either the substance of these positions or the underlying issues that generated them. Moreover, despite persistent disputes about the

---

[14] See, e.g., Friedman, supra note 13, at 576; Hartog, supra note 13.

[15] Essays by a number of these scholars are collected in a special issue of the Journal of American History designed for the bicentennial of the Constitution. See Symposium, The Constitution and American Life, 74 J. Am. Hist. 661 (1987). The essays in Part II of the issue, entitled "Rights Consciousness in American History," focus especially on the interpretations of constitutional rights by various outsiders challenging official legal interpretations. See also William E. Forbath, Law and the Shaping of the American Labor Movement (1991); William E. Forbath, The Ambiguities of Free Labor: Labor and the Law in the Gilded Age, 1985 Wisc. L. Rev. 767 (1985).

meaning of free speech, some views about the subject have always attracted substantial support from Americans.

In contrast to people in many other countries and times, Americans consistently have testified to the underlying value of free speech. Judges who denied free speech claims before World War I, and even vigilantes who physically attacked the soapbox speakers of the Industrial Workers of the World (IWW) during their free speech fights between 1909 and 1913, often emphasized their own deep commitment to what they deemed proper conceptions of free speech. Even if some of these judges and vigilantes were insincere, their efforts to convince others that they believed in free speech at least indicated their perception of its widespread importance to the American people. Some radicals, ranging from IWW members to current legal scholars, have asserted that First Amendment rights are empty formalities for workers, minorities, women, and others who lack social or economic power. These radicals, however, have shared with virtually all Americans the view that meaningful rights to free speech are valuable.

More specifically, since the ratification of the First Amendment, Americans overwhelmingly have agreed that constitutionally protected speech is essential to the proper operation of a democracy. Consensus about the connection between free speech and democracy may be the single unifying free speech theme throughout American history. From this fundamental principle, Americans, with varying degrees of assent, have derived several related corollaries. They have generally believed that speech about public affairs merits more protection than speech about private concerns. Moreover, since the early nineteenth century most commentary on the Sedition Act of 1798 has criticized it for punishing legitimate political speech and has often added that it violated the First Amendment. It is revealing that even the most vigorous proponents of the Espionage Act of 1917 and of earlier antianarchy bills took pains to distinguish this legislation from the admitted faults of the Sedition Act. To a significant extent before World War I and to a much greater extent subsequently, people argued that the role of speech in a democracy requires First Amendment protection of dissenting opinions by unpopular minorities. Since World War I, there has been a similar increase in support for the view that the First Amendment precludes various penalties against speech and is not simply equivalent to Blackstone's prohibition against prior restraints. In justifying substantial protection for unpopular political speech, commentators have frequently claimed that repression often produces more illegal activity than toleration. They have even used the same metaphor, pointing out that speech is a "safety-valve" for discontent, whereas repression creates martyrs. The position that free speech, whatever its social value, is a fundamental right of personal autonomy has always had strong advocates, but it has never achieved as much support as the democratic defense of political expression.

Many doctrines used to analyze free speech have also persisted from the decades before World War I into the present. Throughout this period, commentators and cases have distinguished between protected speech and illegal incitements or actions. They have analyzed the extent of permissible government regulation of election, commercial, and labor speech, and of private speech on public property. They have also identified some categories of speech, such as obscenity, as beyond the protection of law. The claim that government must not favor certain ideas, often characterized today as content or viewpoint neutrality, was an important concern before World War I. Prewar debates about when the public welfare justifies restrictions on speech, and about the relationship between the constitutional rights of property and speech, have counterparts in current controversies.

On the other hand, some prewar views about free speech have largely disappeared, just as some current approaches to the subject lack prewar analogues. Before the war, people asserted limitations on speech that have few defenders today. They frequently maintained that the public owners of property had the same rights as their private counterparts to exclude speakers. Many asserted that free speech did not extend to views that were unpatriotic or that expressed class hatred. Most people assumed that the First Amendment did not apply to the states, and Justice Holmes was far from the only person who understood it as nothing more than the transposition of Blackstone's views on free speech into the United States Constitution. The Supreme Court was not alone in refusing to recognize movies as a form of expression covered by the First Amendment. By contrast, other prewar conceptions of speech were much broader than views asserted today. Serious scholars and lawyers maintained that the First Amendment only allows punishment of speech that actually produces an illegal act. Current uses of individual autonomy as a justification for protecting speech are much more narrow than the conception of autonomy held by libertarian radicals before the war. The prewar libertarian radicals viewed free speech as one of a connected set of fundamental rights to personal autonomy that could not be regulated by the state. These rights covered such diverse subjects as marriage, smoking, medical licensing, and many other activities that most people today would consider unrelated to speech. Correspondingly, some current free speech issues were not addressed before the war. Regulation of mass media and cyberspace obviously were not topics of concern in the decades between the Civil War and World War I.

Although the range of many positions about free speech varied only modestly over time, certain identifiable groups of Americans have had very different beliefs about these positions during different periods of American history. Most dramatically, no group of Americans was more hostile to free speech claims before World War I than the judiciary, and no judges were more hostile than the justices on the United States Supreme Court. Today, by contrast, the judiciary, with the Supreme Court in the lead, is more inclined to protect speech than are most Americans. Views held only by radicals before World War I on subjects ranging from political dissent to sexual expression have in recent decades become holdings of the Supreme Court. On the other hand, prewar scholars had relatively protective views about free speech, and they frequently criticized courts for invoking the public welfare as the basis for denying free speech claims. Today, scholars increasingly criticize the courts for protecting too much speech at the expense of the public welfare. There are, of course, substantial distinctions among the kinds of free speech issues addressed by these different generations of scholars. The prewar scholars protested that judges failed to protect unpopular dissenting speech by placing too much weight on a conception of public welfare as public order. The current scholars protest that judicial enforcement of the free speech rights of wealthy individuals and corporations harm the public welfare by reinforcing and perpetuating inequality. Yet the shift from substantial scholarly defense of free speech during a period of judicial hostility to substantial scholarly concern about the abuse of free speech during a period of judicial protection is nonetheless striking.

Beyond providing a coherent subject of investigation, the history of free speech demonstrates that views about this specialized subject were sometimes linked to more general ideas, but also that people whose broader intellectual orientations were very different could agree on significant free speech issues. The already familiar contrast between the prewar libertarian radicals and the postwar civil libertarians illustrates how social thought influenced positions on free speech. The underlying libertarian commitment to personal autonomy in every aspect of life translated into a strong defense of free speech on all subjects as an individual right beyond state control. The underlying progressive commitment to reforming American society, by contrast, translated after World War I into a belated defense of dissenting political speech as a vital social interest in a democracy. Yet people who had different ideological orientations could have similar positions on many free speech issues. Leading prewar scholars – including inheritors of the liberal traditions of Jefferson and Jackson, libertarian radicals, and even the rare progressives who thought about free speech before World War I – repudiated Blackstone's views on free speech as inconsistent with American popular sovereignty and objected to the judicial reliance on the bad tendency test. And Justice Holmes, whose Social Darwinism and deference to majoritarianism prompted him to dissent from his conservative colleagues in Supreme Court decisions that declared progressive social legislation unconstitutional, wrote several of the Court's most important prewar decisions relying on the bad tendency test to deny free speech claims.

Just as the history of free speech reveals agreement on specialized legal issues among people whose views derived from different intellectual orientations, it illustrates both continuity and change in conceptions of free speech. From the Civil War until World War I, the incompatible free speech positions of libertarian radicals and judges barely changed. Judges continually used the bad tendency test to penalize speech that, according to the equally continual protests of libertarian radicals, deserved protection under the First Amendment. Some relatively minor refinements and elaborations of their respective positions can be detected over this long period, mostly in response to new forms of regulation, but their fundamental positions were little different in 1915 than they were in 1870. The transformation of prewar progressives into postwar civil libertarians, by contrast, shows how quickly people could change their ideas about free speech. Justices Holmes and Brandeis, who moved from writing unanimous opinions that rejected First Amendment challenges to Espionage Act convictions in March 1919 to dissenting in a similar case the following November, provide a particularly dramatic illustration of a rapid shift in free speech views.

As these examples of continuities and changes suggest, relationships between ideas about free speech and external events varied considerably. The extensive repression of antiwar and radical speech during and after World War I made many Americans sensitive to infringements on speech for the first time. Professor Chafee, Justices Holmes and Brandeis, and the founders of the ACLU were among the most influential of these postwar civil libertarians. The war, however, did not alter either the protective free speech views of the libertarian radicals or the restrictive views of most judges, including the majority of the Supreme Court.

Nor did earlier social transformations affect the judicial interpretation or the activist defense of free speech. Important historians, for example, have convincingly identified the decades span-
ning the turn of the twentieth century as a watershed of American
history, marked by the emergence of a mature industrial economy
and the rise of a centralized administrative state.[16] Some free
speech controversies can be connected to these developments,
such as the IWW free speech fights and prosecutions under legislation that prohibited the advocacy of anarchism. But judges denied
protection to IWW and anarchist speech through continued
reliance on the bad tendency test long familiar in the common
law, and libertarian radicals defended it by reiterating arguments
they had previously used to support freethinkers and sex radicals.
While many Americans commented on free speech issues during
these controversies, especially during the IWW free speech fights,
the wide variety of their responses seemed to derive more from
preexisting, though sometimes previously unfocused, views about
free speech than from new or changed perceptions. On the other
hand, the growth of private economic and official government
power in the years around 1900 contributed to the formation of
the progressive movement and influenced progressives in ways
that help to account for their rather unprotective, though largely
submerged, views about free speech. Under these new economic
and political circumstances, progressives believed, American society had become so interdependent that traditional conceptions of
individualism no longer made sense. The emphasis by progressives
on social interests over individual rights, as well as their longing
for consensus and harmony, reflected these beliefs.

Even when external social forces produced changes in ideas
about speech, the content of the new ideas could not simply be
reduced to the social forces that provoked them. The repression
that transformed Chafee into a vigorous defender of First Amendment protection for dissenting political speech, to take the most
striking example, did not determine his creative misrepresenta-
tion of legal history and judicial precedents to articulate his new
position. Nor did the similar impact of repression on Justices
Holmes and Brandeis dictate the ways in which they borrowed and
developed Chafee's arguments. By retaining their prewar prefer-

---

[16] See especially Robert H. Wiebe, The Search for Order 1877–1920 (1967). For
a good overview of historical writing about a watershed around 1900, see
Thomas L. Haskell, Introduction: What Happened in the 1890's?, in The Emergence of Professional Social Science: The American Social Science Association
and the Nineteenth-Century Crisis of Authority (1977).

ence for analysis based on social interests rather than on individual rights, even as they extended this analysis to justify protection for dissent that contributed to a democratic society, many postwar civil libertarians revealed continuities in their thought that survived the war as well as transformations produced by it.

The history of free speech, moreover, provides both examples and counterexamples for the emphasis by current legal historians on interpretive struggles over rights between subordinated outsiders and official interpreters of the Constitution. This model applies in many ways to the IWW free speech fights, during which radical workers and local officials contested the right to speak in public places, and to the struggles of marginalized sex radicals to defend their publications about contraception and marriage from postal authorities and judges who deemed them obscene. Yet substantial commentary on free speech came from legal scholars, journalists, businessmen, ministers, and many other citizens who could not meet any meaningful definition of subordinated outsiders engaged in struggles with officials. More significantly, even the views of outsiders and official interpreters were rarely monolithic. Members of the IWW, for example, differed among themselves about whether First Amendment rights could be vindicated in a capitalist society. Though many local officials refused to recognize any right to speak in public and even participated in vigilante violence against the IWW, other municipal, state, and federal officials explicitly cited the First Amendment in supporting IWW rights to free speech and in resisting strenuous pressure to prosecute the IWW. In addition, a few judges, in IWW cases and in other contexts, reached protective results through reasoning that challenged the overwhelming judicial hostility to free speech claims.

Throughout the prewar period, different interpreters of free speech had little impact on each other. There was virtually no interaction between judicial decisions and popular debate. Scholarly criticisms did not affect judges. A significant number of public officials allowed speech whose restriction most judges would have upheld. This situation only changed with the shared reaction against the repression of speech during and after World War I, as the dramatic intellectual influence of Professor Chafee on Justices Holmes and Brandeis best illustrates.

Difficulties posed by the potentially inescapable barriers current concerns and values place on the study of the past may be the hardest historiographical issue to address. My own experience investigating the history of free speech, however, has convinced me that the genesis of historical inquiry, which may inevitably relate to the contemporary situation of the historian, need not define the scope of the eventual research or preclude recognizing the unfamiliar in the past. My interest in this subject began as a law student in the early 1970s. A strong but unrefined belief in the importance of free speech and a general interest in history prompted me to take several courses in constitutional law and legal history. As I completed these courses, I increasingly was struck by the largely unarticulated assumption that judicial interpretation of the First Amendment began with the Supreme Court's Espionage Act cases in 1919. My rudimentary knowledge of American history made me skeptical about this assumption. I thought that episodes arising before World War I, such as labor and anarchist agitation, surely would have produced litigation over free speech had they occurred in the period since 1919. I suspected such prewar episodes actually did result in at least some legal decisions that addressed First Amendment issues.

I thus began my research with assumptions based on the kinds of issues that generated First Amendment litigation in the present and recent past. I initially searched for cases before World War I that cited the First Amendment or analogous provisions of state constitutions. I found such cases in numbers that seemed significant, particularly in light of the pervasive assumption that none existed. But I also suspected, correctly as it turned out, that prewar courts did not use constitutional analysis in deciding cases that would present clear First Amendment issues to modern judges. These cases vastly exceeded the ones that explicitly referred to constitutional provisions on speech. By reading briefs, which were easiest to find for Supreme Court cases, I realized how many advocates posed First Amendment issues that judges ignored. To obtain a more complete picture of prewar legal analysis of free speech issues, I also examined legal scholarship of the period. The extensive legal literature I uncovered provoked my curiosity about possible free speech views of activists, public officials, intellectuals in various fields, and the broad general public. In this manner, my early discoveries about the past broadened my inquiry from its initial search for First Amendment cases before World War I. In addition, my interest in current First Amendment issues did not prevent me from recognizing that much of what I found, particularly the libertarian radical tradition, was unfamiliar and irreducible to modern categories of analysis.

The chapters that follow focus primarily on the history of ideas about free speech in the forgotten decades between 1870 and 1920. I do not elaborate the historiographical themes I have identified in this introduction, although the contents of the book do so implicitly and should interest the historiographically inclined. At times I devote substantial attention to placing these ideas in broader social context, particularly when I have concluded that context is essential to understanding the ideas and may be relatively unfamiliar to many readers. I thus provide biographical information about leading libertarian radicals and explore the background of the IWW free speech fights. But I found ideas about free speech the most interesting aspect of the history I explored. In their fascinating diversity, complexity, and transformations, they remain the center of this study.

In order to keep this book within manageable length and scope, I have not extended my research earlier than 1870 or used conceptions of free speech uncovered in my historical investigations to interrogate comprehensively current interpretations of the First Amendment. I hope to return to both of these unfinished tasks in future work. Yet the key transformation of prewar progressives into postwar civil libertarians relates directly to a major, and perhaps the central, First Amendment debate of our time. I therefore close this book with a brief analysis of the significant parallels between the prewar views of the progressives and recent scholarly attacks on First Amendment decisions by the Supreme Court since the 1970s.[17]

The typical free speech claimant today, these scholars observe, is no longer the unpopular dissenter who was the focus of the "worthy tradition" that began with the postwar civil libertarians and culminated in decisions by the Warren Court. Instead, the free speech claimant in landmark First Amendment cases has become the economically and politically powerful individual or corporation seeking to prevent regulation of campaign financing, the media, and harmful speech directed against minorities, women, and children. Just as prewar progressives attacked the judicial reliance on formally neutral rights of property and contract under the Fourteenth Amendment to protect the economic advantages of the wealthy, current scholars complain that judicial construction of the First Amendment preserves inequality by relying on formally neutral rights to free speech. And just as prewar progressives argued that social interests limited individual rights of property and contract, current scholars invoke the democratic

---

[17] See, e.g., Mark A. Graber, Transforming Free Speech: The Ambiguous Legacy of Civil Libertarianism (1991); Cass R. Sunstein, Democracy and the Problem of Free Speech (1993); J. M. Balkin, Some Realism About Pluralism: Legal Realist Approaches to the First Amendment, 1990 Duke L. J. 375; Owen M. Fiss, Free Speech and Social Structure, 71 Iowa L. Rev. 1405 (1986).

social interest while advocating restrictions on individual rights to free speech. Current scholars seem unaware of these analogies and may not be familiar with the experience of the progressives. Yet in considering the understandable calls for state action against speech that arguably skews the electoral process or harms the most vulnerable members of society, it is important to remember what the progressives learned so painfully during and after World War I. Government regulation of speech, however well intentioned initially, can easily lead to repression of merely unpopular views. The progressives who became civil libertarians after the war grew to appreciate the social value of First Amendment rights against the state. Their example indicates that the search for alternatives to the Supreme Court's First Amendment decisions over the past twenty years should lead in other directions than the disparagement of "rights talk."

1

The Lost Tradition of Libertarian Radicalism

Just as most commentators have traced judicial interpretation of the First Amendment from the Espionage Act decisions in 1919, they have followed organized advocacy of free speech rights from the creation of the ACLU in the years between 1917 and 1920. The ACLU's initial focus on the protection of unpopular political dissent, they observe, understandably derived from the wartime and postwar repression that generated its founders' interest in free speech. They point out, however, that over time the ACLU developed a fuller conception of free speech that encompassed literary and artistic expression previously considered obscene. The work begun by the small group of brave advocates in the ACLU after World War I, commentators generally conclude, culminated in the 1960s, when the Warren Court gave meaningful constitutional protection to the broad free speech rights that the ACLU had advocated for decades.

The lost tradition of libertarian radicalism obscured by the postwar civil libertarians reveals a substantially different history of free speech. Its defense did not begin with the respectable professionals who founded the ACLU after World War I. Before most of these people ever thought about the subject, an even smaller and braver group of libertarian radicals, often on the intellectual and social fringes of American society, advocated a much more protective conception of free speech that extended well beyond political expression.

Libertarian radicalism defended the primary value of individual autonomy against the power of church and state. It originated before the Civil War in individualist anarchism, in freethought, in radical abolitionism, and in struggles for labor reform and women's rights. Often provoked by disappointment with early experiments in utopian socialism, individualist anarchists instead emphasized the importance of individual sovereignty in social and economic life. Freethinkers rejected the authority of the church and asserted that religious truth can only be interpreted by autonomous individuals. Radical abolitionists insisted that the sinful and coercive laws of the state placed barriers between individuals and God's "higher law." Referring to marriage as a form of slavery, some early feminists claimed that wives, like slaves, lost their individual autonomy to white, male masters. Libertarian radicalism had fewer adherents following the Civil War, but it remained powerfully attractive into the early twentieth century for Americans who rejected both the competitive individualism of laissez-faire capitalism and the emphasis on social harmony in progressive thought.

The ideology and experiences of libertarian radicals produced a broad conception of free speech as an aspect of their underlying belief in individual autonomy. Just as individual autonomy justified freedom of conscience from religious and political authority, freedom to determine the use of one's sexual organs even within marriage, and freedom to retain the value of one's own labor, it justified freedom to express personal opinions on any subject.

Many libertarian radicals, especially those who expressed radical views about sex, suffered in the late nineteenth century from the application of the Comstock Act and analogous state legislation. Passed by Congress in 1873 and amended in 1876, the Comstock Act prohibited the interstate mailing of "obscene" material. Although the statute failed to define obscenity, judicial decisions developed an expansive interpretation and provided postal officials with virtually unreviewable discretion to censor publications as "obscene." Led by Anthony Comstock, postal authorities deemed obscene publications that, in recognizing a woman's right to control her body, opposed legal regulation of marriage and provided sexually explicit information about contraception. They also defined obscenity to include blasphemy.

Censorship and convictions under the Comstock Act provoked many libertarian radicals to move from theoretical support of free speech to active engagement in its defense. Edward Bliss Foote, the author of a popular medical treatise, supplied much of the funding for these efforts. Convicted and heavily fined under the Comstock Act in 1876 for including information about birth control in his book, Foote deleted the offending material from subsequent editions. Foote and his son, however, subsequently devoted themselves to the defense of free speech, especially through financial support to the National Defense Association and the Free Speech League, organizations established by libertarian radicals decades before Roger Baldwin and other postwar civil libertarians created the ACLU.

The National Defense Association, founded in 1878, strenuously opposed the Comstock Act and aided defendants prosecuted under it. Libertarian radicals had more ambitious goals when they organized the Free Speech League in 1902. They were convinced that increased government repression of speech had created a broader group of Americans concerned about its protection. They particularly cited the imperialistic suppression of dissenting speech in the American colonies won during the Spanish-American War of 1898 and the outburst of legislation and prosecutions against anarchist speech after an anarchist assassinated President McKinley in 1901. The Free Speech League, unlike the National Defense Association, committed itself to defending free speech for all viewpoints. Theodore Schroeder, who soon became the key administrator of the League, translated his scholarly views on free speech into arguments during actual controversies. Although the founders of the League and Schroeder were libertarian radicals, more mainstream figures took an active part in its work. The board of directors, for example, included Lincoln Steffens, the nationally recognized "muckraking" journalist, and Gilbert Roe, the best friend and former law partner of Wisconsin Senator Robert M. La Follette.

The Free Speech League followed through on its commitment to defend speech for all viewpoints, but its major beneficiaries were radicals. The League repeatedly assisted Emma Goldman, who was frequently arrested during her national speaking tours on topics such as anarchism and birth control; Margaret Sanger, whose publications linking birth control to class struggle provoked censorship and arrests by Comstock and local authorities; and the IWW, whose free speech fights aroused national attention and extensive popular debate about the meaning of free speech. Among its many other activities, the League participated in two Supreme Court cases. It hired Clarence Darrow and Edgar Lee Masters in 1904 to defend a British journalist deported in the midst of an American lecture tour addressing various anarchist subjects. Beginning in 1912, the League represented an anarchist editor convicted for publishing an article advocating nude bathing. The Supreme Court rejected both appeals, and Justice Holmes wrote the unanimous opinion in the second case. The repression of antiwar speech under the Espionage Act, which transformed the founders of the ACLU and other progressives into civil libertarians, became yet another issue that the Free Speech League added to its already large agenda. Drawing on the commitment to individual autonomy in libertarian radicalism and on their long experience as activists, the leaders of the Free

Speech League tried repeatedly but unsuccessfully to convince the emerging ACLU that the defense of free speech should extend beyond the protection of dissenting political speech.

JOSIAH WARREN AND INDIVIDUALIST ANARCHISM

The relationship between early libertarian radicalism and free speech is best revealed in the individualist anarchism founded by Josiah Warren. Warren became an anarchist in reaction against the utopian socialism of Robert Owen, the British industrialist who established experimental communities in the United States and Britain. Convinced that individuals are shaped entirely by their environments, Owen believed that communal ownership of property would foster cooperation and the development of character.[1] Josiah Warren, an American who in 1826 was among the first settlers of the Owenite community of New Harmony, Indiana, soon became disillusioned. The "communistic experiment" in New Harmony failed, Warren concluded, because it had not recognized and dealt with inevitable differences in human capability, effort, and belief.[2] The "difference of opinion," he observed, "*increased* just in proportion to the demand for conformity."[3] Warren therefore proposed a society designed "to preserve the SOVEREIGNTY OF EVERY INDIVIDUAL inviolate," including the "liberty to dispose of his or her person, and time, and property in any manner in which his or her feelings or judgment may dictate, WITHOUT INVOLVING THE PERSONS OR INTERESTS OF OTHERS."[4] He reasoned that organized government and law, even if approved by the democratic majority, restricted individual autonomy.[5] A society based on the sovereignty of the individual, Warren believed, would represent the culmination of social movements that had already produced the Protestant Reformation and the American Revolution.[6]

Warren himself focused on the economic implications of his anarchist theories. Consistent with his general commitment to individual sovereignty, he maintained that personal labor should be the measure of economic value. Like Owen, Warren established new communities designed to put his economic ideas into prac-

---

[1] James J. Martin, Men Against the State: The Expositors of Individualist Anarchism in America, 1827–1908, at 14–15 (1953).
[2] Id. at 17 (quoting Warren).   [3] Id. at 15 (quoting Warren).
[4] Id. at 18 (quoting Warren).   [5] Id. at 50–51.
[6] Yehoshua Arieli, Individualism and Nationalism in American Ideology 294 (1964).

tice. In these communities, for example, labor notes issued by workers replaced money.[7]

Warren's anarchist views also had clear implications for free speech, as John Stuart Mill realized. In his classic defense of free speech, *On Liberty,* Mill emphasized that "the only purpose for which power can be rightfully exercised over any member of a civilized community, against his will, is to prevent harm to others." Mill added: "Over himself, over his own body and mind, the individual is sovereign."[8] In his subsequent autobiography, Mill acknowledged that he borrowed the concept of individual sovereignty from his reading of Warren, "a remarkable American." Mill accurately reported that Warren and his followers had established a community "which, though bearing a superficial resemblance to some of the projects of the Socialists, is diametrically opposed to them in principle, since it recognizes no authority whatever in Society, over the individual, except to enforce equal freedom of development for all individualities."[9] Some American contemporaries of Warren also derived implications for freedom of expression from individualist anarchism. For example, Lysander Spooner objected to government monopoly over the mails as an infringement of freedom of the press.[10] In the years following the Civil War, Warren was an important influence on libertarian radicals prosecuted under the Comstock Act.

THE COMSTOCK ACT

The energy that many social perfectionists invested in abolitionism found other outlets after the Civil War. Some former abolitionists extended prewar commitments to libertarian radical causes such as freethought, labor reform, and women's rights. Others, who had been equally committed to abolitionism, became active in the broad philanthropic movement for social purity that included prison reform, temperance, aid to the poor, and attacks on prostitution and gambling. Social purists and libertarian radicals, even

---

[7] Martin Henry Blatt, Free Love and Anarchism: The Biography of Ezra Heywood 52–53 (1989); Hal D. Sears, The Sex Radicals: Free Love in High Victorian America 156–57 (1977).

[8] John Stuart Mill, On Liberty 68 (Penguin Classics ed. 1985) (1859). In her introduction to On Liberty, id. at 28, Gertrude Himmelfarb calls this passage "the essence of the book."

[9] John Stuart Mill, Autobiography 217 (Oxford Univ. Press, World's Classics ed. 1935) (1873).

[10] Martin, supra note 1, at 170–71.

though they shared an abolitionist background and a commitment to social perfectionism that generated agreement on some issues, had many incompatible views.[11] Most fundamentally, the libertarian radical vision of individual autonomy often struck social purists as a threat to their goal of a morally cohesive community. For some social purists, including Anthony Comstock, expressions of libertarian radical views about religion and sex were examples of blasphemy and obscenity that should be suppressed in the public interest. The Comstock Act provided the social purists who had lobbied for it with a significant legal weapon against libertarian radicals.

Anthony Comstock had tirelessly lobbied for the law that was popularly known by his name. Raised in Connecticut by a devout family, Comstock moved to New York City in 1867 after serving in the Union army during the Civil War. Both as a soldier and as an employee in the drygoods business, the highly religious Comstock was outraged by the "sin and wickedness" of the people around him. While in New York, Comstock worked to increase police enforcement of laws directed at saloons and obscene literature. In 1872, he succeeded in causing numerous arrests of individuals charged with selling obscene pictures and books, contraceptives, and drugs that induced abortions.[12]

Comstock had arranged for a local newspaper to cover these arrests. The resulting publicity helped him gain the support of Morris K. Jesup, a prominent banker and philanthropist. Jesup was president of the Young Men's Christian Association (YMCA) of New York, a key organization in the movement for social purity. Jesup took the lead in creating within the YMCA a Committee for the Suppression of Vice. The Committee provided a salary and an expense account for Comstock and soon became an independent organization, the New York Society for the Suppression of Vice. The Society received a charter from the New York legislature in 1873 that allowed it to retain half the fines imposed on individuals it helped convict. By early 1874, the YMCA boasted that Comstock had been responsible for seizing 130,000 pounds of books, 194,000 pictures and photographs, and 60,300 "articles made of rubber for immoral purposes, and used by both sexes."[13]

---

[11] Paul S. Boyer, Purity in Print: The Vice-Society Movement and Book Censorship in America 12–13 (1968); David J. Pivar, Purity Crusade: Sexual Morality and Social Control 7, 10–11, 67–68 (1973); Sears, supra note 7, at 26–27.

[12] Heywood Broun & Margaret Leech, Anthony Comstock: Roundsman of the Lord 45–47, 82–84 (1927); Robert Bremner, Editor's Introduction to Anthony Comstock, Traps for the Young ix–xi (1967).

[13] Broun & Leech, supra note 12, at 82–85, 151; Bremner, supra note 12, at xi, xiv.

Anthony Comstock. (Brown Brothers)

After failing to obtain convictions for obscenity in a case that received national attention, Comstock became convinced that no adequate laws existed to meet this "monstrous evil."[14] The case originated in 1872 when *Woodhull and Claflin's Weekly*, the journal published by the sisters and free-love advocates Victoria Woodhull and Tennessee Claflin, carried an article asserting that Reverend Henry Ward Beecher, one of the country's most famous ministers, had a secret adulterous relationship with his best friend's wife. Furious at the abuse that moralists like Beecher directed at open advocates of free love, Woodhull and Claflin emphasized Beecher's hypocrisy rather than his adultery. Comstock had Woodhull and Claflin arrested for publishing an obscene account of Beecher's affair. The prosecution had difficulty identifying precisely what was obscene in this account and more frequently referred to the offense as a libel than as an obscenity. The *Weekly* was temporarily suspended while Woodhull and Claflin were jailed for four weeks before being released. A judge eventually dismissed the case, reasoning that the existing federal obscenity statute, which Congress

[14] Anthony Comstock, Traps for the Young 208 (Robert Bremner ed. 1967).

passed in 1865 to address concerns about material received by soldiers through the mail, did not apply to newspapers.[15]

The unsatisfactory results of this case prompted Comstock to lobby strenuously and successfully for a new and more encompassing federal statute. The official title of the law, which Congress passed hurriedly and without significant debate in 1873, was "An Act for the Suppression of Trade in, and Circulation of, obscene Literature and Articles of immoral Use." The statute created the position of special agent of the Post Office to enforce its provisions. Two days after its enactment, the Postmaster General appointed Comstock to this position, which he held until his death in 1915.[16]

Comstock focused most of his prodigious energy against a wide range of sexually related material that he considered immoral. He bragged in 1913 that he had destroyed 160 tons of obscene literature over the prior forty-one years. Roughly 75 percent of the people Comstock arrested were ultimately convicted. Because Comstock's early successes effectively suppressed a considerable amount of commercial pornography, he expanded his efforts to other evils, such as gambling. Comstock, however, never generated the same enthusiasm when the vice did not involve sex. Suppressing immoral sex was his passionate crusade; eliminating gambling a necessary chore. Shortly before he died, Comstock achieved a fitting end to his long career by helping secure the arrest and prosecution of Margaret Sanger's husband for distributing her famous pamphlet on birth control, *Family Limitations*.[17]

Most American publishers and authors in the late nineteenth century shared literary standards that prevented them from producing books Comstock would consider obscene. On rare occasions, Comstock and his vice-hunting allies tried to censor books by established authors, such as Walt Whitman's *Leaves of Grass* and Leo Tolstoy's *Kreutzer Sonata*. But Comstock generally limited his attacks on books of recognized literary value to editions broadly advertised for their sexual content.[18]

Comstock recognized that many works of genius contained sexually offensive matter. He conceded that such works should be avail-

[15] Blatt, supra note 7, at 73–76; Broun & Leech, supra note 12, at 93–97, 119–22; James C.N. Paul & Murray L. Schwartz, Federal Censorship: Obscenity in the Mail 19–21 (1961).

[16] Bremner, supra note 12, at xii–xiv; Broun & Leech, supra note 12, at 87–89, 128–42; Paul & Schwartz, supra note 15, at 21–24.

[17] Bremner, supra note 12, at xxix; Broun & Leach, supra note 12, at 15–16, 148, 202–3, 209, 249–50.

[18] Boyer, supra note 11, at 15–22; Broun & Leech, supra note 12, at 15.

able to serious readers,[19] and strenuously rejected the "false and misleading" cry that he was "attacking classics." When classic works of literature are "advertised or sold indiscriminately as 'rich,' 'rare,' and 'racy,' or 'amorous books,'" he maintained, the "intent is manifestly to sell an obscene book," and "any person so outraging public decency and good morals ought to be punished."[20] Various "popular and cheap"[21] editions of classics did not, in any event, readily attract Comstock's attention; more often, he would seize books with titles such as *The Lustful Turk* and *Voluptuous Confessions*.[22]

To nonfiction produced by free lovers, freethinkers, and popularizers of medical information, Comstock was unwilling to extend the same exemption from his conception of obscenity that he granted to legitimate editions of literary works. Comstock refused to recognize any legal difference between commercial pornography and the frequently ponderous discussions of sexual issues by serious, though unorthodox, authors.[23] Indeed, he believed that allegedly scientific treatments of sex by "a few indecent creatures calling themselves reformers" were even "more offensive to decency" and "more revolting to good morals" than explicit pornography.[24] According to Comstock, these self-perceived reformers only added hypocrisy to vice.[25]

Comstock included blasphemy within his conception of obscenity and used the Comstock Act to attack both "infidels" and "free lovers," described occasionally by Comstock as "free lusters."[26] Unlike most commercial pornographers, however, libertarian radicals who advocated freedom from sexual and religious constraints were highly educated and articulate.[27] Backgrounds in the abolitionist movement had made many of them skilled veterans of polemical debate, willing to confront government authority in defense of personal liberty and free speech. They organized, spoke, and wrote against Comstock, and, after unsuccessful efforts to repeal the Comstock Act, assisted defendants arrested on obscenity charges. These libertarian radicals provided personal and intellectual links between the abolitionists before the Civil War and the Free Speech League formed in 1902.

[19] Comstock, supra note 14, at 172.
[20] Id. at 175.
[21] Id. at 179.
[22] Broun & Leech, supra note 12, at 16.
[23] Blatt, supra note 7, at 77, 119; Broun & Leech, supra note 12, at 184–86.
[24] Comstock, supra note 14, at 158.
[25] Broun & Leech, supra note 12, at 184–85.
[26] Comstock, supra note 14, at 164, 184.
[27] Broun & Leech, supra note 12, at 188–89.

THE CONTROVERSY OVER *CUPID'S YOKES*

The most significant controversy between Comstock and the libertarian radicals involved *Cupid's Yokes,* a widely distributed pamphlet on free love published in 1876 by Ezra Heywood.[28] Comstock instigated multiple prosecutions of this pamphlet, which led to the key legal precedent under the Comstock Act.

Like many other libertarian radicals of the late nineteenth century, Heywood was influenced by reformers of the antebellum period. His writings reflect personal associations with Josiah Warren, the founder of individualist anarchism, and William Lloyd Garrison, the leading radical abolitionist. Heywood derived his own controversial views about free love from their emphasis on individual autonomy.

Heywood accurately described the range of his reform activities as "negro emancipation, peace, woman's enfranchisement, temperance, labor and love reform."[29] Born in 1829, Heywood followed a familiar path from evangelical Protestantism to social reform. He demonstrated an early interest in civil liberties while preparing for the ministry at Brown University. When he graduated from Brown in 1856, he delivered a commencement address entitled "Milton: The Advocate of Intellectual Freedom," which reflected on Milton's speech, "For the Liberty of Unlicens'd Printing." After meeting Garrison in 1858, Heywood abandoned the ministry to become a traveling lecturer for the Massachusetts Anti-Slavery Society.[30] As Heywood later put it, "I 'fell' from well-dressed and full-stomached religion to abolition 'infidelity.'"[31]

The pressures of the Civil War created a rift between Heywood and most of his colleagues in the Garrisonian abolitionist movement. Although Garrisonians generally abandoned their former pacifism, Heywood continued to oppose war as a means to end slavery. Consistent with his anarchist beliefs, Heywood even affirmed the right of Southern states to secede from the Union. Heywood also opposed government suppression of antiwar speech. At the 1863 meeting of the Massachusetts Anti-Slavery Society, he unsuccessfully introduced several resolutions supporting free speech and criticized the prosecution of an Ohio politician, C. L. Vallandigham, for advocating a negotiated settlement of the war.[32] Although Heywood disagreed with Vallandigham's proposal as an

---

[28] E. H. Heywood, Cupid's Yokes: The Binding Forces of Conjugal Life (1877).

[29] Sears, supra note 7, at 156.

[30] Blatt, supra note 7, 16–20; Broun & Leech, supra note 12, at 172; Sears, supra note 7, at 153–54.

[31] Blatt, supra note 7, at 18.

[32] Blatt, supra note 7, at 29–31; Sears, supra note 7, at 154–55.

"immoral and useless method of conciliating the Slave Oligarchy," he claimed that Vallandigham had the same "undeniable and sacred right of free speech" that the abolitionists had claimed before the war for their own attacks on slavery.[33] Fellow abolitionist Stephen S. Foster charged that Heywood's resolutions favored the South and should not be supported by an organization opposed to slavery. Although the meeting tabled the resolutions, Heywood increasingly became cut off from the Garrisonians.[34]

Heywood's criticisms of Garrisonian abolitionists for refusing to uphold the free speech rights of antiwar Democrats prompted Josiah Warren to visit him soon afterwards. Impressed by his meeting with Warren in 1863, as he had been by Garrison in 1858, Heywood spent the next five years studying and developing Warren's ideas about labor reform.[35] Heywood saw his new interest in labor as an extension of his work as an abolitionist. "What slave oligarchy was to republicanism," he maintained, "our profit-system is to legitimate enterprise."[36] Joined by other former abolitionists, Heywood began in 1867 to form various "labor reform" leagues designed to promote his views.[37]

Like other individualist anarchists, Heywood perceived labor and sexual reform as related concerns. In 1873, Heywood and his wife founded the New England Free Love League as a companion organization to the labor reform leagues.[38] Heywood also linked these issues in the prospectus to *The Word*, a journal he founded in 1872. According to the prospectus, the new journal supported "the abolition of speculative income, of women's slavery, and war government."[39] Consistent with his life-long dedication to free speech, Heywood created a section of *The Word* called The Opposition. This section printed criticisms of the editor's views, a feature seldom found in radical journals of the period.[40]

In 1876, Heywood published *Cupid's Yokes*, a twenty-three page pamphlet whose cover proclaimed "the Natural Right and Necessity of Sexual Self-Government."[41] Heywood's views about "sexual self-government" and his direct attacks on Comstock seemed almost to invite Comstock's prosecutions of the pamphlet, which began within months of its publication.

---

[33] Blatt, supra note 7, at 29. [34] Id., at 29–33.
[35] Id., at 33–34, 41, 52–54; Martin, supra note 1, at 105–10.
[36] Blatt, supra note 7, at 52.
[37] Id. at 44–54; Martin, supra note 1, at 112; David Montgomery, Beyond Equality: Labor and the Radical Republicans, 1862–1872, at 137, 411–14 (1981).
[38] Blatt, supra note 7, at 82; Sears, supra note 7, at 157.
[39] Blatt, supra note 7, at 51. [40] Id.; Martin, supra note 1, at 116–17.
[41] Heywood, supra note 28, at 1.

Heywood called the Comstock Act "the National Gag-Law."[42] Conceding that Congress and President Grant had framed it "with good intentions," he assumed that the lawmakers were "ignorant of the cause of the evils they proposed to correct" and were "probably unaware of the unwarrantable stretch of despotism embodied in their measure, and of the use which would be made of it." Heywood directed his criticism against Comstock himself, the "real author" of the legislation.[43] He called Comstock *a religious monomaniac,* whom the mistaken will of Congress and the lascivious fanaticism of the Young Men's Christian Association have empowered to use the Federal Courts to suppress free inquiry." Comstock's prosecutorial zeal, Heywood observed, revealed "the spirit that lighted the fires of the inquisition."[44]

Throughout *Cupid's Yokes,* Heywood linked free love to abolitionism and labor reform under an umbrella of anarchist commitments to individual autonomy and freedom from state control. Although the pamphlet included some sexually explicit references to birth control,[45] it was essentially a polemical attack on marriage. *Cupid's Yokes* contained few references to sexual activity and no passages that could conceivably be considered prurient or titillating.

According to Heywood, the institution of marriage allowed "the legalized slavery of women,"[46] the "idea that women belong to men" as a form of property.[47] Marriage, the "great social fraud," made sex a "marketable commodity." A prostitute may be bought for a night, but a wife "becomes a 'prostitute' for life." Heywood regarded marriage and capitalism, both sanctioned by the state, as "twin relic[s] of barbarism" that robbed individuals of their personal sovereignty. Free love, Heywood maintained, would liberate women from their husbands, just as using labor as the measure of economic value would liberate workers from capitalists. Emphasizing the relationship between sexual and labor reform, Heywood wrote that "when power to accumulate property without work is abolished, the habits of industry, which both men and women must acquire, will promote sexual temperance."[48]

Heywood asserted that "the right of private judgment, which is conceded in politics and religion," should also be extended to domestic life. He regarded "sexual self-government," the right of individuals to determine for themselves "when, where, and how" their sexual organs will be used, as a key component of "Personal

---

[42] Id. at 10.
[44] Id. at 12.
[46] Id. at 8.
[48] Id. at 21.

[43] Id. at 11.
[45] See id. at 20–21.
[47] Id. at 5.

Liberty and the Rights of Conscience." "If government cannot justly determine what ticket we shall vote, what church we shall attend, or what books we shall read," Heywood asked, "by what authority does it watch at key-holes and burst open bed-chamber doors to drag lovers from sacred seclusion?"[49] Invoking the infamous Beecher case, he mischievously observed that clergymen and legislators are often "the first to violate what they profanely assume to be a divine ordinance."[50] Like Woodhull and Claflin, he criticized Beecher, not for "exercising his natural right to commit adultery," but for his "false and hypocritical attitude, as an official 'solemnizer' of the social crime of marriage."[51]

The growth of individualism over centuries of Western history, Heywood confidently proclaimed, would eventually lead to the reform of marriage and capitalism. He asserted that the right of private judgment – already won for religious beliefs by Luther and for political views by Adams and Jefferson – "is now legitimately claimed in behalf of sexual self-government." According to Heywood, "Protestantism, Magna Charta, Habeas Corpus, Trial by Jury, Freedom of Speech and Press, the Declaration of Independence, Jeffersonian State Rights, Negro-Emancipation, were fore-ordained to help Love and Labor Reformers bury sexual slavery, with profit-piracy, in their already open graves." He believed that the "bonds of affection," which are Cupid's yokes, would eventually replace the "dictation of statutes" regulating marriage.[52]

Heywood stressed that contrary to the "distorted popular view" (and perhaps to his own acceptance of Reverend Beecher's "natural right to commit adultery"), free love opposed rather than advocated "unrestrained licentiousness." The sexual freedom sought by free lovers recognized "that every one's person is sacred from invasion; that the sexual instinct shall no longer be a savage, uncontrollable usurper, but be subject to thought and civilization."[53] Underlining his own opposition to licentiousness, Heywood expressed concern about the "alarming increase of obscene prints and pictures" and the "depraving" influence of obscene literature.[54]

Comstock initiated multiple prosecutions of *Cupid's Yokes*, which he called "a most obscene and loathsome book" and "too foul for description."[55] He considered Heywood the "chief creature" of the "vile creed" of free love.[56] Comstock first prosecuted Heywood in November 1877, arresting him immediately after a free love con-

---

[49] Id. at 22.
[51] Id. at 10n*.
[53] Id. at 19.
[55] Comstock, supra note 14, at 163.

[50] Id. at 6
[52] Id. at 23.
[54] Id. at 11.
[56] Id. at 159.

vention at which Heywood presided and his wife spoke. Comstock wrote a lengthy description of how he "trapped" Heywood from an audience in which he "could see lust in every face."[57]

The trial court limited the evidence to the factual question of whether Heywood had actually mailed his pamphlet. The judge did not allow Heywood to discuss the purpose or philosophy of *Cupid's Yokes,* and instructed the jury that a work is obscene if any part of it has an immoral tendency. The jury found Heywood guilty of mailing an obscene publication in violation of the Comstock Act.[58]

Heywood's lawyers appealed on First Amendment grounds, but the court delayed its ruling pending the Supreme Court decision in *Ex parte Jackson,* a First Amendment challenge to a federal statute that prohibited the mailing of lottery advertisements. The Supreme Court rejected this challenge, reasoning broadly that the Post Office does not violate freedom of the press when it excludes from the mails "matter deemed injurious to the public morals."[59] Probably because the Supreme Court indicated in *Ex parte Jackson* that its reasoning covered obscene publications as well as lottery advertisements, the appellate court rejected Heywood's First Amendment challenge to the Comstock Act. Heywood was ultimately fined and sentenced to two years in jail.[60]

Soon after Heywood's imprisonment, his wife's sister brought copies of *Cupid's Yokes* to the convention of the New York State Freethinkers Association. D. M. Bennett, leader of the most militantly antireligious and socially radical wing of the freethought movement,[61] and other freethinkers sold these copies on her behalf and were immediately arrested under the state counterpart to the Comstock Act. The case, after being postponed, never went to trial. Bennett, however, had already been arrested by Comstock for mailing his tract, "An Open Letter to Jesus Christ." Intervention in Washington by prominent freethinkers had led to the dismissal of this case. Nevertheless, the episode convinced Bennett that Comstock was indirectly responsible for his New York arrest.[62]

Bennett concluded that Comstock had incorporated blasphemy within his definition of obscenity and would continue to use the Comstock Act as a pretext for suppressing radical freethinkers who opposed religion. He decided to challenge Comstock and defend freedom of the press by distributing *Cupid's Yokes* to anyone who

---

[57] Id. at 163–66.   [58] Blatt, supra note 7, at 115–17.

[59] 96 U.S. 727, 736 (1877), discussed infra, Chapter 3, at text accompanying notes 22–23.

[60] Blatt, supra note 7, at 117–18; Sears, supra note 7, at 169–70.

[61] See Sidney Warren, American Freethought, 1860–1914, at 36, 39–40, 126 (1943).

[62] Blatt, supra note 7, at 118; Broun & Leech, supra note 12, at 175–76, 180.

requested it. Although Bennett disagreed with many of Heywood's views on free love, he did not think the pamphlet obscene. According to Bennett, *Cupid's Yokes* was written not "to excite passion, but to elicit thought."[63]

Comstock, predictably, arrested Bennett for mailing *Cupid's Yokes*.[64] Comstock subsequently explained his prosecution by distinguishing "honest infidels," who soberly stated their opinions in religious matters, from Bennett and his followers, who lived "by blaspheming the name of God," provoked laughter and applause from their audiences, and used "scoffs and sneers to wound the feelings" of people with different views.[65] Bennett was fined and sentenced to thirteen months in jail following a trial that produced the key early decision under the Comstock Act, a precedent that would stand for over fifty years.[66]

Bennett maintained that his indictment was defective because it failed to identify the allegedly obscene passages in *Cupid's Yokes,* an argument the court rejected.[67] More fundamentally, he urged the judge to charge the jury that "when the words and sentences claimed to be obscene are used in a social polemic," the author's motives should be determinative. Bennett claimed that words should not constitute an offense under the Comstock Act as long as they "were used by the author in good faith, to properly and reasonably set forth his mistaken and wicked doctrines and sentiments, and not wantonly or unnecessarily, to offend decency or to excite lust or disgust." Jury views about the destructive effect such doctrines "might have upon morals, or society, or the family, or religion, or the welfare of the community" should be irrelevant.[68]

In his charge to the jury, the trial judge expressed a different position. "Freelovers and freethinkers have a right to their views," he conceded, and may express and publish them as long as they are not obscene.[69] But after emphasizing that freedom of the press does not protect obscenity, he added that ideas can be obscene even if "conveyed by words which in themselves are not of an obscene character." The test of obscenity, the judge stressed, is not the motive of the author but the effect of the words upon the reader.[70] The court

[63] Broun & Leech, supra note 12, at 175–76, 180.
[64] D.R.M. Bennett, Anthony Comstock: His Career of Cruelty and Crimes (Da Capo Press 1971) (1878), includes Bennett's account of his own case as part of his survey of Comstock's early prosecutions.
[65] Comstock, supra note 14, at 184.
[66] Blatt, supra note 7, at 119; Sears, supra note 7, at 168.
[67] United States v. Bennett, 24 F. Cas. 1093, 1095–98 (C.C.S.D.N.Y. 1879) (No. 14,571).
[68] Id. at 1100.   [69] Id. at 1101.
[70] Id. at 1102.

of appeals upheld this charge by adopting the test of obscenity from an English decision, *The Queen v. Hicklin*:[71] "whether the tendency of the matter charged as obscenity is to deprave and corrupt those whose minds are open to such immoral influences, and into whose hands a publication of this sort may fall."[72] This bad tendency test, which the English court derived from the existing law of defamation and blasphemy,[73] became the prevailing definition of obscenity in subsequent cases under the Comstock Act.

The prosecutions of Heywood and Bennett prompted the National Liberal League, the leading organization of freethinkers in the United States, to petition Congress against the Comstock Act. In February 1878, the League submitted to Congress a petition signed by 50,000 to 70,000 people, asserting that the Comstock Act had become an instrument of moral and religious persecution. The petition urged Congress to repeal or materially modify the Comstock Act so that it could not "be used to abridge the freedom of the press or of conscience."[74] A House Committee replied by affirming the constitutionality of the Act and by stressing that "the Post-Office was not established to carry instruments of vice, or obscene writings, indecent pictures, or lewd books."[75]

Debate over the Comstock Act produced a schism within the National Liberal League at its 1878 convention. A majority of members endorsed repeal, while a minority, including Robert Ingersoll, the most eminent freethinker in America, advocated only a revision containing a precise and narrow definition of obscenity. This schism prompted Ingersoll and other key figures in the minority to resign, irreparably weakening the League and substantially undermining organized opposition to the Comstock Act. Though substantial disagreement with the law persisted, subsequent attempts to repeal it were weak and sporadic.[76]

---

[71] 3 L.R.-Q.B. 360, 371 (1868). In Hicklin, Chief Judge Cockburn rejected the contention that a book should not be declared obscene if the person selling it did not intend to harm "the public mind, but to expose the practices and errors of the confessional system in the Roman Catholic Church." 3 L.R.-Q.B. at 370. The bad tendency of the book, not the subjective intent of the author or seller, determined whether it was obscene. Id. at 371–73.

[72] United States v. Bennett, 24 F. Cas. at 1104.

[73] Hicklin, 3 L.R.-Q.B. at 366; see 4 William Blackstone, Commentaries *150, *152; Leonard W. Levy, Emergence of a Free Press 7–8 (1985) (at English common law, all four categories of criminal libel – blasphemy, obscenity, private libel, and seditious libel – allowed punishment for the bad tendency of speech).

[74] Comstock, supra note 14, at 190.   [75] Id. at 195.

[76] Blatt, supra note 7, at 126–27; Broun & Leech, supra note 12, at 179; Stow Persons, Free Religion: An American Faith 123–25 (1947).

The most significant continuing source of resistance to the Comstock Act came from the National Defense Association (NDA), an organization formed in 1878 by more radical members of the National Liberal League. Edward Bond Foote, a physician who collaborated with his father, Edward Bliss Foote, in producing medical works for the general public, helped establish the NDA and became its secretary and leading financial supporter. The elder Foote, virtually alone, had opposed the 1872 New York bill that served as the prototype for the federal Comstock Act. He recognized that Comstock's legislative efforts posed a threat to his hugely successful book, *Medical Common Sense,* first published in 1858.[77]

Rejecting the increasing professionalization of medicine, Foote wrote *Medical Common Sense* in a democratic voice accessible to the general public. The book dealt extensively and explicitly with social as well as physiological aspects of sex and laid the groundwork for the birth control movement of the twentieth century. In addition to discussing contraceptive methods and devices, *Medical Common Sense* included information about how to obtain these devices from Foote. After responding to a inquiry from one of Comstock's agents, Foote was arrested in 1874, and in 1876 he was convicted and heavily fined under the Comstock Act.[78] Comstock later wrote that Foote was convicted "not for sending a medical work, but advertisements of an infamous article – an incentive to crime to young girls and women."[79] The court, however, rejected Foote's broader argument that the Comstock Act's exclusion of obscenity from the mail should not be interpreted to cover "medical advice given by a physician in reply to the inquiry of a patient."[80]

Foote reacted to this decision by deleting information about contraceptive methods from his book and pamphlets. In its place, he included protests against the Comstock Act. For example, in a twenty-one page pamphlet entitled *A Step Backward,* Foote conceded that any "decent-minded person" would not "object to the professed design" of the Comstock Act, "the suppression of the traffic in obscene literature, immoral pictures, etc." But he found it "difficult to comprehend why articles and things for the *prevention of conception* should have been so unqualifiedly included" in the definition of obscenity."[81] The conviction and fine also prompted

[77] Sears, supra note 7, at 193, 199–200.
[78] Linda Gordon, Woman's Body, Woman's Right 164–67 (revised ed. 1990); Sears, supra note 7, at 184–85, 194–95, 197.
[79] Anthony Comstock, Frauds Exposed 427 (reprint ed. 1969).
[80] United States v. Foote, 25 F. Cas. 1140, 1141 (S.D.N.Y. 1876) (No. 15, 128).
[81] Edward Bliss Foote, A Step Backward 1 (1875).

Foote and his son to became principal backers of resistance against Comstock, especially through the NDA. The enormous sales of *Medical Common Sense,* which its author estimated at 300,000 copies between its publication in 1858 and 1876, provided the Footes with substantial financial resources for this effort.[82]

The NDA's stated objectives were "to investigate all questionable cases of prosecution under what are now known as the Comstock laws, state and national, and to extend sympathy, moral support, and material aid to those who may be unjustly assailed by the enemies of free speech and free press."[83] As its first project, the NDA organized a mass meeting at Boston's Faneuil Hall in 1878 to protest Heywood's conviction. A crowd of between 4,000 and 6,000 people passed resolutions objecting to the suppression of free speech and urging President Hayes to pardon Heywood.[84] The main speech at the meeting criticized the Supreme Court's decision in *Ex parte Jackson.* Claiming that "depraved theologians" had invented the concept of obscenity, the speaker referred to the Comstock Act as an "unconstitutional espionage-law" because it vested uncontrolled discretion in the Post Office.[85] The meeting generated numerous petitions to President Hayes, who pardoned Heywood six months after his imprisonment.[86]

President Hayes, however, did not respond to the subsequent campaign to pardon Bennett, who was in many respects a more sympathetic figure than Heywood. Bennett distributed but did not write *Cupid's Yokes,* and shared few of Heywood's radical views on sexual relations. Elderly and ill, Bennett attracted the active assistance of Robert Ingersoll, who was convinced that Comstock had really prosecuted Bennett for his anticlerical views, using Bennett's distribution of *Cupid's Yokes* as a convenient pretext. Ingersoll's own conservative positions on marriage and sexuality prevented him from helping Heywood, but he did meet with President Hayes on several occasions to advocate a pardon for Bennett. The NDA, hoping to duplicate its success in obtaining a pardon for Heywood, organized a similar petition campaign, in which it claimed to have gathered 200,000 signatures. Hayes, however, refused to pardon

[82] Sears, supra note 7, at 193, 197.

[83] Samuel D. Putnam, Four Hundred Years of Freethought 538 (1894) (quoting constitution of NDA).

[84] Blatt, supra note 7, at 129–30; Sears, supra note 7, at 171.

[85] T. B. Wakeman, The Comstock Postal Law Unconstitutional: Plain Duty of All Citizens, Speech at Faneuil Hall (Aug. 1, 1878), in The Comstock Laws Considered as to Their Constitutionality 3, 42 (New York, D. M. Bennett 1878); see id. at 19–29 (criticizing Ex parte Jackson).

[86] Blatt, supra note 7, at 131–32.

Bennett, despite the conclusion by his own attorney general that the pamphlet, though offensive, was not obscene. Hayes was probably influenced by the adverse public reaction to his recent pardon of Heywood, opposition to Bennett from religious groups and the president's devout wife, and Comstock's dramatic production of apparently compromising letters Bennett wrote to a young woman, which prompted Ingersoll to withdraw his support.[87]

Over subsequent decades, the NDA distributed anti-Comstock literature, lobbied with some success to prevent extensions of the Comstock Act and analogous state legislation, made fruitless efforts to limit Post Office discretion to censor the mails, and provided aid to defendants prosecuted by Comstock. In 1882, for example, it intervened when the Boston district attorney advised Walt Whitman's publisher that portions of *Leaves of Grass* were obscene. Whitman refused to delete this material from a second edition, and when his publisher stopped publication of the book, Heywood printed two of the offending poems in *The Word*. Comstock had Heywood arrested, but at the NDA's urging the judge dismissed the indictment for failing to identify the allegedly obscene passages in Whitman's poems, the argument rejected by the court in the influential *Bennett* case. The NDA, however, was unsuccessful in helping Heywood in 1890, when he was convicted under the Comstock Act for publishing a letter that contained the word *fuck* and for other alleged obscenities. Heywood and his wife apparently believed that everyday use of such words would help to demystify sex. Despite petitions and pamphlets circulated by the NDA, President Harrison refused to pardon Heywood, who served a two-year jail sentence.[88]

LUCIFER: THE LIGHT-BEARER

Beginning in 1886, material published in *Lucifer: The Light-Bearer* (*Lucifer*) became the main focus of disputes between Comstock and the NDA. *Lucifer* had become the leading radical journal of sex reform and provided the most direct link between the libertarian radicalism of the nineteenth century and the Free Speech League. It originated under another name, the *Valley Falls Liberal,*

---

[87] Blatt, supra note 7, at 127, 133; Broun & Leech, supra note 12, at 180, 182; Sears, supra note 7, at 171.

[88] Blatt, supra note 7, at 128–30, 142–44, 169; Putnam, supra note 83, at 536–47; Sears, supra note 7, at 177, 181. Free Speech: Report of Ezra H. Heywood's Defense 11, 43 (Princeton, Mass., Co-Operative Publishing Co. n.d.), contains Heywood's address to the jury and the judge's charge to the jury.

founded by Moses Harman in 1880. Harman, born in 1830, followed a familiar path for libertarian radicals of his generation. A minister who embraced abolitionism, Harman, like Heywood, eventually abandoned religion for freethought and individualist anarchism. He became an advocate for various secular social causes in the late nineteenth century, including labor and sex reform. Harman's journal, soon renamed the *Kansas Liberal,* contained articles that covered the range of his libertarian views and carried excerpts from Heywood's *Cupid's Yokes* and Whitman's *Leaves of Grass.* Harman helped support his journal through a mail-order business in radical pamphlets and books, including works by Thomas Paine, Josiah Warren, and the Footes.[89]

Through a meeting of the Kansas Liberal League, Harman developed a friendship with Edwin Cox Walker, an individualist anarchist and perhaps the country's most successful organizer of local liberal leagues. Walker became Harman's coeditor at the *Kansas Liberal,* and in 1883 they changed its name to *Lucifer: The Light-Bearer.* Harman and Walker wanted to distinguish the more radical *Lucifer,* which they described as an "Anarchist-Freethought Journal," from other freethought publications that used the term *liberal.*[90] They probably used Lucifer, the devil's name, to mock and enrage their religious opponents. As Harman explained: "The god of the Bible had doomed mankind to perpetual ignorance – they would never have known Good from Evil if Lucifer had not told them how to become wise as the gods themselves. Hence, according to theology, Lucifer was the first teacher of science." Walker helped support *Lucifer* through his popular lectures, which were mostly on freethought themes, but which also dealt with such topics as "The New Sexual Morality" and "Medical Laws and Obscenity Legislation."[91] As an active lecturer and journalist, Walker emphasized the connection between "industrial and sexual emancipation of the race" and criticized economic radicals for failing to recognize that a comprehensive social revolution must remove impediments to free love.[92]

"Our Object," an article published in the first issue after Walker became Harman's coeditor, contained a long list of freedoms to which they were committed: "free press, free rostrum, free mails . . . , free land, free homes, free food, free drink, free medicine, free Sunday, free marriage and free divorce." Emphasizing their anarchist views, the editors concluded by declaring that they "advocate

[89] Sears, supra note 7, at 28–33, 46, 48, 67–69.
[90] Id. at 53–55, 64.   [91] Id. at 54–55.
[92] Id. at 61.

the *Sovereignty of the Individual* or Self Government. We would have every man and every woman to be the proprietor of himself or herself!"[93] Through the 1880s and 1890s, *Lucifer's* editorial focus moved increasingly from advocacy of freethought and anarchism to discussion of sexual matters and related free speech issues.[94]

Harman and Walker lived their beliefs. In an "autonomistic marriage" ceremony conducted by Harman, his daughter Lillian married Walker. The ceremony rejected any role for the church or the state in marriage and recognized the continuing "sovereign" right of both partners to "repulse" the other's sexual advances.[95] In a highly publicized case that reached the Kansas Supreme Court, the couple was prosecuted and imprisoned for violating the state's marriage laws.[96] Only after realizing that *Lucifer's* continued existence depended on their return did the couple decide to pay the court costs enabling their release from jail. Explaining their actions to readers of *Lucifer,* they wrote that they were willing to suffer imprisonment "in the cause of woman's sex emancipation . . . only so long as Pen, Paper, Tongue and Mail were free. When freedom of discussion and investigation is threatened there is no longer any question which can rightfully take precedence to that."[97] In 1888, however, Walker and Lillian Harman left *Lucifer* to start their own journal, perhaps in connection with Walker's criticism of Moses Harman for deviating from anarchist principles by advocating "ballot-boxism," the limited use of voting for social reform.[98]

Both before and after Walker's departure, Harman used *Lucifer* to express his libertarian views on free speech. In 1886, he wrote in *Lucifer* that "words are not deeds, and it is not the province of civil law to take preventive measures against remote or possible consequences of words, no matter how violent or 'incendiary.'"[99] He protested convictions of Heywood as violations of free speech and claimed that the Haymarket anarchists, who were convicted of murder when a bomb exploded at a mass rally they had been addressing, "were hung . . . for exercising their equal right of free speech."[100] In the spring of 1886, Harman informed the readers of *Lucifer* that he would not censor any correspondence based on the language used. This policy led to a decade of repeated arrests and imprisonments under the Comstock Act.[101] Harman published letters protesting that marriage is nothing more than "legal rape,"

---

[93] Id. at 62.
[94] Id. at 68.
[95] Id. at 81, 83–85.
[96] See id. at 86–96.
[97] Id. at 96.
[98] Id. at 136–38.
[99] Id. at 79.
[100] Id. at 137.
[101] Blatt, supra note 7, at 161; Sears, supra note 7, at 74.

objecting to contraception as depriving women of "all excuse for not yielding to the sexual demands of their masters," and containing an anecdote about a married couple who had confessed their sexual improprieties to each other.[102] The publication of these letters, and a subsequent one from a physician referring to oral sex, prompted Harman's own legal problems. Throughout this period, he was supported by Foote and the National Defense Association.[103]

Harman suffered a final arrest and imprisonment in 1905 for publishing obscene articles in *Lucifer*, including one that advised women to refrain from sexual relations during pregnancy. Harman's imprisonment at age seventy-five to one year of hard labor prompted protests from George Bernard Shaw, who claimed that he did not visit the United States out of fear "of being arrested by Mr. Anthony Comstock and imprisoned like Mr. Moses Harman."[104] During his trial, appeal, and subsequent imprisonment, Harman received direct assistance from the Free Speech League, whose founding in 1902 he had eagerly publicized in the pages of *Lucifer*.[105]

THE EMERGENCE OF THE FREE SPEECH LEAGUE

The Free Speech League emerged from the libertarian radicalism of the late nineteenth century. Roger Baldwin, who became acquainted with League members during the years immediately before he founded the ACLU in 1920, later recalled that they included "the anarchists, the agnostics or atheists, the birth-controllers and the apostles of a once slightly 'fashionable' cult on the left, the free lovers."[106] Edward Bond Foote, Edwin Cox Walker, and Moses Harman, veterans of confrontations with Comstock, were instrumental in establishing the League in 1902, and the League's emergence is best documented in the pages of Harman's journal, *Lucifer*.

The League organized in immediate reaction to the flurry of legislation and prosecutions against anarchist speech following an anarchist's assassination of President McKinley in 1901. From its inception, however, the League established ambitious goals that extended beyond any particular threat to free speech. In contrast to the National Defense Association, which had opposed the Com-

---

[102] Sears, supra note 7, at 74–76.

[103] Blatt, supra note 7, at 169; Sears, supra note 7, at 111, 116, 200.

[104] Sears, supra note 7, at 263–65.

[105] See Alice Stone Blackwell, The Postoffice and Free Speech, Woman's J., Aug. 12, 1905, reprinted in Lucifer: The Light-Bearer, Mar. 15, 1906, at 359; The Case of Moses Harman, Lucifer: The Light-Bearer, Mar. 15, 1906, at 478.

stock Act and defended libertarian radicals prosecuted for obscenity, the Free Speech League intended to protect the constitutional free speech of all citizens, whatever their views. A statement published in *Lucifer* identified the League as "a nucleus around which to rally the opponents of a censorship, . . . composed of men and women of every phase of opinion, who believe in preserving the freedom of speech, press, assemblage and mails, guaranteed to us by the constitution of the United States and essential to our existence as a free people."[107] The League's founders were confident that an unprecedented array of threats to free speech would attract a broader public to the Free Speech League than the rather narrow group of libertarian radicals who had previously attempted to combat the Comstock Act. Located in New York City, the League encouraged membership throughout the United States.[108]

Articles in *Lucifer* following the assassination of President McKinley revealed both the lingering impact of libertarian radicalism and the expectation that a more diverse constituency would defend the constitutional right of free speech. Demonstrating the continuing influence of the abolitionist struggle on libertarian radicalism, *Lucifer* invoked the memory of Elijah Lovejoy, an abolitionist killed by a mob in 1837 while defending his printing press, and lauded him as a martyr who died "for the principle of freedom of the press."[109] An editorial advised opponents of the proposed antianarchy laws "to 'AGITATE, AGITATE, AGITATE,' as the old Abolitionists used to say and do." The "only way to prevent such legislative enactments," the editorial stressed, "is to create a public conscience that will be felt and heeded by our national lawmakers."[110]

Just as agitation by an abolitionist minority had ultimately produced a national commitment to end slavery during the Civil War, Harman believed in 1902 that agitation by libertarian radicals could produce a similar expansion of support for the principle of free speech. According to Harman, the repression of dissenting speech in the new American colonies won following the Spanish-American War of 1898 had "opened the eyes of an immense number of peo-

---

[106] The Reminiscences of Roger Baldwin 115 (1954) (Oral History Collection, Butler Library, Columbia University) [hereinafter Baldwin Reminiscences].

[107] Free Speech or Slavery, Lucifer: The Light-Bearer, June 22, 1905, at 327.

[108] Edwin Cox Walker, The Free Speech League, Lucifer: The Light-Bearer, June 22, 1905, at 327.

[109] James F. Morton, Jr., The Fight for Free Speech, Lucifer: The Light-Bearer, Nov. 12, 1903, at 345.

[110] M. Harman, To Our Press Writers, Lucifer: The Light-Bearer, Feb. 13, 1902, at 36.

ple, who were blind to the dangers of Comstockism." No longer
were free speech issues being raised only by "the propaganda of
extreme radicalism," particularly regarding sensitive sexual matters.
Harman confidently proclaimed that "even among those who will
not so much as listen to our more extreme views," some people "will
respond to the plea for free speech, when the hideousness of the
imperialist conspiracy is brought fully home." Once made aware of
the extensive government attacks on free expression, including the
denial of the mails, "even the conservative can never feel himself
wholly safe." Convinced that the "time is ripe for appealing, not
merely to the few radicals, but to the great American public," Harman overcame his anarchist preference for "as little formality as possible in connection with associative effort" and welcomed the newly
formed Free Speech League with enthusiasm. He believed that the
League, if properly supported, could become "the most important
movement of recent years," and he therefore urged the "widest publicity" and the "broadest platform."[111]

A call for "concerted action in defense of speech and utterance"
from the newspaper of the anarchist Home Colony in Washington
State stimulated the efforts that eventually led to the creation of
the Free Speech League. The Manhattan Liberal Club, an organization successively led by Edward Bond Foote and Edwin Cox
Walker, responded to this call by observing the increase in attacks
against free speech under "more and more numerous pretexts."
The Club endorsed the creation of a committee "to devise ways
and means for a united and an effective movement in defense of
that which is fundamental to all progress – liberty of investigation
and expression."[112]

Supporters of this proposed committee hoped that Louis F.
Post, the well-known editor of a progressive journal in Chicago
called *The Public,* would become its chairman and select the other
members.[113] Post, who subsequently served as assistant secretary of
labor in the Wilson administration, had vigorously protested the
prosecution of anarchists following the assassination of President
McKinley. In an editorial in *The Public,* excerpted in *Lucifer,* Post
complained that "plutocrats" were attacking philosophical anarchists for expressing views that "are cordially shared by every one
who opposes the political and economic influences which are
everywhere making a few rich through privilege and keeping the
many consequently poor." Though "nominally against Anarchists,"

---

[111] Ruminations, Lucifer: The Light-Bearer, June 5, 1902, at 161.
[112] A Call for Concerted Action, Lucifer: The Light-Bearer, May 1, 1902, at 122.
[113] Id.

this "crusade of plutocracy," which Post called a "movement for the abrogation of constitutional guarantees of free speech," actually targeted critics of American colonialism and imperialism and, more generally, "all who criticize with any vigor at all the political party which happens to be in power."[114] Perhaps fearing association with radicals to his left, Post apparently declined to serve, for within weeks of publishing the original call *Lucifer* announced the formation of a new organization called the Free Speech League that did not include Post.[115]

Theodore Schroeder became the League's secretary and key administrator, while simultaneously producing substantial scholarship about the meaning of free speech. Gilbert Roe, Schroeder's law school classmate at the University of Wisconsin and the former law partner of Senator Robert M. La Follette, handled many free speech cases for the League. The president of the League, Leonard Abbott, had abandoned the conservative, commercial traditions of his old New England family for anarchist political and journalistic activities.[116] Lincoln Steffens, the famous "muckraking" journalist and author of *The Shame of the Cities,* served on the League's board of directors and publicized its activities. Two of the most visible radicals during the decade before World War I – Emma Goldman, the notorious anarchist, and Margaret Sanger, the activist for birth control – had close associations with the League. Although the leading members of the Free Speech League generally shared libertarian radical views, some of them had broader connections outside the small group of middle-class freethinkers, anarchists, and sex radicals who previously suffered from and opposed the Comstock Act. For example, Roe and Steffens had professional and personal ties with major figures in progressive politics, while Goldman and Sanger had significant contacts with working-class radicals.

The Free Speech League was involved in virtually every major free speech controversy during the first two decades of the twentieth century. League members provided financial and legal assistance to defend free speech principles in court. They publicized free speech disputes, printed and distributed pamphlets, organized protest meetings and demonstrations, corresponded and met with public officials, testified before government commissions, and lectured at scholarly and professional meetings. Operating in a hostile environment, the League generated some public

---

[114] The Crusade of Plutocracy, Lucifer: The Light-Bearer, Oct. 31, 1901, at 342.

[115] By the Way, Lucifer: The Light-Bearer, May 15, 1902, at 139.

[116] Paul Avrich, The Modern School Movement: Anarchism and Education in the United States 165–72 (1980).

and political support for its broad conception of free speech, and even won an occasional legal case.

Both in its writings and in its activities, the League worked hard to fulfill its commitment to defend free speech for all viewpoints. Lincoln Steffens publicized this commitment in his journalism, and Theodore Schroeder underlined it in his articles and correspondence. Schroeder constantly chastised people who supported the principle of free speech for their own opinions, but who were indifferent or hostile to the repression of views they did not share. As members of the League recognized, however, the overwhelming majority of free speech controversies during its existence stemmed from the repression of radical speech. For example, Schroeder claimed that the three major sources of such controversies were attempts by Socialist groups to speak on public streets, efforts to discuss sex, and Emma Goldman's speeches praising anarchism while attacking religion, the "legally maintained family," economic inequities, and government coercion.[117] Few cases involving conservatives or reactionaries arose to test the League's general willingness to protect views its leaders opposed, as cases involving the Ku Klux Klan and neo-Nazis later tested the ACLU. The League, however, did overcome the parochial inability of various single-issue or feuding radical groups to recognize that government repression of speech was a common problem shared by them all.

Nor did the League limit its support to radicals, who often failed to assist each other. It helped religious speakers as well as freethinkers, reformist as well as radical unions, and various nonpolitical speakers, including an attorney disbarred for criticizing a judge,[118] and a man convicted for distributing pamphlets opposing compulsory vaccination.[119] Schroeder protested the suppression of a play in Philadelphia "because it was obnoxious to the Negro population."[120] Moreover, in his administrative capacity Schroeder repeatedly made

---

[117] Theodore Schroeder, Free Speech For Radicals 54–55 (enlarged ed. 1916).

[118] Letter from Charles A. Thatcher to Theodore Schroeder (Apr. 28, 1911), in Theodore Schroeder Papers, Box 9 (Southern Illinois University Library) [hereinafter Schroeder Papers]; Letter from Charles A. Thatcher to Theodore Schroeder (May 3, 1911), in Schroeder Papers, Box 9.

[119] Letter from Herbert A. Thorpe to Theodore Schroeder (Apr. 9, 1916), in Schroeder Papers, supra note 118, Box 12; Letter from Harry Weinberger to Theodore Schroeder (Apr. 28, 1916), in Schroeder Papers, supra note 118, Box 12; Letter from Theodore Schroeder to Harry Weinberger (May 9, 1916), in Schroeder Papers, supra note 118, Box 12; Letter from Theodore Schroeder to Harry Weinberger (May 9, 1916), in Schroeder Papers, supra note 118, Box 12; Letter from Harry Weinberger to Theodore Schroeder (Oct. 27, 1916), in Schroeder Papers, supra note 118, Box 12; see Vaccination Opponent Nabbed, in Schroeder Papers, supra note 118, Box 12 (unidentified newspaper article).

[120] Schroeder, supra note 117, at 27.

clear that the League was organized to defend free speech, not to help needy radicals. To one attorney, for example, Schroeder stressed that the League was not a legal aid society concerned simply with "getting the defendant out of trouble." Rather, the League sought "a judicial precedent favorable to free speech as a constitutional principle or avoiding a precedent which is adverse."[121] When Schroeder believed a case did present a genuine free speech issue, he always tried to help. His voluminous correspondence does not contain a single example of a refusal to assist on ideological grounds.

Despite its widespread activities and consistent commitment to the principle of free speech for all viewpoints, the Free Speech League did not fulfill the high expectations of its founders. The anticipated support for free speech across the political spectrum never materialized. Although local free speech leagues loosely affiliated with the League arose throughout the country in response to various controversies, such as police suppression of Emma Goldman's meetings in Chicago and the free speech fight in San Diego by the Industrial Workers of the World (IWW), the active membership of the League remained limited to a small group in New York City. Even the progressives who in 1920 ultimately founded the ACLU, which for at least ten years was itself a small organization dominated by a self-perpetuating executive committee in New York City,[122] had remained essentially oblivious to the many free speech issues that produced the League's work before World War I. The Free Speech League, however, eventually provided a crucial link to the emerging ACLU when the repression of antiwar speech prompted Roger Baldwin and his early collaborators to organize in defense of civil liberties. The first leaders of the ACLU relied on the knowledge and expertise of League members while developing a narrower conception of constitutionally protected speech.

Theodore Schroeder became the key figure in the Free Speech League, just as Roger Baldwin later became the key figure in the ACLU. Through a combination of personal resources and frugal living, Schroeder was able to devote his full time to the defense of free speech.[123] In 1907, when Roe proposed to Foote that the League greatly expand its activities, Roe stated that the "undertak-

---

[121] Letter from Theodore Schroeder to P. L. Pendleton (Aug. 24, 1916), in Schroeder Papers, supra note 118, Box 12; see also Letter from Theodore Schroeder to William Lloyd Clark (June 26, 1911), in Schroeder Papers, supra note 118, Box 9.

[122] Samuel Walker, In Defense of American Liberties: A History of the ACLU 67 (1990).

[123] See Hutchins Hapgood, A Cold Enthusiast 4–6 (1913), in Schroeder Papers, supra note 118, Box 3; Letter from Theodore Schroeder to Gilbert E. Roe (Feb. 21, 1910), in Schroeder Papers, supra note 118, Box 9.

ing is a very large one, and it ought to have some man as secretary, preferably Schroeder, who can give the whole or the major part of his time to the work." According to Roe, "Schroeder has a better acquaintance for this sort of thing than any other man in the country."[124] Apparently following Roe's advice, in 1909 Foote left Schroeder a secret fund for the "Free Speech League and its propaganda, for defense of victims, for encouragement of papers that favor it and postal progress reforms, and lastly, for comfort and relief of its friends when 'down and out.'" Foote added that the fund could also be used "to promote publishing of [Schroeder's] own particular fad, the sex origin of religious motives," and he encouraged Schroeder to provide that the fund would be passed on to Roe if Schroeder died first.[125]

Schroeder was born in 1864 to a Lutheran father who had left Germany following the revolution of 1848 and a Catholic mother whose family disowned her for marrying a Protestant. Predisposed against religion by the problems that intermarriage had caused his mother, Schroeder became a freethinker at an early age after reading the works of Ingersoll, who became his intellectual hero.[126] As a young man, Schroeder combined formal schooling in his native Wisconsin with extensive travel in the West. There, he worked for various railroads and met immigrants, workers, and hobos.[127] While traveling through Utah, Schroeder became horrified at the persecution of the "downtrodden" Mormons,[128] which influenced his decision to start his law practice in Salt Lake City.[129] Schroeder later wrote that he wanted to help Mormons "even as my mother had once had a need for such a defender" against her religiously intolerant relatives.[130]

Shortly after arriving in Utah, however, Schroeder became a crusader against Mormonism. He blamed his "sentimentalism" about his mother for initially blinding him to the defects in Mormonism

[124] Letter from Gilbert E. Roe to E. B. Foote (Nov. 9, 1909), in Schroeder Papers, supra note 118, Box 8.

[125] Letter from Edward Bond Foote to Theodore Schroeder (Feb. 27, 1908), in Schroeder Papers, supra note 118, Box 8.

[126] Boyer, supra note 11, at 41; David Brudnoy, Liberty's Bugler: The Seven Ages of Theodore Schroeder 20–21 (1971) (unpublished Ph.D. dissertation, Brandeis University); Theodore Schroeder, Books, in Schroeder Papers, supra note 118, Box 1; Theodore Schroeder, Part of My Psychological Evolution 1–2, in Schroeder Papers, supra note 118, Box 1.

[127] Theodore Schroeder, Prospectus for a Psychological Autobiography 2, in Schroeder Papers, supra note 118, Box 1.

[128] Brudnoy, supra note 126, at 25.

[129] Id. at 25, 44; Hapgood, supra note 123, at 3–4.

[130] Brudnoy, supra note 126, at 25.

Theodore Schroeder, around 1914. (Morris
Library, Southern Illinois University)

he discovered while living in Salt Lake City. According to Schroeder,
"the Mormons were quite capable of even more bitter persecution
of apostates than that which was being inflicted upon them."[131] The
timing of Schroeder's conversion to anti-Mormonism, which coincided with the substantial rise of Mormon power in Utah, revealed a
personality trait that later affected his free speech work: abandoning
a cause once it ceased being unpopular.[132]

Schroeder soon began to write anti-Mormon polemics and
founded a journal, *Lucifer's Lantern,* as a vehicle for them.
Schroeder's voracious reading of Mormon texts convinced him
that their theological eccentricities had sexual sources, a view he
captured in his phrase "erotogenesis of religion."[133] Schroeder

---

[131] Id.
[132] Maynard Shipley, A Maverick Psychologist, The New Humanist, Mar.-Apr.
1933, reprinted in Joseph Ishill, Theodore Schroeder: An Evolutionary Psychologist 1, 23 (1964).
[133] Bibliography of the Writings of Theodore Schroeder on the Erotogenesis of
Religion, in Schroeder Papers, supra note 118, Box 54; see Hapgood, supra
note 123, at 9–10.

believed that Mormonism – and probably all religion – fosters prostitution, incest, and other psychosexual problems.[134] In one of his
pamphlets, "Was Joseph Smith an Abortionist?," Schroeder accused
the founder of the Mormon religion of "sexual excesses" and of
illegally "procuring the commission of abortions."[135] That charge
led to Schroeder's prosecution for sending obscene literature
through the mail. Although the grand jury did not return an indictment, the prosecution led Schroeder to conclude that the term
obscenity had no objective meaning.[136] For example, Schroeder
wrote Clarence Darrow that obscenity "is not a quality of literature,
but a quality of the reading mind."[137]

As part of his anti-Mormon activities, Schroeder moved to New
York City in 1901 to participate in the successful effort to exclude
Brigham Roberts, a Utah polygamist, from the Congress.[138] While in
New York, he "met every variety of radicals of that time" and
"debated with them in the open forums."[139] These forums included
the freethinking liberal clubs where he met other eventual members
of the Free Speech League. Schroeder's name does not appear in
the scanty information about the League's founding in 1902, but he
did become an active member by 1905, when he corresponded on
behalf of the League with lawyers representing Moses Harman.[140]

---

[134] Brudnoy, supra note 126, at 266.
[135] Theodore Schroeder, Was Joseph Smith, "The Prophet," an Abortionist?, 9
Lucifer's Lantern 184 (1900).
[136] Ronald Jump, All-Time Champion Menace 3A, in Schroeder Papers, supra
note 118, Box 3; see Jerold S. Auerbach, Introduction to Theodore Schroeder,
"Obscene" Literature and Constitutional Law ix (reprint ed. 1972).
[137] Letter from Theodore Schroeder to Clarence Darrow (May 29, 1905), at 1, in
Schroeder Papers, supra note 118, Box 7.
[138] Roberts initially ran for the territorial Senate in 1895 without the approval of
his superiors in the Mormon Church, who dropped him from his ecclesiastical
positions as punishment. He lost this election, but in 1898 Roberts sought and
received Mormon approval to wage what became a successful campaign for the
House of Representatives. See David Brudnoy, Sinners and Saints: Theodore
Schroeder, Brigham Roberts, and Reed Smoot, 14 J. Church & St. 261, 266–67
(1972). Schroeder had vigorously supported Roberts in his first campaign. Id.
After Roberts submitted to Mormon authorities, however, Schroeder claimed
to have "started a single-handed fight," based on a commitment to "secularist
government," to prevent Roberts from being seated in Congress. Theodore
Schroeder, Suggestions for Publicity in Utah Newspapers, in Schroeder Papers,
supra note 118, Box 2.
[139] Theodore Schroeder, Autobiographical Notes, Varieties of Autobriographical
Technique 11, in Schroeder Papers, supra note 118, Box 3.
[140] Letter from Schroeder to Darrow, supra note 140; Letter from Theodore
Schroeder to Stedman & Soelke (Dec. 5, 1905), in Schroeder Papers, supra
note 118, Box 7.

Schroeder credited Harman with stimulating his own interest in freedom of expression. "Your last imprisonment," Schroeder wrote Harman in 1905, "was the means of my giving much thought to the legal status of our 'freedom of the press.'" After describing his own efforts on behalf of free expression, Schroeder added: "Whatever good may come to the cause of liberty through these efforts of mine, it must in justice be credited to you as one of the fruits of your martyrdom." Schroeder predicted that future generations would list Harman among Socrates, Copernicus, Paine, and other "martyrs of intellectual liberty" who were "despised among their contemporaries." He praised Harman's sacrifices made in defense of the expressive rights of others. "It speaks eloquently for the breadth of your heroism that you have never suffered imprisonment for anything you yourself had written, but only because of your willingness to give others a hearing. Only those deserve liberty who are willing to defend the liberty of others."[141]

Despite his prior success as a practicing lawyer in Utah, Schroeder determined never to be the attorney of record in the free speech litigation he so actively followed and supported. Briefs, Schroeder felt, are "soon lost sight of," but publications "make the court feel that its mental calibre is on trial at the bar of public opinion and that the public has access to all that can be said on the other side." Only through his independent writings would the courts believe "that some one besides the defendant is after them and hard if they carelessly or unfairly decide against my contention."[142]

Schroeder's recognition of his own difficult personality, however, may have been the primary reason for his unwillingness to handle cases directly. Hutchins Hapgood, a well-known journalist sympathetic to the League, recalled Schroeder's "wild swooning desire to talk," a trait that prompted Lincoln Steffens to remark, probably only partially in jest, "I believe in Free Speech for everybody except Schroeder."[143] Roger Baldwin, who met Schroeder in 1917, remembered him as "egocentric, a bit of a crank who conversed only in terms of his preoccupation."[144] Schroeder himself,

---

[141] Letter from Theodore Schroeder to Moses Harmon [sic] (Dec. 5, 1905), in Schroeder Papers, supra note 118, Box 7.

[142] Letter from Theodore Schroeder to Mr. Gautereaux (Jan. 15, 1909), at 2, in Schroeder Papers, supra note 118, Box 9; see Letter from Theodore Schroeder to Bernarr MacFadden (Mar. 25, 1908), at 3, in Schroeder Papers, supra note 118, Box 9 (publications to the Bar under auspices of Free Speech League have more influence on judges than arguments or briefs).

[143] Hutchins Hapgood, A Victorian in the Modern World 279 (1939).

[144] Baldwin Reminiscences, supra note 106, at 114.

in confiding to Gilbert Roe the reasons he did not want to represent clients in free speech litigation, acknowledged that "intro-
spection persuades me that I take the world's troubles too seriously, to enable me to do best work if I must wage a war which
involves contention at close quarters with opponents."[145]

Schroeder's personality, however, should not obscure his substantial achievements as the administrator of the Free Speech
League and as an important scholar of free speech. H. L.
Mencken described Schroeder in 1916 as having "done more for
free expression in America than any other."[146] *"Obscene" Literature
and Constitutional Law,* Schroeder's most important book, was
widely and often favorably reviewed.[147] His writings influenced preeminent contemporary scholars, including Ernst Freund, Roscoe
Pound, and E. A. Ross.[148] Roger Baldwin, despite his reservations
about Schroeder's egocentricity, nevertheless characterized his
publications on free speech as "useful contributions" and "pioneering studies."[149] Henry Miller expressed similar views in his
autobiography,[150] and as late as 1945 Felix Frankfurter responded
to a letter from Schroeder by reporting that he was "of course
familiar with your writings."[151] Justice Frankfurter even cited one
of Schroeder's books in an opinion concurring with the majority's
holding that the First Amendment precludes a state from censor-

---

[145] Letter from Schroeder to Roe, supra note 123, at 1–2.

[146] Theodore Schroeder: A Very Wise Man, in Theodore Schroeder's Last Will
(Leslie Kuhn ed., 1958) (quoting H. L. Mencken).

[147] See, e.g., James F. Morton, Jr., A Monumental Defence of Free Speech, 6 Mother
Earth 307 (1911); G. W. Kirchway, Book Review, 12 Colum. L. Rev. 384 (1912);
I. Maurice Wormser, Book Review, 6 Am. Pol. Sci. Rev. 319 (1912); I. Maurice
Wormser, Book Review, 2 J. Crim. L. & Criminology 959 (1912).

[148] Chafee sent a copy of his 1919 article to Freund, who responded by commend-
ing Schroeder's work to Chafee. Letter from Ernst Freund to Zechariah
Chafee, Jr. (Aug. 13, 1919) (Zechariah Chafee, Jr., Papers, Box 14, Folder 10,
Harvard Law School Library). Commenting in private correspondence about
the problems posed by administrative discretion in determining whether
allegedly improper material should be allowed in the mail, Pound mentioned
that "I was attracted to this matter a number of years ago through the writings
of Mr. Schroeder." Letter from Roscoe Pound to Ella Westcott (Sept. 7, 1916)
(Roscoe Pound Papers, Box 175, Folder 5, Harvard Law School Library). After
spending several hours reading Schroeder's publications in 1912, E. A. Ross
wrote Schroeder that "I was amazed to learn how far we have gone along the
line of a censorship of mail matter." Letter from E. A. Ross to Theodore
Schroeder (Sept. 21, 1912), in Schroeder Papers, supra note 118, Box 10).

[149] Baldwin Reminiscences, supra note 106, at 114.

[150] Henry Miller, Remember to Remember 276–77 (1947).

[151] Letter from Felix Frankfurter to Theodore Schroeder (Mar. 22, 1945), in
Schroeder Papers, supra note 118, Box 20.

ing a film as "sacrilegious."[152] Several modern scholars have also commented on Schroeder's significance and have lamented his relative obscurity.[153]

Schroeder's colleagues were all busy professionals who were unable to match his commitment to the League. It is clear from the material in Schroeder's own files, however, that they corresponded regularly, talked on the telephone, visited each other socially, and held meetings to discuss League business. In general, members informed each other about their individual efforts to promote free speech, and consulted as a group before committing the League to an official position. Many members donated money to the League and participated in the major free speech controversies of the era.

Gilbert E. Roe, Schroeder's most important collaborator in the Free Speech League, moved from Wisconsin to New York City in 1899. Unlike Schroeder, Roe had contacts with important leaders of the progressive movement. Roe was a close personal friend and political confidante of Robert M. La Follette, whose firm Roe joined immediately after his graduation from the University of Wisconsin Law School in 1890.[154] The Roe and La Follette families socialized and communicated frequently, and took vacations together. La Follette's children even referred to Roe as "Uncle." Throughout La Follette's long career as governor of Wisconsin and later as a U.S. senator, Roe often abandoned his own law practice for lengthy periods to participate in La Follette's political campaigns, to serve as his personal lawyer, and to assist in drafting legislation and speeches. Perhaps most significantly, La Follette chose Roe to represent him in Senate expulsion proceedings and related libel actions prompted by an antiwar speech La Follette delivered in 1917.[155]

Roe's close association with La Follette brought him into contact with other major figures. For example, he occasionally dealt with Louis D. Brandeis during La Follette's unsuccessful campaign in

---

[152] Joseph Burstyn, Inc. v. Wilson, 343 U.S. 495, 529 n.51 (1952) (Frankfurter, J., concurring). Justice Frankfurter derived historical examples of "the indefiniteness of the concept 'sacrilegious'" in part from Theodore Schroeder, Constitutional Free Speech 178–373 (1919). 343 U.S. at 528–29 (Frankfurter, J., concurring).

[153] See, e.g., Auerbach, supra note 136, at v; Mark A. Graber, Transforming Free Speech: The Ambiguous Legacy of Civil Libertarianism 54–62 (1991); Leonard W. Levy, Emergence of a Free Press 153 n.36 (1985).

[154] 8 Dictionary of American Biography, pt. 2, at 86 (Dumas Malone ed., 1935).

[155] 1 Belle Case La Follette & Fola La Follette, Robert M. La Follette 112, 127–28, 179–80, 390, 421, 428, 434–38, 491, 623, 656 (1953); 2 id. at 742, 745, 756, 794, 797–816, 822–24, 837–38, 855–57, 875–86, 898, 909–11, 915, 928, 939, 944–46, 950, 1052–53, 1059, 1069, 1122, 1124, 1129; Robert M. La Follette, La Follette's Autobiography 95, 140, 280–82 (revised ed. 1960).

1912 for nomination as a progressive candidate for president and in later efforts to save the financially troubled *La Follette's Magazine*.[156] At La Follette's request, Brandeis made several attempts in 1913 to have Roe endorsed as a candidate for a judicial post in New York, a nomination that ultimately went to Benjamin Cardozo.[157] Roe reciprocated several years later by writing a crucial senator that Brandeis should be confirmed to the U.S. Supreme Court.[158]

Roe suffered another political disappointment in 1915, when he was seriously considered for a position on the Federal Trade Commission. Roe met with Colonel Edward House, President Wilson's key adviser, who immediately wrote Wilson that Roe would be an able and politically popular appointment. Wilson soon solicited more information about Roe at a White House meeting with La Follette, which prompted La Follette to write Roe that "you are most seriously under consideration." Roe, however, did not get the nomination.[159]

Although he never attained a full-time position in public service, Roe remained committed to efforts in New York to implement the progressive legislative agenda he had helped La Follette enact in Wisconsin. In 1905, the governor of New York appointed Roe to a commission that wrote a direct primary law. Roe was also active in efforts to pass workmen's compensation legislation in New York.[160] Roe established a varied and busy law practice in New

---

[156] Letter from Gilbert E. Roe to R. M. La Follette (Aug. 11, 1913), in Gilbert E. Roe Papers, Container H7 (La Follette Family Collection, Series H, Manuscript Division, Library of Congress) [hereinafter Roe Papers]; Letter from Gilbert E. Roe to Louis D. Brandeis (Sept. 9, 1914), in Roe Papers, supra, Container H7; Letter from Gilbert E. Roe to Robert M. La Follette (Sept. 11, 1914), in Roe Papers, supra, Container H7; Letter from Louis D. Brandeis to Gilbert Ernstein Roe (Sept. 18, 1914), in 3 Letters of Louis D. Brandeis 301 (Melvin I Urofsky & David W. Levy eds., 1972) [hereinafter Brandeis Letters]; see 1 La Follette & La Follette, supra note 155, at 510–11 (discussing Roe's efforts to save La Follette's Magazine).

[157] Letter from Louis D. Brandeis to Robert Marion La Follette (July 19, 1913), in 3 Brandeis Letters, supra note 156, at 145; Letter from Louis D. Brandeis to Charles Culp Burlingham (July 24, 1913), in 3 Brandeis Letters, supra note 156, at 150; Letter from Louis D. Brandeis to Robert Marion La Follette (July 28, 1913), in 3 Brandeis Letters, supra note 156, at 153–54. Roe wrote La Follette that "Brandeis had written some corking letters here I understand." Letter from Gilbert E. Roe to R.M. La Follette (Aug. 5, 1913), at 2, in Robert M. La Follette Sr. Papers, Container B74 (La Follette Family Collection, Series B, Manuscript Division, Library of Congress).

[158] Letter from Gilbert E. Roe to William E. Chilton (Feb. 2, 1916), in Roe Papers, supra note 156, Container H5.

[159] 1 La Follette & La Follette, supra note 155, at 516.

[160] 8 Dictionary of American Biography, supra note 154, at 86.

York City. His legal work consisted primarily of bankruptcies, commercial and construction contracts, and personal injury cases.[161] Roe, however, made time to represent numerous defendants in free speech cases, often in association with the Free Speech League and at reduced or no pay.[162] Over the years, Roe spoke frequently on free speech topics,[163] while wishing he could afford to devote more time to writing.[164] Roe did publish one book, *Our Judicial Oligarchy* (1912), for which La Follette wrote the introduction. In classic progressive style, Roe criticized judges for their support of property rights over other social interests and argued that courts had exceeded their proper function within a democracy by their excessive review and invalidation of reform legislation.

Roe seemed equally comfortable with progressives and radicals, both personally and professionally. Neither his close association with La Follette nor his participation in progressive movements in Wisconsin and New York prevented him from having warm relationships with radicals who otherwise had little or no contact with progressives. For example, Emma Goldman repeatedly referred in her autobiography to Roe as a good friend who had provided her the hospitality and refuge of his home, financial assistance, and free legal advice at a time when she was widely ostracized as a dangerous radical.[165]

THE COMMITMENT TO FREE SPEECH FOR ALL VIEWPOINTS

Throughout its existence, the Free Speech League emphasized its commitment to freedom of expression for all viewpoints. When the publisher of *Everybody's Magazine,* a popular journal that fre-

---

[161] For documentation of many of Roe's cases, see Roe Papers, supra note 156, Container H9. See also Commission on Industrial Relations, Industrial Relations: Final Report and Testimony Submitted to Congress, S.Doc. No. 415, 64th Cong., 1st Sess. 10,468, 10,470–71 (1916) (testimony of Gilbert E. Roe) [hereinafter Roe Testimony].

[162] See, e.g., Roe Testimony, supra note 161, at 10,480–81; Letter from Gilbert E. Roe to Theodore Schroeder (June 17, 1913), in Schroeder Papers, supra note 118, Box 11; Letter from Gilbert E. Roe to Theodore Schroeder (Oct. 3, 1914), in Schroeder Papers, supra note 118, Box 11; Letter from Gilbert E. Roe to Leonard D. Abbott (Feb. 19, 1915), in Roe Papers, supra note 156, Container H7; Letter from Gilbert E. Roe to Upton Sinclair (Apr. 26, 1915), in Roe Papers, supra note 156, Container H7.

[163] E.g., American Sociological Society, Ninth Annual Meeting: Papers and Proceedings 35 (1914) (statement of Gilbert E. Roe) [hereinafter Roe Statement]; Roe Testimony, supra note 161.

[164] Letter from Gilbert E. Roe to Vernon Burke (Jan. 15, 1916), in Roe Papers, supra note 156; Letter from Gilbert E. Roe to Theodore Schroeder (Mar. 27, 1913), in Schroeder Papers, supra note 118, Box 10.

[165] 1 Emma Goldman, Living My Life 484–85 (1931); 2 id. at 540–41, 548, 563.

quently carried work by Lincoln Steffens, wrote an editorial in
1911 supporting "a vigorous censorship of plays," Steffens
responded with an article advocating "absolute, unlimited freedom of expression." Identifying himself as a member of the Free
Speech League, Steffens stated that its purpose "is to make it possible for anybody to say anything anywhere." Steffens took pains to
emphasize that he was objecting to more than the censorship of
plays. He also wanted to prevent the public from receiving the
impression that the Free Speech League was "fighting, not for
freedom of speech, but for indecency." Observing that similar confusion could result from backing "the right of Socialists to march
and Anarchists to speak,"[166] Steffens stressed that the League was
not endorsing any particular view. Rather, he explained that those
who believe in the general principle of free speech must make
their point by supporting it for "some extreme cause."[167] Advocating free speech only for a popular or uncontroversial position, he
believed, would not convey the breadth of the principle.

Steffens conceded that most Americans had freedom of expression in the sense that they were free to say whatever they thought,
but he considered this freedom trivial because they had not in fact
"thought very freely." Americans, he maintained, "have been too
busy with facts and acts and things to pay much heed to ideas and
theories and ideals." He predicted that as Americans began to
think more deeply they would discover what members of the Free
Speech League had already realized: "that we have not free speech
in the United States – not by a long way."[168] Steffens closed his article by reminding his readers that "free reports of all the facts" and
the human power of "reason and good feeling" – not legal censorship – are the best ways to combat obscenity.[169]

The publisher responded by praising Steffens's article as a
"remarkable contribution" and expressed his yearning for the day
when the freedom advocated by Steffens would be possible. But he
regretfully concluded that the United States, although "growing
toward" such freedom, was not yet ready for it. If Americans tried
too much freedom too soon, the publisher warned, "civilization
might slip back hundreds of years."[170]

Steffens's article thrilled Schroeder. He immediately wrote
Foote that it made him feel for the first time "as though we had

---

[166] Lincoln Steffens, An Answer and an Answer, 25 Everybody's Mag. 717, 718
(1911).
[167] Id. at 719.   [168] Id. at 717.
[169] Id. at 720.
[170] With "Everybody's" Publishers, 25 Everybody's Mag. 720 (1911).

gotten the Free Speech League and its purposes on the map."[171]
Steffens himself had included a disclaimer of League responsibility for his article, but after receiving Schroeder's congratulations
Steffens modestly replied that it "was really ordered . . . at the last
meeting of the Directors of the League."[172]

Several years later Steffens again tried to publicize the Free
Speech League's position that all expression should be protected
regardless of viewpoint. He sent a letter to the *New York Times* in
response to an editorial entitled "Anarchy," which had called for
Emma Goldman to be "put under lock and key and kept there."
Steffens noted that the editorial "expresses pretty well the idea and
the spirit it deplores," and accused the author of wanting to jail
Goldman "[f]or speaking as you write." Steffens continued:

> The question of free speech is involved. You are, and you
> should be permitted to express your feelings. But so should
> the I. W. W's and the Anarchists be allowed to pour out their
> passions. It is good for you both, and it does nobody harm.
> The public is to be trusted to allow for you both. You, Sir,
> should be permitted even to invite the Mayor and the public
> to club the mob, with heavy clubs. But so should Emma Gold-
> man be permitted to incite the mob to action. Why cannot
> you too understand and make allowances for each other. The
> Free Speech League can, and it does.[173]

The *New York Times* refused to publish the letter.[174] The paper
did bring attention to Steffens and the Free Speech League, however, in various news stories and in a related editorial. For example, a front-page article reported that the League had sponsored a
public protest meeting after an organizer for the IWW, who had
led a march of unemployed workers in New York City, was arrested
for inciting a crowd to riot. According to the article, Steffens spoke
at the meeting, emphasizing the constitutional right of free speech
and proposing "that there should be a place in the city where anybody could say anything he wanted to say."[175]

Schroeder made the protection of free speech for all views the

---

[171] Letter from Theodore Schroeder to E. B. Foote (Oct. 28, 1911), at 2, in
Schroeder Papers, supra note 118, Box 9.

[172] Letter from Lincoln Steffens to Theodore Schroeder (Oct. 28, 1911), in
Schroeder Papers, supra note 118, Box 9.

[173] Letter from Lincoln Steffens to Mr. Wright, Editor, Globe (Mar. 31, 1914), in
Schroeder Papers, supra note 118, Box 11.

[174] Id. Steffens informed the editor of the Globe that the Times had refused to publish his letter, and reproducing the text of this letter, asked the Globe to do so.

[175] I.W.W. Slurs Mayor; Calls Him "Bell Hop," N.Y. Times, Mar. 7, 1914, at 1.

focus of his many published works and the central theme in his correspondence with those who requested League assistance. Concluding that governments have historically suppressed only ideas disliked by the "ruling classes," Schroeder understood the principle of free speech as the demand "that this discrimination should cease" and "that every idea, no matter how unpopular shall, so far as the law is concerned, have the same opportunity as every other idea, no matter how popular, to secure the public favor."[176] Schroeder argued that the Constitution "made no exception for any particular class of intellectual 'evils,' but protected them all alike."[177] As a consequence, the right to speak freely should extend even to those questioning government itself.[178]

A short article by Hutchins Hapgood highlighted Schroeder's commitment to this position:

> If there is anybody, anywhere, whose freedom of expression is interfered with by Comstock, Mrs. Grundy, the courts, the police, Theodore Schroeder takes up the fight, whether it is a clergyman, a lawyer disbarred for contempt of court, an unpopular anarchist, whether Schroeder agrees with the oppressed person or not, and generally he does not, yet he gives him aid and comfort, legally, financially, in written propaganda. No matter how much like a "crank" the suppressed person may appear to be, Schroeder's interest is maintained. His cold logic sustains his interest, even in objects generally supposed to be unworthy.[179]

A statement in Schroeder's papers, apparently written by Schroeder himself, reinforced Hapgood's description:

> Theodore Schroeder holds a unique position among libertarians. Most people will defend the claims of right and of liberty for those whose professions and practices are very similar to their own. Schroeder seems to think that a libertarian must defend the claim for equality of right or liberty, even for his most bitter opponents. If he does not do so, a dangerous precedent may be established. Accordingly, Schroeder has given aid and comfort to a Catholic priest and to atheists; to the Mormons and to agnostics; to socialists, anarchists, sin-

---

[176] Theodore Schroeder, "Obscene Literature and Constitutional Law: A Forensic Defense of Freedom of the Press 153 (1911).

[177] Schroeder, supra note 117, at 63.

[178] Id. at 10.

[179] Hapgood, supra note 123, at 6–7. Mrs. Grundy is an "imaginary English character who typifies the censorship enacted in every day life by conventional opinion." 5 The New Encyclopedia Britannica 523 (15th ed. 1985).

gle taxers, and communists. He has defended the equality of rights for professional Purists and so-called "obscenists."[180]

Schroeder maintained that those who professed agreement with the constitutional protection of speech usually did so only when their own particular viewpoint was threatened.[181] Even worse, they often supported restrictions on speech when others sought to "express anything radically different from their own thoughts."[182] He believed that this inability "to differentiate between their disapproval of an opinion and their opponent's right to disagree with them"[183] prevented Americans from abstracting to a general definition or defense of free speech for all opinions. Too many advocates of free speech, Schroeder lamented, "have no conception of freedom in general, and erroneously conclude that everybody is enjoying the greatest possible freedom when they feel themselves unrestricted." If these "free speech" advocates would only engage in serious reflection, they "would probably know something of the ease with which differences of opinion may arise upon every possible question and of the importance of maintaining the other fellow's right to disagree."[184] Schroeder warned that "the time may come when the descendants of those who will not defend the liberties of others may have to defend their own under the added difficulty of multiple precedents."[185]

Deliberately provoking his most likely supporters, Schroeder maintained that many political conservatives accepted the principle of "unabridged freedom of utterance as a matter of acknowledged natural right,"[186] whereas many "professing radicals" supported free speech only for their allies.[187] For example, some radicals would object to the censorship of sex literature, yet would support the censorship of anarchist literature. "They would limit freedom of speech at the advocacy of what they consider 'invasive' crimes, sexual 'crimes' not being regarded by them as invasive." These radicals, he added, "are more reactionary than the conservatives who framed our charters of liberty . . . because these documents recognize no such exception to our guaranteed freedom of speech and press." Schroeder compared "sex radicals" to Comstock himself, arguing that they differed only on "what constitutes an invasion" justifying the repression of speech.[188]

In addition to criticizing the insensitivity of sex radicals to the

---

180 That Man Schroeder, in Schroeder Papers, supra note 118, Box 2.
181 Schroeder, supra note 176, at 146.   182 Id. at 154.
183 Schroeder, supra note 117, at 3.   184 Schroeder, supra note 176, at 148.
185 Id. at 97.   186 Schroeder, supra note 117, at 68.
187 Id. at 72.   188 Id. at 34.

suppression of anarchist speech, Schroeder complained that various religious groups demanded freedom to express their own views without advocating the same right for atheists or those who held different religious beliefs. Schroeder similarly criticized the mainstream press, which, while attacking the libel indictment of the *New York World* for discrediting government dealings regarding the Panama Canal, would not dream of defending the free speech of sex radicals or anarchists. He also asserted that Samuel Gompers, the president of the American Federation of Labor (AFL), used freedom of speech as a shibboleth to protest judicial injunctions denying labor's right to advocate boycotts, but rejected more general rights to free speech as risking social unrest.[189]

In his private correspondence, Schroeder frequently chastised those who failed to extend their defense of free speech to views they opposed. He criticized Ben Reitman, Emma Goldman's manager, for "a narrow vision" that failed to notice "others who are being deprived of free speech," including socialists, advocates of free love, "anti-Catholic agitators," lawyers held in contempt of court, and people arrested for insulting the flag.[190] Schroeder even felt compelled to urge Leonard Abbott, the president of the Free Speech League, not "to be moved by the sentimental influences of personal relations and affiliations."[191] Schroeder encouraged Abbott to "try the experiment of getting up a free speech enthusiasm concerning the violation of free speech in the person of some one who is an utter stranger to you and whose doctrine you wholly disapprove."[192]

Schroeder's efforts to collect and categorize free speech issues illustrated his broad understanding of the subject. Schroeder subscribed to a clipping service, which informed him of free speech disputes throughout the country, and he corresponded with West Publishing Company to obtain recent judicial decisions involving freedom of expression. He also initiated correspondence with people involved in controversies over free speech that came to his attention. Schroeder kept voluminous files, which are probably the most comprehensive compilations of statutes and cases pertaining

---

[189] Schroeder, supra note 176, at 146–47. Id. at 146. Gompers had denied a similar charge in his correspondence with Schroeder, claiming that he "stood for the fullest freedom of speech and of the press." Letter from Samuel Gompers to Theodore Schroeder (Feb. 19, 1909), in Schroeder Papers, supra note 118, Box 9.

[190] Letter from Theodore Schroeder to Ben Reitman (May 27, 1916), in Schroeder Papers, supra note 118, Box 12.

[191] Letter from Theodore Schroeder to Leonard Abbott (Sept. 23, 1915), in Roe Papers, supra note 156, Container H7.

[192] Letter from Theodore Schroeder to Leonard Abbott (Sept. 27, 1915), at 1, in Schroeder Papers, supra note 118, Box 11.

to freedom of speech during the period immediately preceding World War I. The wide variety of subject headings within the files reveals the range of situations in which Schroeder perceived free speech issues. His major alphabetical categories were advertising (including patent medicine and information on venereal diseases, impotence, and menstrual problems), anarchism, blasphemy, contempt, flag, miscellaneous (including influencing workers to break contracts, abusive language on capitol grounds, pupil insulting teacher, and discouraging volunteering for army service), obscenity, profanity, riot and unlawful assembly, scandal (including publishing details of hangings and printing pictures of prize fights), and treason.[193]

Schroeder's commitment to free speech for all viewpoints generated his insistence that the Free Speech League remain an independent organization. When Schroeder sensed that Abbott might identify the Free Speech League too closely with the IWW, he sent Abbott a copy of a letter "declining union with an anti-Catholic organization fighting as hard and with as much physical violence as the I.W.W. for free speech." Schroeder sought to prevent the League from becoming "the tail of the kite of some other propagandist. Every time that it creates in the public mind the impression of being subordinate to the interests of the I.W.W.'s or of anti-Catholic agitators; of Free Thinkers; or of Socialists, then, it is impairing its efficiency in subsequent activities."[194] Such affiliations would prevent the League from exerting "any influence greater than that other groups already possess in the public esteem." By retaining its own identity, the League would be better able to convince the public that "it has a genuine interest in free speech quite distinct from the person or doctrine of those whom it seeks to help."[195]

---

[193] Schroeder Papers, supra note 118, Boxes 90–91. See Letter from Theodore Schroeder to Charles T. Hallinan (undated in 1913), in Schroeder Papers, supra note 118, Box 11 (subscription to clipping service). Correspondence between Schroeder and West Publishing Company is located in Schroeder Papers, Box 9.

[194] Letter from Schroeder to Abbott, supra note 192, at 2. See also Letter from Theodore Schroeder to F. W. Hubbard (Jan. 24, 1912), in Schroeder Papers, supra note 118, Box 16 (rejecting formal affiliation with another organization because "so many people believe in the phrase Free Speech who would repudiate the organization when it undertook to apply the principles to some concrete cases," but willing to help "as long as our purposes are harmonious").

[195] Letter from Schroeder to Abbott, supra note 191. See Letter from Theodore Schroeder to C. W. Bibb (Sept. 27, 1915), in Schroeder Papers, supra note 118, Box 11 (rejecting as "unwise" affiliation of Free Speech League "with any other organization" because the League's "greatest efficiency for service lies in the maintenance of an independent stand for the free speech of all persons and all kinds or agitations").

THE WORK OF THE FREE SPEECH LEAGUE

Although the Free Speech League was genuinely committed to freedom of expression for all viewpoints, the actual free speech controversies that arose between the League's founding in 1902 and World War I frequently involved sex radicals and anarchists. As its first activity, the League sponsored a dinner for Ida C. Craddock to honor her release from prison after serving a term under the Comstock Act for circulating a booklet entitled "The Wedding Night."[196] Soon rearrested by Comstock and again convicted, Craddock committed suicide before being imprisoned. "I am taking my life," her suicide note began, "because a judge, at the instigation of Anthony Comstock, has decreed me guilty of a crime I did not commit – the circulation of obscene literature."[197]

In 1905, the League unsuccessfully assisted Harman's defense against obscenity charges, publicized his imprisonment, and petitioned President Theodore Roosevelt for a pardon.[198] Writing in *Lucifer*, Foote ranked Harman as a hero equal to Garrison, and asserted that "fifty years hence Harman's assault on the evils of marital slavery will be as much appreciated as is today Garrison's on black slavery."[199] A postal official's comment that "'society would be in a state of chaos'" if Harman's ideas prevailed convinced the League that it "is not obscenity but heresy that is scented and attacked."[200] In a subsequent appeal for funds to defend Harman, the League emphasized that "the test of intelligent devotion to liberty is the defense of the freedom of those who differ from us."[201]

The Comstock Act was not the only statutory threat to libertarian radicals. New federal legislation against anarchist speech, the concern that prompted the organization of the Free Speech League, soon produced the first case the League helped bring to the U.S. Supreme Court. John Turner, a visiting British anarchist, was arrested during a lecture tour of the United States in 1903 for violating the Alien Immigration Act passed by Congress earlier

---

[196] Defense Fund, Lucifer: The Light-Bearer, June 19, 1902, at 181; Eugene H. Porter, Instruction in Sexual Matters, Lucifer: The Light-Bearer, Oct. 29, 1903, at 333.

[197] Sears, supra note 7, at 262.

[198] See Alice Stone Blackwell, The Postoffice and Free Speech, Woman's J., Aug. 12, 1905, reprinted in Lucifer: The Light-Bearer, Aug. 17, 1905, at 359; The Case of Moses Harman, Lucifer: The Light-Bearer, Mar. 15, 1906, at 478.

[199] E. B. Foote, Jr., Alternating Currents, Lucifer: The Light-Bearer, Jan. 4, 1906, at 441–42.

[200] The Free Speech League, The Administrative Process in America, Lucifer: The Light-Bearer, July 6, 1905, at 333.

[201] The Free Speech League, Shall Liberty Be Murdered in the Land?, Lucifer: The Light-Bearer, Aug. 17, 1905, at 357–58.

that year. Turner's lecture topics included "[t]he essentials of anarchism" and, referring to the executions of the Haymarket defendants, "[t]he legal murder of 1887."[202] These topics, the prosecution maintained, required Turner's deportation under the provision of the law excluding anarchists and others who believe in or advocate the overthrow of government by force or violence or the assassination of public officials.[203] The League organized protest meetings and raised money to defend Turner. With the assistance of League funds, Turner hired Clarence Darrow and Edgar Lee Masters to represent him in the Supreme Court.[204] Darrow and Masters based their defense on extended First Amendment arguments, but the Court briefly rejected them while upholding the constitutionality of Turner's deportation.[205]

The Turner case initiated a dozen years of collaboration between the Free Speech League and Emma Goldman, who had previously met Turner through anarchist circles in London[206] and had longstanding associations with the founders of the League. Goldman read *Lucifer,* and described her meeting with Moses Harman and his daughter Lillian in 1897 as a "great event."[207] In discussing her own and Margaret Sanger's efforts on behalf of birth control, Goldman recognized that the "trail was blazed" by the Harmans, the Footes, Walker, and "their collaborators of a previous generation."[208] Goldman began attending the weekly meetings of the Manhattan Liberal Club in 1894, where she met many of the future members of the Free Speech League.[209] Goldman exaggerated in her autobiography by claiming primary responsibility for organizing the League at the time of the Turner case. However, she accurately stated that the "Free Speech Leaguers were mostly professional men and very busy," leaving her to visit various cities to publicize the case and raise funds for Turner's defense.[210]

Goldman herself was eventually deported after the Supreme Court affirmed her conviction for antiwar speech deemed part of a criminal conspiracy to induce men not to register under the Selective Draft Law of 1917.[211] Between the Turner case and her own deportation, however, Goldman and the Free Speech League

---

[202] Turner v. Williams, 194 U.S. 279, 283 (1904).

[203] Act of Mar. 3, 1903, ch. 1012, sections 2, 38, 32 Stat. 1213.

[204] Letter from E. B. Foote Jr., to "Dear Sir" (March 5, 1904), in Schroeder Papers, supra note 118, Box 6; 1 Emma Goldman, supra note 165, at 348.

[205] Turner v. Williams, 194 U.S. 279 (1904), discussed infra, Chapter 3, at text accompanying notes 15–21.

[206] Goldman, supra note 165, at 165, 348–50.

[207] Id. at 219.   [208] 2 id. at 553.

[209] 1 id. at 320, 335.   [210] Id. at 348.

[211] Goldman v. United States, 245 U.S. 474 (1918).

provided frequent mutual support. Goldman made highly successful national speaking tours, which covered anarchism, birth control, and a broad range of other radical topics. Despite her immigrant, working-class background, she drew a significant number of
native, middle-class radicals to her talks. Unlike most immigrant
anarchists, Goldman discovered and accepted the American tradition of individualist anarchism. From her reading of Emerson,
Thoreau, and Whitman, Goldman responded to a welcome
emphasis on individuality and self-expression that American middle-class radicals found attractive. This emphasis, however, alien-
ated many of her fellow immigrant anarchists, who were committed to collective action and class-conscious labor solidarity.[212] For
Goldman, anarchism meant "freedom, the right to self expression," and she complained about immigrant anarchists for whom
commitment to "the Cause" required "the denial of life and joy."[213]

Association with violent acts by other anarchists made Goldman
a figure of widespread notoriety. During the Homestead strike
against the Carnegie Steel Company in 1892, Goldman's lover,
Alexander Berkman, tried unsuccessfully to assassinate Henry
Frick, the designer of the company's intransigent labor policies.
Almost a decade later, Leon Czolgosz assassinated President
McKinley several months after attending a lecture by Goldman on
anarchism.[214] Goldman's notoriety, combined with her controversial subject matter, prompted local authorities throughout the
country to deny her access to lecture halls or to arrest her while
she spoke. Schroeder reported that Goldman had been arrested
nearly forty times and detained for periods ranging from one hour
to several days. "Some of these arrests," he maintained, "were for
speeches actually made, more of them were for merely threatening to make a speech, and sometimes when neither of these facts
existed she was arrested simply because she was Emma Goldman
and had an undeserved newspaper reputation." Schroeder also
pointed out that many of her arrests never led to judicial hearings
and that Goldman had only once been convicted, even under
"unconstitutional laws invading the freedom of speech."[215]

Goldman took advantage of these incidents to highlight the
principle of free expression and occasionally to organize local free
speech leagues loosely affiliated with the national organization.
During the winter of 1907–8, police suppression of her meetings

---

[212] Alice Wexler, Emma Goldman: An Intimate Life 103, 203–6 (1984).
[213] Goldman, supra note 165, at 56.
[214] Richard Drinnan, Rebel in Paradise 39–54, 68–77, 87–89 (1976); Wexler,
    supra note 212, at xv–xvi, 61–70, 110–12.
[215] Schroeder, supra note 117, at 13–14.

in Chicago aroused many liberals and radicals to defend the constitutional right of free speech, and led to the formation of a free speech league there.[216] A similar episode in Philadelphia culminated "with a large meeting under the auspices of the Free Speech League," at which Abbott presided and Schroeder spoke.[217] Goldman wrote repeatedly in her autobiography of the personal, financial, and legal support she received from members of the Free Speech League.[218] In addition, *Mother Earth*, the journal Goldman founded in 1906, published many articles by League members,[219] and frequently publicized and encouraged contributions for League activities in defense of free speech.[220]

The Free Speech League similarly assisted Margaret Sanger, who was a radical activist on behalf of birth control from 1912 until her shift to more conservative tactics after World War I. Sanger, whose father was a freethinker and a supporter of women's suffrage, had personal roots in the libertarian radical tradition. Her first exposure to controversies over free speech occurred as a child, when her father invited Robert Ingersoll to lecture in her home town of Corning, New York. She accompanied her father and Ingersoll as an angry crowd threw fruit at them and effectively prevented Ingersoll from lecturing at the town's only public hall.[221]

After moving to New York in 1912, Sanger met Emma Goldman

---

[216] Goldman, supra note 165, at 419.

[217] Id. at 459.

[218] Id. at 438, 484–85; 2 id. at 548, 609, 618–20. See Theodore Schroeder, Autobiographical Notes, Emman [sic] Goldman 5, in Schroeder Papers, supra note 118, Box 1 (Goldman asked Schroeder to "advise and help" when the New York police repeatedly arrested her to stop her speeches); Letter from Gilbert E. Roe to Theodore Schroeder (Sept. 9, 1910), in Schroeder Papers, supra note 118, Box 9 (reporting Goldman's request for funds and encouraging Schroeder to join him in sending her money).

[219] Goldman, supra note 165, at 393, 395. Four of the chapters in Schroeder, supra note 117, originally appeared in Mother Earth. Schroeder, supra note 117, at viii.

[220] See, e.g., Leonard D. Abbott, The Fight for Free Speech in Tarrytown, 9 Mother Earth 107 (1914) (role of Free Speech League in seeking public meeting for anti-Rockefeller protest); Julia May Courtney, Denver, 9 Mother Earth 104, 106 (1914) (formation of local free speech league "in connection with the National Free Speech League" when Goldman visited Denver); Alden Freeman, The Protest Meeting at Cooper Union, 4 Mother Earth 146 (1909) (meeting chaired by Abbott for the "National Free Speech Committee"); Observations and Comments, 10 Mother Earth 66, 69 (1915) (Free Speech League taking contributions in Sanger birth control case); Ben L. Reitman, Three Years, 6 Mother Earth 84, 88 (1911) (substantial support of free speech for Emma Goldman by "active members of the Free Speech Committee," including Schroeder, Abbott, and Foote).

[221] Ellen Chesler, Woman of Valor: Margaret Sanger and the Birth Control Movement 24–26 (1992); Margaret Sanger, An Autobiography 17–23 (1938).

and key figures in the Free Speech League and absorbed many of their ideas.[222] Sanger reported that she became committed to birth control after witnessing as a nurse the death of a pregnant woman from a self-induced abortion.[223] She viewed birth control both as a weapon for the poor in the class struggle[224] and as "part of the fight for freedom of speech."[225] In 1914 she founded *Woman Rebel,* a magazine "dedicated to the interests of working women."[226] Borrowed from an IWW flyer, the magazine's slogan, "No Gods, No Masters," exemplified the journal's commitment to individual rights.[227] *Woman Rebel* "advocated direct action" and attempted to "put anti-capitalist soapbox oratory in print."[228]

Sanger had her first brush with the Comstock Act in 1913 when the Post Office censored a column she wrote about gonorrhea and syphilis for the *Call,* a popular Socialist daily in New York. The column was part of a series entitled "What Every Girl Should Know." The *Call* published an empty box in place of the censored column, using the headline "What Every Girl Should Know – Nothing!, by order of The Post-Office Department." Several weeks later the Post Office relented and allowed the *Call* to publish Sanger's column.[229]

The following year, federal postal officials determined that various issues of *Woman Rebel* contained nonmailable material and indicted Sanger under the Comstock Act. Sanger was unable to discover the precise articles that led to the Post Office's determinations. Although many articles expressed strident radical views on politics, labor, religion, and marriage, and one advocated birth control to frighten the "capitalist class," none actually gave advice on contraceptive methods. While released on her own recognizance pending trial, Sanger left the country for Europe. She returned a year later, and eventually the government dropped the charges against her.[230]

During this period, the Free Speech League provided substantial assistance to Sanger. She contacted Abbott and Schroeder

---

[222] David Kennedy, Birth Control in America: The Career of Margaret Sanger 8–18 (1970).

[223] Sanger, supra note 221, at 89–92, 107. This incident may have been "an imaginative, dramatic composite of Margaret's experience." Chesler, supra note 221, at 63.

[224] Kennedy, supra note 222, at 110.   [225] Sanger, supra note 221, at 113.

[226] Id. at 106.

[227] Id. at 109–10; see also Kennedy, supra note 222, at 22 (lifting banner slogan from IWW flyer).

[228] Sanger, supra note 221, at 110.

[229] Chesler, supra note 221, at 65–66; Sanger, supra note 221, at 77.

[230] Chesler, supra note 221, at 140; Kennedy, supra note 222, at 22, 25–26, 80; Sanger, supra note 221, at 110–11, 119–20, 189.

upon learning that the Post Office had suppressed *Woman Rebel*.[231] Abbott and Roe acted as her lawyers, and Sanger met periodically with Schroeder to discuss the journal's legal problems.[232] Roe, Abbott, and Emma Goldman joined Schroeder in a heated debate over whether Sanger should plead guilty in return for a light punishment, which would enable her to continue her work, or instead challenge the indictment, which would risk conviction and imprisonment.[233]

The Free Speech League continued its support of Sanger by using the fund left by Foote to print *Family Limitations,* Sanger's pamphlet on birth control intended for "women of extremely circumscribed vocabularies."[234] Probably using Foote's fund again, the League provided Sanger with living expenses during her year abroad.[235] When Comstock, in one of his last acts, arrested her estranged husband William for distributing *Family Limitations*,[236] the League publicized and assisted his defense.[237] At a protest meeting following William Sanger's conviction, Abbott, as president of the League, announced to "all believers in free speech" that radicals would respond, not by appealing to unjust courts, but by distributing "from hand to hand" a million copies of the pamphlet and the details of this "travesty on justice."[238]

The repression of speech associated with labor unrest provided another constant source of work for the Free Speech League and illustrated the range of its activities beyond the problems of sex radicals and anarchists. Demonstrating its commitment to free

---

[231] Sanger wrote the telephone numbers of Roe and Schroeder on the letter she received from the assistant postmaster informing her that the first issue of Woman Rebel was "unmailable." Letter from Assistant Postmaster to Margaret Sanger (Apr. 2, 1914), in Margaret Sanger Papers, Reel 11 (Manuscript Division, Library of Congress) [hereinafter Sanger Papers].

[232] Sanger remembered Schroeder as "a good lawyer and an authority on the constitution" who "gave much sound advice." Sanger, supra note 221, at 113.

[233] See, e.g., Letter from Emma Goldman to Margaret Sanger (Dec. 8, 1915), in Sanger Papers, supra note 231, Reel 8; Letter from Bolton Hall to Leonard Abbott (Dec. 13, 1915), in Sanger Papers, supra note 231, Reel 11; Letter from Gilbert E. Roe to Leonard D. Abbott (Dec. 15, 1915), in Sanger Papers, supra note 231, Reel 11; Letter from Emma Goldman to Margaret Sanger (Dec. 16, 1915), in Sanger Papers, supra note 231, Reel 8; see also Chesler, supra note 221, at 126; Kennedy, supra note 222, at 78–80.

[234] Sanger, supra note 221, at 112.   [235] Kennedy, supra note 222, at 27.

[236] Id. at 72–73; Sanger, supra note 221, at 176–78.

[237] Letter from the Free Speech League to "Friend" (undated), in Sanger Papers, supra note 231, Reel 8; see also Chesler, supra note 221, at 126; Kennedy, supra note 222, at 78–80.

[238] Sanger Trial in Comstock Case Ends in Uproar, in Sanger Papers, supra note 231, Reel 135 (unidentified newspaper article).

expression for all viewpoints, the League assisted both the AFL and the IWW, bitter ideological rivals that generally did not cooperate even in combating attacks on labor speech. Schroeder corresponded with Samuel Gompers, president of the AFL, after a court order enjoined the union from publishing "Unfair" and "We don't patronize" lists in its newspaper as part of a labor boycott.[239] The Supreme Court eventually upheld the injunction, reasoning that it prohibited only "verbal acts" and did not "restrain any form of publication."[240] Apart from the specifics of this case, Schroeder and Gompers exchanged views and literature elaborating their respective positions on First Amendment issues.[241]

The Free Speech League had much closer ties with the IWW, whose "free speech fights" over the right to speak on public streets is the subject of the following chapter. These fights often elicited local repression, widespread attention, and hostility from the AFL's national office. During the highly publicized IWW free speech fight in San Diego in 1912, Abbott played the most active and visible role for the League in providing money and advice. He sent messages on behalf of the League to the governor of California and the mayor and police chief of San Diego. These messages protested the "unconstitutional suppression of free speech" and urged proceedings against "officials and citizens calling themselves vigilantes."[242]

---

[239] Letter from Samuel Gompers to Theodore Schroeder (Jan. 21, 1909), in Schroeder Papers, supra note 118, Box 9; Letter from Samuel Gompers to Theodore Schroeder (Feb. 24, 1909), in Schroeder Papers, supra note 118, Box 9; Letter from Theodore Schroeder to Alton B. Parker (undated), in Schroeder Papers, supra note 118, Box 9.

[240] Gompers v. Buck's Stove & Range Co., 221 U.S. 418, 439 (1911), discussed infra Chapter 3, at text accompanying notes 143–45.

[241] Letter from Gompers to Schroeder (Jan. 21, 1909), supra note 239; Letter from Gompers to Schroeder (Feb. 24, 1909), supra note 239; Letter from Theodore Schroeder to Samuel Gompers (July 22, 1911), in Schroeder Papers, supra note 118, Box 9; Letter from Samuel Gompers to Theodore Schroeder (July 28, 1911), in Schroeder Papers, supra note 118, Box 9.

[242] Letter from Leonard D. Abbott to Theodore Schroeder (May 21, 1912), in Schroeder Papers, supra note 118, Box 10. Abbott's efforts prompted a letter from Vincent St. John, the IWW's general secretary and treasurer, thanking Abbott and the League for their assistance. Letter from Vincent St. John to Leonard D. Abbott (May 23, 1912), in Schroeder Papers, supra note 118, Box 10. Thomas Flynn, the father of Elizabeth Gurley Flynn, one of the key leaders and orators during IWW free speech fights, also wrote to Abbott. Letter from Thomas Flynn to Leonard D. Abbott (Apr. 8, 1912), in Schroeder Papers, supra note 118, Box 10.

Schroeder followed up Abbott's message to the governor with a letter of his own, disapproving of Abbott's wording, but supporting his protest against the "official and semi-official outrages" that had denied free speech in San Diego. Letter from Theodore Schroeder to Governor Hiram Johnson (May 27, 1912), in Schroeder Papers, supra note 118, Box 10.

Roe and Goldman actually traveled to San Diego and relayed first-hand reports of the free speech fight.[243] Schroeder corresponded with several IWW members and attorneys in San Diego and with residents there who formed an affiliated local free speech league. He helped formulate legal arguments against a San Diego ordinance governing street meetings, made financial contributions, and pledged to assist in a potential Supreme Court appeal that never materialized.[244] Schroeder subsequently wrote a lengthy account of the San Diego free speech fight. He published it together with excerpts from an investigative report of the episode, prepared at the governor's request, that had cited substantial violations of freedom of expression.[245] IWW activities on the East Coast also produced work for the Free Speech League. After a 1913 IWW strike in Paterson, New Jersey, Schroeder donated money and arranged for Roe to represent a defendant prosecuted and ultimately convicted under a statute that prohibited advocating, encouraging, or inciting the unlawful destruction of property.[246]

Schroeder and Roe worked together in other labor matters. They defended journalist Max Eastman against a criminal libel indictment for publishing an article in his newspaper, *The Masses*. The article alleged that the Associated Press had suppressed and distorted reports of labor strikes. Roe represented *The Masses* and Schroeder provided research assistance before the government withdrew its indictment.[247] Roe was less successful in defending author Upton Sinclair, who had been arrested while leading a

---

[243] See, e.g., Letter from Emma Goldman to E. B. Foote (May 16, 1912), in Schroeder Papers, supra note 118, Box 10; Letter from Gilbert E. Roe to Theodore Schroeder (May 20, 1912), in Schroeder Papers, supra note 118, Box 10.

[244] See, e.g., Letter from F. W. Hubbard to Theodore Schroeder (Jan. 16, 1912), in Schroeder Papers, supra note 118, Box 10; Letter from Fred H. Moore to Theodore Schroeder (May 29, 1912), in Schroeder Papers, supra note 118, Box 10.

[245] Schroeder, supra note 117, at 116–90.

[246] See, e.g., Letter from Theodore Schroeder to Gilbert E. Roe (Aug. 10, 1914), in Schroeder Papers, supra note 118, Box 11; Letter from Theodore Schroeder to Gilbert E. Roe (Oct. 2, 1914), in Schroeder Papers, supra note 118, Box 11; Letter from Gilbert E. Roe to Theodore Schroeder (Oct. 3, 1914), in Schroeder Papers, supra note 118, Box 11.

[247] See, e.g., Letter from Gilbert E. Roe to Theodore Schroeder (Jan. 10, 1914), in Schroeder Papers, supra note 118, Box 11; Letter from Theodore Schroeder to Gilbert E. Roe (Mar. 24, 1914), in Schroeder Papers, supra note 118, Box 11; Letter from Theodore Schroeder to Gilbert E. Roe (Apr. 7, 1914), in Schroeder Papers, supra note 118, Box 11; Letter from Gilbert E. Roe to Amos Pinchot (June 4, 1915), in Roe Papers, supra note 156, Container H5. For details of this case, see Max Eastman, Enjoyment of Living 464–73 (1948); Art Young, Art Young: His Life and Times: 295–300 (1939).

demonstration in front of the Standard Oil Company building. The demonstrators had blamed John D. Rockefeller for the deaths of women and children during labor unrest in Colorado. Despite Roe's counsel, Sinclair was convicted for behavior "tending to a breach of the peace."[248]

Although much League work involved protecting the speech of Goldman, Sanger, and labor activists, the free speech problems of relatively unknown radicals remained a constant concern. The League maintained a close relationship with Harry Weinberger, a lawyer who often defended radicals, including Emma Goldman. Schroeder provided advice and funding in 1916 while supporting Weinberger's efforts to appeal the case of an anarchist who had been convicted for distributing on a public street pamphlets opposing compulsory vaccination.[249] Abbott, as president of the League, similarly arranged for Weinberger to represent two free-thinkers arrested for delivering antireligious speeches. Both were acquitted.[250] In another matter, Schroeder helped an organization combat the suppression of its "anti-Catholic" agitation.[251]

The League maintained its viewpoint neutrality in religious matters by supporting speech on a variety of religious themes. Schroeder asked Steffens to help a man jailed "more on account of religious mysticism" than for any "real offense."[252] He also wrote a minister that "I am not even a Christian but I believe in Freedom of the Press and am willing to help you defend the principle though I may care nothing about your doctrine or you personally."[253]

In its last major legal case before World War I, the Free Speech League was instrumental in bringing a controversy to the Supreme Court that arose from the same anarchist Home Colony whose call for "concerted action in defense of speech and utterance" had

[248] People v. Sinclair, 86 Misc. 426, 427, 149 N.Y.S. 54, 55 (Ct. Gen. Sess. 1914), aff'd, 151 N.Y.S. 1136 (1915).

[249] Letter from Harry Weinberger to Theodore Schroeder (Apr. 28, 1916), supra note 119; Letter from Theodore Schroeder to Harry Weinberger (May 9, 1916), supra note 119; Letter from Harry Weinberger to Theodore Schroeder (Oct, 27, 1916), supra note 119, see also Harry Weinberger, A Rebel's Interrupted Autobiography, 2 Am. J. Econ. & Soc. 111, 116–17 (1942).

[250] Letter from Leonard Abbott to Theodore Schroeder (July 2, 1915), in Schroeder Papers, supra note 118, Box 12.

[251] Letter from Theodore Schroeder to C. W. Bibb (Sept. 27, 1915), in Schroeder Papers, supra note 118, Box 11.

[252] Letter from Theodore Schroeder to Lincoln Steffens (Feb. 19, 1912), in Schroeder Papers, supra note 118, Box 10.

[253] Letter from Theodore Schroeder to Rev. A. Mylnarczyk (Sept. 17, 1912), in Schroeder Papers, supra note 118, Box 11.

prompted the League's founding in 1902.[254] Ten years later, the League came to the defense of Jay Fox, a member of the Home Colony arrested for editing an article that advocated a boycott against local citizens who had interfered with nude bathing. Schroeder, who corresponded at length with Fox's original attorney, became dissatisfied when the attorney, in his briefs for Fox, failed to include the constitutional arguments Schroeder had supplied. Schroeder then arranged for Roe to become the attorney of record, and the League financed Fox's appeal to the Supreme Court.[255] Writing for a unanimous Court in 1915, Justice Holmes upheld Fox's conviction, finding that the article indirectly but "unmistakably . . . encourages and incites a persistence in what we must assume would be a breach of the state laws against indecent exposure."[256]

In addition to their involvement with individual legal disputes, Schroeder and Roe engaged in broader activities on behalf of free speech. Both lobbied the police commissioner of New York City for greater freedom of assembly.[257] Schroeder also attempted to limit censorship by the U.S. Postal Service. He wrote to a congressional postal commission requesting that it "enlarge the scope of [its] inquiry" in order to hear arguments "for the Amendment or repeal of the laws which make it a crime to send through the . . . mails, so-called 'obscene and indecent' literature." Schroeder protested that under these laws "all scientific books upon the sub-

---

254 See supra text accompanying note 112.
255 Letter from Theodore Schroeder to James J. Anderson (May 11, 1912), in Schroeder Papers, supra note 118, Box 10; Letter from Theodore Schroeder to Jay Fox (May 11, 1912), in Schroeder Papers, supra note 118, Box 10; Letter from Theodore Schroeder to Jay Fox (Sept. 3, 1912), in Schroeder Papers, supra note 118, Box 10; Letter from Gilbert E. Roe to Theodore Schroeder (Jan. 16, 1913), in Schroeder Papers, supra note 118, Box 10; Letter from Gilbert E. Roe to Theodore Schroeder (Mar. 21, 1913), in Schroeder Papers, supra note 118, Box 10; Letter from Gilbert E. Roe to Theodore Schroeder (June 17, 1913), in Schroeder Papers, supra note 118, Box 11; Receipt from Gilbert E. Roe to Theodore Schroeder (June 25, 1913), in Schroeder Papers, supra note 118, Box 11; Letter from Gilbert E. Roe to Theodore Schroeder (Oct. 6, 1913), in Schroeder Papers, supra note 118, Box 11; Letter from Theodore Schroeder to Gilbert E. Roe (July 6, 1914), in Schroeder Papers, supra note 118, Box 11.
256 Fox v. Washington, 236 U.S. 273, 277 (1915), discussed infra Chapter 3, at text accompanying notes 24–32.
257 Letter from Theodore Schroeder to "the Honorable Commissioner of Police, New York City" (Dec. 10, 1906), in Schroeder Papers, supra note 118, Box 7; Letter from Gilbert E. Roe to Edward A. Ross (Oct. 24, 1914), in Roe Papers, supra note 156, Container H4. In 1916, Roe wrote to Police Commissioner Arthur Woods, protesting Emma Goldman's harassment by New York City police. Letter from Gilbert E. Roe to Arthur M. Woods (Oct. 21, 1916), in Roe Papers, supra note 156, Container H5.

ject of sex are penalized and their circulation, even among physicians, is a matter of toleration in spite of the law."[258] The Commission rejected his request as "an unwarranted stretch of [its] authority." Undaunted, Schroeder wrote to Senator La Follette proposing "a searching Congressional investigation as to the postal censorship over literature."[259] Schroeder also wrote the League's protest to the New York legislature about proposed legislation that would have punished doctors who advertised cures for venereal disease. "Whatever may be legitimately done," Schroeder maintained, "may be legitimately advertised."[260]

Schroeder and Roe tried to reach a broader audience by addressing major forums. In 1906, for example, Schroeder spoke to the National Purity Federation Conference in Chicago, although he was undoubtedly disappointed that Anthony Comstock, with whom Schroeder had been corresponding extensively, did not appear for his scheduled reply.[261] The substance of Comstock's position, however, emerged in a long letter he wrote Schroeder. While conceding "the fullest latitude" for one's personal views, Comstock did not accept the absolute right of an individual to advocate and publish those views, no matter what their possible tendency upon others. In rejecting this absolutist position he ascribed to Schroeder, Comstock cited the *Hicklin* and *Bennett* cases, as well as numerous decisions of the U.S. Supreme Court that upheld the "police power" of government. Comstock emphasized "that we are living under a System of Government, where the Government is organized with a view to the preservation of Good Order and Public Morals."[262]

In the years immediately preceding World War I, Schroeder participated in the National Newspaper Conference in Wisconsin,[263] and Roe lectured on legal aspects of free speech at the 1914 annual meeting of the American Sociological Society.[264] Schroeder

---

[258] Letter from Theodore Schroeder to "the Honorable Postal Commission" (Oct. 2, 1906), in Schroeder Papers, supra note 118, Box 7.

[259] Letter from Theodore Schroeder to Hon. Robert M. La Follette (Sept. 3, 1909), in Schroeder Papers, supra note 118, Box 9.

[260] Protest of the Free Speech League (1911), in Schroeder Papers, supra note 118, Box 54.

[261] Sears, supra note 7, at 263.

[262] Letter from Anthony Comstock to Theodore Schroeder (Jan. 12, 1906), at 1–2, in Schroeder Papers, supra note 118, Box 5.

[263] Extension Division of the University of Wisconsin, General Information and Welfare, Proceedings of the First National Newspaper Conference 31–32 (Bulletin of the University of Wisconsin Serial No. 561, General Series No. 386, 1913). For a newspaper interview with Schroeder during this conference, see For Free Speech Is This Visitor, Madison Democrat, July 30, 1912.

[264] Roe Statement, supra note 163.

and Roe probably received the most attention when they testified in 1915 at widely publicized hearings before the Commission on Industrial Relations about the repression of speech during labor unrest.[265] Schroeder subsequently received an appreciative letter about his testimony from AFL President Samuel Gompers.[266]

Schroeder, who was an indefatigable publicist, regularly sent multiple copies of his own works, along with other literature, to libraries throughout the country. In 1913, Schroeder estimated that he had distributed several thousand pamphlets in this manner.[267] He also sent selected literature to federal and state judges, governors, and state legislatures and congressional committees considering "invasive bills." Always on the alert for potential free speech controversies, Schroeder and his colleagues in the League responded to any "local excitement" that involved free speech by sending "some of the good stuff" to "local newspapers and others."[268] This activity may have reached its extreme when, at the conclusion of the IWW free speech fight in San Diego, Schroeder mailed a reprint of a pamphlet by Hutchins Hapgood "to all persons whose residence address was given in the San Diego Telephone Directory."[269]

Despite its many achievements, the Free Speech League never fulfilled the high expectations of its founders. The anticipated support for free speech across the political spectrum never materialized. Even the progressives who ultimately founded the ACLU in 1920 had remained essentially oblivious to the many free speech issues that produced the League's work before World War I. The League's disappointments derived more from the process by which commitment to free speech developed in the United States than from any internal difficulties, such as financing or leadership. In the decades before World War I, Americans generally needed to experience repression of views they shared before formulating a theory of free speech that extended to ideas they opposed. During this period, radicals generally suffered from the repression of speech. The struggles of the IWW, advocates of birth control, and anarchists, like the previous problems of free lovers and freethinkers under the Comstock Act, did not prompt many Ameri-

---

[265] Roe Testimony, supra note 161; S. Doc. No. 415, supra note 161, at 10,840–52, 10, 866–96 (testimony of Mr. Theodore Schroeder).

[266] Letter from Samuel Gompers to Theodore Schroeder (Aug. 19, 1915), in Schroeder Papers, supra note 118, Box 11.

[267] Letter from Schroeder to Hallinan, supra note 193.

[268] Letter from Theodore Schroeder to Edmund Norton (Feb. 3, 1909), in Schroeder Papers, supra note 118, Box 9.

[269] Letter from Schroeder to Hallinan, supra note 193.

cans to worry about First Amendment guarantees. Even radicals, as Schroeder reiterated throughout his career, often did not support the free speech rights of each other.

The Free Speech League, however, achieved many of its most important goals. It became the first organization in American history to demonstrate a principled commitment to free expression for all viewpoints on all subjects. It overcame the parochial inability of various single-issue or feuding radical groups to recognize that government repression of speech was a common problem shared by them all. Operating vigorously, and generally alone, the League defended the speech of any individual or group whose expressive rights were threatened or abridged, including radicals who failed to help each other. During World War I, it provided a crucial link to the emerging ACLU, which relied on the knowledge and expertise of League members. The ACLU, however, developed a narrower conception of constitutionally protected speech. Whereas the underlying belief in individual autonomy at the core of libertarian radicalism generated an extensive general commitment to free speech by the Free Speech League, the ACLU initially limited its defense of free speech to the democratic value of political expression. The more visible and ultimately more successful defense of political speech by the ACLU following World War I obscured the broader prewar conception of free speech supported by the Free Speech League as well as the League's distinctive and deeply rooted ideology of libertarian radicalism.

The career of Roger Baldwin, the key figure in the ACLU, highlights the newly discovered interest in political speech by the postwar civil libertarians. It is ironic that much of Baldwin's early free speech work involved the defense of the IWW, whose entire leadership was indicted under the Espionage Act following Justice Department raids on IWW offices throughout the country in September 1917. In 1919, after serving a prison term for refusing induction based on his conscientious objection to the war, Baldwin himself joined the IWW and worked for a time as a laborer.[270] Earlier, however, when the Free Speech League was energetically supporting the IWW free speech fights between 1909 and 1913, Baldwin and most of his future colleagues in the ACLU were essentially bystanders. Instead, they devoted most of their energy to the social work movement and other causes of progressive reform. In contrast to the leaders of the Free Speech League, none of them had become free speech activists before the war.

[270] Walker, supra note 122, at 25–26, 42; Roger Baldwin, Recollections of a Life in Civil Liberties – 1, 2 Civ. Lib. Rev., Spring 1975, at 39, 59–72.

2

The IWW Free Speech Fights

Among the many controversies in which the Free Speech League became involved before World War I, none generated more popular discussion of free speech than the dramatic and highly publicized IWW free speech fights. These fights typically arose when local communities tried to prevent the IWW from using downtown street corners to express its radical ideology in deliberately provocative language. They began in 1906 and ceased before the American entry into World War I in 1917. Although the IWW did not keep statistics itself, a contemporary investigator identified free speech fights in twenty-six different communities. At least twenty-one of them took place between 1909 and 1913.[1]

During the free speech fights, the members of the IWW, frequently called "Wobblies," explicitly invoked their First Amendment rights and devoted substantial attention to the legal and practical importance of free speech. Various municipal, state, and federal officials responded to IWW free speech claims. Most significantly, the free speech fights, which often received national publicity, prompted the diverse American public to confront free speech issues. Commentators included editorial writers and journalists, ministers, teachers, businessmen, politicians, workers, farmers, and members of a variety of organizations, such as veterans' groups, charities, the Socialist Party, the American Federation of Labor (AFL), and the Daughters of the American Revolution.

Labor historians have written extensively about the IWW free speech fights,[2] but they have not thoroughly investigated what the

[1] Paul L. Brissenden, The I.W.W.: A Study of American Syndicalism 76–77, 88–89 (2d ed. 1920).

[2] Id. For two more recent, comprehensive studies of the IWW, see Melvyn Dubofsky, We Shall Be All: A History of the Industrial Workers of the World (1969); Philip S. Foner, History of the Labor Movement in the United States: The Industrial Workers of the World 1905–1917 (1965). Periodical literature examining IWW free speech fights in particular places supplements this more general information. See, e.g., Ronald Genini, Industrial Workers of the World and Their Fresno Free Speech Fight, 1910–1911, 53 Cal. Hist. Q. 100 (1974); Charles P. LeWarne, The Aberdeen, Washington, Free Speech Fight of 1911–1912, 66 Pac. Nw. Q. 1 (1975); Grace L. Miller, The I.W.W. Free Speech Fight: San Diego, 1912, 54 S. Cal. Q. 211 (1972); Robert L. Tyler, The Everett Free Speech Fight, 23 Pac. Hist. Rev. 19 (1954).

Wobblies or their audiences actually thought about the meaning of free speech. They have thereby left the impression that the free speech fights were merely a tactic lacking intellectual content. Presenting the range of views provoked by the free speech fights corrects this impression while responding to the call by current legal historians to investigate the "rights consciousness" of Americans who were not official interpreters of the Constitution.[3] The diversity of opinions about free speech issues, however, also challenges the prevailing assumption that attention to "rights consciousness" will reveal interpretive struggles between legal elites and subordinated outsiders asserting alternative visions of rights. Most commentators observed rather than participated in the free speech fights, and even the views of Wobblies and public officials were far from monolithic.

While commentators overwhelmingly stressed their antipathy to the ideology and tactics of the IWW, a large number relied on the constitutional principle of free speech to support the right of Wobblies to express their offensive views in public places. Many also protested official and vigilante repression during the free speech fights. Others, who claimed that the Wobblies had hypocritically "abused" the right of free speech while engaging in impermissibly "licentious" behavior, nevertheless endorsed the value of constitutional protection for speech. Many elaborated their own views about the proper contours of lawful speech at the same time that they declared the illegality of the free speech fights and sometimes even justified vigilante violence. To a significant extent, the issues and categories of analysis that arose during the free speech fights are similar to those that dominate current interpretation of the First Amendment. And in contrast to the mechanistic rejection of free speech claims by most judges before World War I, popular commentators on the IWW free speech fights often expressed their diverse views thoughtfully and in detail.

AN OVERVIEW OF THE FREE SPEECH FIGHTS

The IWW free speech fights emerged from the commitment to direct action at the core of its syndicalist ideology. Dissatisfaction with the trade unionism promoted by the AFL prompted the found-

---

[3] Essays by many of these legal historians are collected in a special issue of the Journal of American History designed for the bicentennial of the Constitution. See Symposium, The Constitution and American Life, 74 J. Am. Hist. 661 (1987). The essays in Part II of the issue, entitled "Rights Consciousness in American History," focus especially on the interpretations of constitutional rights by various groups challenging prevailing legal understandings.

ing of the IWW in 1905. Unlike the AFL, which by then had committed itself to improving the economic position of workers within a free market economy, the IWW advocated the revolutionary overthrow of capitalism. The IWW rejected the AFL's focus on organizing skilled workers by craft and on negotiating binding trade agreements with employers. It determined instead to create a broad union based initially on the unskilled and stressed direct action by workers as the key tactic in the struggle against capitalism.[4]

While never defining direct action succinctly, the IWW understood it to include spontaneous strikes and slowdowns at the workplace, as well as various forms of mass activity, such as picketing, parades, demonstrations, and the public speaking in downtown areas that provoked the free speech fights. Singing from the *"Little Red Song Book,"*[5] the IWW's famous collection of class conscious songs, often accompanied and supported these forms of direct action. The IWW officially endorsed sabotage as a tactic of direct action even as it cautioned members against violence. Talk of sabotage often frightened employers and the public while titillating fellow workers, but Wobblies used the term to describe a huge range of activities from uncooperativeness at work to disabling and even destroying employer property. Various forms of direct action, the IWW believed, would ultimately lead to a general strike, which would paralyze industry and bring about the abolition of capitalism.[6]

Although resembling contemporary developments within European syndicalism, the IWW emphasis on direct action arose essentially from indigenous American conditions, particularly frustration with the AFL. Wobblies stressed the American origins of their direct action by comparing themselves to eighteenth-century revolutionaries and nineteenth-century abolitionists who openly defied

---

[4] Brissenden, supra note 1, at 57, 76–77, 88–89; Nick Salvatore, Introduction to Samuel Gompers, Seventy Years of Life and Labor: An Autobiography xxv (1984); Philip Taft, The A.F. of L. in the Time of Gompers xviii (1970). Salvatore observes that Samuel Gompers, the president of the AFL when the IWW was founded, once had a broader view of the labor movement "that looked toward a fundamental transformation of the society." Gompers's views narrowed after 1886, and especially after 1900. Id. at xxiii, xxxix. William Forbath similarly claims that in the late 1890s AFL leaders abandoned their earlier "radical republican claims upon the government" and "began to echo the freedom-of-contract rhetoric of liberal constitutional doctrine and late-nineteenth century common law." William E. Forbath, Law and the Shaping of the American Labor Movement 130 (1991).

[5] I.W.W. Songs: To Fan the Flames of Discontent (photo. reprint 1989) (1923).

[6] Dubofsky, supra note 2, at 151–57, 161–66; Foner, supra note 2, at 134–40, 160–64; David Montgomery, The Fall of the House of Labor: The Workplace, the State, and American Labor Activism, 1865–1925, at 310–27 (1987).

existing law to bring about a better society.[7] In his dramatic opening address to the first IWW convention in 1905, "Big Bill" Haywood called the gathering "the Continental Congress of the working class."[8]

Seeking to organize unskilled workers who were generally
neglected by the AFL, the IWW focused especially on migratory
workers in the West and immigrant industrial workers in the East.
The geographical diffusion of Western agriculture, mining, and
lumber made it difficult for Wobbly organizers to reach migratory
workers at job sites. Employer harassment of organizers who did
reach these remote locations compounded the underlying logisti-
cal obstacles. The IWW decided that it could organize workers
more effectively in Western cities, where migratory workers congre-
gated when looking for jobs. Employment agencies in these cities
typically hired workers on commission from employers. Many agencies also received fees from workers, who frequently discovered on
arrival that the "jobs" for which they had been "hired" no longer
existed. Wobbly organizers attempted to attract the migratory workers in these cities as a preliminary step to gaining influence at the
place of employment. They spoke and distributed literature on
street corners, often near the employment agencies whose control
over hiring they attacked and attempted to displace.[9]

IWW support of striking workers through picketing, meetings,
and demonstrations also provoked confrontations over free
speech. Although labor historians often confine their usage of the
term *free speech fights* to IWW organizing efforts, strikes raised similar free speech issues. The famous IWW strike against silk manufacturers in Paterson, New Jersey, probably produced more extensive press coverage, government study, and judicial opinions about
free speech than any other single incident involving the IWW.

Many free speech fights followed a familiar pattern. Wobblies,
often after traveling long distances, attempted to speak on soap-
boxes at downtown street corners and deliberately courted arrest.[10]
If police did not arrest them at a particular street corner, Wobblies
moved elsewhere and, as a government investigator reported,

[7] Brissenden, supra note 1, at 231, 274–76; Dubofsky, supra note 2, at 147;
Dubofsky, "Big Bill" Haywood 64, 67–68 (1987); Foner, supra note 2, at 23,
157–60.
[8] Brissenden, supra note 1, at 83 (quoting Proceedings of the First IWW Convention 1 [1905] [statement of William D. Haywood]).
[9] Brissenden, supra note 1, at 158–59, 214; Dubofsky, supra note 2, at 174–75;
Foner, supra note 2, at 115–23, 177–78.
[10] Foner, supra note 2, at 173–75.

"practically demanded that they be incarcerated."[11] Police frequently arrested Wobblies when they mounted the soapbox, sometimes before they had even begun to speak. Hundreds of Wobblies were arrested[12] and charged with various offenses, such as obstructing the sidewalk, blocking traffic, vagrancy, unlawful assembly, or violating a local ordinance against street speaking.[13]

Arrested Wobblies generally pleaded not guilty and attempted to get jury trials to extend the jury selection process as long as possible. Applicable laws, however, often provided for trials by police magistrates or judges without juries. Many arrested Wobblies, sometimes after spending several weeks or longer in jail, were released before trial, and frequently were arrested again on the

---

[11] Daniel O'Regan, Free Speech Fight in Spokane 4 (Nov. 2, 1914) (Reports of the U.S. Commission on Industrial Relations, 1912–1915 [National Archives, Microfilm Publication T4, Roll 2]; General Records of the Department of Labor, Record Group 174; National Archives, Washington, D.C. [hereinafter CIR Microfilm Collection]).

[12] The number of arrests in IWW free speech fights can only be approximated. As an investigator for the Commission on Industrial Relations pointed out in writing about incidents that had occurred one to three years previously, "exact facts are hard to obtain as they are dim in the minds of the authorities and the I.W.W.'s as a general thing cannot be located." Daniel O'Regan, Free Speech Fights of the I.W.W.'s 6 (Nov. 10, 1914) (Civil Liberties; Commission on Industrial Relations ["CIR"]; Records Relating to CIR Studies, 1912–1915; General Records of the Department of Labor, Record Group 174; National Archives, Washington, D.C. [hereinafter Civil Liberties Collection], Folder: Free Speech Fights of the I.W.W.'s). He was, however, able to estimate 150 arrests, involving approximately 60 individuals, in Missoula, Montana, id., 500 in Fresno, id. at 14–15, and 320 in Spokane. O'Regan, supra note 11, at 2. In testimony before the Commission, Wobbly leader "Big Bill" Haywood estimated arrests at 500–600 in Spokane, 150–200 in Fresno, and 135 in San Diego. 11 Commission on Indus. Relations, Industrial Relations: Final Report and Testimony, S. Doc. No. 415, 64th Cong., 1st Sess. 10573 (1916) (hereinafter Final Report) (testimony of William D. Haywood). A judge in San Diego asserted during the free speech fight that it had produced more than 200 arrests. I.W.W. Chiefs Fined and Sentenced to Jail, San Diego Union, Aug. 6, 1912, at 9, 12. Commission investigators of the IWW strike and demonstrations in Paterson, NJ, put the number of arrests at slightly over 2,000. Patrick F. Gill & Redmond S. Brennan, Report on the Inferior Courts and Police of Paterson, N.J. 21 (Oct. 1914) (Numerical Series of CIR Report, No. 109, Commission on Industrial Relations; Records Relating to CIR Studies, 1912–1915; General Records of the Department of Labor, Record Group 174; National Archives, Washington, D.C.). By contrast, the lawyer for the arrested Wobblies in Paterson testified that he had slightly under 2,000 cases. 3 Final Report, supra, at 2530.

[13] B. F. Moore, Constitutionally Protected Personal Liberties 17 (Feb. 1915) (Civil Liberties Collection, supra note 12, Folder: Moore: Constitutionally Protected Personal Liberties); O'Regan, supra note 11, at 2–3.

same or a similar charge. Wobblies generally submitted passively to arrests, but later created ruckuses in increasingly overcrowded jails. They sang ideologically charged Wobbly songs, attempted to speak to people gathered outside the prison, and engaged in hunger strikes.[14]

Officials in several communities escalated the charges against Wobblies as the free speech fights continued. In both San Diego and Paterson, for example, police initially arrested speakers on a variety of misdemeanor charges. When mass arrests failed to stop the street speaking, officials charged the speakers with felonies, which carried longer sentences.[15] Officials also responded to the free speech fights by effectively pressuring owners of local halls to refuse rentals to Wobblies, by confiscating newspapers sympathetic to IWW positions, and by arresting people selling those newspapers.[16]

Although large numbers of arrested Wobblies were released rather than prosecuted,[17] many others were tried and convicted in local courts. Convicted Wobblies frequently received fines, but most did not pay them and instead served prison terms of several days or weeks. Wobblies rarely sought appellate review of their convictions, in part because they lacked sufficient financial resources, but primarily because they preferred the pressure of direct action over recourse to a legal system they ridiculed as a tool of the employing class.

The free speech fights produced mixed results for the IWW. Some communities capitulated to IWW demands for freedom of speech in centrally located public areas, but others effectively resisted. In two of the largest and most publicized confrontations between the IWW and local authorities, the IWW failed to achieve

---

[14] Moore, supra note 13, at 17, 23; O'Regan, supra note 11, at 3–5, 7, 9; O'Regan, supra note 12, at 5, 15.

[15] 57 Free-Speech Advocates Face Prosecution by State, San Diego Union, Feb. 10, 1912, at 5; see Forty Strikers Arrested For Picketing Held Under Bail by the Recorder in the Police Court this Morning, Paterson Evening News, Mar. 27, 1913, at 1 (editorial); To Charge I.W.W.'s with General Conspiracy, San Diego Union, Mar. 25, 1912, at 5.

[16] Dubofsky, supra note 2, at 180, 185; A Straight from the Shoulder Talk on the Strike Situation and the Truth of the Whole Matter in Plain Language, Paterson Evening News, May 20, 1913, at 1 (editorial); Situation of the Strike Today, Paterson Evening News, May 20, 1913, at 1 (editorial).

[17] Arrests without prosecutions remained common long after the IWW free speech fights. According to Professor LaFave, "The making of an arrest intended to culminate in release of the suspected offender rather than in his prosecution is said to be both illegal and unlikely. Yet in current criminal justice administration arrests for purposes other than prosecution are common." Wayne R. LaFave, Arrest: The Decision to Take a Suspect into Custody 437

its primary goals: the repeal of a restrictive street ordinance in San Diego and the protection of picketing and street meetings during the strike in Paterson.[18] Failures in San Diego and Paterson exacerbated debate within the IWW over the strategic value of free speech fights. Wobbly activists increasingly argued that they diverted attention and energy from the primary goal of organizing workers. Soapbox oratory and civil disobedience could be exciting, but they took personal and financial resources from the hard and unglamorous work of developing an effective union. Rather than fighting for, and even winning, the right to free speech in one city and then moving on to another fight elsewhere, the IWW became convinced that the admittedly difficult work of organizing workers at the job site must take precedence. Building strong local unions replaced free speech fights as the focus of Wobbly activity, particularly after 1913.[19]

THE IWW IDEOLOGY OF FREE SPEECH

During the free speech fights, Wobblies repeatedly invoked the First Amendment. IWW publications called on "footloose rebels"[20] throughout the country to travel to the location of a fight to test and win the constitutional right of free speech. One activist explained the Wobbly view that "it was we who were upholding constitutional Law and the city officials who were disregarding it." He claimed that crowds of Wobblies shouted at police comments such as "Have you ever read the Constitution?"; "Don't you believe in free speech?"; "Go home and read your history"; and "What is

---

[18] See Dubofsky, supra note 2, at 189–96 (describing the San Diego free speech fight); id. at 263–85 (describing the Paterson, NJ, strike); Foner, supra note 2, at 194–205 (describing the San Diego Free speech fight); id at 351–72 (describing the Paterson, NJ, strike).

[19] Dubofsky, supra note 2, at 196–97; Foner, supra note 2, at 210–11, 463, 467, 552–53. IWW organizing activity was never very successful for reasons historians continue to debate. IWW opposition to American intervention in World War I led to severe government repression, but its syndicalist ideology, its inattention to bureaucratic details, and the inherent difficulties of organizing unskilled and often migratory workers also account for its weaknesses as a union. See Dubofsky, supra note 2, at 480–83; Foner, supra note 2, at 462–72, 558.

[20] See Assignment of Errors in Admitting Government's Exhibit No. 375 into Evidence 3a–4a, United States v. Haywood, No. 6125 (N.D. Ill. 1918), aff'd, 268 F. 795 (7th Cir. 1920), cert. denied, 256 U.S. 689 (1921) (IWW Collection, Walter P. Reuther Archives of Labor and Urban Affairs, Wayne State University, Detroit, Mich. [hereinafter IWW Collection], Box 119, Folder 10) (quoting Letter from I. K., IWW General Secretary and Treasurer, Chicago, Ill., to G. J. Bourg, IWW Secretary No. 61, Kansas City, Mo. (Nov. 13, 1914)).

this, Czarist Russia, or Free America?"[21] Another veteran of free speech fights reported that Wobblies, confronted by a police demand for a permit when mounting a platform to speak, replied that they "had none save the First Amendment to the Constitution of the U.S."[22]

Wobblies often accompanied their assertions of First Amendment rights with detailed discussion of free speech issues. Many exhibited strong consciousness of free speech as a fundamental and valuable right incorporated by the Framers into the First Amendment, enjoyed by all Americans in the early republic, but subsequently denied to workers by capitalists and their judicial agents. By contrast, other Wobblies claimed that workers never had meaningful rights to free speech in the United States, that the Framers viewed the First Amendment as a guarantee of free speech only for themselves, and that the history of the First Amendment had been nothing more than the self-interested manipulation of constitutional language by successive elites who abridged the dissenting speech of others. For these Wobblies, it was a waste of time to think about the meaning of free speech because true freedom of expression for workers could only be realized in the utopian classless society that would follow revolutionary action.

Throughout the free speech fights, many Wobblies characterized their repression as a dangerous deviation both from the original understanding of the First Amendment and from basic American traditions. Referring to the First Amendment, an IWW article complained that the "right of free speech, provided by the Constitution of the United States, has been perverted into 'no right to free speech.'"[23] The IWW observed that the "old English common law" of seditious libel, which "was supposed to have been overthrown by the First Amendment to the U.S. Constitution during Jefferson's administration," was revived by local authorities "as a last resort" in the "administration of justice directed against the working class."[24] As a result, "even those parts of the employers' national constitution which working people used to value are more and more a dead letter."[25] IWW publications maintained that "America today has abandoned her heroic traditions of the Revolution and

---

[21] Richard Brazier, Looking Backward to the Spokane Free Speech Fight 10, 16 (IWW Collection, supra note 20, Box 146, Folder 13).

[22] See George V. Carey, Free Speech Fight in Aberdeen, S.D. 2 (1914) (CIR Microfilm Collection, supra note 11).

[23] Which Is the More Dangerous?, Indus. Worker, Dec. 1, 1909, at 2.

[24] "Seditious Libel" in New Jersey, Solidarity, June 21, 1913, at 2.

[25] Grafters Hate Free Speech, Indus. Worker, Apr. 1, 1909, at 2.

the War of 1812 and has turned to hoodlumism and a denial of free speech and assembly to a large and growing body of citizens."[26] Yet because "Americans have been accustomed to eulogize the freedom of speech since the foundation of the republic," the IWW predicted that "multiplied thousands will continue to speak and protest against its denial, for they realize that in the imprisonment of one class of men in defiance of all constitutional guarantees, the liberties of all are invaded and placed in peril."[27]

Beyond its "originalist" account of a capitalist perversion of the First Amendment's true meaning, the IWW occasionally engaged in more technical analysis of First Amendment issues. The editor of *Solidarity*, one of the two major IWW publications, acknowledged the effectiveness of the First Amendment's explicit prohibition against federal legislation that abridged free speech. He complained, however, that "minor municipalities could do that very thing on some excuse such as 'disturbing the peace', 'interfering with traffic', or just because the 'leading citizens' couldn't tolerate that particular kind of 'free speech'." Even though the text of the First Amendment refers only to abridgments by Congress, he concluded that these municipalities "obviously" had violated it by interfering with IWW free speech fights.[28]

Wobblies sometimes advanced general arguments for free speech virtually identical to ones subsequently incorporated into constitutional analysis. Responding to concerns that the angry talk of workers could spur illegal activity, an IWW organizer asserted during a trial that repressing free speech poses the greater threat. "Whenever there exists in any society a class who suffers," he observed, "if that class is allowed to freely discuss their grievances, they may get hot under the collar in splitting hairs, but after a while they will agree upon a plan." On the other hand, if authorities deny such freedom of discussion, "then ideas ridiculous and dangerous to all classes of society will develop; ideas that can live in the dark, but which could not live in the open air; nothing will kill an unsound idea quicker than to air it." Only people "who are afraid of the truth," he added, "are afraid of free speech."[29]

This reasoning was not for judicial consumption alone. Articles in IWW publications made similar points in more highly charged

---

26 "Heroic" Contrasts, Solidarity, July 26, 1913, at 2.
27 Why Free Speech Is Denied the I.W.W., Indus. Worker, Nov. 17, 1909, at 4.
28 Ben H. Williams, Saga of the "One Big Union": American Labor in the Jungle 42 (IWW Collection, supra note 20, Box 146, Folder 14).
29 Record at 4977, 4978, United States v. Haywood, No. 6125 (N.D. Ill. 1918) (testimony of James P. Thompson), aff'd, 268 F. 795 (7th Cir. 1920), cert. denied, 256 U.S. 689 (1921) (IWW Collection, supra note 20, Box 109, Folder 1).

language. "Let one man stop Freedom of Speech," one warned, "and hell breaks forth." The article explained that if the government prohibits workers from discussing "the evil that afflicts them" and if the workers "cannot fight their common enemy in the open, they will resort to other means to carry on the war against the capitalist class."[30] During the free speech fight in Spokane, Wobblies characterized it as a struggle between two classes of anarchists. "The first belongs to that officialdom and money power that ignores and sneers at the right of free speech – a right granted by the constitution. The second class is being clubbed into anarchistic thoughts by the first."[31] Another article warned that ideas can be suppressed but cannot be killed. Revolutionary ideas, it pointed out, will last as long as the economic conditions that produce them. Wobbly organizers maintained that civilization itself depended on freedom of expression, and defined free speech and free press as the right "to say what the other fellow doesn't like."[32]

Wobblies were convinced that their own understandings of free speech and the First Amendment would not be accepted by judges. IWW commentary on the legal treatment of free speech frequently invoked basic Marxist class analysis and exhibited contempt for American law and legal institutions. The IWW claimed that the courts, like other state institutions, "are but the mirrors reflecting the prevailing mode of ownership in the means of production." Courts judge workers "with the consciousness of the class whose interest they reflect."[33] All Americans benefit from free speech, the IWW added, "so long as they keep their mouths shut about the boss and his ill-gotten gains." There is no freedom of expression, however, "for workers who want more or all of the product of their toil."[34]

Members of the "ruling class," Wobblies maintained, do not regard the First Amendment as a general guarantee of free speech. Rather, they interpret the Constitution as if it read, "Freedom of speech shall be guaranteed to all capitalists, politicians, preachers and other representatives of law and order in good and regular standing. It shall be abridged to socialists and utterly denied to anarchists, to the I.W.W., and to all inciters of strikes and other riots." Capitalists do not amend the First Amendment to reflect its

[30] Freedom of Speech Gone?, Indus. Worker, July 6, 1911, at 2.
[31] Which Is the More Dangerous?, supra note 23.
[32] J. J. Ettor, Press Freedom, Solidarity, June 14, 1913, at 1 (quoting Elizabeth Gurley Flynn).
[33] Why Free Speech Is Denied the I.W.W., supra note 27.
[34] Freedom of Speech, Indus. Worker, Dec. 14, 1911, at 2.

current meaning because it is in their interest "to leave the WORDS exactly as they are in order to fool the gullible workers into thinking that they had 'constitutional rights' and into wasting their time and breath talking about their being 'in jeopardy.'" The "toiling slaves" are misled into believing that they have enforceable rights to free speech "while the masters and their obedient hirlings go on with the every-day demonstration of the fact that the 'constitutional rights' of a working man are an idle dream."[35]

Wobblies cited the free speech fights as evidence of capitalist control of the legal system. Before the fights began, Wobblies claimed, capitalists never cared about the right to free speech on public streets. Capitalists effectively exercised their own free speech rights in their homes, clubs, libraries, and universities. They tolerated the street speaking "by religious bodies and other toothless institutions whose inane propaganda can never interfere with business."[36] But when workers decided to use the streets to "voice their opinion of the wrongs inflicted upon the producers of wealth," capitalists made the government officials they control pass ordinances restricting street speaking.[37] Wobblies were also convinced that libel law "will never be used except against workers" when they condemn "employment sharks."[38]

For many Wobblies, contempt for the capitalist legal system, perhaps exacerbated in the course of the free speech fights, extended to rejection of the underlying worth of constitutional rights under any circumstances. "Historically and logically," Wobblies maintained, "the constitution has nothing to do with the American working class of the twentieth century."[39] Rather, it is a "joke," a "mere mask of anarchy for the employing class." The language of the "rotten constitution," they protested, provided no more protection to workers "than it did to the negro slaves whose slavery was confirmed and upheld by it."[40] These Wobblies claimed to value freedom of speech, but believed that for working people it "can never be considered as a permanent and universal conquest so long as there remains a ruling class." Rather than "waste money and energy on the shell game of the law," they sought "the chance to appeal not to the 'Supreme Court,' but to their fellow workers against the common enemy." Workers must realize that

[35] Herbert Sturges, "Free Speech," Solidarity, Sept. 6, 1913, at 2.
[36] Bruce Rogers, Free Speech Fights, Indus. Worker, Jan. 25, 1912, at 3.
[37] What San Diego Need Expect, Indus. Worker, Apr. 18, 1912, at 2.
[38] Free Speech and Free Press, Indus. Worker, June 10, 1909, at 2.
[39] Sturges, supra note 35.
[40] The "Constitutional" Joke, Indus. Worker, Oct. 7, 1909, at 2.

"force is law" and "nothing else is a supreme court." They must win free speech for themselves through their own "power and fighting spirit."[41]

Many Wobblies, as their most vigorous opponents charged, viewed the free speech fights as only incidental to the more fundamental goals of unionization, economic power "to deal with the masters on the job," and, ultimately, the revolutionary abolition of capitalism.[42] "EDUCATE, AGITATE, ORGANIZE!!!,"[43] Wobbly publications exhorted. Class consciousness and revolutionary action would follow.

POPULAR REACTIONS

Popular reactions to the free speech fights ranged from support and collaboration to hostility and vigilante violence. Socialists, labor unions, and other groups affected by restrictive street ordinances supported the free speech fights, as did the Free Speech League, a few important intellectuals, and members of the general public. Many of these people, without accepting the IWW call for revolution, reiterated its claims of class bias in the legal system and agreed that the working class had no meaningful constitutional right to free speech. Over time, however, some supporters increasingly criticized the IWW for intemperate language, incendiary tactics, and the misuse of funds. Numerous other organizations and people, including the national AFL, opposed the free speech fights from their inception.

Socialists, who themselves had experienced repression of speech in connection with their own organizing and political efforts,[44] provided the most dependable and active allies for the IWW. Socialists raised money to support the free speech fights, protested violations of free speech, and sometimes participated directly in the fights. During the San Diego free speech fight, a member of the Socialist Party's national executive committee wrote two letters to Governor

---

[41] Basis of Free Speech, Solidarity, Dec. 7, 1912, at 2.

[42] Jacob Fuchrenberger, Local 13 Issues Statement, Indus. Worker, May 16, 1912, at 3.

[43] See, e.g., Grafters Hate Free Speech, supra note 25.

[44] See generally Information Dep't, The Socialist Party, Violations of the Right of Free Speech: 1905–1914 (Civil Liberties Collection, supra note 12, Folder: Thompson: Violations of the Right of Free Speech) (summarizing first-hand reports by Socialists of alleged violations of their free speech); John W. Wertheimer, Free-Speech Fights: The Roots of Modern Free-Expression Litigation in the United States 175–215 (1992) (unpublished Ph.D. dissertation, Princeton University, on file with author) (discussing free speech fights of Socialists).

Hiram Johnson of California complaining that the city ordinance restricting street speaking violated both the federal and the state constitutional protections for free speech.[45] "Must the brave struggle of noble-hearted citizens for the elemental rights guaranteed under the Constitution," he asked, "be turned from a badge of good citizenship into the marks of a criminal?"[46]

Labor unions lent similar support to the IWW. For example, the Western Federation of Miners refused to buy supplies from Spokane merchants to "punish the suppression of free speech" in that city.[47] Stating its belief "that the right of free speech, of a free press and of public assemblage, are fundamental requisites in a free society," the Federated Trades of San Diego urged organized labor throughout California to aid the fight in that city "to exercise our constitutional rights."[48] Despite the unwavering efforts of the national AFL to prevent any cooperation with the IWW, local affiliates of the AFL assisted free speech fights in many communities.[49]

Other groups affected by restrictive street ordinances, such as the Salvation Army and advocates of the single tax,[50] sometimes joined or supported free speech fights, as did Emma Goldman and her anarchist followers.[51] The IWW, while acknowledging difficulty finding "common grounds" with the middle-class activists in the Free Speech League, accepted assistance from both the national League and the local affiliated leagues that formed in response to individual free speech fights.[52]

Broader segments of the general public also endorsed the rights of free speech and assembly advocated by the IWW. The San Diego chief of police expressed surprise and disappointment that people "one would never suspect" were supporting and even con-

---

[45] Letter from J. Stitt Wilson, Representative, Socialist Party National Executive Committee, to Hiram W. Johnson, California Governor 2 (Aug. 1, 1913) (Civil Liberties Collection, supra note 12, Folder: J. Stitt Wilson: Two Letters Protesting Imprisonment of Officials in San Diego "Free Speech" Riots); Letter from J. Stitt Wilson, Representative, Socialist Party National Executive Committee, to Hiram W. Johnson, California Governor 2, 4 (July 7, 1913) (Civil Liberties Collection, supra note 12, Folder: J. Stitt Wilson: Two Letters Protesting Imprisonment of Officials in San Diego "Free Speech" Riots) (hereinafter July 7 Wilson-Johnson Letter).

[46] July 7 Wilson-Johnson Letter, supra note 45, at 2.

[47] Free Speech and Business, N.Y. Call, Nov. 18, 1909, at 6 (editorial).

[48] Chief Wilson and Head Detectives are Accused in Federated Trades Charges, San Diego Sun, Apr. 5, 1912, at 1, 2.

[49] See Foner, supra note 2, at 183 (Spokane); id. at 193 (Aberdeen); id. at 193, 195, 197, 199–205 (San Diego).

[50] See, e.g., Restrict Street Oratory? 'Never,' Cry Orators, San Diego Union, Dec. 14, 1911, at 11.

[51] Foner, supra note 2, at 201–02.

[52] A Free Press, Indus. Worker, Feb. 27, 1913, at 2.

tributing money to the IWW free speech fight.[53] The police chief did not specify who these people were, but newspapers reported sympathetic comments from the president of a local consortium of charities, a minister, a Republican high school teacher, and a member of the Daughters of the American Revolution.[54] A group of farmers boycotted local merchants during the free speech fight in Minot, North Dakota, and instead ordered supplies from Sears, Roebuck.[55] Addressing businessmen at the Commercial Club of Minot, the president of a local bank defended the constitutional right of Wobblies to speak on street corners, a position that prompted members of the audience to call him a traitor.[56] Other commentators, without directly addressing the IWW's free speech claims, asserted that communities had provoked and exacerbated the free speech fights.[57] They protested police and vigilante brutality, employer exploitation of labor, and "inflammatory stories" and "yarns" by "yellow" journalists.[58]

The IWW free speech fights occasionally provoked expressions of support from important figures in intellectual and public life. They influenced Professor Edward A. Ross, the president of the American Sociological Society, to devote the Society's Annual Meeting in 1914 to the subject "Freedom of Communication."[59]

---

53 More Free Speech Advocates Placed Under Arrest, Feb. 14, 1912, San Diego Union, at 10.
54 Free Speech and Great Industrial Problems Are Discussed in Pulpit, San Diego Sun, Apr. 29, 1912, at 6; Settle Question in Christian Way, Pleads Col. Ed. Fletcher, San Diego Sun, Apr. 6, 1912, at 1; May Stout, Woman's Views on Free Speech, San Diego Sun, Mar. 26, 1912, at 4; Teacher Must Explain, N.Y. Times, June 8, 1912, at 24.
55 Jack Allen, A Review of the Facts Relating to the Free Speech Fight at Minot, N. Dak. from Aug. 1st to Aug. 17th 1913 (Civil Liberties Collection, supra note 12, Folder: Various Letters, etc., Addressed to Vincent St. John, Document: Letters, etc., Addressed to Vincent St. John), in Fellow Workers and Friends: I.W.W. Free Speech Fights as Told by Participants 164 (Philip S. Foner ed., 1981) [hereinafter Fellow Workers].
56 Grant S. Youmans, Extract from "Legalized Bank Robbery" (Civil Liberties Collection, supra note 12, Folder: Reports of the Denial of Freedom of Speech in Various U.S. Communities, Document: Letters Relating to Free Speech Fights, from William D. Haywood), in Fellow Workers, supra note 55, at 166, 168–73.
57 See, e.g., City Officials Adopt Repressive Measures, 30 Survey 82, 82 (1913); Lawlessness in San Diego, 15 Public 482, 482 (1912).
58 Austin Adams' Letter to Weinstock, San Diego Sun, Apr. 22, 1912, at 4; Facts and Insults, and What They Mean for This Fine City, San Diego Sun, Apr. 22, 1912, at 4 (editorial); Patriotism and the American Flag. What It Means, Paterson Evening News, Mar. 15, 1913, at 4 (editorial).
59 Symposium, Freedom of Communication, 9 Am. Soc. Soc'y: Papers & Proceedings (1915); see Dorothy Ross, The Origins of American Social Science 229–40 (1991) (describing Ross's background and ideology).

"Speaking of Anarchy." (Cartoon by Art Young
in the January 1913 issue of *The Masses*)

Ross referred to the IWW throughout his presidential address and cited the locations of many free speech fights while bemoaning that the "constitutional rights of free communication have been denied to socially insignificant persons." "Could any apostasy to principle be more contemptible," Ross asked, "than depriving the weak of the chief weapon by which they may achieve common economic action?" Unfortunately, Ross added, "nothing less sordid than this seems to lie behind the multiplying interferences with free assemblage, free discussion, and liberty of the press."[60]

Amos Pinchot, an important progressive journalist, sent a substantial check to defray the legal costs of a Wobbly leader arrested in Paterson. "I am not in sympathy with the theories of the I.W.W.," he emphasized in an accompanying letter, "but I believe that in your case as in the case of scores of people . . . a very vital principle of American life is at stake – the right of free speech – of public discussion and protest." In many places throughout the United States, Pinchot lamented, alliances between "capital and local government" have taken the position that the IWW, simply by refusing "to recognize certain vested rights of capital," has forfeited the protection of the Constitution.[61] Pinchot also joined a group of thirty-one eminent progressives who signed a petition to President Wilson alleging the denial of free speech and assembly in Paterson and calling for an investigation and action by Wilson and the Congress.[62]

Some who were initially sympathetic to the free speech fights, including members of the IWW, grew disillusioned by evidence that the IWW itself deviated from its professed commitment to free speech, used gratuitously offensive language unrelated to its central message of industrial unionism, and spent money donated to the cause of free speech for personal living expenses. For example, William E. Trautmann played a dominant role in founding the IWW, and he subsequently served as its secretary-treasurer and general organizer before leaving the organization in 1913.[63] Yet he objected in 1911 to "the anti-political politicians and the never-will-I work scavengers who pose as organizers and spokesmen" of

---

[60] Edward A. Ross, Freedom of Communication and the Struggle for Right, 9 Am. Soc. Soc'y 1, 5 (1915).

[61] Quinlan Gets $500 To Help Pay Court Costs, Paterson Evening News, May 26, 1913, at 7.

[62] Paterson Morning Call, June 5, 1913, at 11. Frederic C. Howe presented the petition to President Wilson. The 31 signers included many eminent progressives, including Lillian D. Wald and Paul U. Kellogg. Id.

[63] Brissenden, supra note 1, at 79; Dubofsky, supra note 2, at 78, 86, 108; Foner, supra note 2, at 14, 19–20.

the IWW.[64] By 1913 Trautmann referred to many free speech fights as "free speech grafts." While continuing to approve of "free speech fights to maintain guaranteed rights," Trautmann called it "criminal to exhaust the resources and energies of the proletariat to further designs of elements who in their philosophy and psychology are anti-proletarian, although they have and play with a vocabulary of revolutionary phrases." Based on his own experience as treasurer of an IWW defense fund, Trautmann charged that much of the money raised to support the free speech fights had been misused. He warned against contributing to a free speech fight in Denver "pulled off by those who never will work, who will always be there when the general secretary and the general organizer of the Industrial Workers of the World call for volunteers, to live on the funds collected for the support of real militants and struggling toiler[s]."[65]

Eugene Debs, the Socialist Party's frequent presidential candidate, supported the founding of the IWW, attended its first convention in 1905, and initially reacted with enthusiasm to the free speech fights. By 1912, however, Debs cited IWW selfishness while supporting the expulsion of Wobblies from the Socialist Party.[66] When the IWW "gets into trouble," Debs observed, "it frantically appeals to the Socialist party for aid, which has always been freely rendered, and after it is all over the I.W.W. kicks the Socialist party in the face." Debs accused the IWW of being "an anarchist organization in all except in name." "Anarchism and socialism," he concluded, "have never mixed and never will."[67]

Disillusioned former supporters accused the IWW of using tactics that unnecessarily provoked the free speech fights and harmed the IWW's more responsible allies. The treasurer of the San Diego Free Speech League alleged that the Wobblies, rather than preaching industrial unionism, slung "vile epithets" that no civilized community would tolerate, such as referring to police as "dogs" and "pimps." If the Wobblies had used more temperate language, he concluded, there would have been no need for a free speech fight that prompted contributions and sacrifices from socialists and other genuine defenders of free expression. Moreover, once the free speech fight started Wobblies undermined the strategy of the Free Speech League, which intended to minimize

---

[64] Brissenden, supra note 1, at 268 (quoting Letter from William E. Trautmann to Eugene V. Debs (1913), in Wkly. People, July 26, 1913, at 2).

[65] William E. Trautmann, Free Graft Fights, N.Y. Call, May 2, 1913, at 6.

[66] Nick Salvatore, Eugene V. Debs: Citizen and Socialist 206, 247, 254–56 (1982).

[67] Letter from Eugene V. Debs to William E. Walling (Mar. 5, 1913), in 2 Letters of Eugene V. Debs, 1913–1919, at 11–12P (J. Robert Constantine ed., 1990).

disruption and public hostility by having only a few orderly speakers risk arrest to test the validity of the restrictive ordinance. Instead, the IWW urged massive civil disobedience and brought people to San Diego who only wanted to be fed and lodged. This tactic, the Free Speech League complained, turned the free speech fight into a fiasco.[68]

Even IWW leaders began to question the language used in free speech fights. A member of its general executive board suggested to delegates at the 1913 IWW convention that they limit their street speaking to issues of industrial unionism. He complained that too many Wobblies "attack everybody, the police, the city officials, religion, politics, and everything else." This undisciplined approach, he warned, provided excuses for removing speakers and diverted attention from the IWW's primary message.[69]

Many organizations and people vehemently opposed the IWW throughout the free speech fights. Though some unions affiliated with the AFL supported the IWW in particular locations, the national AFL and many other AFL leaders attacked the free speech fights as vigorously as anyone. Samuel Gompers, the national president of the AFL, maintained that the sensationalism of Wobbly tactics, although effective in generating substantial press coverage for the IWW, brought disaster to the relatively few American workers who had adopted them.[70] Gompers condescendingly invoked the widespread perception that many Wobblies were recent immigrants to undermine their First Amendment claims. "In America the people have a right to free assemblage," Gompers observed, "but it is hard for people coming from foreign countries to understand what this means."[71] Other AFL officials refused IWW requests for assistance, often by referring to the IWW as an un-American and unprincipled organization.[72] The AFL executive council, while denying financial aid during the San Diego free speech fight, pointed out that the AFL "is constantly contending for the right of free speech."[73] In fact, the AFL had been relying vigorously on "inherent, natural human rights guaranteed by the constitution of

---

[68] San Diego Free Speech Facts Made Public, Miners Mag., May 1, 1913, at 8.
[69] Brissenden, supra note 1, at 265.
[70] Letter from Samuel Gompers to Ole C. Lian 4 (Oct. 14, 1916), microformed on American Federation of Labor Records: The Samuel Gompers Era, Reel 81, Frames 507–11 (Microfilming Corp. of Am.) [hereinafter AFL Records].
[71] Some Can't Understand, Spokane Daily Chronicle, Nov. 18, 1909, at 4 (quoting unidentified Samuel Gompers letter).
[72] See, e.g., Unions Refuse Support, San Diego Sun, Mar. 30, 1912, at 1.
[73] AFL Executive Council, Minutes of Meetings, Aug. 12–17, 19, 1912, at 72 (Aug. 19, 1912), microformed on AFL Records, supra note 70, Reel 4, Frames 1183–1249.

our country"[74] in opposing an injunction that prohibited it from using its journal to publicize a labor boycott.[75] The AFL's defense of its own First Amendment rights, however, did not extend to supporting IWW free speech activities, as its executive council demonstrated again in refusing a subsequent request to protest the imprisonment of an editor during the IWW strike in Paterson.[76]

Worker opposition to the IWW free speech fights was not limited to the organizational differences between the IWW and the AFL. A group of war veterans in Portland, Oregon, claiming that more than eighty percent of them were working class, asked the police to prevent Wobblies from speaking at the base of a monument to the war dead. The veterans objected to the "mob tactics of the I.W.W." and to speakers who "gather around this monument and defame the nation, society, humanity, religion, decency, and everything else."[77] Even socialists, who generally supported the free speech fights, occasionally found it impossible to cooperate with the IWW. In Paterson, for example, socialists refused to talk from the same platform as IWW orators they felt were insulting the flag and advocating sabotage.[78] Echoing former supporters who had become disillusioned with the free speech fights, many opponents of the IWW accused the IWW, frequently derided as the "I Won't Workers,"[79] of subsidizing a dissolute lifestyle through the financial contributions of people genuinely concerned about alleged threats to freedom of expression.

Moreover, many people agreed with the Free Speech League that the IWW, instead of using massive civil disobedience as the primary tactic to force repeal of ordinances restricting street speaking, should have challenged the ordinances through test cases in court.[80] A Spokane newspaper summarized the argument

---

[74] American Federation of Labor: History, Encyclopedia Reference Book 233 (1919).

[75] Gompers v. Bucks Stove & Range Co., 221 U.S. 418 (1911), discussed in Chapter 3, text accompanying notes 143–44.

[76] AFL Executive Council, Minutes of Meetings, Sept. 22–27, 1913, at 73 (Sept. 27, 1913), microformed on AFL Records, supra note 70, Reel 4, Frames 1387–1435.

[77] Spanish War Veteran's [sic] To Clean Out the I.W.W., L.A. Times, Jan. 31, 1912, § 1, at 3.

[78] Socialists Take Determined Stand in Case of Boyd, Paterson Evening News, Apr. 1, 1913, at 1.

[79] See, e.g., Infamies of the I.W.W.'s, L.A. Times, May 26, 1912, § 6, at 7 (editorial); Tar and Feathers, L.A. Times, May 19, 1912, § 2, at 4 (editorial).

[80] The Class War in San Diego, 15 Public 529, 530 (1912) (editorial); Council Upholds Mayor and Police, Spokane Spokesman-Rev., Nov. 11, 1909, at 7; I.W.W. Band Retreats to Camp Near Capistrano, San Diego Union, Apr. 25, 1912, at 9; The I.W.W. Problem, Fresno Morning Republican, Feb. 15, 1911, at 4 (editorial); Says Law Is Sound, Spokane Daily Chron., Nov. 11, 1909, at 7; Uphold the Law, San Diego Union, Feb. 9, 1912, at 4 (editorial).

against Wobbly civil disobedience: "If the I.W.W. men believe the
law is wrong, they have a perfect right to test it, or work to have it
changed. They have no right, however, to clog the wheels of the
law and to stop its action."[81] After provoking riots and creating
martyrs, Wobbly complaints about "czarism," "despotism," and
"oppression," according to the paper, were "worse than
nonsense."[82] A Baptist minister in San Diego cited Jesus as an
instructive counterexample to the IWW free speech fighters.
Stressing that Jesus took care to observe Roman law, the minister
rejected the argument of some that "if Jesus came to San Diego he
would go straightaway to Fifth and E streets." The declaration by
Jesus – "Render to Caesar the things that are Caesar's, and unto
God the things that are God's" – was "the mightiest principle that
should govern every man in his relations to human government."
This principle demonstrated that "Jesus cannot be claimed among
the lawbreakers of the world." The minister, after identifying his
own family background as working class, advised his congregation
that the remedy for a bad law in a democracy "is repeal, and not
lawlessness."[83]

In addition to opposing IWW civil disobedience, some critics
observed the irony that Wobblies, who advocated anarchism and
violated the law for tactical advantage, seemed to have no com-
punction about alleging violations of their own constitutional
rights. An army veteran in Spokane complained that the Wobblies
came into court "with unclean hands."[84] In more florid style, an
editorial about the IWW strike in Paterson noted that "these men,
after spending their breath and ink berating the authorities and
the constituted government and the laws of the nation, and excori-
ating the constitution of the United States and this state . . . as soon
as they find themselves in trouble, endeavor to place themselves
behind the legal breastworks they have been blackguarding and
condemning."[85] Socialists, who disagreed with the IWW's rejection
of political activity, pointedly observed that the Constitution, on
which the IWW relied throughout the free speech fights, is itself "a
political document, a product of parliamentary enactment."[86]

Even worse, many maintained, Wobblies hypocritically invoked

---

[81] No Compromise Needed, Spokane Daily Chron., Nov. 3, 1909, at 4 (editorial).
[82] Here the People Rule, Spokane Daily Chron., Nov. 8, 1909, at 4 (editorial).
[83] Man Who Will Listen to I.W.W. Preachings and Not Contradict Them Is Cow-
    ard, Says Geistweit, San Diego Union, Mar. 4, 1912, at 6.
[84] Council Upholds Mayor and Police, supra note 80.
[85] Editorial Comments, Paterson Morning Call, June 9, 1913, at 4.
[86] Frederic Heath, Current Comment, Soc.-Democratic Herald (Milwaukee), Feb.
    15, 1913, at 1.

the constitutional protection of the First Amendment while themselves denying the free speech of others. After a professor
mounted a soapbox to defend the police, a newspaper reported,
Wobblies shouted "lynch him!" and "take away his soap box!"[87]
Wobblies also disrupted a speech by an important officer of the
California AFL after he accused the IWW of untruthfulness. The
AFL officer then commented, "Yes, they are in favor of free speech
– for themselves."[88] The IWW's vociferous derision of a parade led
by the mayor of San Diego provided an editorial writer with
"[p]roof of the oft-repeated assertion that the howling dervishes of
the soapbox are absolutely insincere in their demand for 'the right
of free speech,' except so far as that right is accorded to themselves."[89] Another editorial found proof that Wobblies were "malicious and not actuated by the 'principles' which they pretend to
advocate" in their decision to move their soapbox opposite a hotel
for no conceivable reason other than to annoy the guests.[90]

At times, unapologetic Wobblies acknowledged that they
repressed the speech of internal dissenters. Speakers' deviations
from official IWW policies at street meetings prompted physical
removal from the soapbox. A leading Wobbly organizer frankly
admitted this policy in federal court. The more the IWW gained
power, he explained, the more it "insisted that our speakers should
not get on the box and tell us what they think." Instead, speakers
should express the views adopted in the IWW's own constitution.[91]

Outrage against the IWW prompted some people to defend vigilante action during free speech fights. Responding to a minister
who had opposed vigilantes, one editorial observed that similar
arguments "were uttered from disloyal pulpits before and during
the Civil War on behalf of the institution of slavery." The editorial
characterized those who violated the fugitive slave laws as "ardent
anti-slavery 'vigilantes.'" Jesus himself, the editorial added, removed

---

87 Street Speaker Talks Heresy; Is Dethroned From Soap-Box Perch, San Diego
   Union, Jan. 13, 1912, at 6.
88 I.W.W.'s Bolt When Labor Leader Scores Them, San Diego Union, Apr. 20,
   1912, at 11 (quoting Paul Scharrenberg, Secretary of the California State Federation of Labor); see 3 Final Report, supra note 12, at 2612, 2617–18 (James
   Starr, corresponding secretary of the Horizontal Warpers' Benevolent Association, testifying that organized "howl" by Wobblies disrupted labor meeting).
89 They Want a Liberty Trust, San Diego Evening Trib., Feb. 6, 1912, at 4 (editorial).
90 One Way To End an Intolerable Nuisance, San Diego Evening Trib., Mar. 11,
   1912, at 4 (editorial).
91 Record at 4982, United States v. Haywood, No. 6125 (N.D. Ill. 1918) (testimony of James P. Thompson), aff'd, 268 F. 795 (7th Cir. 1920), cert. denied,
   256 U.S. 689 (1921) (IWW Collection, supra note 20, Box 109, Folder 1).

"the chief priests and scribes, the traitors and moneychangers" from the temple in Jerusalem in much the same lawless manner as vigilantes did in "cleansing San Diego of anarchists, agitators, hoboes, trouble-breeders, and those who preach the propaganda of 'direct action,' 'sabotage' and treason."[92]

The same people who opposed the free speech fights frequently emphasized their own deep commitment to free expression both as an important social value and as a fundamental constitutional right. They often portrayed themselves as defending a legitimate interpretation of free expression and the First Amendment against devious and cynical IWW attempts to manipulate free speech ideology for its own revolutionary purposes. Some of these critics of the free speech fights may not have really believed what they said. They may have manipulated free speech ideology themselves for their own, very different purposes. The perceived need for ideological manipulation, however, itself suggests the importance of free speech to many in their audience.

Impassioned tributes to free speech often accompanied arguments for restricting it. "In the American mind free speech is something sacred – and it should be," commented an editorial in the midst of advocating stronger laws to combat the "emergency" conditions created by the IWW and other anarchists.[93] The *New York Times*, while referring to free speech as a "noble and indispensable right," denied that "IWW ranters" and "breeders of anarchy" deserved legal protection.[94] Similarly, a minister supported the restrictive ordinance at issue in the San Diego free speech fight, but he also maintained that "[n]o nation and no city ever permitted freer speech and action than the one we live in" and observed that "this controversy is not between people who believe in free speech and those who oppose it."[95]

Some opponents of the IWW referred explicitly to the Constitution while defending free speech. They vigorously rejected claims by the IWW and others that local authorities had violated the constitutional right to free expression. "Only the unthinking"[96] and people who "have been deceived by their advisers either by deliberate purpose or through gross ignorance"[97] could conceivably believe such wild untruths, editorials assured readers. Another edi-

---

[92] Shall San Diego Submit to This?, San Diego Union, May 21, 1912, at 4 (editorial).
[93] The Remedy for Treason Talk, San Diego Union, Apr. 27, 1912, at 4 (editorial).
[94] Good for Paterson, N.Y. Times, Sept. 14, 1915, at 10 (editorial).
[95] License, Not Liberty, Is Free Speech Aim, San Diego Union, Feb. 19, 1912, at 9.
[96] Uphold the Law, supra note 80.
[97] Revising an Inscription, San Diego Union, Feb. 25, 1912, at 4 (editorial).

torial advocated additional legislation to punish Wobbly speakers while urging the preservation of the "constitutional right of free speech."[98] Quoting the state constitution, the same paper emphasized that Californians have "great freedom in expressing their views," but warned that "the constitutional guarantee of liberty of speech does not mean that a person may say anything anywhere."[99] Even a letter sent by self-described vigilantes to justify their tarring and deporting "undesirable citizens as fast as we can catch them" observed that the state constitution "guarantees the right of free speech and public assembly" to all citizens "who respect the laws of the state and the nation."[100]

Defenders of municipal authorities during the free speech fights frequently distinguished between freedom of speech and license or abuse. For example, one editorial asserted that freedom of the press should not protect "utter licentiousness of thought," as when "freedom is permitted to be translated into insolence, defiance of law, authority, and social order."[101] Another editorial noted that the California constitution protects free speech and holds speakers "responsible for the abuse of that right."[102] Expressing this theme in more literary language, a San Diego pastor built a sermon around Milton's comment: "None love freedom heartily but good men; the rest love not freedom but license."[103]

Many who proclaimed their own commitment to free speech while rejecting IWW claims of repression observed that the IWW asserted rights other citizens neither possessed nor desired. "These misguided and contentious men," a newspaper in Spokane remarked, "are demanding privileges outside the law that are not accorded to other citizens." The editorial claimed that the IWW wanted to "harangue bystanders" while obstructing streets and sidewalks "to any extent that may suit their whim or purpose." For this "imaginary right" to be characterized as a fight for free speech, the editorial concluded, is "fallacious and wholly unfounded."[104]

The IWW did not respond directly to these attacks, just as its

[98] Free Speech and Treasonable License, San Diego Union, June 7, 1912, at 4 (editorial).

[99] The Question of Speaking on the Streets, San Diego Union, Jan. 14, 1912, at 4 (editorial).

[100] Vigilantes Send Warning to Paper, San Diego Sun, Apr. 12, 1912, at 3.

[101] Editorial Comments, Paterson Morning Call, June 11, 1913, at 4.

[102] The Remedy for Treason Talk, supra note 93; see also Right of "Free Speech" is Qualified, Paterson Press, Mar. 6, 1913, at 6 (editorial).

[103] License, Not Liberty, Is Free Speech Aim, supra note 95.

[104] Misguided and Contentious, Spokane Spokesman-Rev., Nov. 3, 1909, at 4 (editorial).

opponents did not respond directly to the IWW claim that workers had no meaningful rights to free speech under capitalism.
Yet just as the content and tone of the IWW critique of American institutions struck many as beyond the bounds of protected
speech, the distinction between free speech and license or
abuse must have reinforced the IWW position that First Amendment protection had been reduced to speech that did not
offend capitalists or their official agents. Wobbly organizer Elizabeth Gurley Flynn complained that "the United States, like Russia, is a place where, if you say the government is all right and
the police are good and kind, you can talk as much as you
want."[105] Even a mainstream progressive journal, in attacking
the repression of IWW speakers who protested the labor policies
of John D. Rockefeller, commented that Americans "never think
of objecting to 'freedom of speech' until someone stands to say
something disagreeable."[106]

OFFICIAL REACTIONS

The IWW free speech fights generated a range of responses from
various government officials that corresponded roughly with attitudes expressed by the general public. Many local officials whose
actions provoked or exacerbated free speech fights vigorously
defended themselves against claims of repression by stressing their
own commitment to free speech and the extent of IWW provoca-
tions. For example, the chief of police in Spokane informed the
city council that the IWW had freely used the town's public streets
for evening meetings that lasted until midnight for nearly five
years. By smashing the windows of employment agencies and street
cars, he added, Wobblies themselves provoked citizens to request
the city council for an ordinance limiting street speaking.[107] A joint
statement by key law enforcement officials in San Diego, including
the district attorney, the city prosecutor, and the chief and superintendent of police, similarly emphasized that for a long time they
had not disturbed street speaking, even when IWW speakers
encouraged people to cross the border and join a revolt against the
Mexican government. A defensive "memorial" to Governor Johnson passed unanimously by the city council reiterated this point

---

[105] "No God – No Law" of I.W.W. Exemplified, Paterson Morning Call, June 5,
     1913, at 1.
[106] Tarrytown Disgracing the Nation, 17 Public 591, 591 (1914) (quoting Chicago
     Evening Post).
[107] Council Upholds Mayor and Police, supra note 80.

while stressing that the "anarchistic tendency" of Wobbly speakers had been "consistently increasing" for more than a year before it received the petition that prompted passage of a restrictive ordinance. The final version of the ordinance, the council added, limited street speaking in six downtown blocks rather than the forty-two block area requested by a group of local merchants.[108]

In many places, especially where socialists or progressives controlled city government, IWW street speaking did not lead to free speech fights. Citing the constitutional guarantee of free speech, the socialist mayor of Haledon, New Jersey, allowed a public meeting organized by the IWW after officials in neighboring Paterson repeatedly arrested IWW street speakers.[109] Progressive police commissioners, such as George Creel in Denver and Arthur Woods in New York City, worked hard to protect IWW speech and to prevent free speech fights. In his autobiography, Creel described a Wobbly "invasion" of Denver led by Big Bill Haywood. According to Creel, the "Wobblies had been turning other cities into bedlams by street meetings that invited arrest. Jail was exactly what they wanted, for it gave them the opportunity to raise a cry against 'America's Cossacks' and attack the whole democratic process." "Knowing this," Creel continued, "and happening to believe in free speech, I gave the wobblies the right to talk their heads off." Civic groups throughout Denver denounced Creel "as Haywood's secret partner in the conspiracy to overthrow American institutions." As Creel had expected, however, people soon lost interest in IWW orators. Creel reported that Haywood then begged for a "crack-down." When Creel refused, "the hulking agitator and his followers left town."[110]

New York City Police Commissioner Arthur Woods became the most prominent official spokesman for the position that all people, including the IWW and other radical groups, should enjoy substantial free speech and assembly in public parks and streets. Woods expressed his views most thoroughly in his paper, "Reasonable Restrictions Upon Freedom of Assemblage," delivered at the 1914 Annual Meeting of the American Sociological Society organized by Edward A. Ross.[111] Woods reiterated his major themes

---

[108] Officials of San Diego Take Weinstock to Task, L.A. Times, May 20, 1912, § 1, at 4.
[109] Strikers Will Be Welcomed to Haledon By Mayor Brueckmann, Paterson Evening News, Feb. 28, 1913, at 1.
[110] George Creel, Rebel at Large: Recollections of Fifty Crowded Years 103 (1947).
[111] Arthur Woods, Reasonable Restrictions Upon Freedom of Assemblage, 9 Am. Soc. Soc'y: Papers & Proceedings 29 (1915).

and illustrations in testimony before the federal Commission on Industrial Relations.[112]

Free speech and freedom of assembly, Woods emphasized, are fundamental constitutional rights that police should actively protect and not merely tolerate. He maintained that the law allows states and municipalities to regulate these rights, but not in ways that undermine or abrogate them. Reasonable regulations, Woods reasoned, protect rather than limit speech by creating optimal conditions for expression in ways that do not interfere with the rights of others.[113]

Woods illustrated his general approach with examples from his experience in New York City. Just prior to his becoming police commissioner, he reported, weekly Saturday meetings in Union Square by socialists, advocates of the single tax, anarchists, and Wobblies had provoked disorder and significant police force in response, resulting in a number of arrests, "broken heads," and "a great deal of bad feeling between some of the people assembled and the police." Upon taking office, Woods decided to change "the policy, the methods, and the orders given to the police." Woods realized that many in the Saturday crowds believed firmly, though perhaps inaccurately, that the police had used excessive force. "A large number of the people were foreigners," he reasoned, "and they naturally had a conception of the police which was tinctured with memories and traditions of violent police action in the countries of Europe from which they had come."[114]

Woods therefore decided to have a relatively small contingent of police visible at Union Square. He personally instructed them to guard the speakers, emphasizing the role of police in protecting the constitutional rights of free speech and assembly. Woods further instructed the police to intercede against the meeting only if obstructions to the streets or sidewalks resulted or if the speakers incited immediate violence. Woods reported that no incidents occurred at the meeting, prompting the crowd to applaud the police.[115]

Newspaper reports and police files confirm that Woods's public statements reflected his actual practices. An article in the *New York Times* reported that one man was arrested and fined for attempting to disrupt the soapbox orations of Wobbly speakers. Leonard Abbott, president of the national Free Speech League, hailed the

[112] 11 Final Report, supra note 12, at 10,550–58 (testimony of Arthur Woods).
[113] Id. at 10,550–51; Woods, supra note 111, at 30–31.
[114] 11 Final Report, supra note 12, at 10,551; Woods, supra note 111, at 29–30.
[115] 11 Final Report, supra note 12, at 10,551; Woods, supra note 111, at 30–31.

police for abandoning their prior policy of arresting IWW speakers and for deciding instead to support free speech by acting against the rowdies who bothered the speakers.[116] Another article reported that Abbott and Woods negotiated an agreement ending a controversy over the picketing by the IWW and others of John D. Rockefeller's home and office. The picketers claimed that Rockefeller was responsible for deaths during a violent miners' strike in Colorado. They carried signs reading "Thou Shalt Not Kill" and wore black bands of mourning. Numerous people had been arrested and jailed during this picketing on charges such as loitering and disorderly conduct. After a conference with Woods, Abbott stated that the police would "permit the fullest possible play of public emotion through free speech, free assemblage, and free passage through the streets of all people not engaging in organized parades." The police would not molest picketers as long as they "only wear crape on [their] arms and do not display banners."[117]

Police Department files also demonstrate Woods's commitment to freedom of speech and assembly. When the mayor of New York received a letter complaining that Wobblies and other "notorious speakers" at Madison Square Park used blasphemous language while instigating thousands to commit crimes,[118] he asked Woods to respond. Woods did so by enclosing the report of the police investigator, who found no merit in these charges.[119] In another incident, the police department specifically cited the constitutional rights of free speech and assembly to justify its refusal to interfere with unpopular IWW public meetings.[120]

U.S. Attorney General George Wickersham, in resisting vigorous lobbying to prosecute the IWW under federal law, further revealed the diversity of official responses to the free speech issues posed by IWW activities. During the height of the San Diego free

---

116 Fined for Hazing I.W.W., N.Y. Times, Apr. 30, 1914, at 5.
117 Night Picketing at Rockefeller's, N.Y. Times, May 1, 1914, at 4.
118 Letter from Thomas J. Havey to Hon. John Purroy Mitchel, Mayor, New York City (July 16, 1914) (Mayor's Papers; Record Group: Mitchel, John P., 1914–1917; Record Series: Departmental Correspondence Received; Police Dep't, New York City Municipal Archives [hereinafter Mitchel Papers], Box: MJP-130, Folder: Police Dept [22] Mitchel, 1914 July).
119 Letter from Arthur Woods to Hon. John Purroy Mitchel (July 14, 1914) (Mitchel Papers, supra note 118, Box: MJP-130, Folder: Police Dep't [22] Mitchel, 1914 July); Letter from New York City Inspector, 3d District, to New York City Police Commissioner (July 28, 1914) (Mitchel Papers, supra note 118, Box: MJP-130, Folder: Police Dep't [22] (Mitchel, 1914 July).
120 Letter from New York City Third Deputy Commissioner to Sidney Kaufman (July 19, 1915) (Mitchel Papers, supra note 118, Box: MJP-154, Folder: Police Dep't [12] Mitchel, 1915 July).

speech fight, the United States Attorney in Los Angeles, the superintendent of the San Diego Police Department, and a U.S. Senator
from California wrote Wickersham requesting federal action
against the IWW. A coded message from A. J. McCormick, the U.S.
Attorney in Los Angeles, reported that his office had received
information indicating an IWW conspiracy in San Diego to form
an "expedition" to Mexican "Lower California."[121] This expedition, he warned, might violate the sections of the federal penal
code dealing with "inciting or engaging in rebellion or insurrection" and with "seditious conspiracy."[122]

At the same time, John L. Sehon, the superintendent of police
in San Diego, wrote Wickersham and Senator John D. Works long
telegrams giving a more detailed description of the perceived
IWW conspiracy and tying it to the ongoing free speech fight. "It is
urgently desired," he wrote both Wickersham and Works, "to
secure support of the Federal government in every possible
way."[123] Senator Works, who had been a justice of the Supreme
Court of California,[124] immediately wrote Wickersham that Sehon
was "not an alarmist." Works mentioned the prior IWW free
speech fight in Fresno, which gave "the authorities there a great
deal of trouble," as an additional reason to take Sehon's message
seriously.[125] After receiving a similar request for federal assistance
from H. S. Utley, the San Diego district attorney,[126] Wickersham
instructed U.S. Attorney McCormick in Los Angeles to present the
IWW situation to a grand jury. In the same message, Wickersham
informed McCormick that the "Department does not wish indictments returned unless evidence clearly warrants it."[127]

Approximately six weeks later, McCormick reported to Wicker-

---

[121] Telegram from A. J. McCormick to George Wickersham (May 3, 1912) (Central Files and Related Records; Straight Numerical Files, 1904–1937; File
150139 sec. 1; General Records of the Department of Justice, Record Group
60; National Archives, Washington, D.C. [hereinafter Wickersham Collection],
Folder 2, Series No. 150139-6).

[122] Act of Mar. 4, 1909, ch. 321, sections 4, 6, 35 Stat. 1088 (1909).

[123] Telegram from John L. Sehon to George Wickersham 4 (May 3, 1912) (Wickersham Collection, supra note 121, Folder 2, Series No. 150139-7); Telegram
from John L. Sehon to John D. Works 4 (May 3, 1912) (Wickersham Collection, supra note 121, Folder 2).

[124] Zechariah Chafee, Jr., Freedom of Speech 84 (1920).

[125] Letter from John D. Works to George Wickersham (May 4, 1912) (Wickersham Collection, supra note 121, Folder 2, Series No. 150139-10).

[126] Telegram from H. S. Utley to George Wickersham (May 10, 1912) (Wickersham Collection, supra note 121, Folder 2, Series No. 150139-15).

[127] Letter from George Wickersham to A. J. McCormick (May 11, 1912) (Wickersham Collection, supra note 121, Folder 2, Series No. 150139-15).

sham that the federal grand jury in Los Angeles was prepared to return indictments against the IWW for violating the federal law on "seditious conspiracy." Citing Wickersham's previous cautions, McCormick sought his instructions about pursuing these indictments.[128] Assistant Attorney General Harr, who had been following this case, advised Wickersham that McCormick's report "fails to disclose a sufficient basis for a prosecution against the leaders of the Industrial Workers for conspiracy to overthrow the Government of the United States by force." Harr determined that the Wobblies were "self-confessed liars and lawbreakers," that their purpose was "vague and indefinite," and that there was "nothing indicating a specific attack upon the Government of the United States." He concluded that IWW activities in San Diego were "at worst only an attack on the local government," and not a "demonstration against the Federal authorities."[129] Wickersham agreed and instructed McCormick not to seek an indictment.[130] Despite continued pressure from Sehon and Works,[131] and ultimately from President Taft himself, who urged Wickersham to "show the strong hand of the United States" against the IWW, Wickersham remained firm in refusing to prosecute.[132]

Nothing in Department of Justice files indicates that its officials viewed themselves as vindicating free speech in this episode. Yet the Department's decision against seeking indictments of Wobblies for "seditious conspiracy" during the charged atmosphere of the San Diego free speech fight contrasts sharply with its broad use of similar language in the Espionage Act of 1917 to prosecute and punish the IWW and many others for antiwar speech a few years later. The Department of Justice protected free speech in a significant sense simply by acting professionally in resisting efforts by California officials to use federal law against unpopular IWW speakers.

---

[128] Letter from A.J. McCormick to George Wickersham 1 (June 28, 1912) (Wickersham Collection, supra note 121, Folder 2, Series No. 150139-20).

[129] Letter from William R. Harr to George Wickersham 1–2 (July 5, 1912) (Wickersham Collection, supra note 121, Folder 2, Series No. 150139-20).

[130] Letter from George Wickersham to A.J. McCormick (July 5, 1912) (handwritten note by George Wickersham, U.S. Attorney General (July 6, 1912)) (Wickersham Collection, supra note 121, Folder 2, Series No. 150139-20); see Telegram from George Wickersham to William R. Harr (July 6, 1912) (Wickersham Collection, supra note 121, Folder 2, Series No. 150139-21).

[131] Letter from John D. Works to George Wickersham (Aug. 23, 1912) (Wickersham Collection, supra note 121, Folder 2, Series No. 150139-26); Letter from John L. Sehon to John D. Works (Aug. 16, 1912) (Wickersham Collection, supra note 121, Folder 2).

[132] Dubofsky, supra note 2, at 195; Foner, supra note 2, at 203.

Two important government commissions provided official responses to the IWW free speech fights based on extensive investigations. Governor Johnson of California appointed Harris Weinstock, a California businessman and political ally, special commissioner to report on "disturbances" in San Diego during the IWW free speech fight. The federal Commission on Industrial Relations had the broader charge of examining a wide range of labor issues, but it devoted substantial attention to the IWW and its free speech fights. The Commission consisted of three public representatives, three employer representatives, and three union representatives recommended by AFL president Samuel Gompers. Weinstock was one of the three employer representatives chosen by President Wilson.

Both the California and the federal investigations spread blame broadly for the free speech fights. Testimony by Wobblies and others convinced Weinstock that many popular criticisms of the IWW were accurate. He concluded that the IWW's purpose was only "incidentally to test the validity of the so-called anti-free speech ordinance." Its primary goal, he maintained, was "to clog the machinery of and to overwhelm the city and county government of San Diego and to put upon the taxpayers of the city and county the greatest possible burden." Weinstock claimed that IWW behavior during the free speech fight, including its decision to attack the ordinance through civil disobedience rather than through a test case, deserved "the severest condemnation" by good citizens and "the most extreme punishment within the law." According to Weinstock, IWW teachings, if accepted, "would make society impossible" by creating "a nation of thieves, liars and scoundrels."[133] Citing previous IWW free speech fights elsewhere, he warned that they could eventually lead to civil war. Weinstock urged both the California legislature and the federal Congress to devise laws to "meet this new and menacing condition" posed by the IWW.[134]

Daniel O'Regan, a staff investigator for the federal Commission on Industrial Relations, made additional criticisms of the IWW. He condemned Wobbly language during the free speech fights as outrageously abusive and blasphemous, especially when it ridiculed "Pay-triotism," religion, and the American flag. O'Regan, like many unofficial commentators, observed that Wobblies inconsis-

---

[133] Report of Harris Weinstock, Commissioner To Investigate the Recent Disturbances in the City of San Diego and the County of San Diego, California 8–9 (1912) [hereinafter Weinstock Report].
[134] Id. at 22.

tently demanded the constitutional right to free speech while themselves repressing views they rejected. O'Regan specifically cited the tension between the IWW and the Salvation Army, whose members often competed directly with the IWW on the same street corners for the same working-class audience. On numerous occasions, O'Regan reported, Wobblies broke up meetings of the Salvation Army and other religious groups, sometimes by "jeers and threats of bodily harm," and sometimes by singing IWW songs. These famous songs frequently parodied Salvation Army hymns, using their music while subverting their religious themes. O'Regan added that Wobblies had made barely veiled threats to him when he criticized the discrepancies between their talk and their actions. "We can imagine," he concluded, "how they'd act if they had any real power."[135]

While severely condemning the IWW, both Weinstock and the federal commission simultaneously protested vigilante and official action that violated constitutionally protected speech. Weinstock pointedly compared the Wobblies with the vigilantes. The Wobblies, Weinstock emphasized, had not committed any acts of violence during the San Diego free speech fight. "Their plan," he declared, "was purely one of passive resistance; annoying, aggravating, burdensome, but not inimical to life or property." By contrast, the vigilantes, encouraged by local newspapers and commercial bodies, violently attacked Wobblies, depriving them of fundamental personal liberties while hypocritically preaching "the sacredness of the constitution and its inviolability." The vigilante, Weinstock insisted, was "a far greater criminal than those whom he brands as 'anarchists,' 'revolutionists,' 'dynamiters' and 'the scum of the earth.'"[136] Weinstock also declared that "the right of free speech should be inviolable and that it should not be left to the police, in their discretion, to prevent men from exercising this constitutional right on the ground of anticipating an improper use thereof." He found that the police in San Diego had violated the constitutional rights of Wobblies by preventing them from holding street meetings outside the restricted zone defined in the ordinance.[137]

Many investigators for the federal Commission on Industrial Relations focused particularly on official misconduct during the free speech fights. In a lengthy report on "constitutionally protected personal liberties," B. F. Moore reported that police, by deciding when to disperse crowds, determined in practice the defi-

---

[135] O'Regan, supra note 12, at 2–4.
[136] Weinstock Report, supra note 133, at 16–20.
[137] Id. at 11.

nition of an unlawful assembly.[138] He especially criticized the power of police to define "constructive crime" by interfering with "[w]ould-be speakers . . . before they actually speak and before anyone can have definite knowledge of what they intend to say." Police, Moore protested, "assume in advance that the speech will have a criminal aspect."[139] Moore observed that police frequently caused IWW free speech fights by refusing to issue permits for street speaking. Based on his review of many free speech fights, Moore emphasized "the undesirability of uncontrolled police authority over speaking and congregating, and the undesirability of having the ordinary police act as special censors."[140]

Two other members of the commission's staff, Patrick F. Gill and Redmond S. Brennan, reiterated these criticisms in a detailed report on Paterson, New Jersey. The report especially condemned "the officers of the inferior courts," who, with the police, "seemed intent on driving out the I.W.W. leaders." Conceding that these officials had acted in good faith to protect their conception of community interests, the report maintained that court officers should not have sole authority to determine individual rights or to decide, even before arrest or trial, who should be punished. The report stressed the existence of "certain rights that have grown to be among our most invaluable possessions" and that must be protected by the "legal machinery."[141] As examples of such rights, it cited IWW expressions of unpopular ideas. The report concluded that the inferior courts and the police, institutions that worked well in times of industrial peace, "broke down completely" during labor unrest, "became tools of oppression," and "trespassed every natural right and constitutional guarantee of the citizens." Gill and Brennan were confident that this "arrogant and illegal assumption of authority would not have stood the test of judicial review in the higher courts."[142] In practice, however, largely unreviewed actions by local officials effectively suppressed the strike. Arrests of striking workers on charges of disorderly conduct and unlawful assembly, the report concluded, constituted the functional equivalent of injunction and contempt proceedings, a more familiar response attempted by employers but previously rejected by a judge early in the Paterson strike.[143]

The final report of the Commission on Industrial Relations adopted many of the criticisms contained in these staff reports. In a section titled "Free Speech," the report directed special attention

---

[138] Moore, supra note 13, at 15.

[139] Id. at 19.

[140] Id. at 17, 25.

[141] Gill & Brennan, supra note 12, at 27.

[142] Id. at 1, 3.

[143] Id. at 3, 6.

to the "attitude of the police toward public speaking" as a major source of "social unrest and bitterness" in the United States. The report found that police throughout the country, "either arbitrarily or under cloak of a traffic ordinance," frequently prohibited people associated with disapproved organizations from speaking in halls or in outdoor meetings. Some police "suppression of free speech," it concluded, could be attributed to "sheer brutality and wanton mischief." More typically, however, police and their superiors, even while invading personal rights, acted on the honest belief that they were upholding the public interest.[144] Elsewhere, the report listed the sites of many IWW free speech fights to support its charge that local officials and citizens repressed, brutally but with impunity, the "guaranteed rights" of workers.[145] The report singled out Paterson as the scene of especially outrageous injustice, mentioning "ridiculous" arrests for alleged unlawful assembly, disorderly conduct, and criminal libel.[146]

ANALYSIS OF FREE SPEECH THEMES

Popular and official responses to the IWW free speech fights often extended to fairly detailed analysis of free speech themes. People occasionally engaged in direct debate and responded explicitly to views they opposed. More frequently, commentators simply expressed different positions on related themes. Regulation of street speaking, the issue most clearly presented by the free speech fights, generated discussion about the importance of access to public property, the nature of reasonable limitations, and the danger of discriminatory or pretextual application of apparently fair rules. People did not use modern legal terms such as public forum, content neutrality, and time, place, and manner restrictions. But they did address similar issues in analyzing these topics. Illustrating additional structural analogies to current First Amendment interpretation, people also distinguished between legal speech and illegal action, identified various categories of unprotected speech, and confronted the especially vexing and controversial problem of determining when legitimate criticism of government crossed over the boundary into an illegal form of speech.

Virtually all commentators on the IWW free speech fights agreed that constitutional protection of free speech did not cover

---

[144] 1 Final Report, supra note 12, at 98–99.
[145] Id. at 49.
[146] Id. at 55. Although the final report produced major rifts within the Commission, none of these rifts involved the report's comments about free speech.

certain categories of expression. Some disagreement arose over
the proper treatment of a particular category, such as sedition, but
most discussion revolved around competing definitions of admittedly unprotected categories. Speech that to some clearly constituted illegal incitement, libel, or obscenity was to others nothing
more than vigorous criticism of government and important individuals, criticism that must be protected by the Constitution in a
democracy. Virtually everyone similarly agreed that public speaking could be limited by reasonable regulations, but many disputed
the reasonableness of particular restrictions.

REGULATION OF STREET SPEAKING

Because the free speech fights arose from conflicts between Wobblies and local communities over IWW attempts to speak on downtown street corners, it is not surprising that they provoked substantial debate about what constitutes reasonable regulation of street
speaking. The IWW and its supporters maintained that freedom of
expression could be meaningful for working people only if it
included the right to speak where fellow workers could be
reached. Public streets downtown, many maintained, provided the
most effective location.[147] An IWW leader objected to ordinances
limiting public speaking to places outside the business district
"where there was no audience to talk to."[148] Others observed that
soapbox orators often did not have the funds or connections to
hire a hall. "The street corner was their only hall," remarked a rare
banker sympathetic to IWW organizing efforts, "and if denied the
right to agitate there then they must be silent."[149] *The New Republic,*
a leading progressive journal, made the related point that those
who already had power did not need to agitate in public to achieve
their goals. Corporate directors could alter conditions in their
plants without mass meetings and parades, but workers did not
have this luxury.[150]

While maintaining that any meaningful right of free speech
must include access to busy downtown areas, the IWW and its supporters acknowledged that public speaking could be subject to rea-

[147] See, e.g., Council Upholds Mayor and Police, supra note 80.
[148] Record at 4981, United States v. Haywood, No. 6125 (N.D. Ill. 1918) (testimony of James P. Thompson), aff'd, 268 F. 795 (7th Cir. 1920), cert. denied,
256 U.S. 689 (1921) (IWW Collection, supra note 20, Box 109, Folder 1)
[hereinafter Thompson Testimony].
[149] Youmans, supra note 56, at 1; see Free Speech and Great Industrial Problems
Are Discussed in Pulpit, supra note 54.
[150] So-Called Industrial Peace, New Republic, Jan. 30, 1915, at 7.

sonable restrictions. An IWW official testified that he did not object to regulation of speech on crowded corners during the day, after 10:00 P.M. in front of residences, or in places where the activity would interfere with traffic and access to public transportation.[151] He pointed out that Wobblies placed speaking boxes at least forty feet from curbs to avoid interfering with traffic.[152] During the San Diego free speech fight, various citizens and organizations, including the local free speech league, unsuccessfully proposed a less restrictive ordinance than the one the council ultimately passed. The proposed ordinance would have limited public speaking to places at fixed distances from curbs and would have allowed police to maintain passage both in the center of the street and on adjoining sidewalks. It also would have required prior notice to the police about planned street meetings and would have prohibited more than one meeting on a block at the same time.[153]

The IWW and its supporters, even when conceding the legitimacy of reasonable restrictions on street speaking, maintained that local authorities had applied ordinances discriminatorily or pretextually. The editor of *Solidarity* rejected claims by municipal officials that they restricted speech only to preserve the peace or to prevent congested traffic. These claims, he maintained, were not supported by the facts. He asserted that many free speech fights occurred in large public squares in the early evening and thus did not disturb either sleep or traffic. Religious and other groups, he added, were never molested when they held meetings on the same streets where Wobblies were arrested.[154] Objecting to the repression of IWW meetings and demonstrations in Tarrytown, New York, the national Free Speech League issued a statement admitting "the right of any community to regulate outdoor meetings and to shift the place of meetings in cases where traffic would be impeded." The Free Speech League argued, however, that "this contention must be bona fide and not a mere pretext."[155]

IWW supporters provided specific illustrations of discriminatory

---

151 Thompson Testimony, supra note 148, at 4980–81.

152 Id. at 5003.

153 Peace Plan Started; Ordinance Prepared, San Diego Sun, Apr. 8, 1912, at 1.

154 Williams, supra note 28, at 42; see also I.W.W. Protest Against Ordinance, Fresno Morning Republican, July 15, 1911, at 9 (reporting IWW protest of ordinance forbidding public speaking on county property on Sundays and holidays but allowing exceptions for Ministerial Union and band).

155 League To Push Fight, N.Y. Times, June 8, 1914, at 1 (quoting statement of Free Speech League [June 7, 1914]).

156 Observations and Comments, 5 Mother Earth 338 (1911).

applications of ordinances against the IWW. An article in *Mother Earth* complained that the IWW was not permitted to hold street meetings in Fresno, California, although the same right "was granted freely to the Salvation Army and other concerns that are not considered dangerous to the master class."[156] Speakers before the Spokane City Council claimed that police enforced an ordinance against the IWW soon after President Taft and William Jennings Bryan spoke in the same place. According to these speakers, Taft's appearance blocked traffic for four hours and Bryan used language "more inflammatory than any of the IWW speeches."[157] A participant in another free speech fight observed that local authorities even allowed disruptive and illegal gambling to continue on the same street corners where Wobblies were arrested simply for speaking.[158]

Opponents of the free speech fights, on the other hand, viewed the ordinances violated by the IWW as examples of reasonable regulations.[159] Many observed that free speech can conflict with other legitimate rights. An editorial defending the Spokane ordinance proclaimed, "Every American citizen has a right to talk when he pleases, if he is not interfering with the rights of others."[160] But when public speaking does interfere with the rights of others, another editorial asserted, it "is un-American, unfair, and intolerant." According to the editorial, "to contend that this contumacious conduct is justified in the name of free speech, is preposterous."[161] Just as the constitutional right of free press gives no right to set up printing plants in a public street, a newspaper observed, the constitutional right of free speech gives no right to hold disruptive street meetings.[162] A Unitarian minister in San Diego stressed that the ordinance was "aimed just as much against the man that preaches salvation on the street corner as against the

---

[157] Council To Hear Free Speech Plea, Spokane Spokesman-Rev., Nov. 10, 1909, at 9; Council Upholds Mayor and Police, supra note 80.

[158] See George V. Carey, Free Speech Fight in Aberdeen, S.D. 1 (1914) (CIR Microfilm Collection, supra note 11.)

[159] Opponents of the free speech fights generally ignored accusations of discriminatory treatment against the IWW. One newspaper editorial, however, responded that Taft and Bryan spoke on a vacant lot in Spokane, not on a public street. Dealing With Agitators, Spokane Spokesman-Rev., Nov. 4, 1909, at 4 (editorial).

[160] No Compromise Needed, supra note 81.

[161] Misguided and Contentious, supra note 104.

[162] Dealing with Agitators, supra note 159; see also "Free" Speech, Fresno Morning Republican, Nov. 29, 1910, at 4 (editorial) (stating that free speech does not include the right to set up a "printing press in the public streets" or to "[write] on the face of a public monument").

social reformer." Rather than abridging free speech, he reasoned, the ordinance assured "that all the citizens have equal rights" to use city streets.[163]

The property rights of business owners provided another justification for the ordinances. The attorney for the Merchants' Association of San Diego argued before the city council that the right of people whose businesses were blocked by crowds listening to speeches outweighed any expressive rights of the speakers.[164] A newspaper complimented the ordinance passed by the council and expressed sympathy for owners and lessors of property who "complained that their right to carry on legitimate business is obstructed by the persistent acts of those who insist that they shall be permitted to exercise their right of free speech irrespective of the rights of anybody and everybody else."[165] The right of free speech, another newspaper observed more succinctly, is not the right to "stop business."[166] And the *Los Angeles Times* criticized editorials in newspapers sympathetic to IWW free speech claims for maintaining, in effect, that the framers of the Constitution "ought to have provided for the security of personal liberty alone, and not guarded the rights of property."[167]

To many people, the availability of public speaking outside downtown areas revealed the absurdity of IWW free speech claims. Commentators pointed out that communities regularly permitted outdoor meetings on vacant lots[168] and observed the existence of "a fine natural amphitheatre" for public speaking.[169] Noting that the famous speakers' corner in London's Hyde Park "would not be tolerated for one moment in any of the public thoroughfares," a letter writer concluded that the controversy over a restrictive ordinance, rather than posing fundamental issues about free speech, was "a matter of location and nothing else."[170]

The unpopularity of IWW ideology, many argued, accounted for its refusal to accept modest geographical restrictions on street

---

[163] License, Not Liberty, Is Free Speech Aim, supra note 95.
[164] Restrict Street Oratory? 'Never,' Cry Orators, supra note 50.
[165] Revising an Inscription, supra note 97; see The Question of Speaking on the Streets, supra note 99.
[166] No Compromise Needed, supra note 81.
[167] "Buts," L.A. Times, May 19, 1912, § 2, at 4.
[168] See, e.g., Council Upholds Mayor and Police, supra note 80; Dealing with Agitators, supra note 159; In Justice to Labor, Spokane Spokesman-Rev., Nov. 7, 1909, at 4 (editorial); No Compromise Needed, supra note 81.
[169] E. F. Buss, Argues Against Use of Street by Orators, San Diego Union, Jan. 11, 1912, § 2, at 16.
[170] Not Free Speech but a Place to Speak, San Diego Union, Feb. 17, 1912, § 2, at 13.

speaking. "If the themes, the doctrines, the theories and political ideals of street speakers are not enough to draw an audience to halls which can be rented or to lots which can be occupied," a minister concluded, "then they must admit utter failure in their systems." To demonstrate his consistency, he added that churches should not be able to hold meetings in the restricted district whenever their messages are unable to attract people to regularly scheduled indoor services.[171] An army veteran told the Spokane city council that Wobblies wanted to speak on crowded streets only because "they cannot create an audience any other place where they can cram their damnable teaching down our throats."[172] No legitimate conception of free speech, others added, justifies forcing utterances on "unwilling ears."[173] Wobblies could not convincingly protest laws that prevented them from imposing "their radical doctrines upon citizens who have no desire to be bothered with their rant."[174] Allowing Wobblies to speak outside the central business district, by contrast, would enable them to "talk all night if they saw fit without discomfort to anyone" except those who voluntarily choose to listen.[175]

Consistent with these defenses of local ordinances, many urged cities to establish centrally located outdoor forums for public speaking in places that would not interfere with traffic or commercial activity.[176] A staff member of the Commission on Industrial Relations advocated the "desirability of every city setting apart a certain accessible public place where all may speak as they wish." Although the Commission's final report did not comment directly on this proposal, the report did recommend that state and local governments "provide by law for the fullest use of schools and other public buildings for public meetings and lectures."[177]

Some opponents of the free speech fights, however, rejected any right to speak in public. They reasoned that the public, like private owners, should be able to exclude unwanted speakers from its property. A letter to the editor asked during a free speech fight, "Is it right to go into a man's private residence to have 'free speech'? That is his personal property and no one would even think of doing it." City streets, the letter pointed out

---

171 License, Not Liberty, Is Free Speech Aim, supra note 95.
172 Council Upholds Mayor and Police, supra note 80.
173 Misguided and Contentious, supra note 104.
174 Dealing with Agitators, supra note 159.
175 The Question of Speaking on the Streets, supra note 99.
176 See, e.g., id; Some Free Speech Suggestions, San Diego Sun, March 12, 1912, at 4 (editorial).
177 Moore, supra note 13, at 25; 1 Final Report, supra note 12, at 100.

by analogy, "are public property, laid out for the benefit of the whole people, and not for an individual or representative of any organization who has an ax to grind." However excellent the speaker or the cause, "no one has a right to blockade the streets."[178] Editorials proclaimed that the public can rid itself of undesirable intruders on its streets, "just as an individual citizen would rid himself of a gang of gypsies camping on his lawn or in his back yard"[179] or as a church could expel someone who interrupted services.[180] During an IWW free speech fight in Minot, North Dakota, the president of the city commission declared that there is "no constitutional right to hold meetings in the streets," although street speaking can be permitted by "courtesy or sufferance."[181] A report to the Commission on Industrial Relations supported this position. After a review of legal decisions that did not specifically involve the IWW, it concluded that local officials could constitutionally restrict or forbid public speaking in "streets, parks and other public places."[182]

In the few legal decisions that arose directly from IWW activities, judges generally upheld restrictive street ordinances. A judge in San Diego rejected a constitutional attack on the ordinance challenged by the free speech fight. He cited a recent state appellate court decision sustaining a Los Angeles street ordinance that had been the model for the one in San Diego.[183] In Los Angeles, as in San Diego, the ordinance prohibited street speaking in a defined area, and the San Diego judge quoted the key language from the opinion: "This ordinance does not attempt to suppress freedom of speech, or seek to interfere with the citizen in the right to express his views upon any subject, political, religious, or otherwise, as is suggested by the petitioner. It simply specifies a certain district within the city wherein no one may do the things prohibited." The appellate court added that this restriction was a reasonable judgment within the discretion of the legislative branch of city government. Given the city's power to enact the ordinance, "the character or object of the assemblages prohibited are of no materiality," whatever the alleged public benefit they might have had.[184] The judge in San Diego observed that the existence of this clear precedent

---

178 Buss, supra note 169.
179 Why San Diego Has Taken Some of the Law into Its Own Hands, San Diego Evening Trib., May 10, 1912, at 4 (editorial).
180 Enforce the Law at Any Cost, San Diego Union, Feb. 11, 1912, at 4 (editorial).
181 To the People of Minot, Minot Daily Optic, Aug. 20, 1913, at 1.
182 Moore, supra note 13, at 14.
183 See I.W.W. Chiefs Fined and Sentenced to Jail, supra note 12.
184 Ex parte Thomas, 102 P. 19, 20 (Cal. Dist. Ct. App. 1909).

helped explain why the Wobblies "showed so little anxiety to bring the matter to the test of a legal ruling."[185]

A police court judge in Spokane upheld a similar ordinance prohibiting street speaking within a defined area, but he declared unconstitutional a subsequent one that made an exception for street speeches by religious organizations, such as the Salvation Army.[186] The judge called freedom of speech "an inalienable and God given right." Yet this judge, like judges elsewhere, did not consider this right violated by a law that applied without discrimination to all street speakers. In fact, he convicted all Wobblies arrested under the initial ordinance.[187] Rejecting the Wobblies' talk of "constitutional rights," the judge asserted without citation that he "could feed them a whole volume of decisions in cases like this, where the people have regulated street fights."[188]

DEFINING THE BOUNDARIES OF PROTECTED SPEECH

Commentators on the IWW free speech fights occasionally distinguished between legal speech and illegal action. They also identified various kinds of unprotected speech, such as incitement, sedition, obscenity, and a vague, inclusive category of "indecent" expression. Debate over the application of First Amendment prohibitions to state action further addressed the boundaries of protected speech.

Editorials and public officials maintained that speakers should not be prosecuted unless they commit illegal acts. The *New York Times,* which frequently denounced the IWW, was moved by vigilante violence in San Diego to stress that "mere error of opinion is hardly warrant for indictment." "Prosecution for opinion," it editorialized, "too much resembles persecution." It suggested instead that speakers in appropriate circumstances should be prosecuted under the theory that a breach of the peace occurs when people violate laws governing public meetings.[189] During the free speech fight in Paterson, a local newspaper similarly observed the "growing sentiment that the police made a mistake in arresting out-of-town strike agitators without their having committed any overt acts." According to the newspaper, such arrests violated the inalienable right of peaceful speech and assembly, "a principle of

---

[185] I.W.W. Chiefs Fined and Sentenced to Jail, supra note 12, at 12.
[186] O'Regan, supra note 11, at 2.
[187] Id. at 9.
[188] Council Upholds Mayor and Police, supra note 80.
[189] Free Speech, N.Y. Times, May 20, 1912, at 8 (editorial).

American citizenship as old as the republic and as deep-rooted as the American love of liberty."[190] Several years later, a new mayor of Paterson accepted this reasoning while reversing an official policy of prohibiting public speeches by Wobbly organizer, Elizabeth Gurley Flynn. The mayor stressed that Flynn could speak as long as she did not violate any law.[191]

People had very different views about when legal speech becomes illegal action, as contrasting results in two state appellate courts revealed. Upton Sinclair, the famous muckraking author, appealed his conviction under a New York law prohibiting "disorderly conduct." Sinclair had been convicted in a magistrate's court for leading demonstrations against John D. Rockefeller that ultimately led to the agreement between Police Commissioner Woods and the Free Speech League. The state statute defined *disorderly conduct* as including behavior "whereby a breach of the peace may be occasioned."[192] Invoking the public interest in the "preservation of order," the judge upheld Sinclair's conviction because the demonstration, even if entirely "peaceable" and "courteous," could have provoked a breach of the peace either by people whose passage was impeded or by people holding different views. The judge emphasized that his decision did "not militate against the right of free speech or against the right of assembly," although he never addressed the potential impact on free expression of holding people legally responsible whenever disagreement with their views could conceivably prompt others to breach the peace.[193]

By contrast, the Supreme Court of New Jersey set aside the conviction of IWW leader Big Bill Haywood for violating a state law "concerning disorderly persons." A police court judge had convicted and sentenced Haywood to a six-month jail term. According to the judge, Haywood had displayed disorderly conduct by obstructing and interfering with people on a public street. The state supreme court found "not a particle" of evidence supporting the claim of obstruction and interference. While acknowledging that a large crowd had followed Haywood, the court stressed that one cannot be guilty of disorderly conduct without the intent to obstruct or interfere. Otherwise, "almost every person having something more than a local reputation sufficient to arouse the

---

[190] Workingmen of Paterson Want to Know Where Mayor M'Bride Stands – It Is Up to Him To Tell Them, Paterson Evening News, Mar. 4, 1913, at 4 (editorial).

[191] Lets Miss Flynn Speak, N.Y. Times, Jan. 21, 1916, at 20.

[192] People v. Sinclair, 149 N.Y.S. 54, 55–56 (Ct. Gen. Sess. 1914). See supra text accompanying notes 116–17 for the agreement between Woods and the Free Speech League.

[193] Id. at 60–61.

curiosity of the public would be liable to be apprehended as a disorderly person." The court did not explicitly refer to free speech
issues.[194] Another judge, however, dismissed an unlawful assembly
charge that arose out of the same incident, emphasizing that the
intent requirement protects the traditional right of people "to
gather to discuss their grievances, whether these grievances have
any foundation or not."[195]

A significant amount of commentary maintained that speech,
even if not itself construed as action, could be unlawful when it
incited illegal activity. A report on free speech by the National Civic
Federation, drafted by a special committee whose membership
included a former attorney general of the United States and other
eminent lawyers, concluded that "civil authorities are not required
to sit idly by while incendiary speeches incite mobs to destroy order,
peace, and property, which it is the duty of those authorities to preserve and maintain."[196] Free speech, a typical editorial observed during the Spokane free speech fight, does not encompass the right to
"incite a half-thinking crowd to disorderly actions."[197]

Some people defined incitement quite broadly. A San Diego
newspaper, for example, justified the forced expulsion of Emma
Goldman and her manager, Ben Reitman, from the city before
they had an opportunity to speak. The newspaper conceded that
Goldman and Reitman may have had "no intention of inciting riot
here." It believed, however, that "their very presence was an overt
act, and if they had been permitted to exercise their 'constitutional' right of free speech, riot would have been incited."[198]

Advocacy of illegal activity, although never systematically differentiated from incitement, was also frequently considered beyond
the bounds of protected speech.[199] Similarly unprotected was
speech deemed to have a general tendency or likelihood to lead to
crime, the rubric under which most courts of the period denied
many varieties of free speech claims. The belief of town officials
that a speech could create a disturbance, according to the *New York*

[194] Haywood v. Ryan, 88 A. 820, 821 (N.J. 1913).
[195] Haywood Discharged Is Now Free, Paterson Evening News, Apr. 5, 1913, at 1;
see Gill & Brennan, supra note 12, at 30.
[196] Free Speech a Nuisance, N.Y. Times, Dec. 27, 1914, at C2.
[197] No Compromise Needed, supra note 81.
[198] These People Must Not Disturb Our Peace, San Diego Evening Trib., May 16,
1912, at 4 (editorial); see San Diego Sets the Example, San Diego Union, May
17, 1912, at 4 (editorial).
[199] See, e.g., Enforce the Law at Any Cost, supra note 180; Free Speech a Nuisance, supra note 196, at C2; San Diego Free Speech Facts Made Public, supra
note 68.

Times, was sufficient grounds for denying a permit. "A man may not harangue a crowd," a San Diego newspaper maintained, "if his language tend[s] to cause a riot or merely a breach of the peace."[200]

Others agreed that freedom of expression does not include incitement to illegal activity, but they defined incitement more narrowly. For example, New York City Police Commissioner Woods maintained that constitutional rights of public speakers do not extend to speech that is "provocative of immediate violence."[201] According to Woods, speech "cannot be considered provocative of immediate disorder if speakers criticize, no matter how vehemently, the existing order of things, or if they recommend, no matter how enthusiastically, a change which they believe would improve things."[202] In addressing when speech becomes unlawful, the Free Speech League admitted "that the police have a right to arrest any speaker whose words lead to crime," but denied that they could "forbid speaking because they conjecture that it may be the intention of a speaker to use such words."[203]

In several cases arising from the IWW strike in Paterson, New Jersey courts construed statutes prohibiting the advocacy or incitement of illegal action. One decision reversed the conviction of Alexander Scott, the editor of a socialist newspaper. Scott had published an article that accused the Paterson police of overriding the Constitution by brutally attacking peaceful strikers. The article called the police "brass buttoned anarchists" and "professional strikebreakers" who, "at the behest of the silk manufacturers, rushed at the defenseless workers like a bunch of drunken Cossacks." Scott was indicted and convicted by a jury under a statute that punished persons who "advocate the subversion and destruction by force of any and all government." The prosecutor argued that the statute supplemented "all" with "any" to encompass opposition to a particular government, such as the city of Paterson, as well as anarchist opposition to all government.[204]

The court observed that this statute was the "product of feverish and political excitement, caused by the assassination of the late President McKinley" by an anarchist. It warned that such laws are

---

200 Soap Boxes Anywhere, N.Y. Times, June 25, 1914, at 8 (editorial); Enforce the Law at Any Cost, supra note 180.

201 Woods, supra note 111, at 31–32.

202 Id.; see 11 Final Report, supra note 12, at 10,550–51 (testimony of Arthur Woods; see also Keep Cool, Fresno Morning Republican, Feb. 17, 1911, at 4 (editorial) (arguing that free speech includes right "to denounce the police" but not to "incite to violence or other crimes in doing so")).

203 League to Push Fight, supra note 155.

204 State v. Scott, 90 A. 235, 235–36 (N.J. 1914).

"very apt to reflect the crude and undigested sentiment of a public upheaval at the cost of encroachments on constitutional rights." The prosecutor's proposed construction, the court added, would "clearly" violate the New Jersey Constitution because it would "prevent all free discussion relating to a change in the administration of municipal and state governments." Moreover, this construction "would preclude fair criticism on the conduct of public officials" and "would silence the public press." The court avoided such constitutional problems by interpreting the statute to prohibit only "the advocacy of anarchy." The court defined the "vice of anarchy" not as "the belief of a state or condition of society where there is no law or supreme power," but as "the promotion and encouragement of disobedience to and contempt of existing laws." Under this interpretation, the court concluded that the article did not violate the statute, though it was "couched in hot and intemperate language" that could subject the author and publisher to indictment for libel against the police department.[205]

In two other cases, the Supreme Court of New Jersey affirmed the convictions of Wobblies in Paterson based on a statute that made it a high misdemeanor to "advocate, encourage, justify, praise or incite the unlawful burning or destruction of public or private property" or "the killing or injuring" of any person. One defendant, referring to the silk manufacturers and the nonstriking workers, moved at a meeting "that we go to the silk mills, parade through the streets, and club them out of the mills; no matter how we get them out, we got to get them out."[206] The other defendant urged striking workers to "put a kink into the warp" and "fix up a little something in the dye box."[207] The court held that the statements of both defendants violated the statute, rejecting arguments that the statute was uncon-

---

[205] Id. at 236–37. The local prosecutor considered bringing a libel action against the newspaper, but determined that "the law of libel could not be brought against an inanimate body." Editor Scott Guilty, Paterson Evening News, June 3, 1913, at 1, 7 (quoting Prosecutor Dean).

[206] State v. Quinlan, 91 A. 111, 112 (N.J. Sup. Ct. 1914), aff'd, 93 A. 1086 (N.J. 1915).

[207] State v. Boyd, 91 A. 586 (N.J. Sup. Ct. 1914), rev'd on other grounds, 94 A. 807 (N.J. 1915). According to a local newspaper, IWW leaders "were indignant in their repudiation of the sentiments expressed by this rampant agitator." Editorial Comments, Paterson Morning Call, Apr. 2, 1913, at 4. Yet the paper wondered why they let the speech be made. "If they mean what they say," an editorial suggested, "they should shoo him out of town without further ado." Id. A news article in the same issue reported that IWW leaders did cut short this speech and warned the speaker against similar comments. Boyd Must Be Good, Paterson Morning Call, Apr. 2, 1913, at 11.

stitutional under the First Amendment and the free speech clause
of the New Jersey constitution. Stressing the "well settled" principle
that "the right of free speech is not unlimited," the court denied
Gilbert Roe's contention on behalf of one of the defendants that
advocacy could constitutionally be punished only if it were "coupled
with some acts of destruction in pursuance of such advocacy."[208]

These decisions seem entirely consistent with the reversal of
Scott's conviction by the same court. The defendants used highly
inflammatory language, which arguably could be punished even
under the much more protective First Amendment standards that
apply today, whereas Scott's language did not come close to advocating illegal actions. As a group, these New Jersey decisions generated by IWW activities in Paterson recognized free speech interests
to a much greater extent than did the typical judicial decision
addressing free speech claims before World War I.

Many commentators identified categories of unprotected
speech in addition to incitements or other words that might provoke illegal action. People frequently attached the label *indecent* to
speech they considered beyond the protection of law. They
observed that freedom of expression had never encompassed various forms of indecent speech, such as blasphemy, obscenity, and
profanity,[209] a point conceded even by those who advocated
greater expressive rights. For example, the final report of the
Commission on Industrial Relations revealingly urged that "every
barrier to the freedom of speech [should] be removed as long as it
is kept within the bounds of decency and as long as the penalties
for libel can be invoked."[210]

People opposed to the free speech fights attempted to apply
categories of indecent speech traditionally unprotected at common law to the language of Wobblies and their supporters. When
Emma Goldman and Ben Reitman published accounts of their
mistreatment by vigilantes in San Diego,[211] a local newspaper
called it obscene. The paper warned that the distributors of this

---

[208] Boyd, 91 A. at 588; cf. Quinlan, 91 A. at 113–14 (finding "unsound" the argument that "in order to charge a crime within the purview of the statute, the
indictment must set out [that] as a result of uttering the words, there was a
killing or injury").

[209] Free Speech a Nuisance, supra note 196; Free Speech and Treasonable
License, supra note 98; The Remedy for Treason Talk, supra note 93.

[210] 1 Final Report, supra note 12, at 99.

[211] Emma Goldman, The Outrage of San Diego, 7 Mother Earth 115, 115 (photo
reprint 1968) (1912); Ben L. Reitman, The Respectable Mob, 7 Mother Earth
109, 109 (photo. reprint 1968) (1912).

"filthy 'propaganda,'" if caught, would probably be prosecuted under the federal Comstock Act.[212] Without actually calling speech obscene, some drew direct parallels between obscenity and other indecent speech that does not merit legal protection. "Nobody would ever dream of saying," one editorial observed, that a person arrested for public use of obscene language "had only exercised his right of free speech." According to the editorial, there is a far greater abuse of free speech "when a man publicly asks people to join him in an attempt to destroy the government, and when he calls the Republic's emblem a 'filthy rag.'" Morality and decency, it concluded, require punishing unpatriotic language as well as profanity and obscenity.[213] The president of the Washington Federation of Labor wanted to prohibit even "language bordering on the indecent." IWW songs such as "Hallelujah, I'm a Bum," and "How in Hell Can I Work When I Ain't Got a Job?," he conceded, "may be highly humerous" to the Wobblies, "but they should not be permitted in any assemblage."[214]

More frequently, people simply considered language that others declared indecent or obscene to be beyond the bounds of free speech. A paper asserted that the public did not have to tolerate "scurrilous language" that "coarsely vilified and falsely assailed" respected members of the community.[215] Another paper observed that freedom of expression did not extend to "preaching class hatred and denunciation of the law's representatives."[216] In one of his reports on IWW free speech fights to the Commission on Industrial Relations, Daniel O'Regan expressed similar views while attempting to illustrate the point at which speech loses its protection:

> Freedom to use the streets as their forum, freedom to organize the workers by means of this forum, freedom to practice and preach whatever religion they want, or none at all, freedom to attack the policies of any party or organization should certainly be accorded them[,] but when they use this freedom of speech for the purpose of denouncing our country and our flag, condemning our soldiers and our sailors, holding

---

212 Mercenary Anarchists and Their "Literature," San Diego Evening Trib., July 2, 1912, at 4 (editorial).

213 The Remedy for Treason Talk, supra note 93; see Free Speech and Treasonable License, supra note 98.

214 Fix the Responsibility for Seattle Outrage, Miners Mag., Aug. 7, 1913, at 9, 9.

215 Enforce the Law at Any Cost, supra note 180.

216 A Straight from the Shoulder Talk on the Strike Situation and the Truth of the Whole Matter in Plain Language, supra note 16, at 2.

them up to ridicule as misguided puppets of an unscrupulous government[,] a halt should be called and measures adopted to see that the border line is not crossed.[217]

Some people accused municipal authorities of using various local ordinances essentially to prosecute the Wobblies for sedition without explicitly so stating. In a speech to the Commonwealth Club of San Francisco following his report to Governor Johnson about the San Diego free speech fight, Harris Weinstock asserted that the Wobblies should have been prosecuted and jailed only if they had preached sedition on the streets. Weinstock reported that he had tried to determine whether any Wobbly speeches constituted sedition, but had discovered nothing more than vague accusations before a grand jury that some unidentified speakers mocked the Constitution and the American flag. Using an ordinance against street speaking for the real purpose of punishing attacks on government that fall short of sedition, Weinstock indicated, was an improper manipulation of the legal system that only aided the Wobblies' own strategy of undermining local authorities.[218] Weinstock was probably unaware of the pressure by public officials in California on Attorney General Wickersham to seek federal indictments for "seditious conspiracy" against IWW agitators in San Diego, but this episode provided evidence for Weinstock's view that fear of sedition lay behind local enforcement of the ordinance against street speaking.

Others expressed concern that notions akin to sedition prompted government repression of speech. While Scott's appeal was pending in New Jersey, the *New York Tribune* observed that his alleged crime was "hostility to the government." It characterized this crime as an extremely vague offense, "something like, we imagine, what our own good mayor calls 'sedition.'" According to the *Tribune*, numerous mainstream publications throughout the country, and even an appellate court judge in another case that arose from the IWW strike in Paterson, had made virtually identical accusations of official lawlessness against Paterson officials. Upholding Scott's conviction, the paper stated, would indicate that "the freedom of the press means very little." The editorial sardonically added that the next step would be to put the appellate court judge in jail for "hostility to the government."[219]

By contrast, some opponents of the IWW worried that the tradi-

---

[217] O'Regan, supra note 12, at 3.
[218] Threats Sent to Weinstock, L.A. Times, May 26, 1912, § 1, at 4.
[219] New York's Idea of the Scott Case, Paterson Evening News, June 5, 1913, at 4 (editorial) (quoting New York Tribune).

tional American aversion to sedition laws created an intolerable barrier to punishing the new threat of anarchist speech. Many people viewed Wobblies as anarchists, and sometimes differentiated advocacy of anarchism from mere criticism of government. Speech critical of government, they conceded, should be and is protected by law. On the other hand, they considered advocacy of anarchism to be a form of sedition or treason beyond any legitimate conception of free speech.[220]

People who held this view acknowledged and even agreed with the widespread national opposition to the Sedition Act of 1798, one of the "most unpopular measures" Congress ever enacted.[221] "To the average American who cherishes the traditions of the republic," wrote a newspaper that justified vigilante action against the IWW, "there is something abhorrent about the thought of enacting either federal or state sedition laws." The Sedition Act of 1798, it added, "was invoked for unworthy purposes." The American people were pleased when this law expired and hoped that there would never be another law "under which, by using pretexts, it might be possible to prosecute persons who indulged in even the most severe criticism of government."[222]

Such sentiments, the paper stated, were appropriate in the early republic, but "times have changed." The problem was not that criticism of government had become more offensive. Indeed, the paper indicated that it would be impermissible to punish speech based on its degree of offensiveness. Anarchists, however, did not simply criticize government; they engaged in "open advocacy of its destruction." Moreover, anarchists presented a serious national problem, for "their propaganda is gaining recruits from the ignorant, the dissatisfied and the criminal."[223] At the time of the unpopular Sedition Act, the paper pointed out, "the anarchist and his propaganda was unknown." It was confident that Americans of earlier periods, "whatever their aversion to sedition laws, would never have tolerated the speeches that are heard nowadays." The current generation of Americans, it predicted, "will say that the time has come to call a halt."[224]

Even while differing about the wisdom of a sedition law, these commentators generally assumed that Congress had the power to pass one. Only much later did decisions by the Supreme Court

---

[220] Colonel Weinstock's Accusation, San Diego Union, May 20, 1912, at 4 (editorial); The Remedy for Treason Talk, supra note 93; Under Which Flag, San Diegan?, San Diego Union, May 24, 1912, at 4 (editorial).

[221] The Remedy for Treason Talk, supra note 93.

[222] Sedition Laws Will Come, San Diego Union, May 28, 1912, at 4 (editorial).

[223] Id.

[224] The Remedy for Treason Talk, supra note 93.

hold that the First Amendment precludes punishment for seditious libel. The IWW free speech fights, however, did provoke substantial debate about whether the First Amendment applied
beyond its explicit prohibition that "Congress shall make no law
. . . abridging the freedom of speech." In response to IWW assertions that local ordinances violated the constitutional right to free
speech, some defenders of official action pointed out that the First
Amendment operates only against Congress. "The Constitution of
the United States," one editorial stressed, "does not guarantee free
speech to the citizens of the Republic; it leaves that matter to the
discretion of the states themselves."[225] The states, therefore, have
the power under the federal Constitution "to abridge the right of
free speech and to prohibit or regulate the privilege of popular
assembly."[226] Relying on this federalism argument, an editorial
referred to "the arrogant assumption of the street orators that they
were 'exercising a constitutional privilege' – a deliberate misinter-
pretation" of the First Amendment.[227]

B. F. Moore, a staff member of the Commission on Industrial
Relations, wrote a sophisticated analysis of "constitutionally pro-
tected civil liberties" that did not find the narrow reach of the First
Amendment so obvious. Moore recognized that the text of the First
Amendment limits only the federal government and that the entire
bill of rights essentially left the protection of "personal rights" to
the states. Yet he found the subsequent adoption of the Fourteenth
Amendment problematic because it explicitly imposed requirements of due process and equal protection on the states. The U.S.
Supreme Court, Moore reported, had interpreted these terms as
prohibiting state "infringement on property rights rather than on
personal rights." However, in a cautious and ultimately prescient
comment that predated by a decade the Supreme Court's "incorporation" of the First Amendment into the Fourteenth Amendment, Moore concluded that "it is not positively known at present
just what protection is given to certain personal rights by certain
clauses of the U.S. Constitution, especially the 14th amendment."
He indicated the possibility that the Fourteenth Amendment in
fact "guarantees free speech and press in the states."[228]

---

[225] Revising an Inscription, supra note 97.
[226] What San Diego Desires of the State's Lawmakers, San Diego Evening Trib.,
June 6, 1912, at 4 (editorial); see also The Remedy for Treason Talk, supra
note 93 (United States Constitution "merely forbids the enactment of any federal law 'abridging the freedom of speech'"; it contains "nothing that forbids a
state to regulate free speech").
[227] A Plain Statement of the San Diego "Free Speech" Fuss, San Diego Evening
Tribune, March 13, 1912, at 4 (editorial).
[228] Moore, supra note 13, at 1.

FREE SPEECH AND MAJORITY RULE

In addition to analyzing important technical issues, substantial popular debate during the free speech fights addressed the extent to which an individual's right to free speech limits majority rule in a democracy. Free speech and majority rule, some observed, are both fundamental values. For example, a minister in Spokane insisted that the responsibility of "the minority [to] submit to the majority . . . is as sacred a principle in our democratic form of government as is the principle of free speech." At least in some situations, he suggested, the power of speech justifies a community's fear of letting "the man speak too freely who does not agree with us."[229]

Many commentators seemed unable to conceive of the constitutional right to free speech as posing barriers to the kinds of laws communities could pass by democratic majorities. These commentators deferred to existing laws as long as communities enacted them "for their convenience, safety and general welfare," or "in the interest of public safety and good morals."[230] Even when calling for more democratic procedures in enacting laws governing speech, people assumed that speech could be restricted by majority rule. A single-tax society in San Diego urged a referendum "to submit the whole matter to a vote of the people and let the citizens decide whether or not the streets are to be open for the use of all classes of citizens at all times." The society stated its view that the council "cannot legally pass a law that violates the right of free speech and peaceable assembly guaranteed by state and federal constitutions." The society believed, however, that a majority of the people could adopt such a law through a referendum,[231] a position endorsed by a local newspaper.[232]

Editorials frequently elaborated the view that democratic majorities could restrict the speech of minorities. A Boston paper

---

[229] Free Speech His Theme, Spokane Spokesman-Rev., Nov. 8, 1909, at 7.

[230] Bowers Denounces Soap Box Orators, San Diego Union, Feb. 25, 1912, § 2, at 13 (letter from self-described "laboring man"); Free Speech and Treasonable License, supra note 98.

[231] Society Asks Council to Re-Consider Plan, San Diego Sun, Jan. 10, 1912, at 10 (quoting letter from Henry George Society to San Diego City Council (Jan. 10, 1912)). The San Diego city council subsequently maintained that it had openly welcomed a petition to submit its ordinance to a popular referendum. City Council Protests Against State Interference: Prepares Memorial to Governor Outlining I.W.W. Situation in This City: Declares City Capable of Handling Invaders, San Diego Union, Apr. 25, 1912, at 9 (quoting Memorial from San Diego City Council to Hiram Johnson, Governor of California [Apr. 24, 1912]).

[232] See, e.g., Some Free Speech Suggestions, San Diego Sun, Mar. 12, 1912, at 4 (editorial).

commenting on the San Diego free speech fight asserted that an advocate of controversial and divisive minority views, such as "class hatred" and anarchism, "puts the burden of proof as to his or her right to continue therein upon himself or herself and not upon representatives of the collective will, if at any time there is a question of checking utterances and stopping acts that a majority of persons deems obnoxious." The rights of society should "not be held up or undermined by a few persons, not even for liberty's sake." Moreover, minority rights to free speech do not contribute significantly in a complex society like the United States, where there is only a small probability that "a radical solution based on an individual's expertise or reasoned belief will be the only way out."[233] An editorial in the *New York Times* regretting vigilante violence in San Diego distinguished between the "public" and "private" speech of minorities. "Privately," the paper reasoned, "everybody has a license to be as wrong as he or even she pleases." By contrast, public speech can legitimately be regulated by "a majority standing for the public welfare." People "whose views differ from the generality's" should "observe moderation in the expression of them in public." The editorial concluded that those who disobey this etiquette and attempt to "browbeat" the community can lawfully be restrained.[234]

Others, however, stressed that the Constitution protects free speech from popular majorities. A deputy to New York City Police Commissioner Woods made this point explicitly. Writing on behalf of Woods, the deputy stressed that "it is very often the duty of the police to protect the minority." Although majority rule generally governs "daily life and customs," the Constitution provides an exception for "the right of free assemblage and speech," whose protection is "vital to the maintenance of the basic principles of our form of government."[235]

---

[233] What Newspapers Say of I.W.W. Situation, San Diego Union, May 30, 1912, at 7 (quoting Boston Monitor).

[234] Free Speech, N.Y Times, May 20, 1912, at 8 (editorial).

[235] Letter from Third Deputy Commissioner to Sidney Kaufman, supra note 120, at 1. Although the deputy wrote in response to a letter protesting pro-German open air meetings at a time when large portions of the American public were advocating United States intervention in World War I to help the Allies fight Germany, the Police Department also applied this policy to speech by the IWW. See supra text accompanying notes 118–120; see also Letter from Theodore Rousseau, Secretary, City of New York, Office of the Mayor, to Arthur Woods, Police Commissioner (July 1, 1915) (Mitchel Papers, supra note 118, Box: MJP-154, Folder: Police Dep't [12] Mitchel, 1915 July) (directing the Commissioner to respond to the letter concerning pro-German open air meetings).

More general commentary, without referring explicitly to the First Amendment, asserted the importance of protecting the free speech of minorities. During the San Diego free speech fight, an editorial suggested that the underlying cause of any free speech controversy "is small in comparison with the large question of the maintenance unimpaired of the rights of men, whether they belong to minorities or majorities."[236] Another editorial, after observing how "many of us will disagree wholly with much of the perfervid remarks which are shot forth" by the IWW, added that "a free chance to talk is about as American an institution as we can have."[237] In an article reprinted by the Free Speech League, Hutchins Hapgood argued for community toleration of subversive ideas instead of legislation against them. While observing that the suppression of ideas increases the probability of violence, Hapgood also suggested that the most unpopular ideas could "serve to modify our prejudices and our injustice and our routine habits."[238]

The New Republic offered its readers pragmatic reasons for protecting the free speech of unpopular Wobblies. The magazine maintained that agitation by radicals often prompts "the careful improvements of the more reasonable reformers" and the "'constructive' plans of statesmen." Wise reformers realize "that we are all of us freer today to speak, to make proposals, to offer criticisms which would have got no hearing whatever if loud threats had not been made and ugly fists raised in anger." Moreover, in a democratic society "the quiet of those who submit is often far more ominous than the disturbance of those who rebel."[239]

Commentary generated by the IWW free speech fights refutes the conventional understanding that Americans before World War I did not pay much attention to the meaning of free speech. The general public, officials at various levels of government, and even members of the IWW expressed a wide range of views on a large number of free speech issues raised by the free speech fights. This commentary overwhelmingly took place outside the judicial system. Most of it was more sophisticated analytically, and more sensitive to free speech concerns, than typical judicial decisions of the period responding to free speech claims in any context.

---

[236] Fredericks Is Right, San Diego Sun, May 4, 1912, at 4 (editorial) (quoting the New York World, described in the article as "not an I.W.W. organ by a good deal").

[237] A Question of Common Sense, San Diego Sun, Jan. 30, 1912, at 1 (editorial).

[238] Basis of Free Speech, supra note 41.

[239] So-Called Industrial Peace, supra note 150, at 6, 7.

3

The Courts and Free Speech

Cases that arose from the IWW free speech fights and from the activities of libertarian radicals represented only a small fraction of judicial encounters with free speech issues between the Civil War and World War I. An enormous variety of cases at all levels of the judicial system refutes the widespread assumption that litigation over free speech began abruptly with prosecutions under the Espionage Act of 1917. These cases, however, have been obscured ever since Chafee minimized and mischaracterized them in his 1919 article, "Freedom of Speech in War Time."[1] Relying uncritically on Chafee, subsequent scholars have not independently examined the prewar period. They exceed even Chafee in their neglect of the substantial litigation over free speech before World War I. For example, no major casebook on constitutional law includes a single decision before 1917 in its section on freedom of expression.[2]

Only a few scholars have tried to explain the assumed absence of earlier judicial encounters with free speech issues. Like most people interested in constitutional matters, these scholars think mostly about the federal courts, particularly the Supreme Court. As a result, they have focused on possible factors limiting federal jurisdiction. The text of the First Amendment prohibits only Congress from abridging free speech. Some have asserted that the

---

[1] Zechariah Chafee, Jr., Freedom of Speech in War Time, 32 Harv. L. Rev. 932 (1919).

[2] See, e.g., Daniel A. Farber, William N. Eskridge, Jr., and Philip P. Frickey, Constitutional Law (1993); Gerald Gunther, Constitutional Law (12th ed. 1991); William B. Lockhart, Yale Kamisar, Jesse H. Choper, Steven H. Shiffrin, and Richard H. Fallon, Jr., The American Constitution (8th ed. 1996); Geoffrey R. Stone, Louis M. Seidman, Cass R. Sunstein and Mark V. Tushnet, Constitutional Law (3rd ed. 1996). Some of these casebooks do refer in passing to Commonwealth v. Davis, 162 Mass. 510, 39 N.E. 113 (1895), aff'd, 167 U.S. 43 (1897), in connection with the later case, Hague v. CIO, 307 U.S. 496 (1939). See Gunther at 1250; Lockhart, at 881; Stone, at 1335. Professor Van Alstyne's innovative casebook on the First Amendment departs from the general constitutional law casebooks by including a pre-World War I case, Patterson v. Colorado, 205 U.S. 454 (1907). William W. Van Alstyne, First Amendment 9 (2nd ed. 1995).

Sedition Act of 1798, which expired in 1801, was the only federal legislation before the Espionage Act of 1917 that posed significant threats to free speech. An important Supreme Court decision in 1812 held that federal courts did not have jurisdiction over common-law crimes,[3] thereby reducing their exposure to free speech issues. The ratification of the Fourteenth Amendment following the Civil War introduced federal jurisdiction over various forms of state action, but the Supreme Court did not "incorporate" First Amendment freedoms into the rights protected by the Fourteenth Amendment until 1925.[4] During the period before incorporation, scholars assumed, state deprivations of free speech could not be litigated in federal courts. Hardly anyone thought about developments within the states. An occasional comment, however, observed that states rarely passed legislation that implicated their own constitutional guarantees of free speech.[5]

Examination of legal decisions before World War I reveals that some of these explanations for the assumed lack of free speech litigation are incorrect or incomplete. The Sedition Act of 1798 was not the only federal legislation that raised free speech issues before 1917. As discussed in the chapter on libertarian radicalism, Congress passed the Comstock Act of 1873, which prohibited the interstate mailing of obscene material, and the Alien Immigration Act of 1903, which provided for the exclusion of aliens who advocated anarchist doctrines. Both of these acts produced Supreme Court decisions that affected speech, as did other postal legislation and an 1876 statute that prohibited federal employees from financial involvement in political campaigns. Requests for injunctions against labor leaders for expression alleged to violate federal law provided another source of free speech litigation in the federal courts, including a Supreme Court case brought by Samuel Gompers, the president of the American Federation of Labor. The Supreme Court, moreover, occasionally addressed free speech issues arising under state law without resolving debate over the relationship between the First and Fourteenth Amendments. The most significant example was the 1907 decision by Justice Holmes in *Patterson v. Colorado*,[6] which limited the First Amendment to Blackstone's prohibition against prior restraints. Holmes reached

---

[3] United States v. Hudson & Goodwin, 11 U.S. (7 Cranch) 32 (1812).

[4] Gitlow v. New York, 268 U.S. 652 (1925).

[5] See Walter Berns, The First Amendment and the Future of American Democracy 147–48 (1976); Paul L. Murphy, The Meaning of Freedom of Speech: First Amendment Freedoms from Wilson to FDR 14, 22, 248 (1972).

[6] 205 U.S. 454 (1907).

this conclusion without resolving Colorado's claim that the Supreme Court lacked jurisdiction over the case because the Colorado Supreme Court had relied only on state common law in upholding an editor's conviction for contempt.

Although the Supreme Court and other federal courts decided many more free speech cases than Chafee revealed and subsequent scholars assumed, a significantly larger number of cases in state courts even more clearly refutes the conventional wisdom that litigation over the constitutional meaning of free speech began in 1917. State courts frequently addressed whether various crimes and torts at common law violated the First Amendment or state constitutional protection for free speech, and more state than federal statutes presented free speech issues. Major topics of litigation included libel, contempt, obscenity, speech in labor disputes, political campaigning, public speaking, and the relationship between speech and crime.

As Chafee correctly reported in 1919, few prewar cases analyzed free speech issues in any depth. The public commentary on the IWW free speech fights was generally more thoughtful than most judicial opinions of the period. As part of his propaganda for more judicial protection of dissenting antiwar speech, however, Chafee falsely asserted that the Espionage Act decisions by the lower federal courts had "revived"[7] the bad tendency test that had expired with the Sedition Act of 1798. In fact, the bad tendency test was the predominant judicial approach in scores of prewar cases affecting speech.

Throughout the period from the Civil War to World War I, the overwhelming majority of decisions in all jurisdictions rejected free speech claims, often by ignoring their existence. This judicial response might account for the many instances in which counsel did not assert free speech claims made by some of their colleagues in other cases. No court was more unsympathetic to freedom of expression than the Supreme Court, which rarely produced even a dissenting opinion in a First Amendment case. Most decisions by lower federal courts and state courts were also restrictive. Radicals fared particularly poorly, but the widespread judicial hostility to free speech claims transcended any individual issue or litigant. This historical record poses a substantial challenge to current constitutional theorists who identify an independent judiciary as the best protection for individual rights in a democracy.

The prewar judicial landscape, however, was not unrelievedly restrictive. A few Supreme Court opinions contained some frag-

[7] Chafee, supra note 1, at 952, 965.

mentary analysis and hints of a more tolerant attitude toward freedom of expression. In addition, a minority of state and lower federal courts upheld free speech claims, and several examined the constitutional meaning of speech with care and sophistication. A significant number of state court decisions, in contrast to Justice Holmes's opinion for the Supreme Court in *Patterson,* vigorously rejected Blackstone and the English common law as guides to American constitutional provisions on speech. The possibility of substantial legal protection for speech, therefore, was not beyond the conceptual universe of American judges before World War I.

THE BAD TENDENCY TEST

The most pervasive and fundamental judicial approach to free speech issues between the Civil War and World War I used the bad tendency test derived from Sir William Blackstone's *Commentaries* on the English common law in the eighteenth century. Many decisions, like Justice Holmes in *Patterson,* followed Blackstone's conclusion that the legal right of free speech precludes prior restraints, but permits the punishment of publications for their tendency to harm the public welfare. In striking contrast to their increased oversight of economic and social legislation that infringed "liberty of contract" and property rights, judges gave great deference to the "police power" of legislators and administrators to determine the tendency of speech. Judges also readily found that speech, even if not directly prohibited, had a tendency to produce an action proscribed by statute and therefore could be penalized as a violation of the more general law.

The details of Holmes's opinion in *Patterson* highlights the reliance on Blackstone's bad tendency test in judicial decisions before World War I. Thomas Patterson was a U.S. Senator from Colorado. He also owned and edited newspapers in his home state. Through his newspapers, Patterson had actively supported reformers who in 1902 won a referendum that amended the state constitution by providing home rule to Denver. Patterson, who was a populist, became outraged when Republican members of the recently enlarged state supreme court overturned elections in Denver by invalidating the home rule amendment on state constitutional grounds. Editorials, cartoons, and letters in his newspaper ridiculed the court. Their common theme was that the judges essentially acted as the tools of the utility corporations, which controlled the Republican Party. The attorney general of Colorado brought criminal contempt proceedings against Patterson on behalf of the state supreme court. The court convicted Patterson and fined him and his publishing company $1,000 without allowing him to prove truth as a defense. It recognized that contempt applied only to criticism of judges in pending cases, but held that the decisions Patterson criticized remained pending because the losing parties could still request a rehearing.[8]

In his brief to the Supreme Court, Patterson argued that the state supreme court had violated his federal and state constitutional rights by precluding him from demonstrating the truth of his accusations. He stressed that the American conception of popular sovereignty, contained in the federal and in all state constitutions, protected truthful criticism of "public officials as to their official conduct." Only through public discussion, Patterson reasoned, "are the people who possess sovereign power informed of the merits or demerits of those who are chosen to rule over them." Patterson did not link this right of truthful public discussion to the First Amendment, but to "those general rights not specifically named in the constitution, which are reserved by the people." By contrast, in discussing the Colorado constitution Patterson found direct support in its provision "that every person shall be free to speak or write and publish whatever he will on any subject, being responsible for all abuse of that liberty; and that in all suits and prosecutions for libel, the truth thereof may be given in evidence." Patterson maintained that this provision, although explicitly limited to libel, announced a general principle that "whenever the freedom of the press is called in question in any form of proceeding, it shall be sufficient to establish the truth of what is published as a defense to the action." Truthful criticism of judges, Patterson emphasized, is not an abuse of free speech. Invoking the federal constitution generally, Patterson asserted that "being armed with truth no man in this country must face the open jail doors before he dares to speak it, and having spoken it, to hear them close behind him."[9]

Holmes tersely rejected Patterson's attack on his contempt conviction. The First Amendment, Holmes declared, prevents all "*previous restraints* upon publications," but allows "the subsequent punishment of such as may be deemed contrary to the public welfare." "The preliminary freedom," he added, "extends as well to the false as to the true; the subsequent punishment may extend as well to the true as to the false." Holmes supported this holding with a citation to Blackstone's *Commentaries* and to state court decisions in

---

[8] See Owen M. Fiss, Troubled Beginnings of the Modern State, 1888–1910, at 340 (1993); Lucas A. Powe, Jr., The Fourth Estate and the Constitution: Freedom of the Press in America 1–7 (1991).

[9] Brief of Plaintiff in Error at 87–95.

1788 and 1826 that had relied on Blackstone in libel cases.[10] In the section of the *Commentaries* cited by Holmes, Blackstone defined criminal libels as writings "of an immoral or illegal tendency" and considered them a subcategory of crimes, such as "challenges to fight," that tend to provoke breaches of the peace. Blackstone emphasized that "the provocation, and not the falsity, is the thing to be punished criminally."[11]

Holmes believed that Blackstone's reasoning, developed in the context of the common law of criminal libel, was particularly applicable to contempts of court. Publications criticizing judicial behavior in pending cases, he asserted, "tend to obstruct the administration of justice," whether or not the allegations are true.[12] Patterson's brief had pointed out that Colorado law allowed a petition for rehearing to be filed at any time, and thus placed no limit on the state supreme court's definition of when a case is pending. As a result, Patterson argued, Colorado could impose a perpetual ban on criticism of judicial conduct. Without directly responding to this argument, Holmes simply maintained that the definition of when a case is pending should be decided under local law "without interference from the Constitution of the United States" as long as there was no showing that "innocent conduct has been laid hold of as an arbitrary pretense for an arbitrary punishment."[13] Holmes found no such showing by Patterson.

Justice Harlan's dissent in *Patterson* contained a vigorous, if undeveloped, defense of free speech under the First Amendment. Harlan explicitly opposed Holmes's conclusion that the First Amendment prevents only prior restraints. Holmes's view, Harlan feared, would allow a legislature to "impair or abridge the rights of a free press and of free speech whenever it thinks that the public welfare requires that to be done." According to Harlan, legislative determinations of the public welfare "cannot override constitutional privileges," a position he stressed in interpreting the Constitution generally.[14] Although Harlan did not elaborate his views on the First Amendment in other decisions, his analysis in *Patterson* provided a doctrinal alternative to the widespread practice of invoking the alleged bad tendency of speech as an automatic barrier against free speech claimants.

Although *Patterson v. Colorado* was the case that most clearly

---

[10] Patterson v. Colorado, 205 U.S. 454, 462 (1907). See Commonwealth v. Blanding, 20 Mass. (3 Pick.) 304 (1826) and Respublica v. Oswald, 1 Dall. 319 (Pa. 1788).

[11] 4 William Blackstone, Commentaries *150.

[12] 205 U.S. at 462.   [13] 205 U.S. at 461.

[14] 205 U.S. at 465.

relied on the bad tendency test and best revealed its source in Blackstone's *Commentaries,* other Supreme Court decisions demonstrated the pervasive use of this approach. In the *Turner* case that attracted the attention of the Free Speech League, the Court relied on the tendency of anarchist speech in upholding the conviction and deportation of John Turner, a visiting English anarchist, under the Alien Immigration Act of 1903. This legislation, passed soon after President McKinley was assassinated by an anarchist, excluded "anarchists, or persons who believe in or advocate the overthrow by force or violence of the Government of the United States or of all government or of all forms of law, or the assassination of public officials."[15] In their brief for Turner, financed by the Free Speech League, Clarence Darrow and Edgar Lee Masters asserted that arresting Turner for the contents of his lectures in the United States violated his First Amendment right to free speech. "Anarchists," they stressed, "are distinguished by a definite creed and not by the *means* proposed to propagate the creed or render it paramount." They argued that anarchists do not necessarily believe in or advocate the overthrow of government by force or violence and therefore are not, solely by definition, guilty of violating the Alien Immigration Act.[16] No evidence against Turner, Darrow and Masters emphasized, indicated that he personally urged the use of force or violence.[17] At a more general level, Darrow and Masters asserted that the "fundamental basis of free opinion demands that convictions shall be freely spoken to the end that the truth shall be known. Upon this freedom all progress depends."[18]

The government's brief, written by future Supreme Court Justice James McReynolds, called Turner's First Amendment claims "incomprehensible." The brief's treatment of the First Amendment issue revealed its general hostility to free speech, particularly for aliens. "Abridgement of the freedom of speech or of the press," it contended, "is no more brought about by the exclusion or expulsion of anarchists than by similar treatment of the followers of Confucius." The brief added that "the right to talk is no more sacred than the right to work" and pointed out that not all alien workers could be admitted. It claimed that the statute, rather than violating the First Amendment, protected the country from aliens seeking to overthrow the government.[19]

Although the Court did not refer to this portion of the govern-

---

[15] Turner v. Williams, 194 U.S. 279, 293 (1904).
[16] Brief and Argument of Appellant at 36.
[17] Id. at 6.   [18] Id. at 49.
[19] Brief for Appellee at 21–22.

ment's brief, it firmly rejected the arguments of Darrow and Masters on behalf of Turner. If Congress defined an anarchist as one who supports the violent overthrow of government, the majority reasoned, then any alien "who avows himself to be an anarchist, without more," necessarily adopts that definition and is subject to deportation. In any event, the Court added, Turner's speech and proposed lecture topics justified the inferences that "he contemplated the ultimate realization of his ideal by the use of force" and that "his speeches were incitements to that end." For example, Turner predicted and endorsed a general strike throughout the industrial world. In addition, he protested as "legal murder" the execution of the Haymarket defendants, who were found guilty of aiding and abetting murder when in 1886 a fatal bomb exploded in Chicago's Haymarket Square while they were advocating anarchist doctrine. Invoking the bad tendency of speech, the Court also asserted that there could be no constitutional objection to the Act even if it defined anarchists as "political philosophers innocent of evil intent." Congress could legitimately conclude, the Court reasoned, "that the tendency of the general exploitation of such views is so dangerous to the public weal that aliens who hold and advocate them would be undesirable additions to our population." While defending the punishment of speech for its possible tendency, the Court went out of its way to emphasize that its decision should not "be understood as depreciating the vital importance of freedom of speech and of the press." This freedom, the Court felt, was not involved in *Turner,* apparently because "as long as human governments endure they cannot be denied the power of self-preservation."[20]

Concurring in *Turner,* Justice Brewer questioned the majority's treatment of philosophical anarchism. He agreed that it was "not an unreasonable deduction" from the record that Turner himself was "an anarchist in the commonly accepted sense of the term, one who urges and seeks the overthrow by force of all government." Brewer, however, considered it unnecessary for the majority to consider the rights of "a philosophical anarchist, one who simply entertains and expresses the opinion that all government is a mistake, and that society would be better off without any."[21] His concurrence was far from a ringing affirmation of First Amendment rights. The distinction between expressing general opposition to government, which could conceivably influence others to commit acts of violence, and urging its overthrow by force might

---

[20] 194 U.S. at 293–95. See generally Paul Avrich, The Haymarket Tragedy (1984).
[21] Id. at 296.

imply some limitations on the punishment of speech for its possible tendency. Yet Brewer never specified any reservations about the bad tendency approach. He did not even assert that it would be unconstitutional to deport philosophical anarchists. But at least he acknowledged that the treatment of philosophical anarchism presented a potential problem that the majority should not have addressed and resolved so facilely.

Patterson and *Turner* were the two Supreme Court decisions that explicitly invoked the bad tendency of speech to justify the rejection of First Amendment claims. In other cases, however, the Court used the same rationale for denying protection to speech even when it did not use the word *tendency* or refer to the First Amendment. In its *Ex parte Jackson* decision of 1877, for example, the Court did not respond directly to the argument that an 1868 federal statute, which excluded lottery advertisements from the mail, violated the First Amendment by permitting the punishment of speech for its bad tendency. Louis F. Post, in his brief for the petitioners, warned that if Congress can exclude lotteries from the mail "by virtue of their asserted injurious tendency," it could also "cut off all means of epistolary communication upon any subject which is objectionable to a majority of its members." Legislation proposed in 1836, Post reminded the Court, would have excluded material on slavery from the mail out of fear that it might incite slaves to revolt against their masters. Post emphasized that Congress had "signally defeated" this measure. The opposition voiced in Congress on First Amendment grounds by "the most eminent statesmen of that day," he asserted, conclusively demonstrated the unconstitutionality of the subsequent statute prohibiting the mailing of lottery advertisements. Post maintained that whatever was mailable when the Constitution was adopted cannot subsequently be excluded by legislation.[22]

The Court's unanimous opinion rejected Post's arguments while upholding the constitutionality of the statute and making clear that the Comstock Act's prohibitions against mailing "obscene" and otherwise "indecent" publications would also withstand scrutiny under the First Amendment. Justifying its position, the Court observed that lotteries and obscenities "are supposed to have a demoralizing influence upon the people." Although the Court did not refer explicitly to the bad tendency of speech, a "demoralizing influence" seems very similar to a "bad tendency." Responding to Post's First Amendment arguments, the Court acknowledged that Congress, in exercising its power "to establish

[22] Ex parte Jackson, 96 U.S. 727, 730–31 (1877).

post-offices and post-roads," may not "interfere in any manner with the freedom of the press." It also recognized that liberty of publication has no value without liberty of circulation; if Congress could block all avenues of communication, then freedom of the press would suffer a "fatal blow." Yet Congress, the opinion reasoned, has no power to prevent the circulation, through private channels, of matter it excludes from the federal mails. Denying lotteries and obscene material access to the mails, it asserted, is therefore not an unconstitutional interference with freedom of the press, but a legitimate refusal by Congress to use "its facilities for the distribution of matter deemed injurious to the public morals." The Court distinguished the prior congressional controversy over mailing material about slavery by asserting without any elaboration that lotteries – unlike the letters, newspapers and pamphlets at issue in 1836 – can be transported in other ways than through the mail.[23] The Court did not discuss the viability of alternative means of circulation or whether, even if alternatives are not viable, public morals could override free speech.

The Supreme Court sometimes punished speech for its bad tendency without even referring to the First Amendment. Ironically, the Supreme Court case over which the Free Speech League had most control provides the best example. Jay Fox, the editor of the newspaper published by the anarchist Home Colony, challenged a Washington state statute that made it a gross misdemeanor to publish, edit, or circulate written matter "in any form, advocating, encouraging or inciting, or having a tendency to encourage or incite the commission of any crime, breach of the peace or act of violence, or which shall tend to encourage or advocate disrespect for law or for any court or courts of justice." Fox was convicted under this statute for editing an article entitled "The Nude and the Prudes," which predicted and encouraged a "boycott" against those who interfered with nude bathing in the community. The Home Colony had helped stimulate the organization of the Free Speech League in 1902, and this article expressed libertarian radical views shared by the League's founders. It described the Home Colony as "a community of free spirits, who come out into the woods to escape the polluted atmosphere of priest-ridden, conventional society." Bathing "with merely the clothes nature gave them" was "one of the liberties enjoyed by the Homeites." Unfortunately, "a few prudes got into the community and proceeded in the brutal, unneighborly way of the outside world to suppress the people's

[23] Id. at 732–33, 735–36.

freedom" by securing the arrests of nude bathers on charges of indecent exposure.[24]

After his conviction, Fox sought and received the assistance of Theodore Schroeder, who arranged for Gilbert Roe to represent Fox in the Supreme Court when Fox's original attorney did not follow Schroeder's legal suggestions.[25] It is somewhat surprising that Roe did not use this opportunity to pursue First Amendment claims, especially because he viewed this case, among the many that came to his attention through his work with the Free Speech League, as a particularly promising vehicle for a useful decision from the Supreme Court.[26] Roe referred to the First Amendment in only two sentences at the end of his brief. He simply reminded the Court that *Patterson v. Colorado* raised, but did not decide, the issue of whether the Fourteenth Amendment applied the First Amendment to state action, and pointed out that the record in *Fox* preserved that question.[27] Roe made no substantive First Amendment arguments, perhaps concluding, based on the Court's prior decisions, that it would avoid or reject First Amendment claims. The Court in *Patterson,* however, had addressed the meaning of the First Amendment without resolving the relationship between the First and Fourteenth Amendments. It might have done so again if Roe had briefed more thoroughly the potential free speech issues in *Fox.* And even if the Court in *Fox* had been no more responsive to the value of free speech than it was in its previous *Patterson* decision, *Fox* might have produced a useful dissent, such as the one Justice Harlan wrote in *Patterson.*

Instead of making First Amendment arguments directly, Roe translated potential claims about free speech into Fourteenth Amendment terminology. Using analysis clearly adopted from

---

[24] Fox v. Washington, 236 U.S. 273, 275–77 (1915).

[25] See, e.g., the following correspondence in the Theodore Schroeder Papers, Southern Illinois University Library [hereinafter Schroeder Papers]: Letter from Theodore Schroeder to James J. Anderson (May 11, 1912), Box 10; Letter from Theodore Schroeder to Jay Fox (May 11, 1912), Box 10; Letter from Theodore Schroeder to Jay Fox (Sept. 3, 1912), Box 10; Letter from Gilbert E. Roe to Theodore Schroeder (Jan. 16, 1913), Box 10; Letter from Gilbert E. Roe to Theodore Schroeder (Mar. 21, 1913), Box 10; Letter from Gilbert E. Roe to Theodore Schroeder (Jun. 17, 1913), Box 11; Receipt from Gilbert E. Roe to Theodore Schroeder (June 25, 1913), Box 11; Letter from Gilbert E. Roe to Theodore Schroeder (Oct. 6, 1913), Box 11; Letter from Theodore Schroeder to Gilbert E. Roe (July 6, 1914), Box 11.

[26] Letter from Gilbert E. Roe to Theodore Schroeder (Dec. 31, 1912), Schroeder Papers, supra note 25, Box 10.

[27] Brief for Plaintiff-in-Error at 17.

Schroeder's scholarly writings, Roe's brief concentrated on demonstrating the vagueness of the statute and on asserting that it deprived Fox of the liberty protected by the Fourteenth Amendment.[28] Roe attempted to distinguish *Fox* from the many cases upholding statutes that punished "language naturally tending to produce" crimes such as breach of the peace and assault and battery, and from cases sustaining statutes that prohibited sending obscenity through the mails. Roe privately did not approve of these other cases and often litigated for different results. He argued in his brief, however, that in all of them the "character and causes of the prohibited act are known, and it is possible to determine with some degree of certainty, what language induces the commission of such act." In *Fox,* by contrast, "the mental state of the reader or hearer described as 'disrespect for law' is the ultimate fact to be produced by the use of the language penalized, and who can say what language will produce that state of mind?"[29]

Decided eight years after *Patterson, Fox* gave Justice Holmes another opportunity to consider the relationship between the bad tendency of speech and crime. As in *Patterson,* Holmes allowed the punishment of speech for its bad tendency and upheld Fox's conviction. But in *Fox,* unlike in *Patterson,* Holmes did not address First Amendment issues, perhaps because Roe's brief only referred to them in passing. Typically, Holmes stressed that the decision of the Court had "nothing to do with the wisdom of the defendant, the prosecution, or the act. All that concerns us is that it cannot be said to infringe the Constitution of the United States." With evident discomfort, Holmes strained to limit a statute he apparently did not like. He rejected the argument that the act was "an unjustifiable restriction of liberty and too vague for a criminal law." Holmes contended that, "by implication at least," the state court had "read the statute as confined to encouraging an actual breach of law." Straining, he reasoned that it "would be in accord with the usages of English to interpret disrespect as manifested disrespect, as active disregard going beyond the line drawn by the law." Moreover, Holmes doubted that the statute would be "construed to prevent publications merely because they tend to produce unfavorable opinions of a particular statute or of law in general."[30]

In *Fox,* "the disrespect for law that was encouraged was disregard of it – an overt breach and technically criminal act." The offensive article, Holmes found, "by indirection but unmistakably . . . encourages and incites a persistence in what we must assume

28 Id. at 15–17.   29 Id. at 15.
30 236 U.S. at 277–78.

would be a breach of the state laws against indecent exposure." He noted that even without statutory prohibitions such statements, "if directed to a particular person's conduct, generally would make him who uttered them guilty of a misdemeanor if not an accomplice or a principal in the crime encouraged." Holmes acknowledged that Fox's article was directed to "a wider and less selected audience," but he added, as if to dispose of this problem, that "[l]aws of this description are not unfamiliar."[31]

Thus, in the *Fox* case, as in his famous dissent in *Lochner v. New York*[32] and in other cases that construed economic regulations, Holmes was eager to emphasize the irrelevance of his own views about legislation while upholding statutes against constitutional attacks based on the Fourteenth Amendment. His colleagues on the Supreme Court, by contrast, showed no such consistency. Most of them, unlike Holmes, regularly invalidated economic legislation as a violation of the liberty protected by the Fourteenth Amendment. Yet they unanimously joined Holmes in denying Roe's assertion that the Washington statute, by punishing unspecified language for its tendency to produce "disrespect for law," deprived Fox of his constitutionally protected liberty under the Fourteenth Amendment.

Free speech cases in the lower federal and state courts, even more than Supreme Court decisions, often relied on the supposed bad tendency of speech for doctrinal support. Cases that involved libel law, the context in which Blackstone set forth the bad tendency test, frequently used this theory even when they, unlike Blackstone, allowed truth as a defense. A decision by the Michigan Supreme Court in 1878 was typical. "The doctrine is elementary," the court held, "that written articles which in any way tend to bring ridicule, contempt or censure on a person are libelous, and are actionable unless true or privileged."[33] The Washington Supreme Court extended this approach to dead people when it upheld in 1916 a conviction for a libel against George Washington. The court rejected First Amendment and state constitutional attacks on a statute that defined libel to include a "malicious publication . . . which shall tend to expose the memory of one deceased to hatred, contempt, ridicule or obloquy." According to the court, the state legislature could reasonably have concluded that "all publications tending to defame the memory of deceased persons might have the tendency to excite some persons to breaches of the peace."[34] Like Justice Holmes in *Patterson*, many lower court judges

---

[31] Id.   [32] 198 U.S. 45, 74 (1905).
[33] Foster v. Scripps, 39 Mich. 376, 379–80 (1878).
[34] State v. Haffer, 162 P. 45, 46–47 (Sup. Ct. Wash. 1916).

applied the bad tendency standard to contempts of court and upheld convictions for articles "tending to embarrass or influence the court in its final conclusion."[35]

Moreover, numerous obscenity cases followed the *Bennett* decision of 1879 in relying on the bad tendency test announced in the 1868 English case, *The Queen v. Hicklin*.[36] Even Judge Charles Amidon, one of the rare federal judges who subsequently refused to convict defendants under the Espionage Act for antiwar speech, applied the bad tendency test to a publication he described as glorifying fornication and praising geniuses who were illegitimate children. The constitutional guarantee of a free press, Amidon insisted, has "nothing to do" with legislation against obscenity. Amidon described the Comstock Act as a criminal law designed not to restrict "a free press, but to protect society against practices that are clearly immoral and corrupting."[37]

State courts extended the bad tendency test from obscenity to other publications that harmed the "public morals." The Supreme Court of Errors of Connecticut affirmed a conviction under a law prohibiting publications "principally made up of criminal news, police reports, or pictures and stories of deeds of bloodshed, lust, or crime." "It is impossible to say," the Court reasoned, "that such publications do not tend to public demoralization as truly as descriptions of mere obscenity."[38] The Supreme Court of Minnesota similarly upheld the indictment of a defendant who, contrary to law, published an account of an execution. The court acknowledged that the article was "moderate" and did not "emphasiz[e] the horrors of executing the death penalty," but it rejected as "altogether too restricted a view" the argument that the liberty of the press could not constitutionally be limited unless the publication was blasphemous, obscene, seditious, or scandalous. As long as the subject matter was "of such character as naturally tends to excite the public mind and thus indirectly affect the public good," the article could be penalized. The court therefore deferred to the legislative judgment that "it is detrimental to public morals to publish anything more than the mere fact that the execution has taken place."[39]

In more politically charged contexts, courts frequently found that articles, speeches, and demonstrations by radicals had a bad

[35] See, e.g., State v. Tugwell, 52 P. 1056, 1061 (Sup. Ct. Wash. 1898).
[36] See Chapter 1, text accompanying notes 74–76.
[37] Knowles v. United States, 170 F. 409, 411–12 (8th Cir. 1909).
[38] State v. McKee, 73 Conn. 18, 27, 46 A. 409, 412, 413 (1900).
[39] State v. Pioneer Press Co., 100 Minn. 173, 176–77, 110 N.W. 867, 868–69 (1907).

tendency to cause unrest in an impressionable public. New York's highest court twice affirmed convictions of Johann Most, a prominent anarchist editor. The first conviction, under a statute that prohibited assembling with others to attempt or threaten "any act tending towards a breach of the peace," was based on a speech Most delivered to a meeting of anarchists the day after the Haymarket defendants had been hanged in Chicago. He urged his audience to "arm yourself, as the day of revolution is not far off; and when it comes, see that you are ready to resist and kill those hirelings of capitalists" who, in his opinion, were responsible for the executions. Most argued that his speech consisted of prophecies of what would be likely to happen, and not threats that he or others in sympathy with him would commit violence or murder. The court concluded that the jury's conviction was based on sufficient evidence. "Incendiary speeches before a crowd of ignorant, misguided men," it reasoned, "are not less dangerous because . . . [they] are accompanied with the suggestion that the time is not quite come for action." Noting that the audience was sympathetic and highly excited, the court stressed that "[n]o one can foresee the consequences which may result from [such] language."[40] The court viewed this uncertainty, not as a consideration against punishing speech, but as an added reason to do so.

Eleven years later, the same court affirmed another conviction of Most, this time for endangering the public peace by republishing an article in his newspaper the day President McKinley was shot by an anarchist. The article argued that all government is founded on murder, and maintained that revolutionary forces sometimes have a duty to kill "a professional murderer." The court concluded that the article "manifestly tended toward" a breach of the public peace by using language that was "an invitation to murder" and could not be considered legitimate criticism of public affairs. Although the article neither addressed a specific person nor advocated the murder of any particular individual, the court observed that its readers would include "reckless and aggressive" persons "who are ready to act on such [general] advice, and to become the assassins of those whom the people have placed in authority." Such articles "naturally lead" to assassination, and their "punishment and repression are essential to the welfare of society and the safety of the state." By invoking the familiar distinction between "free" speech and its "license" or "abuse," the court stressed that its holding was consistent with the provisions in the state constitution forbidding the abridgment of speech. Although

---

[40] People v. Most, 128 N.Y. 108, 109, 111, 114–16, 27 N.E. 970, 970–73 (1891).

the article had been written fifty years earlier by another author, the court found that Most, by his introductory comment stating that the article "is true even to-day," had endorsed the sentiments and ratified the advice given.[41]

Emma Goldman confronted similar reasoning when she asked for an injunction to prevent officials in Philadelphia from denying a public hall for her lectures. Refusing to issue an injunction, a Pennsylvania state court rejected her reliance on the free speech clause of the state constitution. If Goldman lectured, the court concluded, "dangerous and disturbing sentiments tending to disturb the peace would be uttered." Even worse, Goldman wanted to "advocate ideas which, if carried out, would naturally lead to the destruction of government." In words close to those of the Supreme Court in *Turner v. Williams,* the Pennsylvania court held that the government's "right of self-preservation" overrides "such abuse of the right of free speech." Like many other decisions of the prewar period, the court closed its opinion by invoking the importance of free speech while denying its exercise in a particular case.[42]

State courts sometimes used the bad tendency rationale to attribute responsibility to radicals for the potential lawlessness of hostile audiences, however moderate the expression or unreasonable the response. The conviction of Upton Sinclair for leading a peaceful demonstration, consisting mostly of Wobblies, in front of the Standard Oil Company building provides a good example. If public "reprobation" is likely "to be resented," the court held, "the behavior evidencing such reprobation," however peaceable and courteous, "is unlawful as tending to a breach of the peace." The court declared that Sinclair's conviction protected "the public interest in the enforcement of law and the preservation of order" and did not violate his right to free speech.[43]

The Supreme Judicial Court of Massachusetts also relied on the bad tendency of speech on a potential audience while sustaining a conviction for the public display of a red flag. The court held constitutional a statute forbidding the use in a parade of a red or black flag or of any flag "which may be derogatory to public morals." According to the court, statutes designed to preserve the public safety "cannot be stricken down as unconstitutional unless they manifestly have no tendency to produce that result." Citing dictionary definitions of the red flag as a "revolutionary and terroristic

---

[41] People v. Most, 171 N.Y. 423, 426–28, 431, 64 N.E. 175, 176–78 (1902).

[42] Goldman v. Reyburn, 18 Pa. Dist. R. 883, 884–885 (1909).

[43] People v. Sinclair, 86 Misc. 426, 438, 149 N.Y.S. 54, 61 (Ct. Gen. Sess. 1914).

emblem," the court reasoned that the legislature could legitimately view it as the symbol of ideas hostile to established order and therefore "likely to provoke turbulence" if carried in parades.[44]

The Supreme Court of Michigan similarly upheld the convictions of socialists for having "infuriated the local public" by displaying the red flag. Without using the words *bad tendency*, the court found that the socialists had actual knowledge that this display "would excite fears and apprehension" and "provoke violence and disorder" as a "natural and inevitable consequence." The fact that the public peace was disturbed by "those whose sentiments they offended" rather than by the socialists themselves provided no excuse; both groups "jointly invaded" the rights of the public. Although acknowledging the socialists' right "to propagate their political views," the court "emphatically" denied that in so doing they were permitted to violate the law.[45]

In a few rare cases, courts applied the bad tendency test without finding a violation of law. For example, the Supreme Court of Washington reversed a contempt conviction after determining that the article in dispute did not have "a reasonable tendency to prevent a fair and impartial trial." The court stressed the "well settled" rule that in a criminal case all doubts must be resolved in favor of the accused.[46] This rule, however, did not prompt most courts to reach similar results, and atypical sensitivity to the rights of the accused probably does not account for the reversal in Washington. The fact that the article attacked the prosecuting attorney and not, as in most contempt cases, the presiding judge, provides a more likely explanation for this unusual result. In another contempt case, the Supreme Court of California found that testimony in a divorce proceeding was not the type of publication that "tends to impede, embarrass, or obstruct the court in the discharge of its duties."[47] As in the Washington case, the alleged contempt was not directed against the judge, and the California court clearly rejected the newspaper's claim that the constitutional rights of free speech and a free press preclude contempt for any discussion of judicial proceedings.

Other, equally rare cases protected free speech in contexts where most courts might have been tempted to use the bad tendency theory to reach the opposite result. The decisions by New Jersey courts that arose from IWW activities in Paterson provide

[44] Commonwealth v. Karvonen, 219 Mass. 30, 31–32, 106 N.E. 556, 556–57 (1914).
[45] People v. Burman, 154 Mich. 150, 155–57, 117 N.W. 589, 591–92 (1908).
[46] State v. Hazeltine, 143 P. 436, 440 (1914).
[47] In re Shortridge, 34 P. 227, 229 (1893).

the best examples. The New Jersey Supreme Court refused to hold Wobbly leader Big Bill Haywood responsible for the crowd he attracted,[48] and another New Jersey decision, in contrast to the U.S. Supreme Court in the *Turner* case, cited constitutional considerations in refusing to apply a state statute passed during the "feverish and political excitement" following the McKinley assassination to an article expressing philosophical anarchism "in hot and intemperate language."[49]

Moreover, one important judge criticized the reliance on bad tendency as the test for obscenity even though he felt compelled by precedent to apply this approach. In a 1913 decision, *United States v. Kennerley,* Judge Learned Hand characterized *Hicklin* as an anachronistic example of "mid-Victorian morals." Hand believed that anything "which is honestly relevant to the adequate expression of innocent ideas" should not be judged obscene, no matter what language that expression takes. Assuming that this "abstract definition" would not be adopted, Hand argued in the alternative that a community standard of obscenity, defined on a case-by-case basis by jurors, would be a major improvement over *Hicklin.* According to Hand, the *Hicklin* bad tendency test forced society "to accept for its own limitations those which may perhaps be necessary to the weakest of its members." Allowing jurors to define "the average conscience of the time" would be "perhaps tolerable."[50] Hand never mentioned the First Amendment in *Kennerley,* but this decision, like his later opinion construing the Espionage Act in *Masses Publishing Co. v. Patten,* criticized the bad tendency test and favored significantly more protection for speech than analogous cases decided by his contemporaries.

TOPICAL ANALYSIS OF FREE SPEECH ISSUES

The widespread judicial reliance upon the bad tendency test between the Civil War and World War I did not preclude the development of more specific analysis of free speech issues in connection with various discrete topics. Many cases dealt with familiar categories of the common law, such as libel and contempt of court. Others arose from federal and state statutes that regulated areas as disparate as mail delivery and political campaigns. Labor unrest generated free speech cases over public speaking and the growing

[48] Haywood v. Ryan, 85 N.J.L. 116, 88 A. 820 (1913).
[49] Scott v. State, 86 N.J.L. 133, 136, 139, 90 A. 235, 236–37 (1914), discussed supra, Chapter 2, at text accomaning notes 204–5.
[50] United States v. Kennerley, 209 F. 119, 120–21 (S.D.N.Y. 1913).

use of the injunction to restrain union activities. Moreover, in cases ranging from film censorship to commercial advertising, judges, and sometimes even counsel for the parties, ignored what today would be recognized as obvious free speech issues. On the other hand, federal courts occasionally addressed free speech issues that arose from state action without resolving the logically preliminary question of whether the First Amendment's prohibitions against Congress extended to the states through the Fourteenth Amendment.

THE FIRST AMENDMENT AND STATE ACTION

The Supreme Court did not explicitly apply the First Amendment to the states until its 1925 decision in *Gitlow v. New York*,[51] when it included free speech as one of the liberties protected against state action by the Fourteenth Amendment. The potential relationship between the First and Fourteenth Amendments, however, began to generate substantial litigation soon after the ratification of the Fourteenth Amendment in 1868. Before the Supreme Court addressed this issue, a fascinating lower federal court decision in 1871 took an interpretive path that the Supreme Court soon rejected. In *United States v. Hall*, a federal judge in Alabama sustained the indictments, under the federal Enforcement Act of 1870, of a mob of whites for unlawfully conspiring against a political meeting of black Republicans with intent to violate the rights of free speech and assembly. Judge William Woods, who subsequently served on the U.S. Supreme Court from 1881 to 1887, held that the Fourteenth Amendment extended First Amendment prohibitions against the states by providing that no state "shall abridge the privileges or immunities of citizens of the United States." According to Woods, these privileges included "the right of freedom of speech, and the right peaceably to assemble." In addition, Woods maintained, the Fourteenth Amendment empowered Congress to legislate if states failed to safeguard these rights from abridgment even by private parties.[52]

Three years later, the Supreme Court reached a different result in another case brought under the Enforcement Act of 1870. The federal government alleged a conspiracy to deprive citizens "of African descent and persons of color" of the lawful right to peaceable assembly. In *Cruikshank v. United States*, the Court acknowledged that the Fourteenth Amendment prevented "an encroach-

---

[51] 268 U.S. 652 (1925).
[52] United States v. Hall, 26 F. Cas. 79, 81 (C.C.S.D. Ala. 1871) (No. 15, 282).

ment by the States upon the fundamental rights which belong to every citizen as a member of society." Yet contrary to *Hall*, the Court held that the Fourteenth Amendment added "nothing to the rights of one citizen as against another." The Court never specified whether the First Amendment contains "fundamental rights" protected by the Fourteenth Amendment against state encroachment, although it did assert that the very idea of a republican form of government "implies a right on the part of its citizens to meet peaceably for consultation in respect to public opinion and to petition for a redress of grievances." The decision in *Cruikshank* thus suggested the possibility that the Fourteenth Amendment protected First Amendment freedoms against state action. Purely as a matter of First Amendment interpretation, the Court in *Cruikshank* indicated that citizens have a constitutional right, perhaps protected even against private abridgment, to assemble to petition Congress about matters "connected with the powers or the duties of the national government." The Court emphasized, however, that freedom to participate in a "meeting for any lawful purpose whatever" did not qualify for the same protection.[53]

The Haymarket anarchists raised similar issues in 1887. In *Spies v. Illinois,* they asserted that the "fundamental rights" protected against federal power by the Bill of Rights are "privileges and immunities" of citizens of the United States "that cannot now be abridged by a State under the Fourteenth Amendment." According to the anarchists, the state of Illinois, by convicting them for "mere general advice" intended to change the existing social order, had unconstitutionally violated their right to free speech.[54] The Supreme Court, however, did not address these contentions while dismissing the anarchists' petition for a writ of error.

By contrast, as *Patterson* and *Fox* illustrate, the Supreme Court occasionally analyzed free speech issues arising from state action without initially resolving the relationship between the First and Fourteenth Amendments. Holmes, in *Patterson,* explicitly left "undecided the question whether there is to be found in the Fourteenth Amendment a prohibition similar to that in the First." He immediately added, however, that "even if we were to assume that freedom of speech and freedom of the press were protected from abridgment on the part not only of the United States but also of the States," Patterson's constitutional argument would fail.[55] In addition to disagreeing with Holmes's equation of the First Amend-

---

[53] United States v. Cruikshank, 92 U.S. 542, 544, 552–54 (1875).

[54] Spies v. Illinois, 123 U.S. 131, 139, 166 (1887).

[55] 205 U.S. at 462.

ment with Blackstone, Justice Harlan in dissent asserted that the Fourteenth Amendment applies the First Amendment to the states. Citing *Cruikshank*, Harlan maintained that First Amendment rights are "attributes of national citizenship" protected against violation by the states under the "privileges or immunities" clause of the Fourteenth Amendment. He added that free speech constitutes part of the liberty secured against state action by the Fourteenth Amendment.[56] Justice Harlan dissented alone. But other Supreme Court majority decisions, tacitly assuming jurisdiction without discussing the Fourteenth Amendment, addressed and rejected claims that states had deprived citizens of free speech.

POSTAL REGULATION

Litigation over federal postal regulation continued after the 1877 decision in *Ex parte Jackson*,[57] when the Supreme Court rejected the First Amendment attack on federal legislation that excluded lottery advertisements from the mail and indicated that the exclusion of obscene publications by the Comstock Act would similarly survive a First Amendment challenge. A case brought fifteen years later against newspapers containing lottery advertisements, *In re Rapier*, prompted James C. Carter, counsel for one of the petitioners, essentially to relitigate *Ex parte Jackson*. Carter mistakenly suggested that First Amendment issues had been inadequately presented in the earlier case.[58] In fact, Lewis F. Post had opposed the lottery statute in *Ex parte Jackson* by cleverly stressing the key historical precedent from 1836, the congressional refusal on First Amendment grounds to exclude material on slavery from the mail.[59] The Supreme Court, not counsel, had ignored the First Amendment in *Ex parte Jackson*, but Carter probably made the strategic decision to deflect responsibility from the Court while seeking a different result. Carter maintained that the First Amendment only excepted from its protection speech previously defined by the law of libel in England and the colonies.[60] Hannis Taylor, counsel for another petitioner in the case, warned that the rationale used in *Ex parte Jackson* would permit Congress to act as "official censor of public morals." A political party in control of government, Taylor argued, could "resolve to silence the journals of its adversaries" by enacting a law that "all utterances which dispute its

---

[56] Id. at 464–65.   [57] 96 U.S. 727 (1877).
[58] In re Rapier, 143 U.S. 110, 123 (1892).
[59] See supra text accompanying note 22.
[60] 143 U.S. at 120.

tenets and policy are *hostile to the public interests and morals,*" and therefore should be excluded from the mails.[61]

The government's brief responded that the First Amendment, like all constitutional provisions, "is subordinate to the great leading purposes for which the Constitution was ordained," including "the promotion of the general welfare." The federal statute excluding lotteries from the mail, the brief maintained, was a legitimate exercise of the legislative "police powers" to determine what laws are needed to protect public health, safety, and morals.[62] The Supreme Court agreed while substantially reiterating its prior approach from *Ex parte Jackson.* In language that tracked the government's brief and gave an elliptical response to Taylor, Chief Justice Fuller concluded his opinion with the statement that the danger of abuse of power "furnishes no grounds for a denial of its existence, if government is to be maintained at all."[63]

On occasion, however, the Supreme Court overruled decisions to confiscate mail. In an 1896 decision, *Swearingen v. United States,* a closely divided Court held that a newspaper article attacking populists did not constitute obscenity. The article's reference to "the red headed mental and physical bastard that flings filth under another man's name," the majority conceded, "is exceedingly coarse and vulgar, and, as applied to an individual person, plainly libelous." The majority emphasized, however, that the word *obscene* relates to "sexual impurity," and it found nothing in the article "calculated to corrupt and debauch the mind and morals of those into whose hands it might fall."[64]

Six years later, in *American School of Magnetic Healing v. McAnnulty,* the Court held that the Postmaster General acted unlawfully in refusing to deliver payments mailed to a business selling Christian Science treatments. The Court rejected the Postmaster General's determination that Christian Science is fraudulent by definition. Noting that "[e]ven intelligent people" differ as to the influence of the mind on the body, the Court reasoned that "[t]here is no exact standard of absolute truth" by which to judge the claims of Christian Scientists. Since the statute dealing with fraudulent use of the mails was not directed at "mere matters of opinion upon subjects which are not capable of proof as to their falsity," the Court held that the Postmaster General had violated the law.[65] *Swearingen* and *Magnetic*

---

[61] Argument of Hannis Taylor upon a Petition for Writs of *Habeas Corpus* and *Certiorari* at 48, 49.

[62] 143 U.S. at 131–32.   [63] Id. at 135.

[64] Swearingen v. United States, 161 U.S. 446, 447 n.1, 451 (1896).

[65] American School of Magnetic Healing v. McAnnulty, 187 U.S. 94, 104 (1902).

Healing indicated that there could be some limits to federal censorship of ideas, although neither opinion referred to the First Amendment. The Court, however, was not similarly solicitous of differences of opinion in more controversial settings. *Ex parte Jackson, In re Rapier,* and subsequent cases gave judicial approval to federal censorship over the mails. Legislation initially excluded lotteries and obscene material, but in 1917 the Espionage Act added treasonable and seditious language to the list of prohibited subject matter.[66]

Lewis Publishing Co. v. Morgan presented the Court with related issues. Congress historically had provided lower postal rates to newspapers and magazines in order to encourage "the dissemination of current intelligence."[67] As a condition for these rates, a 1912 statute required newspapers and magazines to label paid advertisements and to furnish information regarding ownership, managerial and editorial personnel, and circulation. Appellants attacked this statute as unconstitutional on First Amendment grounds. They claimed that the First Amendment prohibits all restrictions on the press "either by anticipation through a licensing system or retrospectively by obstruction or punishment," except in matters of "recognized morality" and common-law libel.[68] If the Court upheld this statute, one of the briefs asserted, Congress could also deny mailing privileges or impose severe penalties "with respect to any newspapers owned or financially influenced by individuals advocating certain public questions or the policies of political parties." Although the brief writer assumed that "no one would attempt to uphold the right of Congress to so legislate,[69] the solicitor general proved him wrong. The government's brief maintained that if views held by the owner, including political theories, "*are expressed in the paper* Congress can doubtless exclude them, just as Congress could now exclude all papers advocating lotteries, prohibition, anarchy, or a protective tariff if a majority of Congress thought such views against public policy."[70]

The Supreme Court rejected the publishers' arguments against the statute. The same interest in "the dissemination of knowledge of current events" that had prompted Congress to establish lower rates for second-class mail, the Court observed, justified the new requirement to disclose the financial interests that might influ-

[66] Act of June 15, 1917, ch. 30, tit. 12, sections 1, 2, 40 Stat. 217.
[67] Lewis Publishing Co. v. Morgan, 229 U.S. 288, 302 (1913).
[68] 229 U.S. at 292; see Brief for Appellant, Lewis Publishing Company at 32–36.
[69] Brief of Counsel for Appellant, The Journal of Commerce and Commercial Bulletin at 38–39, Journal of Commerce & Commercial Bulletin v. Burleson, 229 U.S. 288 (1913) (brief submitted in case consolidated with *Lewis Publishing Co.*).
[70] Brief for the United States at 46–47.

ence the reporting of news. Because the low postal rates gave newspapers an "influence unequaled in history," the Court reasoned, the public had the right to know this information. The Court emphasized that its decision did not involve "any general regulation of what should be published in newspapers" or any absolute exclusion from the mails, but only the conditions for a publisher "to continue to enjoy privileges and advantages at the public expense." Implicitly rejecting the position of the solicitor general, the opinion concluded by making clear that "we do not wish even by the remotest implication to be regarded as assenting to the broad contentions concerning the existence of arbitrary power through the classification of the mails."[71]

Later decisions under the Espionage Act, however, substantiated the concern that Congress might deny lower rates to punish newspapers publishing unpopular political views. Postmaster General Burleson revoked the second-class rates for the *Milwaukee Leader* in 1917 because, in his opinion, strongly antiwar articles in that newspaper violated the recently passed Espionage Act. The Supreme Court upheld his action in 1921, provoking a lengthy dissent by Justice Brandeis and a separate dissent by Justice Holmes.[72] The *Milwaukee Leader* case incorporated *Lewis Publishing Company* into the line of decisions, inaugurated by *Ex parte Jackson*, that used the content of a publication as the basis for restricting access to the federal mails.

REGULATION OF POLITICAL CAMPAIGNS

Statutory regulation of political campaigns provided another fertile source of controversies over free speech. The Supreme Court's 1882 decision in *Ex parte Curtis* upheld the constitutionality of a federal statute forbidding employees of the United States to solicit or receive from each other money or property for political purposes. The petitioner protested that the statute, "under the banner of 'reform!'," gave a "deadly stroke" to the freedom of expression protected by the First Amendment. "[F]reedom of speech and of the press is *abridged*," he contended, "if every citizen cannot, *at will*, contribute to cause the speech to be made, in a suitable place; and, when made, that it may be disseminated, to accomplish the 'political purpose' for which it is intended." Although the government's brief dismissed this claim as unworthy of serious attention, the petitioner could not

---

[71] 229 U.S. at 312, 315–16.
[72] United States ex rel. Milwaukee Social Democratic Publishing Co. v. Burleson, 255 U.S. 407 (1921).

imagine a "more secure blow at free discussion."[73] The majority of the Court, however, had no such difficulty. Without even referring to the First Amendment, it viewed the statute as simply a constitutionally legitimate means to the valid legislative ends of promoting efficiency, integrity, and discipline among public servants.[74]

Many lower court decisions reached similar results, but at least gave some attention to constitutional arguments. While still serving on the highest state court in Massachusetts in 1892, Holmes rejected constitutional objections to the dismissal of a police officer for violating a regulation that prohibited solicitation of money for political purposes. "The petitioner may have a constitutional right to talk politics," Holmes declared in one of his most famous epigrams, "but he has no constitutional right to be a policeman."[75] A federal district court in 1916 denied the assertion by the United States Brewers' Association that a federal law prohibiting campaign contributions by corporations violated First Amendment rights to free speech and a free press. The purpose of the statute, the court declared, "is to guard elections from corruption, and the electorate from corrupting influences in arriving at their choice." The court apparently felt that no further elaboration was necessary.[76] In 1910 the Supreme Court of Idaho upheld a statute that limited campaign expenditures to 15 percent of the salary for the office sought. Rejecting an attack based on the free speech provision of the state constitution, the court declared that the law "does not attempt to prevent a candidate from freely speaking, writing, and publishing his views on all subjects."[77]

By contrast, in other cases state courts held that election reform laws violated constitutional guarantees of free speech. The Supreme Court of Virginia invalidated a statute that prohibited a variety of public officials, including judges and educators, from making political speeches and from official involvement in political meetings. After an unsuccessful attempt to distinguish *Ex parte Curtis*, decided two years earlier, the court stressed that the state constitutional protection of free speech is "guaranteed to all the citizens of the state, not to any portion or any class of citizens." To deprive some citizens of free speech solely because they are public officials, the court held, is unconstitutional.[78]

---

[73] Brief for the Petitioner at 28–29; Brief for the Government at 12.
[74] Ex parte Curtis, 106 U.S. 371, 373 (1882).
[75] McAuliffe v. Mayor of New Bedford, 155 Mass. 216, 220, 29 N.E. 517, 517 (1892).
[76] United States v. United States Brewers' Ass'n, 239 F. 163, 169 (W.D. Pa. 1916).
[77] Adams v. Lansdon, 110 P. 280 (1910).
[78] Louthan v. Commonwealth, 79 Va. 196, 197, 204, 206 (1884).

The Supreme Court of Wisconsin invoked both the federal and the state constitutions while invalidating a corrupt practices act that placed severe limitations on spending for political purposes by persons other than candidates or members of a party committee. This decision protected the right of a private citizen to spend money "in investigating the governmental, political, and financial affairs of the state and communicating the results of his investigations" to the voters. "Almost every forward step in political and governmental affairs," the court concluded, "comes as the result of long agitation and discussion in the press, on the rostrum, and in the open forum of personal contact," often continuing "for years before the idea is formally endorsed by any party." Moreover, the court asserted, at times "devoted citizens firmly believe that no organized political party stands for the right or deserves support and that an independent candidacy is necessary." If the spending restrictions were not an abridgment of freedom of speech, the court concluded, "it would be difficult to imagine what would be."[79]

Relying on the state constitutional protection of speech, the Supreme Court of Missouri overturned a law that required all groups publishing reports or recommendations on candidates for public office to state the supporting facts and the names and addresses of all persons who furnished them. "If a publication is neither blasphemous, obscene, seditious or defamatory," the opinion held, "then under the Constitution of this State, no court has the right to restrain it, nor the Legislature power to punish it."[80] In another case that struck down a law that limited criticism of candidates for public office, the Supreme Court of Nebraska held that the state's "nonpartisan judiciary act" violated the free speech provision of its constitution. The act provided that candidates for various judicial and educational offices shall not be "nominated, endorsed, recommended, censured, criticized, or referred to by any political party." The court described political parties as "the great moving forces in the administration of public affairs" and held that "their influence in elections cannot be eliminated by the legislature as long as the right to assemble and speak the truth remains in the charter of our liberties." "Published criticisms of candidates, officers, and policies," the court added, "are potent factors in the struggle for civic virtue and cannot be suppressed by legislative enactment."[81] The state courts thus exhibited substantial

---

[79] State v. Pierce, 163 Wis. 615, 618–20, 158 N.W. 696, 697–98 (1916).
[80] Ex parte Harrison, 212 Mo. 88, 93, 110 S.W. 709, 710 (1908).
[81] State v. Junkin, 122 N.W. 473, 474 (1909).

diversity in addressing the tension between election reform legislation and the constitutional protection for free speech.

LIBEL AND CONTEMPT

The common law of libel and the related doctrine of contempt, like statutes regulating political campaigns, tested the constitutional protection for speech about public affairs. Cases frequently observed that the First Amendment and analogous state constitutional provisions did not preclude punishment for libel[82] or contempt.[83] The language of many state constitutions explicitly differentiated between the right of free speech and its abuse, a distinction often invoked in libel and contempt cases. The constitution of Washington state was typical: "Every person may freely speak, write, and publish on all subjects, being responsible for the abuse of that right."[84] Other decisions in libel and contempt cases relied on the analogous distinction between protected free speech and unprotected license.[85] The judges who decided these cases sometimes made a special point of emphasizing that the press has no greater right to freedom of expression than any individual member of the public.[86]

Many cases developed a distinction between protected criticism of public officials and libelous attacks on their character. For example, a decision by the Supreme Court of Maryland stressed the right of a citizen in a free country to criticize official conduct "boldly and fearlessly." The exercise of this right, the court observed, often provides the social benefit of uncovering "official abuse and corruption." The court, however, proceeded to highlight "a broad distinction between fair and legitimate discussion in regard to the conduct of a public man, and the imputation of corrupt motives, by which that conduct may be supposed to be governed." If a citizen "goes out of his way to asperse the personal character of a public man," the court warned, "and to ascribe to

---

[82] See, e.g., State v. Pape, 96 A. 313 (Sup. Ct. Err. Conn. 1916); Diener v. Star Chronicle Pub. Co., 132 S.W. 1143 (Sup. Ct. Mo. 1910).

[83] See, e.g., State v. Bee Pub. Co., 83 N.W. 204 (Sup. Ct. Neb. 1900); State v. Tugwell, 52 P. 1056 (Sup. Ct. Wash. 1898).

[84] See, e.g., State v. Hafner, 162 P. 45, 48 (Sup. Ct. Wash. 1916); State v. Tugwell, 52 P. 1056, 1058 (Sup. Ct. Wash. 1898).

[85] See, e.g., In re Shortridge, 34 P. 227, 230 (Sup. Ct. Calif. 1893) (contempt); State v. Pape, 96 A. 313, 315 (Sup. Ct. Err. Ct. 1916) (libel).

[86] See, e.g., Coleman v. MacLennan, 98 P. 281, 286 (Sup. Ct. Kan. 1908) (libel); Foster v. Scripps, 39 Mich. 376, 380 (1878) (libel); State v. Shepherd, 76 S.W. 79, 91 (Sup. Ct. Mo. 1903) (contempt).

him base and corrupt motives, he must do so at his peril; and must either prove the truth of what he says, or answer in damages to the party injured."[87] Using a similar approach, the highest court of New York emphasized that protected criticism included sarcasm and ridicule of official acts.[88] Elevating the rhetorical stakes, the Supreme Court of Missouri identified criticism of public officials regarding matters of public concern as the foundation of free government. "It is only in despotisms," the court observed, "that one must speak sub rosa, or in whispers, with bated breath, around the corner, or in the dark on a subject touching the common welfare." The court claimed that "the brightest jewel in the crown of the law" is "to seek and maintain the golden mean between defamation, on one hand, and a healthy and robust right of free public discussion, on the other."[89]

Although courts frequently assumed that the essential democratic right to criticize official conduct would be preserved by limiting the common law of libel to attacks on the character of public officials, the distinction between conduct and character often did not work in practice. Applying this distinction, many courts upheld libel convictions of people who had charged public officials with misconduct. For example, in the Maryland case the court affirmed the damages awarded to a Republican state senator accused by a newspaper article of changing his vote when he received a valuable contract through the auspices of the state Democratic party. The majority was not persuaded by the dissenting judge, who asserted that the senator's votes "were the proper subjects of the fullest and freest criticism among his constituents" and that the free press provision of the state constitution protected the allegedly libelous article.[90] The disagreement between the majority and the dissent about whether the attack on the senator constituted political criticism or an attack on his personal character underlined the general difficulty in making this distinction.

Similar cases did not even produce dissenting opinions. Charges that an inspector of the board of health received stock in a company he recommended for a city contract,[91] that a policeman had a criminal record,[92] and that a coroner had stolen prop-

---

[87] Negley v. Farrow, 60 Md. 158, 176–77 (1883); see also Neeb v. Hope, 2 A. 568, 571 (Sup. Ct. Pa. 1886); Williams Printing Co. v. Saunders, 73 S.E. 472, 478 (Va. Sup. Ct. App. 1912).

[88] Hamilton v. Eno, 81 N.Y. 116, 126–27 (1880).

[89] Diener v. Star Chronicle Pub. Co., 132 S.W. 1143, 1149 (1910).

[90] Negley v. Farrow, 60 Md. 158, 184 (1883).

[91] Hamilton v. Eno, 81 N.Y. 116 (1880).

[92] Post Pub. Co. v. Moloney, 33 N.E. 921 (Sup. Ct. Ohio 1893).

erty from deceased people while performing his official functions[93] all resulted in unanimous decisions upholding libel awards
for attacks on character. A rare decision, however, reached the
opposite result. The assertion in a newspaper article that a coroner had failed to investigate when the health commissioner's
chauffeur killed a child in a car accident, the court concluded, was
nothing more than "honest criticism."[94]

Contempt cases developed an analogous distinction between
protected criticism of judges and contemptuous language that
interfered with the administration of justice. Proclaiming that it
"would not for a moment sanction any contraction of freedom of
the press," the Supreme Court of Colorado asserted the right of
every citizen to criticize the fitness of candidates for judicial office,
their fidelity to duty once elected, and the soundness of their decisions. The court added, however, that "the right to attempt, by
wanton defamation, to prejudice the rights of litigants in a pending case, degrade the tribunal, and impede, embarrass, or corrupt
that due administration of justice which is so essential to good government, cannot be sanctioned."[95] Similarly, the Supreme Court
of Idaho, while welcoming the "freest criticism of all decisions of
the court," warned that "criticism ceases and contempt begins
when malicious slander, vilification, and defamation bring the
courts and the administration of the law into dishonor and disre-
pute among the people."[96] Somewhat more specifically, the
Supreme Court of California maintained that the constitutional
liberty of the press does not give a newspaper a "right to assail litigants during the progress of a trial, intimidate witnesses, dictate
verdicts or judgments, or spread before juries its opinions of the
merits of cases which are on trial."[97] Nor could a newspaper
attempt to affect the judgment of a court in a pending case.[98]

The attempt to differentiate protected criticism worked no better for contempt than it did for libel. As in the *Patterson* case, courts
found it easy to respond to journalistic attacks on judicial neutrality
by holding newspapers in contempt. For example, almost two
decades before *Patterson* the Supreme Court of Colorado affirmed
the contempt conviction of a newspaper that had criticized a judge
for committing "a judicial outrage" by granting a writ of habeas cor-

---

[93] Neeb v. Hope, 2 A. 568 (Penn. Sup. Ct. 1886).
[94] Diener v. Star Chronicle Pub. Co., 132 S.W. 1143 (Sup. Ct. Mo. 1910).
[95] Cooper v. People, 22 P. 790, 799–800 (1889).
[96] McDougall v. Sheridan, 128 P. 954, 966 (1913).
[97] In re Shortridge, 34 P. 227, 230 (1893).
[98] State v. Bee Pub. Co., 83 N.W. 204, 206 (Sup. Ct. Neb. 1900).

pus despite precedents to the contrary. A concurring judge would have allowed the paper to criticize the issuance of the writ "in temperate and respectful language," but he stressed that a paper had no right during pending proceedings "to subject the judge to ridicule, or to make insinuations against his good faith."[99] According to the Supreme Court of Nebraska, a newspaper article asserting that state judges had decided cases in a politically partisan manner, and had even given advance notice of decisions to political allies, constituted a contemptuous attempt to influence pending cases. The court stressed that in reaching this decision it had, "of course, no desire to restrain, in the slightest degree, the freedom of the press."[100] Accusations by a newspaper that judges of the state supreme court decided a case "by reason of a political trade or bargain, and not on the law and facts" convinced those judges to fine and imprison the publisher and editor for contempt. The failure of the defendants to publish the text of the decision they criticized demonstrated their maliciousness to the court.[101]

Other contempt cases emphasized that the fundamental issue was not free speech or a free press, but the right of litigants to a fair trial[102] or maintained that the right to a fair trial outweighed expressive rights. Acknowledging that the right of free speech is sacred, the Supreme Court of North Dakota observed that even a sacred right "must give way to others, even more sacred." Just as the right of free speech does not protect interruption of political meetings or obstruction of the street, the court reasoned, it does not allow interference with "the rights of other men to unhampered justice."[103] The constitutional requirement of maintaining the courts as a coordinate branch of government, which could be undermined by improper attacks, provided another justification for the contempt power.[104]

By contrast, some courts relied on the constitutional protection of free speech to reverse contempt convictions. Citing the First Amendment and the state constitution, the Supreme Court of Wisconsin overruled a judge who, while running for reelection, had held a critic of his judicial record in contempt. The court held that the judge could bring an action for libel, but that sustaining the contempt power in these circumstances would "gag the press,

[99] Cooper v. People, 22 P. 790, 792, 801 (1889).
[100] State v. Bee Pub. Co., 83 N.W. 204, 206 (1900).
[101] McDougall v. Sheridan, 128 P. 954, 966 (Sup. Ct. Idaho 1913).
[102] See, e.g., State v. Rosewater, 83 N.W. 353 (Sup. Ct. Neb. 1900); State v. Tugwell, 52 P. 1056, 1061 (Sup. Ct. Wash. 1898).
[103] State v. Nelson, 150 N.W. 267, 269 (Sup. Ct. N.D. 1914).
[104] McDougall v. Sheridan, 128 P. 954, 966 (Sup. Ct. Idaho 1913).

and subvert freedom of speech." In passing, the court found Blackstone's interpretation of constructive contempt, which prohibited "the mere writing contemptuously of a superior court or judge," inconsistent with the free speech clause of the state constitution.[105] Emphasizing the fundamental incompatibility of prior restraints with constitutional protection for free speech, the Supreme Court of California reversed a lower court order that prohibited performances and advertisements of a play based on a pending murder trial. The publicity from the play, the lower court believed, would constitute a contempt by interfering with a fair trial. Conceding the validity of this concern, the state supreme court nevertheless held that an order not to commit a contempt was precisely the type of censorship prohibited by the state constitution. The judge hearing the murder trial, the higher court reasoned, could protect "the administration of justice after the contempt was committed" by granting a new trial.[106]

While reconciling the constitutional protection for speech with the common law of libel and contempt, many American courts, in contrast to Holmes in *Patterson*, differentiated the American common law from its English predecessor. Even courts that relied on Blackstone's bad tendency theory frequently departed from his rejection of truth as a defense in libel actions. Several courts emphasized that the English common law as summarized by Blackstone in the eighteenth century should not define the common law in American states over one hundred years later. The Supreme Court of California pointedly observed that Blackstone had synthesized precedents "promulgated at a time when ministers of the crown claimed and exercised the right to seize a newspaper, and stifle the voice of its editor," and "when books were destroyed and speeches suppressed" for "political purposes." The framers of American federal and state constitutions provided explicit guarantees for free speech and a free press, the court stressed, precisely to prevent such actions in the United States.[107] Without explicitly mentioning Blackstone, the Supreme Court of Washington similarly attributed the American constitutional protections for freedom of expression to the perceived inability of the previous English common law to safeguard the discussion of public affairs necessary in a democracy. In the aftermath of the American Revolution, the court added, statutes in virtually all states abrogated the

---

[105] State ex rel. Attorney General v. Circuit Court, 97 Wis. 1, 12, 72 N.W. 193, 193, 196 (1897) (citing 4 Blackstone Comm. 285).

[106] Dailey v. Superior Court, 112 Cal. 94, 99–100, 44 P. 458, 460 (1896).

[107] In re Shortridge, 34 P. 227, 230 (1893).

"arbitrary" English common law of libel and provided that the
truth of a publication could be introduced by the defense.[108]

A Virginia court expressed the typical American approach,
holding that the defendant "must stand prepared to prove the
truth of his statement under a plea of justification; otherwise the
presumption is that the defamatory language, written or spoken, is
false and will, without more, support a verdict for substantial damages."[109] While still a federal circuit court judge, William Howard
Taft provided an explanation for the majority rule. According to
Taft, "the danger that honorable and worthy men may be driven
from politics and public service by allowing too great latitude in
attacks upon their characters outweighs any benefit that might
occasionally accrue to the public from charges of corruption that
are true in fact, but are incapable of legal proof." Taft added that
the "freedom of the press is not in danger from the enforcement
of the rule we uphold," but he did not elaborate his reasoning.[110]

A number of important decisions, however, questioned the prevailing approach and argued for interpretations of libel law that
would protect more speech about public concerns. The most significant challenge came from Thomas M. Cooley, a justice on the
Supreme Court of Michigan and the author of *Constitutional Limitations,* the leading treatise on American constitutional law.[111] Cooley presented his most complete judicial analysis of libel law while
dissenting in *Atkinson v. Detroit Free Press Co.,* an 1881 decision that
upheld a libel award against a newspaper. The offending article
alleged financial improprieties by a member of the Detroit board
of trade. Cooley criticized the majority for holding the newspaper
"responsible for every injurious deduction that can legitimately be
drawn from the article" and for insisting that every justification by
the newspaper "be made out with a literalness and strictness such
as is demanded in the criminal law to convict one of a felony." He
maintained instead that a qualified privilege should protect publications about matters of public concern motivated by a desire "to
bring about a reform of abuses, or to defeat the re-election or re-
appointment of an incompetent officer." The privilege should be

---

[108] State v. Tugwell, 52 P. 1056, 1060 (1898).
[109] Williams Printing Co. v. Saunders, 73 S.E. 472, 478 (Va. Sup. Ct. App. 1912);
see also State v. Pape, 96 A. 313, 316 (Sup. Ct. Err. Conn. 1916); Hamilton v.
Eno, 81 N.Y. 116, 126–27 (1880).
[110] Post Publishing Co. v. Hallam, 59 F. 530, 541 (6th Cir. 1893).
[111] Norman L. Rosenberg, Protecting the Best Men: An Interpretive History of the
Law of Libel 161–89 (1986), contains an excellent, detailed discussion of Cooley's views about libel law. I find more consistency in Cooley's views over time
than does Rosenberg.

overcome, he asserted, only if the plaintiff proves malice. According to Cooley, malice exists "if one publishes as true what he knows to be false, or what by proper investigation he might have assured himself was false."[112]

Cooley protested that the standard of proof imposed by the majority would make "any attempt at public discussion practically worthless." He doubted that anyone would expose a swindler or a blackmailer, or expose corporate misconduct, "if every word and sentence must be uttered with judicial calmness and impartiality" and every fact and inference "be justified by unobjectionable legal evidence." Cooley was so outraged by the majority position that he preferred the restoration of despotic censorship to the granting of "a liberty which can only be accepted under a responsibility that is always threatening and may at times be ruinous."[113]

In developing his argument for a privilege, Cooley stressed that he was following a more general analysis of rights. Whenever rights are exercised, he observed, "incidental injuries" inevitably occur. "If the law should require every man to indemnify others from all injuries resulting from his doing those acts which are his lawful right," Cooley reasoned, "it would by this very penalty strip him of some which are most important and vital, by rendering them practically valueless." Instead, the law allows the exercise of rights "with due regard to the corresponding and coincident rights of others," and imposes liability if a person "causes injury through malice or negligence, but not otherwise." This principle, Cooley stressed, "is as true of the right to free speech as it is of the right to the free enjoyment of one's property." In addition to this rare judicial equation of individual rights to speech and property, Cooley made the more specific point that in libel cases involving matters of public concern "the public interest is paramount to that of individuals." Conceding that under his approach "a person whose character and actions are impugned may suffer without remedy when in fact he is free from blame," Cooley maintained that this regrettable injury to reputation must be tolerated as an "incidental" byproduct of the socially valuable right of individual free expression.[114]

Two other opinions by Cooley indicated the limits of his proposed privilege. Concurring in a case decided three years earlier, Cooley maintained that not all publications about matters of public concern should be entitled to a qualified privilege. He advocated balancing "the public benefits of free discussion" against the

---

[112] Atkinson v. Detroit Free Press Co., 9 N.W. 501, 520–21, 523–24 (1881).
[113] Id. at 521, 524.   [114] Id. at 520.

"individual injury" to the person defamed. Evaluating an article that charged a city physician with gross professional misconduct resulting in the death of a child, Cooley distinguished candidates for official positions from incumbents. He reasoned that the accusation against the physician, in addition to causing him "grievous private injury," created "serious public injury" by undermining confidence in an important official. The combination of public and private injuries in this case, Cooley concluded, outweighed the admitted public benefit that could result if the accusation prompted the removal of an unfit city physician. Emphasizing that his concurrence was confined "to the exact case before us," Cooley made clear that the same charge against a candidate for city physician would have prompted him to reach a different result. The danger to the public interest would not have existed, and the public benefit from the publication would have outweighed the private injury to the physician.[115]

The year after his dissent in *Atkinson*, Cooley convinced the Supreme Court of Michigan to accept a qualified privilege for libel while refining its scope. The court reviewed a libel award against a newspaper that had criticized a police justice for unfairly jailing a "Chinaman" who had not been charged with a crime and for setting unreasonably high bail. The newspaper called the actions of the police justice "inexcusable," "contemptible," and "cowardly." Claiming that the newspaper article was based on unsupportable assertions rather than on underlying facts, the trial court awarded damages to the police justice. In his opinion for the majority of the state supreme court, Cooley relied on his dissent in *Atkinson* to reverse the libel award and did not even address the trial court's distinction between assertions and facts. Cooley stressed the qualified privilege to criticize the administration of justice regarding a matter "which concerns every member of the political community," but he made clear that matters of public concern did not extend to "merely private gossip and scandal."[116]

The facts of the cases Cooley decided prompted him to focus his criticism of prevailing law on the rule that defendants in libel actions had the burden of proving the literal truth of all potentially defamatory statements. Although Cooley suggested in his *Atkinson* dissent that a qualified privilege should extend even to actual defamatory falsehoods made in good faith, the most sustained defense of this position appeared in an exceptionally thorough opinion by the Supreme Court of Kansas in the 1908 case,

---

[115] Foster v. Scripps, 39 Mich. 376, 383–84 (1878).
[116] Miner v. Post & Tribune Co., 13 N.W. 773, 774–76 (1882).

Coleman v. MacLennan. In a thoughtful historical discussion, the court recognized that the relationship between the First Amendment and the law of defamation had not been clarified and that "judicial decisions had often been narrow, illiberal and confusing." It cited the "ill-starred" Sedition Act of 1798 as an example of "how far ideas relating to the protection of personal character and governmental institutions were then unreconciled in legal theory with freedom of thought and expression upon public questions." As a result, the court considered it necessary to take into account "the needs and the will of society at the present time" in deciding cases involving liberty of the press.[117]

Following this approach, the court in *MacLennan* rejected the claim by the state attorney general that an article published during his reelection campaign libeled him while criticizing his role in a school fund transaction for which he had official responsibility. The attorney general had relied heavily on Judge Taft's statement that honorable people would be driven from political life if they could not recover for statements "that are true in fact, but are incapable of legal proof." The Supreme Court of Kansas believed that Taft's assertion lacked empirical support even in the more serious context of actual falsity. In those jurisdictions that allowed a privilege for defamatory falsehoods made without malice, the court observed, many honorable people still ran for political office.[118]

On a more theoretical level, the court concluded that a democratic government requires the "freedom to canvass in good faith the worth of character and qualifications of candidates for office." While recognizing that "at times, the injury to the reputations of individuals might be great," it held that a privilege for defamation in good faith appropriately balanced "public need and private right" and best served the combined interests of individuals, the press, and the public. As a general principle, the court added, the "history of all liberty, religious, political, and economic, teaches that undue restrictions merely excite and inflame, and that social progress is best facilitated, the social welfare is best preserved, and social justice is best promoted in presence of the least necessary restraint."[119]

As the Supreme Court of Kansas conceded, most states did not recognize a privilege for false statements about public officials or events, even if "made in good faith, without malice and under the honest belief that they are true."[120] Oliver Wendell Holmes con-

---

[117] Coleman v. MacLennan, 78 Kan. 711, 716–18, 98 P. 281, 283 (1908).
[118] Id. at 288–89.   [119] Id. at 285–86, 292.
[120] Id. at 286.

tributed to this approach while still on the highest Massachusetts court in his 1891 decision, *Burt v. Advertiser Newspaper Co.* Holmes distinguished in *Burt* between the "privilege of fair criticism upon matters of public interest" and statements about them, which are not privileged if false. Holmes found that allegations of fraud in the New York custom house constituted statements of fact, but he ordered a new trial to provide the defendant an opportunity to prove their truth.[121] The court in *MacLennan,* claiming that the "distinction between comment and statements of fact cannot always be clear to the mind," protested that it in effect tells a newspaper "you have full liberty of free discussion, provided, however, you say nothing that counts."[122] Even while disagreeing with the majority of jurisdictions about privilege in libel, however, *MacLennan* specifically approved restrictions on speech in other contexts, including the punishment of Johann Most following the McKinley assassination and of newspapers reporting scandal, criminal news, and immoral conduct.[123]

Libel and contempt cases rarely reached the Supreme Court. The Court explicitly addressed the relationship between the First Amendment and the common law of libel and contempt only in the *Patterson* case. In two other decisions, however, it reinforced the indication by Holmes in *Patterson* that the First Amendment offered no more protection to speech than had the prior common law of England. *Robertson v. Baldwin,* a case decided under the Thirteenth Amendment in 1897, declared that the Bill of Rights did not set forth "any novel principles of government," but simply embodied "certain guaranties and immunities which we had inherited from our English ancestors, and which had from time immemorial been subject to certain well-recognized exceptions arising from the necessities of the case." The exceptions "continued to be recognized as if they had been formally expressed." To illustrate this point, the Court stated that free speech did not "permit the publication of libels, blasphemous or indecent articles, or other publications injurious to public morals or private reputation."[124]

United States v. Press Publishing Co. is consistent with the *Robertson* dicta. The case arose when Joseph Pulitzer's New York *World* published a series of articles claiming that President Theodore Roosevelt had misled the American people by acquiring the Panama Canal for an inflated price that secretly benefited his friends. In a special message to Congress in 1908, Roosevelt called the articles

---

[121] Burt v. Advertiser Newspaper Co., 154 Mass. 238, 242, 28 N.E. 1, 4 (1891).
[122] 98 P. at 290–91.   [123] Id. at 284.
[124] Robertson v. Baldwin, 165 U.S. 275, 281 (1897).

"scurrilous and libelous in character and false in every particular."
According to Roosevelt, Pulitzer's libels extended beyond individuals and included the United States government. Because "the great injury done is in blackening the good name of the American people," Roosevelt maintained, Pulitzer "should be prosecuted for libel by the governmental authorities."[125]

Prosecuting this case posed difficulties for the federal government because the Supreme Court had abolished federal common law in criminal cases in 1812 and no federal statute prohibited criminal libel. The government based its case on the federal "assimilative act," which made state law applicable to federal reservations within a state. Claiming that these articles had been circulated at West Point and the Post Office Building in New York City, both federal reservations, the government attempted to apply the New York criminal libel statute through the assimilative act. After the government obtained an indictment, the publisher moved to quash on the ground that a trial would "abridge the liberty of speech and of the press" and create an atmosphere in which "no owner or editor of a paper could with safety freely discuss public affairs." Sustaining the indictment, the publisher argued, would give the federal government power "to prosecute any publisher who had attacked the government, or the character of government officials, by criticizing their public acts."[126]

The Supreme Court denied the applicability of the assimilative act and quashed the indictment without reaching the First Amendment issues raised by the publisher. By concluding that state law would provide "adequate means" for punishing the alleged libel, however, the Court hinted that a state conviction for criminal libel would not violate the federal Constitution.[127] Thus, the Court suggested that the common-law crime of libel, possibly including seditious libel, survived the ratification of the First Amendment.

REGULATION OF PUBLIC SPEAKING

Other controversies over free speech arose out of attempts to regulate public speaking. More than a decade before the IWW free speech fights publicized this issue, a Boston minister, William F. Davis, brought the case that presented the constitutional status of

---

[125] Clyde Peirce, The Roosevelt Panama Libel Case: A Factual Study of a Controversial Episode in the Career of Teddy Roosevelt, Father of the Panama Canal 77 (1959).

[126] Brief for the Defendant in Error at 11, 23.

[127] United States v. Press Publishing Co., 219 U.S. 1, 15 (1911).

public speaking to the Supreme Court. Arrested on the Boston Commons under a city ordinance that prohibited public addresses "in or upon any of the public grounds . . . except in accordance with a permit from the mayor,"[128] Davis asserted that the ordinance established an unjustified censorship and "violate[d] the rights of free public speech, of free assembly, and of free public religious worship." He maintained that the city's justifications for the ordinance, the dangers of breaches of the peace and damage to the public grounds, were "most improbable and *never threatened.*" Davis also objected to the mayor's "Pontifical and Princely Power to *Dispense with* the prohibition."[129] He alleged that the municipal authorities, contrary to the equal protection clause of the Fourteenth Amendment, enforced the ordinance solely against preachers of the gospel and ignored the many other men in public life who had given speeches on the common without obtaining a permit. In support of his equal protection claim, Davis cited cases that permitted parades by the Salvation Army. Emphasizing that the Supreme Court had construed the Fourteenth Amendment to protect Chinese immigrants from discriminatory municipal ordinances, Davis asserted that, as an American citizen and a preacher of the gospel, he should also receive the benefit of equal protection.[130]

The attorney general of Massachusetts responded to Davis by maintaining that the First Amendment protects "freedom as to substance, rather than as to place" and by denying that the ordinance was administered unjustly.[131] The Supreme Court used similar reasoning to sustain the ordinance without even addressing Davis's constitutional claims. After denying as empirically inaccurate his assertion that people had preached the gospel on Boston Common "from time immemorial," the Court, like the most restrictive nonjudicial reactions to the IWW free speech fights, simply denied any right to speak in public. To make this point, the Court repeated verbatim the key sentence from the decision in this case by the Supreme Judicial Court of Massachusetts, which was written by Holmes while he served on that court. "For the legislature absolutely or conditionally to forbid public speaking in a highway or public park," Holmes proclaimed, "is no more an infringement of the rights of a member of the public than for the owner of a private house to forbid it in his house." The Supreme Court added that the mayor's power to exclude anyone from pub-

---

[128] Davis v. Massachusetts, 167 U.S. 43, 44 (1897).
[129] Brief for Plaintiff in Error, at 4, 43, 45.
[130] Id. at 19, 55–61.   [131] Brief of Defendant in Error at 10.

lic grounds necessarily included the lesser power to issue permits for their use.[132]

A broader array of lower court cases commented on the right to speak in public. Organized efforts by the Salvation Army and the Socialist Party to convey their very different messages prompted many of these cases before the IWW free speech fights made the issue a major topic of national debate.[133] In contrast to the Supreme Court in *Davis,* some lower court decisions, like opinions in California and Washington during the IWW free speech fights, at least addressed assertions of constitutional rights to free speech while upholding restrictions on public speaking. Sustaining the conviction of a socialist professor for deliberately speaking without a permit required by local ordinance, the Supreme Court of Georgia pointed out that the "primary object of streets is for public passage" and that a "man has many constitutional and legal rights which he can not lawfully exercise in the streets of a city." The court observed that the "constitutional right to exercise one's lawful vocation is quite as sacred and often more important than the right to make speeches, but the exercise of either right must yield to the municipal power properly exercised over the streets." Neither the First Amendment nor the free speech clause of the state constitution, the court concluded, "confers any constitutional right to gather crowds and make public orations in the streets of a city regardless of the municipal control over them." Throughout its opinion, the court remained unmoved by the fact that the city authorities had withdrawn without explanation a permit previously issued to the professor.[134]

A few countervailing decisions, without relying explicitly on federal or state constitutional protection for speech, recognized the importance of public speaking and demonstrations in a democratic society. For example, during Reconstruction the Supreme Court of North Carolina affirmed a jury verdict of "not guilty" in the case of defendants indicted for riot, nuisance, and obstructing the streets during a noisy but peaceful celebration of the Emancipation Proclamation. The court concluded that the celebration was not a riot because there was no unlawful assembly or threat of violence. The sound of a fife and drum, the court added, did not constitute a nuisance. "To render an act indictable as a nuisance,"

---

[132] 167 U.S. at 46–48.
[133] See generally John W. Wertheimer, Free-Speech Fights: The Roots of Modern Free-Expression Litigation in the United States 129–237 (1992) (unpublished Ph.D. dissertation, Princeton University).
[134] Fitts v. City of Atlanta, 121 Ga. 567, 570–71, 49 S.E. 793, 794–95 (1905).

the court reasoned, "it is not sufficient that it should annoy particular persons only, but it must be so inconvenient and troublesome as to annoy the whole community." Nor was there any evidence that the celebration blocked the streets in ways that prevented travel and business. Indicting under these circumstances would extend the doctrines of riot and common nuisance "far beyond the limits heretofore circumscribing them, and would put an end to all public celebrations, however innocent or commendable the purpose." The court stressed that in "a popular government like ours, the laws allow great latitude to public demonstrations, whether political, social or moral."[135]

Several of the cases in which courts overturned ordinances giving local authorities broad discretion over the time, place, and manner of parades and public speeches involved members of the Salvation Army. For example, the Supreme Court of Michigan invalidated a city ordinance by pointing out that "unregulated official discretion" to control parades "would enable a mayor or council to shut off processions of those whose notions did not suit their views or tastes, in politics or religion, or any other matter on which men differ." Acknowledging that reasonable restrictions on the "times and occasions" of public assemblies may be necessary, the court emphasized that regulation could only be justified because of actual or threatened harm rather than "because of the sentiments or purposes of the movement, if not otherwise unlawful." It added that "to suppress things not absolutely dangerous, as an easy way of getting rid of the trouble of regulating them, is not a process tolerated under free institutions."[136]

The Supreme Court of Wisconsin similarly declared unconstitutional a local ordinance that excepted only funerals, fire and militia companies, and political parties from the requirement of obtaining a discretionary permit from the mayor before parading on certain public streets while singing, shouting, or playing musical instruments. The court labeled the ordinance "entirely un-American and in conflict with the principles of our institutions and all modern ideas of civil liberty." In the court's opinion, the ordinance more closely resembled "petty tyranny" than "any fair or legitimate provision in the exercise of the police power of the state to protect the public peace and safety." While conceding the police power of a legislative body to impose reasonable regulations on rights such as parading, the court insisted that these rights cannot be suppressed, directly or indirectly, by giving discretionary

[135] State v. Hughes, 72 N.C. 25, 39–40 (1875).
[136] In re Frazee, 63 Mich. 396, 404–7, 30 N.W. 72, 74–76 (1886).

power to public officials.[137] "The spirit of our free institutions," an Illinois appellate court observed in another Salvation Army case, "allows great latitude in public parades and demonstrations, whether religious or political." As long as they are not a threat to the public peace and do not violate the rights of others, "every measure repressing them, whether by legislative enactment, or municipal ordinance, is an encroachment upon fundamental and constitutional rights." The court noted that since the landing of the Mayflower, the right to parade in a peaceable manner and for a lawful purpose has been "among the fundamental rights of a free people." When public officials have the discretionary power to "shut off the parades of those whose notions do not suit their views and tastes in politics and religion, and permit like parades of those whose notions do," the court warned, "liberty is subverted, and the spirit of our free institutions violated."[138]

It is, of course, revealing that courts were often more sympathetic to the Salvation Army than to similar claims raised by socialists or the IWW. Most dramatically, the Supreme Court of Michigan, which warned against "suppress[ing] things not absolutely dangerous" in its Salvation Army case in 1886, held in 1908 that socialists could not parade with red flags because their display would offend and arouse the general public. In the Salvation Army case the court pointed out that parades "with banners and other paraphernalia" have been "customary, from time immemorial, in all free countries, and in most civilized countries, for people who are assembled for common purposes." The same court was later unmoved by the socialists' argument that the red flag "is an emblem of their order, and signifies brotherhood." The court justified this different result by quoting the passage from the Salvation Army case warning that "there may be times and occasions when such assemblies may for a while be dangerous in themselves because of inflammable conditions among the population."[139]

LABOR INJUNCTIONS

As Felix Frankfurter and Nathan Greene disclosed in their classic 1930 study, *The Labor Injunction,* the development of injunctions as the "central lever" in "the administration of justice between

---

[137] State ex rel. Gerrabad v. Dering, 84 Wis. 585, 594–95, 54 N.W. 1104, 1107–8 (1893).
[138] Rich v. City of Naperville, 42 Ill. App. 222, 223–24 (1891).
[139] Compare People v. Burman, 154 Mich. 150, 153, 155–57, 117 N.W. 589, 591–92 (1908) with In re Frazee, 63 Mich. 396, 404, 30 N.W. 72, 74 (1886).

employer and employee" provided another source of litigation over free speech issues. Toward the end of the nineteenth century, the courts expanded the injunction into "an enveloping code of prohibited conduct." Courts issued injunctions to forbid various activities of union leaders and their supporters, thereby employing "the most powerful resources of the law on one side of a bitter social struggle." Judges often used the same broad and vague injunction in numerous cases, without adaptation to the facts of the particular labor dispute. Many of the most outrageous injunctions were directed against speech and prohibited "opprobrious epithets," language that was "bad," "abusive," "annoying," or "indecent," and words such as *scab, traitor,* and *unfair.*[140] Some judges held that all picketing is unlawful. For example, a federal judge in Iowa reasoned that "[t]here is and can be no such thing as peaceful picketing, any more than there can be chaste vulgarity, or peaceful mobbing, or lawful lynching. When men want to converse or persuade, they do not organize a picket line."[141]

Injunctions against Eugene Debs and Samuel Gompers, two of the major labor leaders of the late nineteenth and early twentieth centuries, generated important litigation that reached the Supreme Court. During the nationally significant Pullman strike of 1894, the federal court in Chicago issued an injunction against Debs and other officers of the American Railway Union. The injunction forbade them "from sending out any letters, messages, or communications directing, inciting, encouraging, or instructing any persons whatsoever to interfere" with the business of named railroad companies "or from persuading any of the employees" of the railroad companies "to fail or refuse to perform the duties of their employment." Neither counsel for Debs nor the Supreme Court, however, addressed the implications of this injunction for free speech.[142] The Supreme Court's affirmance in this case became the major precedent for the use of injunctions in labor disputes, but the decision had no impact on First Amendment analysis.

---

[140] Felix Frankfurter and Nathan Greene, The Labor Injunction 52, 81, 89–106 (1930).

[141] Atchison, T. & S.F. Ry. v. Gee, 139 F. 582, 584 (C.C.S.D. Iowa 1905).

[142] Fiss points out that the Supreme Court decision in the case, In re Debs, 158 U.S. 564 (1895), did not even quote this provision of the injunction, which Fiss uncovered in the report of a commission that subsequently investigated the strike. Fiss, supra note 8, at 324 and n.6. The commission acknowledged the legitimacy of those who "seriously questioned . . . whether courts have jurisdiction to enjoin citizens from 'persuading' each other in industrial or other matters of common interest." Id. at 324 n.5. See generally Nick Salvatore, Eugene V. Debs: Citizen and Socialist 126–38 (1982), for a discussion of the Pullman strike and its impact on Debs.

Samuel Gompers, by contrast, relied heavily on the First Amendment when challenging a 1907 injunction that ordered him and other officers of the AFL not to publish or otherwise state that the company was on the union's "Unfair" and "We don't patronize" lists. *Gompers v. Buck's Range & Stove Co.* became a major confrontation between the AFL and the American Anti-Boycott Association, a group organized by employers in 1902 to confront organized labor through litigation and lobbying. Reflecting the importance of this case, Gompers retained Alton B. Parker, an eminent lawyer and former judge who had become president of the American Bar Association in 1906 after running unsuccessfully as the Democratic presidential candidate against Theodore Roosevelt in 1904.[143] Numerous articles in the *American Federationist,* the official journal of the AFL, attacked the injunction as a violation of the First Amendment, a position the AFL elaborated in its legal briefs. When the case reached the Supreme Court, Gompers and Parker relied on the opinion by Justice Holmes in *Patterson v. Colorado.* Conceding that a legislature could punish the publication at issue, they denied that courts of equity had authority to impose by injunction a prior restraint on speech.[144]

The Supreme Court barely discussed the First Amendment in its 1911 opinion. It held without explanation that "the general provisions of the injunction did not, in terms, restrain any form of publication." The opinion went on to imply a distinction between normal speech, which is protected by the First Amendment, and "verbal acts," which have "a force not inhering in the words themselves, and therefore exceeding any possible right of speech which a single individual might have." Such "verbal acts," the Court reasoned, are "as much subject to injunction as the use of any other force whereby property is unlawfully damaged." When speech becomes a means for accomplishing an unlawful purpose – in *Gompers,* a union boycott conspiring in restraint of trade – it is no longer speech but a "verbal act."[145] This distinction probably explains why the Court did not consider the injunction a forbidden prior restraint. The First Amendment prohibits only prior restraints upon speech and, under the Court's analysis, "verbal acts" are apparently a form of conduct.

Many lower courts reached similar results, as an 1898 decision

---

143 Daniel R. Ernst, Lawyers Against Labor: From Individual Rights to Corporate Liberalism 5, 133 (1995). Ernst devotes a chapter to the Buck's Stove case, id. at 124–46.
144 Brief for Appellants at 12–13, 26; Supplemental and Reply Brief for Appellants at 18.
145 Gompers v. Buck's Stove & Range Co., 221 U.S. 418, 436–37, 439 (1911).

by the Supreme Court of Michigan illustrates. While acknowledging that the free speech clause of the Michigan Constitution prohibits injunctions against libels, the court, in order to avoid irreparable injury to property rights, upheld an injunction against a circular urging a boycott. The court found that the purpose of the circular was to intimidate and prevent the public from doing business with the employer, and not just to libel him. Although the court did not use the term *verbal act,* it anticipated the *Gompers* decision by viewing speech used in connection with a labor boycott as beyond the constitutional protection for free speech.[146] By contrast, the free speech provisions of state constitutions often provided the basis for decisions invalidating "blacklisting" statutes, which required employers to provide written explanations to discharged employees. Judges asserted that free speech implies a "correlative" right not to speak and that the blacklisting statutes violated this implicit right.[147]

Not all courts accepted the growing use of the labor injunction. For example, in 1902 the Supreme Court of Missouri cited the state constitution while refusing to enjoin a boycott. If members of a union "are not permitted to tell the story of their wrongs, or, if you please, their supposed wrongs, by word of mouth or with pen or print, and to endeavor to persuade others to aid them by all peaceable means, in securing redress of such wrongs," the court asked, *"what becomes of free speech, and what of personal liberty?"* After observing the responsibility of all persons under the state constitution for injuries that result from the exercise of free speech, the court stressed that "such responsibility is utterly incompatible with authority in a court of equity to prevent such responsibility from occurring." The court conceded that a court of equity could enjoin threats of personal violence or of the destruction of property. When made with the "present ability to be carried into execution," the court reasoned, such threats constitute "verbal acts." Unlike the Supreme Court in *Gompers* a decade later, however, the Supreme Court of Missouri did not construe speech in support of a labor boycott as a "verbal act" beyond the constitutional protection of free speech.[148]

Other courts, without citing constitutional provisions, conceded

---

146 Beck v. Railway Teamsters' Protective Union, 118 Mich. 497, 526–27, 77 N.W. 13, 24–25 (1898).
147 See, e.g., Atchison, T. & S.F. Ry. v. Brown, 80 Kan. 312, 315, 102 P. 459, 460 (1909); St. Louis S.W. Ry. v. Griffin, 106 Tex. 477, 485, 171 S.W. 703, 705 (1914).
148 Marx & Haas Jeans Clothing Co. v. Watson, 168 Mo. 133, 150, 67 S.W. 391, 395–96 (1902).

that picketing was not necessarily unlawful. For example, a federal appellate court sharply contrasted permissible picketing for purposes of communication, which appeals to a person's free judgment, with unlawful duress, which "intimidate[s] . . . as effectually as . . . physical assault." The court acknowledged that "[u]nder the name of persuasion, duress may be used," but it cautioned that "it is duress, not persuasion, that should be restrained and punished." Applying this distinction, the court refused to prohibit "picketing, as such."[149] Justice Holmes made a similar point in a famous dissent while still on the Supreme Judicial Court of Massachusetts. He objected to an injunction that, in his view, prohibited "organized persuasion or argument, although free from any threat of violence, either express or implied." Holmes thought that the majority made the unwarranted assumption that picketing "necessarily carries with it a threat of bodily harm."[150]

IGNORING FREE SPEECH ISSUES

Throughout the period from the Civil War to World War I, many judges and lawyers ignored free speech issues that their counterparts recognized in other cases. For example, the Supreme Court did not address the First Amendment implications in the *Debs* injunction case, the *Davis* case restricting public speaking on the Boston Common, the *Curtis* case upholding statutory restrictions on political fundraising, or the *Fox* case punishing advocacy of nude bathing for its supposed bad tendency to produce a breach of the peace. In *Rosen v. United States*, which affirmed in 1896 a conviction for mailing obscene literature, the appellant and the Court focused on the specificity of the indictment under the Sixth Amendment without alluding to the First Amendment or free speech.[151] Moreover, in some areas of the law virtually no courts discussed free speech in cases that today would be recognized as raising First Amendment issues. *Halter v. Nebraska*, a 1907 decision by the Supreme Court, provides an illustration. The Court sustained a Nebraska statute that prohibited the use of the United States flag in advertisements, but not in newspapers or magazines. The defendants attacked this statute as a deprivation of property under the Fourteenth Amendment and on a variety of other con-

---

[149] Iron Molders' Union No. 125 v. Allis-Chalmers Co., 166 F. 45, 51 (7th Cir. 1908).

[150] Vegelahn v. Guntner, 167 Mass. 92, 104–5, 44 N.E. 1077, 1080 (1896).

[151] Rosen v. United States, 161 U.S. 29, 42–43 (1896).

stitutional grounds, but neither their brief nor the Court's opinion mentioned freedom of speech or "commercial" speech.[152]

Although film censorship provoked strong free speech arguments from the emerging movie industry, the Supreme Court, like the lower courts, essentially ignored them.[153] In *Mutual Film Corp. v. Industrial Commission of Ohio,* the appellants attacked, as a prior restraint in violation of the free speech provision of the Ohio Constitution, a state law that required approval of all films by a board of censors before exhibition. The briefs of both parties concentrated on free speech arguments to a much greater extent than was typical during this period. The brief of the Ohio attorney general is especially revealing because it recognized the potential First Amendment concerns lurking in prior Supreme Court cases decided on other grounds. Citing *Gompers* and cases that prohibited the use of the mails for lotteries, the brief asserted that the Supreme Court would have based its decisions on the First Amendment if the right to free speech were *"as broad as claimed by the appellants in this case."*[154] The Supreme Court's 1915 decision in *Mutual Film* began with generalities about the certainty, value, and breadth of "freedom of opinion and its expression," asserting "'that opinion is free and that conduct alone is amenable to the law.'" After invoking these pieties, however, the Court promptly rejected the argument of the film corporation that movies are "publications of ideas" deserving the same constitutional protection as other publications. The Court found this position inconsistent with "common sense" and "judicial sense." According to the Court, the exhibition of films was simply a profit making business and should not be regarded "as part of the press of the country or as organs of public opinion."[155]

The Supreme Court of Minnesota did not even mention free speech while upholding the right of the mayor of Minneapolis to revoke the license of a movie theater for showing "The Birth of a Nation." The mayor claimed that the glorification of the Ku Klux Klan in the movie was historically false, that it dehumanized and caricatured black people, and that it generated racial hatred. Upholding the discretion of the mayor to act in a situation where "reasonable people can differ," the court cited evidence that per-

---

[152] Halter v. Nebraska, 205 U.S. 34 (1907); Brief for Plaintiffs in Error at 49–59.

[153] See generally Wertheimer, supra note 133, at 68–128; John Wertheimer, Mutual Film Reviewed: The Movies, Censorship, and Free Speech in Progressive America, 37 Am. J. Legal Hist. 158 (1993).

[154] Brief of Appellees at 25.

[155] Mutual Film Corp. v. Industrial Comm'n of Ohio, 236 U.S. 230, 243–44 (1915).

formances of a related play in Minneapolis had "resulted in disparaging remarks regarding negroes and in subjecting them to indignities in public places." There was no reason to doubt, the court added, that the mayor's threat to revoke the theater's license was made honestly "in the interest of the public welfare and the peace and good order of the city."[156]

THE JUDICIAL TRADITION

The overwhelming weight of judicial opinion in all jurisdictions before World War I offered little recognition and even less protection of free speech interests. Although radical activity prompted many of the prosecutions, it alone cannot account for the restrictive results. Film censorship, political speech by government employees, public sermons by ministers, and newspaper reports of crime also produced decisions that rejected First Amendment claims. A general hostility to the value of free expression permeated the judicial system. This pervasive hostility had few doctrinal underpinnings, nor was it openly expressed. Judges often emphasized the sanctity of free speech in the very process of reaching adverse decisions in concrete cases. Even in the relatively threatening context of the IWW free speech fights, much public and official reaction was more sensitive to free speech concerns and more thoughtful about the meaning of free expression than was the typical judge deciding less controversial cases.

Just as most judges valued speech less than many other Americans, the justices on the U.S. Supreme Court afforded less protection for speech than their counterparts on lower federal and state courts. In striking contrast to its vigilant identification and protection of "liberty of contract" and individual property rights, the Supreme Court rejected First Amendment claims whenever it confronted them directly. But confrontation, even in rejection, at least lent these claims some status. In rendering decisions that today would be based on an analysis of the First Amendment, the Court frequently did not address free speech issues at all, even when counsel raised them. The Court repeatedly denied that cases implicated freedom of expression, and often made no reference to the First Amendment.

Some opinions, predominantly in the state courts, reveal that restrictive decisions did not reflect the entire judicial spectrum. Courts occasionally protected freedom of expression and pointed to issues that contemporary scholars and postwar judicial decisions

---

[156] Bainbridge v. City of Minneapolis, 154 N.W. 964, 966 (1915).

addressed more systematically. For the most part, however, the few relatively libertarian opinions were not analytically more rigorous than the norm for this period. Even when supporting free speech claims, they generally did not explain in any meaningful detail the basis for the result. They did not attempt to develop guidelines for determining what constitutes speech or when speech may be unlawful, perhaps because they devoted so little attention to considering the interests the constitutional protection for speech was designed to safeguard.

The analytical sterility of most opinions, regardless of outcome, was self-perpetuating. Judges did not challenge each other to think deeply about free speech and were therefore less likely to revise their views. There were, however, a sufficient number of protective decisions to suggest that judges were not simply unable to conceive of more generous approaches to constitutional guarantees of free speech. Free speech claimants in some cases cited protective decisions by other courts. Even without the assistance of counsel, it seems likely that many judges who reached restrictive decisions knew some of the protective precedents and consciously, if seldom explicitly, rejected them. In any event, the fact that some prewar judges could be sympathetic to free speech claims suggests that the tradition of insensitivity was not so dominant that only an intellectual breakthrough in constitutional interpretation could have created the possibility of different results. The existence of protective decisions, even more than their relative paucity, emphasizes the general judicial hostility toward free speech before World War I.

4

Legal Scholarship

Scholars as well as judges considered the meaning of freedom of expression between the Civil War and World War I. Just as many legal decisions confronted free speech issues before the Espionage Act cases, treatises and articles preceded Chafee. This legal scholarship stands in striking contrast to the tradition of judicial hostility to free speech claims. Unlike the prewar decisions, which were generally restrictive and poorly reasoned, much of the legal writing of this period used sophisticated analysis to reach protective standards. The authors included some of the most eminent scholars in the country. They offered convincing doctrinal support for freedom of expression, but their ideas did not gain significant judicial acceptance until after the United States entered World War I.

Within this scholarship, five authors were particularly important. The prodigious writings of Theodore Schroeder, the guiding force behind the Free Speech League, were the most extensive and libertarian treatments of free speech in the first two decades of the twentieth century.[1] Two respected and widely cited treatises, Thomas Cooley's *Constitutional Limitations,* first published in 1868 and reissued in numerous subsequent editions,[2] and Ernst Freund's *The Police Power,* published in 1904, included sections on free speech.[3] Henry Schofield, a professor at Northwestern University Law School, presented a comprehensive paper on "Freedom of the Press in the United States" at the annual meeting of the American

---

[1] Schroeder's major essays on free speech are collected in two volumes: Theodore Schroeder: Free Speech for Radicals (enlarged ed. 1916) [hereinafter Schroeder-Free Speech] and Theodore Schroeder, "Obscene" Literature and Constitutional Law (1911) [hereinafter Schroeder-"Obscene" Literature].

[2] Cooley's treatment of free speech issues did not change significantly over time. I cite from the 1883 edition, the last edition written solely by Cooley. Thomas M. Cooley, Constitutional Limitations (5th ed. 1883). Subsequent editions appeared in 1890 and 1903.

[3] Ernst Freund, The Police Power (1904).

Sociological Society in 1914.[4] Roscoe Pound, perhaps the most influential legal scholar of his generation, wrote two articles in the *Harvard Law Review* in 1915 and 1916 that, while limited in scope, offered highly original and provocative interpretations of the First Amendment.[5]

The prewar scholars had remarkably similar views on many important free speech issues, even though they often derived these views from vastly different social theories. They were most united in their criticism of judicial decisions. Given his personality and beliefs, it is not surprising that Schroeder was the most vitriolic. Courts, he frequently complained, "have destroyed and evaded the constitutional guarantee of freedom of speech and of the press" by "dogmatically" creating "new exceptions and limitations, which are not represented by a single word in the constitution itself."[6] Yet Schofield, the careful law professor, also complained about unauthorized "judge-made law" covering a range of free speech issues, and concluded that "the courts are a failure up to date" in interpreting constitutional declarations protecting freedom of expression.[7] Cooley, Freund, and Pound made similar criticisms.

The prewar scholars objected particularly to the common judicial position that the First Amendment and analogous provisions of state constitutions simply incorporated Blackstone's account of the English common law of free speech in the eighteenth century. The abuses of government power allowed by this English common law, many stressed, contributed to the grievances that provoked the American Revolution. They maintained that the constitutional protection for free speech in the United States helped to secure the revolutionary victory by overturning the prior English common law. In particular, they emphasized that the American constitutions precluded the punishment of speech on matters of public concern for its alleged bad tendency. An expanded definition of free speech, they believed, was an essential element of the distinctively American conception of popular sovereignty and democratic government. The American constitutions, they added, provided

---

[4] Henry Schofield, Freedom of the Press in the United States, 9 Am. Soc. Soc'y: Papers & Proceedings 67 (1914), reprinted in 2 Henry Schofield, Essays on Constitutional Law and Equity 510 (1921).

[5] Roscoe Pound, Equitable Relief Against Defamation and Injuries to Personality, 29 Harv. L. Rev. 640 (1916) [hereinafter Pound-Equitable Relief]; Roscoe Pound, Interests of Personality (pts. 1–2), 28 Harv. L. Rev. 343, 445 (1915) [hereinafter Pound-Personality].

[6] Schroeder-Free Speech, supra note 1, at 81; Schroeder-"Obscene" Literature, supra note 1, at 155.

[7] Schofield, supra note 4, at 115.

safeguards for speech that could be further expanded, but not limited, as society developed.

At the same time that they vigorously condemned judges for continuing to apply the English common law to speech on matters of public concern, many of these scholars conceded that American constitutional guarantees did not eliminate liability for various torts and crimes involving speech, such as libel, obscenity, and incitement to violence. They often complained, however, that judges exhibited insensitivity to free speech values while deciding cases on these subjects. Several believed that broad protection for freedom of speech would reduce the threat of disorder and that its repression would be more likely to lead to actual violence. Moreover, the scholars did not simply criticize the courts. They developed sophisticated alternative approaches for analyzing free speech claims.

THEORETICAL SOURCES FOR FREE SPEECH VIEWS

The writing on free speech by several of these scholars reflected broader and sometimes competing social theories. Schroeder, like his colleagues in the Free Speech League, derived many of his views about free speech from the libertarian radicalism that originated before the Civil War. Cooley, who was born in 1824, was not the apologist for laissez-faire capitalism demonized by progressive historians and their ideological successors. Revisionist scholars have convincingly demonstrated that Cooley remained committed to the political tradition of liberal individualism derived from Jefferson and Jackson. Though much less individualistic than libertarian radicalism, this tradition emphasized the need to protect the equal rights of all citizens from the danger that government power would be exercised on behalf of class interests.[8] By contrast, Pound was the leading legal figure in the effort by political progressives and philosophical pragmatists in the early twentieth century to promote the use of government power for the public welfare. Progressives and pragmatists maintained that the liberal individualism of Jefferson and Jackson, while perhaps appropriate for the early Republic, had produced the very inequality its founders abhorred in the period of corporate consolidation following the Civil War. Freund, somewhere between Cooley and

---

[8] Alan Jones, Thomas M. Cooley and "Laissez-Faire Constitutionalism": A Reconsideration, 53 J. Am. Hist. 751 (1967); see also Michael Les Benedict, Laissez-Faire and Liberty: A Re-Evaluation of the Meaning and Origins of Laissez-Faire Constitutionalism, 3 Law & Hist. Rev. 293 (1985).

Pound, combined relatively progressive views on government regulation of the economy with traditional concerns about the need
to protect individual intellectual and political liberty from government interference.

Most of Schroeder's writings did not explicitly reveal the
broader sources of his views on free speech. Unlike his libertarian
radical predecessors such as Josiah Warren, Ezra Heywood, Edwin
Walker, and Moses Harman, Schroeder did not focus on the connection between his treatment of free speech and his fundamental
commitment to individual autonomy. Although Schroeder privately credited Moses Harman, the anarchist, freethinker, and sex
radical, with stimulating his own interest in free speech, he never
acknowledged this debt in his published work. The background
and membership of the Free Speech League, combined with
Schroeder's personal correspondence, provide the best evidence
of his libertarian radicalism. Other evidence, however, can be
found in Schroeder's many publications on free speech. These
publications revealed that he had a much more libertarian conception of protected speech in all contexts than any other legal
scholar of the period. Alone among his colleagues, he claimed
that all speech, including the advocacy of criminal conduct, is constitutionally protected unless it directly results in an actual and
material injury designated as a crime. Under this standard,
Schroeder opposed any restrictions on allegedly obscene speech.
The title of his major collection of essays on free speech, *"Obscene"
Literature and Constitutional Law,* highlighted his emphasis on this
subject. Schroeder was also the only prewar scholar who took seriously the Supreme Court case in which Jay Fox, the editor of the
newspaper published by the anarchist Home Colony, asserted the
right to advocate the liberty of nude bathing.

On some occasions, Schroeder explicitly revealed his general
libertarianism in his scholarly work on free speech. He viewed
freedom of expression as a natural right as well as a constitutional
guarantee.[9] Moreover, for Schroeder history disclosed "the evolution of organized government toward liberty," and ultimately
toward a utopian anarchism. He divided the progress of history
into three stages. The first stage restrains the arbitrary power of
autocratic sovereigns by subjecting their authority to law. The second stage subordinates law to principles of natural justice, which
require uniformity in the application of law. The third stage
increasingly limits legislative power "so as to conserve a larger

[9] Schroeder-"Obscene" Literature, supra note 1, at 208

human liberty" even from uniform laws. Schroeder believed that legislation would eventually prohibit "only such conduct as in the nature of things necessarily, immediately and directly involves an invasion of the liberty of another, to his material and ascertainable injury." He claimed that he had "no doubt it was such a government, of limited power to regulate human affairs, that the framers of American constitutions intended to establish."[10]

Schroeder agreed with "the leaders of libertarian thought" that the United States at the turn of the twentieth century was near the beginning of the third stage of this evolution. In a few thousand years, he believed, the country might approximate "real liberty under the law." It would take another million years, however, to attain "the anarchist's ideal, which is liberty without state-enforced law, made possible because no one has the inclination to invade his neighbor, and all are agreed as to what constitutes an invasion." Schroeder regretted that his fellow Americans seemed willing to accept "tyranny under the forms of law" and knew "nothing of liberty in the sense of an acknowledged claim of right to remain exempt from invasive authority."[11]

The writings of Cooley, Freund, and Pound more explicitly disclosed the broader sources of their views about free speech. In his 1871 preface to the second edition of *Constitutional Limitations,* Cooley emphasized that "he had written in full sympathy with all those restraints which the caution of the fathers had imposed upon the exercise of the powers of government." He cited his discussions "of jury trials and the other safeguards to personal liberty, of liberty of the press, and of vested rights" as examples of this sympathy. Reflection since the initial publication of his treatise, Cooley added, confirmed "his previous views of the need of constitutional restraints at every point where agents are to exercise the delegated authority of the people."[12] These introductory comments strongly support the conclusion of revisionist scholars that Cooley's commitment to "constitutional limitations" on government power extended to personal as well as to economic liberties. In his edition of Story's *Commentaries,* Cooley similarly asserted that the word *liberty* "embraces all our liberties – personal, civil, and political." Cooley's examples of liberty included "the freedom of speech" and "the right freely to buy and sell as others may." In a footnote, Cooley quoted from Mill's introduction to *On Liberty,*

---

[10] Schroeder-Free Speech, supra note 1, at 73–74.
[11] Id. at 74.
[12] Thomas M. Cooley, Constitutional Limitations iii–iv (2d ed. 1871).

which emphasized the fundamental "liberty of expressing and publishing opinions."[13]

In some passages, Cooley indicated that he valued freedom of expression even more than other liberties. Cooley began his long chapter on "liberty of speech and of the press" in *Constitutional Limitations* by observing that the protection "against unfriendly legislation by Congress" provided through the First Amendment "is almost universally regarded not only as highly important, but as essential to the very existence and perpetuity of free government." For the same reason, Cooley added, the states have guarded this liberty "with jealous care, by provisions of similar import in their several constitutions, and a constitutional principle is thereby established which is supposed to form a shield of protection to the free expression of opinion in every part of our land."[14] Discussion of economic liberties did not arouse similar passion in Cooley.[15]

Like Cooley's *Constitutional Limitations*, Ernst Freund's influential 1904 treatise, *The Police Power*, reflected the traditional individualism of American law. A law professor at the University of Chicago Law School, Freund was widely and accurately regarded as a progressive. Progressivism explicitly challenged the viability of liberal individualism for the United States in the twentieth century. Freund, however, might have recognized the extent to which liberal individualism permeated the American legal system and might have felt compelled as a scholar writing a treatise to report his findings accurately. In any event, Freund made room for some progressive views in his treatise by asserting that the government could exercise its police powers to a much greater extent in regulating the economy than in restricting speech.

American federal and state constitutions, Freund maintained, rejected the subordination of individual interests to society. Instead, they guaranteed individual liberty against the state. According to Freund, the framers believed that constitutional guarantees of liberty would ultimately lead to a better society even though they would frequently present obstacles to realizing current conceptions of the public welfare. Undoubtedly influenced by his familiarity with German philosophy, Freund acknowledged that the highest individual and social interests might ultimately converge. But "until the conditions of that harmony are discovered," Freund warned, the dangerous possibility existed that genuine individual interests could be subordinated to "interests which

---

[13] Joseph Story, 2 Commentaries on the Constitution of the United States 668–69 (Fourth Edition, With Notes and Additions by Thomas M. Cooley 1873).

[14] Cooley, supra note 2, at 512.   [15] See Jones, supra note 8, at 765.

while being put forward as social are not such in reality." Under American constitutions, he reiterated, "the idea of a public welfare bought at the cost of suppressing individual liberty and right" is "inadmissible."[16]

Freund identified three broad spheres affected by the police power of the state: (1) safety, order, and morals; (2) the "proper production and distribution of wealth;" and (3) "moral, intellectual and political movements." The government's right to exercise the police power, Freund maintained, varies across these spheres. He asserted that the moral, intellectual, and political sphere is "exempt" from the police power. "The exercise of the police power," Freund recognized, "might conceivably serve the purpose of guiding and checking intellectual movement so as to further the ideas of the government of what is beneficial to society or state." The protection for free expression in American constitutions, however, "removes the pursuit of ideal interests on the whole from the operations of the police power." Moreover, this constitutional protection withdraws from the police power the ability to control, in the interest of order and stability, "public opinion and agitation" that does not incite to violence or injure private rights.[17]

By contrast, use of the police power to regulate the economy seemed more "debatable" to Freund.[18] He viewed the American economic system as "based upon peaceful struggle and conflict," not simply as "essentially individualistic." Substantial government regulation of the economy would be appropriate in a socialistic state, but in the United States it would "operate largely as interference and disturbance, as favoritism or oppression." Freund, however, recognized "important exceptions" in which the police power should be exercised in economic matters "where the benefit bestowed is tolerably equal for all." He contrasted legitimate economic legislation, which provides "equal benefit to the whole community," with improper "class legislation," which favors "certain economic interests against injurious competition" and is often justified by "the supposed necessity of maintaining the established order of society." Reflecting his progressive views, Freund conceded that much recent class legislation was "modern and benevolent," passed "on the theory that the power of the state should come to the aid of those who are economically and socially weak, and should temper the natural inequalities in the struggle for life."[19] Freund did not comment further on whether the police

[16] Freund, supra note 3, at 12–13.
[18] Id. at 11.
[17] Id. at 9–11.
[19] Id. at 8–9.

power justified such "modern and benevolent" class legislation, but he found the position that the police power should be used to protect the community's safety and morals "generally admitted." In this third sphere, people disagreed only about the proper extent of regulation.

After examining the application of the police power appropriate to each of these three spheres, Freund observed that the spheres often overlapped. For example, he pointed out that "conditions affecting health and morality are primarily subject to the police power, but all restrictive legislation should have the utmost regard for the freedom of science, art and literature." Similarly, he added, "religion and speech and press are primarily free, but that does not prevent them from being subjected to restraints in the interest of good order or morality." Freund confidently but unconvincingly concluded that reconciliation of these overlapping interests had been easily resolved in American law.[20]

Unlike Freund, a progressive whose treatise largely reflected the prevailing liberal individualism of American law, Pound frequently described his work as the application of pragmatism to law.[21] Pound directly incorporated into his legal writings the widespread progressive belief that the American legal system, by adopting the destructive individualism of the broader society, perpetuated inequality and obstructed social justice. Moreover, Pound's primary interest in jurisprudence prompted him to articulate his fundamental principles much more directly and comprehensively than other legal scholars who wrote about free speech. Pound called for "the socialization of law,"[22] which would "lead our law to a more even balance between individualism and socialism."[23] His views about free speech are best understood as an application of the "sociological jurisprudence" he developed as an alternative to the "mechanical jurisprudence" of the past.[24] Sociological jurisprudence, Pound emphasized, recognized that the ultimate function of the law is to balance competing social interests.[25] He viewed free speech as one among many social interests that the law must balance.

---

[20] Id. at 11.

[21] See, e.g., Roscoe Pound, Liberty of Contract, 18 Yale L.J. 454, 464 (1909) [hereinafter Pound-Liberty of Contract]; Roscoe Pound, Mechanical Jurisprudence, 8 Colum. L. Rev. 609, 609–10 (1908) [hereinafter Pound-Mechanical Jurisprudence].

[22] Roscoe Pound, Legislation as a Social Function, 18 Am. J. of Soc. 755, 756, 761 (1913).

[23] Roscoe Pound, Do We Need a Philosophy of Law?, 5 Colum. L. Rev. 339, 352 (1905).

[24] Pound, supra note 22, at 761.

[25] Pound-Personality, supra note 5, at 344, 349.

Pound located the unfortunate individualism of the American legal system in both common law and constitutional law. The individualism of the common law, Pound observed, is best expressed in Blackstone's classic commentary that "the public good is in nothing more essentially interested than in the protection of every individual's private rights." Pound pointed out that American judges frequently cited this commentary. The antipathy of the common law to legislation, Pound added, can be traced to the individualistic assumption that private rights are best protected by keeping law to a minimum.[26]

The preoccupation of the common law with individual rights, Pound complained, diverted its attention from questions of social justice. He protested that in the United States, even more than in England, the common law viewed litigation as nothing more than "a fair fist fight" in which the role of the court is simply to insure "fair play and prevent interference." Because issues of great social importance are tried only as private controversies between the litigating parties,[27] the common law often sacrificed the public welfare to exaggerated notions of individual rights.[28] "The individual," Pound tersely concluded, "gets so much fair play, that the public gets very little."[29]

The individualism of the American legal system, Pound frequently observed, manifested itself in constitutional law as well as in common law. He pointed out that to a substantial extent the individualistic assumptions of the common law had simply been extended to constitutional analysis. As examples, he cited references to Blackstone in constitutional cases that developed the doctrine of liberty of contract and judicial skepticism about the constitutionality of legislation.[30] Pound also maintained that the Constitution, and especially the Bill of Rights, supported individualism by identifying individual rights with natural law. He regretted that the individualistic emphasis of the Constitution itself, which was framed at the zenith of the natural law school of jurisprudence, became reinforced by the influence of individualistic theories in economics and ethics during the subsequent growth of American law in the nineteenth century.[31]

Pound conceded that legal individualism had served useful historical functions. It had helped to emancipate people from the

[26] Pound-Liberty of Contract, supra note 21, at 461–62.
[27] Pound, supra note 23, at 346–47.
[28] Pound-Liberty of Contract, supra note 21, at 457.
[29] Pound, supra note 23, at 348.
[30] Pound-Liberty of Contract, supra note 21, at 461–62.
[31] Id. at 457, 459–60, 465.

decadence of medieval society. More recently and relevantly for American purposes, the development of the common law in England was part of the understandable struggle for individual liberty against the powers of the king. Pound, however, believed that "times have changed." The common law, he maintained, served no contemporary purpose by protecting individuals, and especially corporations artificially designated individuals by the law, whose legitimate interests had become secure and who frequently abused their individual rights by harming society. Individualism in constitutional doctrine similarly enabled "a fortified monopoly to shake its fist in the face of a people and defy investigation or regulation."[32]

The American legal system, Pound complained, had failed to adapt to changed historical circumstances. Lawyers seemed to believe that the individualistic doctrines of the common law "are part of a universal jural order." Even worse, courts most fully developed these doctrines after they had lost their vitality for the general public and for scholars in other fields.[33]

Pound maintained that popular dissatisfaction with the American legal system should be addressed by harmonizing law with contemporary social thought. In contrast to the individualistic conception of law sustained by "mechanical jurisprudence," he stressed "the need of a sociological jurisprudence"[34] sensitive to actual social conditions. Pound identified "a general movement in all departments of mental activity away from the purely formal, away from hard and fast notions, away from traditional categories which our fathers supposed were impressed upon the nature of things for all time."[35] Jurisprudence, he observed, was the last discipline still under the sway of formalistic deduction from predetermined conceptions.[36]

By developing sociological jurisprudence, Pound intended to bring jurisprudence, and eventually legal rules,[37] into the twentieth century. As part of the technical exposition of his sociological jurisprudence, Pound asserted that the law recognizes three sets of interests: individual, public, and social. Individual interests, Pound believed, in turn could usefully be divided into three categories:

---

[32] Pound, supra note 23, at 348–52.

[33] Pound-Liberty of Contract, supra note 21, at 460, 466.

[34] Roscoe Pound, The Need of a Sociological Jurisprudence, 19 The Green Bag 607 (1907).

[35] Roscoe Pound, A Practical Program of Procedural Reform, Proceedings of the Illinois State Bar Association 372, 375 (1910).

[36] Pound-Liberty of Contract, supra note 21, at 474; Pound-Mechanical Jurisprudence, supra note 21, at 610.

[37] Pound, supra note 35, at 375.

interests of personality, domestic interests, and economic interests.[38] He defined public interests as the "interests of the state as a juristic person" and social interests as the "interests of the community at large."[39]

Individual interests, Pound maintained, were the first to be analyzed critically. They developed as the law slowly differentiated private rights from group rights. The process culminated in the eighteenth century with the distinction of individual interests from public interests. The most important individual interests, such as those recognized in the Bill of Rights, achieved the status of natural rights. Pound emphasized, however, that natural rights and other individual interests arose independently of the law. They are distinct from legal rights, which are only those individual interests the law actually secures.[40] Thus, Pound concluded, "the law recognizes but does not create" individual interests.[41]

Although Pound acknowledged the legal recognition of individual and public interests, he believed that law essentially involves the analysis of social interests. Pound maintained that law exists for social ends. It recognizes and secures individual interests, not as a primary function, but because "there is a social interest in the individual moral and social life." "Strictly the concern of the law is with social interests," he concluded in two major articles, "since it is the social interest in securing the individual interest that must determine the law to secure it."[42]

The ultimate role of the law, Pound maintained, is to balance competing social interests. The social interest in "individual moral and social life" is just one of many social interests that must be balanced. Securing a particular individual interest, therefore, depends on whether it "is a suitable means of achieving the result which such a balancing demands."[43] Consistent with his general pragmatism, Pound did not believe in an absolute formula for balancing social interests; however, he did believe that balancing should "secure at all times the greatest number of interests possible, with the least possible sacrifice of other interests." He also pointed out that the intensity and even the nature of interests change over time. "The legal system," he therefore concluded, "must be kept flexible and law-making must accommodate itself

---

[38] Pound-Equitable Relief, supra note 5, at 349.

[39] Id. at 344; Pound supra note 22, at 763.

[40] Pound-Equitable Relief, supra note 5, at 343–46, 349; Pound, supra note 22, at 760, 763.

[41] Pound-Equitable Relief, supra note 5, at 347.

[42] Id. at 344, 347, 349; Pound, supra note 22, at 763.

[43] Pound-Equitable Relief, supra note 5, at 349.

perennially to shiftings in the quantity and quality of the interests it has to meet."[44]

Pound applied his analysis of interests to the specific issue of free speech, although he repeatedly regretted in private correspondence that he did not have more time to study this subject. It is intriguing that he indicated his familiarity with the work of Theodore Schroeder.[45] E. A. Ross, Pound's former colleague at the University of Nebraska, who had become the president of the American Sociological Society, asked Pound in 1914 to prepare a paper on "Freedom of Speech in the United States Since 1890" as part of the Society's general discussion of "Free Communication" at its next annual meeting. This is the meeting at which Schofield, also at Ross's request, presented his important article on freedom of the press. Pound, who by then had joined the faculty of Harvard Law School, agreed, but unfortunately never wrote the paper he promised.[46] Pound did address the subject of free speech, however, in an important 1915 article in the *Harvard Law Review* entitled "Interests in Personality."

Pound viewed free speech as both an individual interest and a social interest. Just as Schroeder and the members of the Free Speech League extended the nineteenth-century tradition of libertarian radicalism by associating free speech with the broader right to personal autonomy, Pound characterized the individual interest in free speech as an aspect of "the interest in the physical person." The social interests in free speech, according to Pound, derived from its role in promoting political efficiency and social progress. Although the Bill of Rights guaranteed free speech as an individual natural right, Pound believed that, except in cases of physical interference, social interests in free speech are more significant.[47]

[44] Pound, supra note 22, at 765–66.
[45] Letter from Roscoe Pound to Ella Westcott (Sept. 7, 1916) (Roscoe Pound Papers, Box 157, Folder 10, Harvard Law School Library) [hereinafter Pound Papers].
[46] See E. A. Ross to Roscoe Pound (May 18, 1914) (Pound Papers, supra note 45, Box 227, Folder 28) (inviting Pound to present paper); E. A. Ross to Roscoe Pound (May 27, 1914) (Pound Papers, supra note 45, Box 227, Folder 28) (regretting that Pound cannot present paper in person but welcoming his written contribution); Roscoe Pound to Morris R. Cohen (Nov. 9, 1914) (Pound Papers, supra note 45, Box 156, Folder 3) ("The American Sociological Society is bombarding me with reference to an old promise to take part in a symposium on freedom of speech and are expecting me to work up the decisions and statutes on freedom of speech in this country since 1890"); E. A. Ross to Roscoe Pound (Dec. 10, 1914) (Pound Papers, supra note 45, Box 227, Folder 28) (Ross reports receipt of all papers except Pound's). See 9 Am. Soc. Soc'y: Papers & Proceedings (1914) (published version of papers presented at this meeting).
[47] Pound-Personality, supra note 5, at 453.

Following his general approach, Pound added that social interests in securing individual interests applied to free speech as much as they did to other interests of personality. Free speech implicates the social interest in general security because the "individual will fight for his beliefs no less than for his life and limb and for his honor." In addition, restraints on free speech, by undermining mental and spiritual life, harm "the social interest in the moral and social life of the individual."

Pound maintained that free speech had only recently been recognized in morals and in law. He cited examples of continuing community intolerance of unpopular religious, economic, and sociological opinions. Mormons had been persecuted simply for preaching the abstract doctrines of their religion, as had other new and unusual sects. Pound, who was active in founding the American Association of University Professors, also mentioned that professors had to insist upon academic freedom in the face of strong popular disapproval of their ideas.[48]

Although obviously concerned about threats to free speech, Pound sympathetically remarked that many of them could be explained by legitimate social interests in the security of institutions and in the personality of the state. Interests in free speech, he pointed out, must be balanced against these other interests. Pound believed that free speech had historically been undervalued by "an over-insistence upon the countervailing interest of the state."[49] He apparently felt that threats to religious minorities and to academic freedom extended this unfortunate historical tradition. Moreover, in advocating "a balancing of interests" in regulating public speaking Pound observed that if people "are not allowed a certain amount of loud talk which accumulates in their systems it is apt to ferment and produce worse explosions than those involved in their talk at social centers." He added, however, that "in time of insurrection, riot, or war the general interest in public security may require us to put the lid on for the time being."[50]

THE REJECTION OF BLACKSTONE

The different and often inconsistent social theories underlying the First Amendment views of these prewar scholars did not preclude substantial agreement about many fundamental free speech values and doctrines. Perhaps most dramatically, these scholars vigorously

[48] Id. at 453–54.   [49] Id. at 454.
[50] Letter from Roscoe Pound to Harry A. Forster (April 27, 1916) (Pound Papers, supra note 45, Box 157, Folder 4).

rejected Blackstone's limitation of free speech to the prohibition of prior restraints. They condemned the many American judges who relied on Blackstone, including the justices of the Supreme Court for the opinion written by Holmes in the *Patterson* case.

Schofield and Schroeder provided compelling historical arguments for rejecting Blackstone. They emphasized that the framers of the First Amendment and the initial state constitutions intended to overturn the antirepublican English common law of free speech summarized by Blackstone in his *Commentaries.* Schofield pointed out that many publications about politics in the American colonies before the Revolution "were seditious and even treasonable under the English common law and its administration." An object of the American Revolution, he maintained, "was to get rid of the English common law on liberty of speech and of the press."[51]

Schofield emphasized that in creating a new government Americans adopted a conception of sovereignty that required a new understanding of free expression. The view that "the governed are the master and the governors are the servants," Schofield asserted, "was promulgated in the Declaration of Independence, was vindicated by the Revolutionary War, and was made the foundation stone of the law of the land by our written constitutions."[52] In order to perform their responsibilities under this conception of sovereignty, the people needed more free speech than the "antirepublican precedent"[53] provided by Blackstone's *Commentaries,* which reflected the very different view that the ruler is superior to his subjects.[54] The framers of American constitutions included written provisions guaranteeing freedom of speech and of the press, Schofield observed, because they wanted to base the recognition of greater expressive rights in the United States on more than an "inference from the legal fact of the supremacy of the people." He called the courts "a failure" for holding that these provisions "are only declaratory of the anti-republican English common law of the days of Blackstone,"[55] and described the opinion by Holmes in *Patterson* as simply "wrong."[56] American judges, he complained, "seem to have forgotten that the founders of the government are not distinguished for their reception of the English common law but for their adaptation of the democratic leaning and tendency of the constitutional side of it to a new career of popular freedom and equal justice."[57]

[51] Schofield, supra note 4, at 76.
[53] Id. at 85.
[55] Id. at 115.
[57] Id. at 83.

[52] Id. at 75–76.
[54] Id. at 75.
[56] Id. at 110.

Schroeder reinforced Schofield's major historical points in more colorful language. "Can it be," he asked incredulously, "that the only object of the framers of our constitution was the mere abolition of a censorship before publication, in favor of a censorship after publication, without any actual enlargement of intellectual liberty?"[58] He observed that the English licensing acts, which allowed prior censorship, had expired in 1694.[59] "Did the makers of our constitution," Schroeder asked with equal incredulity, "believe the people before the revolution enjoyed adequate liberty of the press?"[60] To accept Blackstone's definition of free speech, as the Supreme Court did in *Patterson*, struck Schroeder as an acknowledgment that "for nearly a century preceding our Revolution the agitation for larger freedom of speech and of the press was a vain demand for something already enjoyed by the agitators, but not known by them to exist." Schroeder considered this position "ridiculous," despite "the official eminence" of the numerous American judges who relied on Blackstone. He maintained that

> unabridged liberty of discussion did not obtain in England, or its American Colonies, from 1694 until the American Revolution, and that our Constitutions were designed to change the prevailing system of an abridged and *abridgeable liberty of discussion by permission,* to an unabridged and *unabridgeable liberty of discussion as a constitutionally guaranteed, natural right,* not to be ignored, as in England, or Russia, where the claim of such freedom was and is denied, on the plea of furthering the public welfare.[61]

Like Schofield, Schroeder pointed out that Blackstone's belief in the British monarchical theory of government accounted for his acceptance of the abridgments on free expression under the English common law he summarized in his *Commentaries.* Schroeder also mentioned Blackstone's belief in witchcraft in an apparent attempt to portray his views on free expression as equally absurd. The framers of the American constitutional guarantees of free speech, Schroeder stressed, adopted the views of Blackstone's opponents, not of Blackstone himself.[62] "The whole controversy over 'freedom of speech,'" Schroeder argued, "was a demand that speakers might be free from . . . subsequent punishment as well as previous restraint, . . . and it was that controversy which the

---

[58] Schroeder-"Obscene" Literature, supra note 1, at 158.
[59] Id. at 207.   [60] Id. at 158.
[61] Id. at 208.   [62] Id. at 225–26.

framers of our constitutions intended to decide for all time."[63] If the framers wanted to prohibit only prior restraints, Schroeder argued, "the easiest way would have been to have had the Constitution say, 'No censor shall ever be appointed,' or 'No *previous* restraints shall be put upon speech or press.'"[64]

Although Cooley did not base his rejection of Blackstone on historical arguments and died before the Supreme Court decision in *Patterson,* he, too, believed that the constitutional protections for speech and press secured more than "mere exemption from previous restraints." After pointing out that oral statements cannot be censured, he maintained that "the liberty of the press might be rendered a mockery and a delusion, and the phrase itself a byword, if, while every man was at liberty to publish what he pleased, the public authorities might nevertheless punish him for harmless publications." The framers of American constitutions, Cooley asserted, wanted to prevent not just censorship of the press, but any government action that might interfere with "such free and general discussion of public matters as seems absolutely essential to prepare the people for an intelligent exercise of their rights as citizens."[65] While avoiding direct criticism of Blackstone or the American courts that relied on his *Commentaries,* Freund asserted his objections to many forms of subsequent punishment for expression throughout *The Police Power.* Freund even maintained that criminal anarchy statutes, which prohibited advocacy of the overthrow of government by force, violated the constitutional guarantees of free speech, press, and assembly.[66]

Consistent with his general attack on "mechanical jurisprudence," Pound criticized Blackstone for a "merely formal" position on free speech that did not respond to social realities. Pound observed that if a legislature could impose subsequent liability for expression, it could "effectually prevent indirectly" the same publications it could not directly censor, and could thereby evade the formal guarantee against prior restraints. He cited and agreed with the typical criticism of Blackstone's approach to free speech "as not going far enough in securing against imposition of liability after publication upon arbitrary or unreasonable grounds." Blackstone's approach, Pound protested, "proceeds on a formal interpretation of the guarantee that deprives it of substantial efficacy when applied to legislation imposing prohibitive penalties." Pound believed, however, that Blackstone also "goes too far in

---

[63] Schroeder-Free Speech, supra note 1, at 41.
[64] Schroeder-"Obscene" Literature, supra note 1, at 210.
[65] Cooley, supra note 2, at 520–21.   [66] Freund, supra note 3, at 513.

denying to the law all power of restraint before publication." He rejected the argument that "the constitutional guarantee of free speech and free publication absolutely precludes an injunction against speaking and writing under any circumstances." Such a prohibition, he pointed out as a good progressive, would mean that "the constitution would forbid administrative prevention of false labels under a pure food law."[67] Without Pound's elaborate conceptual apparatus, Schofield also described as "untenable" decisions that refused to issue injunctions against threatened union activity or defamatory falsehoods solely because the courts assumed that any prior restraint on publications violates the constitutional protection for free speech.[68]

LIMITING THE BAD TENDENCY TEST

Many of the prewar scholars, similarly departing from prevailing judicial opinion, also asserted that American constitutional protection for free expression limited the punishment of speech for its alleged bad tendency, especially regarding matters of public concern. Schofield was the scholar who relied most heavily on the American rejection of the English common law of free speech to deny the legitimacy of the bad tendency test. He pointed out that the English common law at the time of the American Revolution divided unlawful publications into four categories of libel: defamation, sedition, blasphemy, and obscenity or immorality. The tendency of a publication "to create and diffuse among the people an ill opinion" was the key factor in determining whether it constituted one of these four categories of libel. Thus, a defamatory tendency related to "the personal or professional reputations of the persons referred to," a seditious tendency to "existing public officers, government, institutions, and laws," a blasphemous tendency to the Christian religion, and an obscene tendency to "existing standards of morality." With respect to defamatory libel, Schofield observed, "it seems actual objective tendency as a matter of fact was more emphasized than in the other cases of seditious, blasphemous, and obscene and immoral libels, where supposed tendency as a matter of abstract, subjective speculation seems to have been controlling and decisive." All four categories of libel were criminal under English law, although charges of defamatory libel could also be brought in a civil action by the person alleging injury to reputation. In a civil action, truth was an absolute defense, but the bur-

---

[67] Pound-Equitable Relief, supra note 5, at 651, 654.
[68] Schofield, supra note 4, at 105 n.1, 106 n.1.

den of proving truth rested with the defendant. By contrast, in criminal prosecutions the truth or falsity of the publication was irrelevant, as revealed by the common maxim, "the greater the truth the greater the libel."[69]

Schofield pointed out that religion and politics were the major subjects of public debate in England before the American Revolution.[70] He summarized the English common law of free speech on the eve of the Revolution as subject to "the opinion of the judges of the King's Bench on the tendency of publications, true or false, to excite and move the people to change the existing order." Schofield also observed that the English common law considered the Christian religion a fundamental part of this order. "As it was popularly put," Schofield disparagingly reported, "the English judges were proceeding on the view that God had a reputation to maintain and needed the help of the English common law to support it."[71]

Explicitly relying on history rather than on judicial opinions he believed mistaken, Schofield maintained that American constitutional provisions on free speech "obliterated the English common-law test of supposed bad tendency to determine the seditious or blasphemous character of a publication," and thereby abolished sedition and blasphemy as crimes at common law. He placed great weight on the Virginia Religious Liberty statute of 1777, which provided that government officials should interfere only "when principles break out into overt acts against peace and good order." Schofield pointed out that Thomas Jefferson, the author of the Virginia statute, himself acknowledged that neither his ideas nor his language were original. Rather, Jefferson drew on the earlier laws of several other states and on the best previous English literature advocating religious liberty and freedom of the press.[72]

A key document in this literature, Schofield asserted, was a letter from Dr. Furneaux to Blackstone himself, published in England and in Philadelphia before Jefferson wrote the Virginia statute. Furneaux, a popular independent minister in England, published his *Letters to Mr. Justice Blackstone* in 1770 to provide arguments against Blackstone's treatment of religious nonconformity as a crime in the 1769 volume of his *Commentaries*.[73] In a passage quoted by Schofield, Furneaux wrote that "the tendency of principles" should not be punished until "it issues in some overt acts against the public peace and order." The magistrate "may

---

[69] Id. at 71–72.   [70] Id. at 71.

[71] Id. at 74.   [72] Id. at 77–79, and at 78 n.1.

[73] Alexander Gordon, Furneaux, Philip, 7 Dictionary of National Biography 770–72 (Leslie Stephen and Sidney Lee eds. 1908–9).

punish the *overt acts,* but not the tendency." "Punishing a man for the tendency of his *principles,*" Furneaux added, "is punishing him *before* he is guilty, for fear he *should be guilty*" and could lead to "the total destruction of civil liberty." While conceding that Jefferson might not have relied on Furneaux's letter to Blackstone in drafting the Virginia statute, Schofield was certain that he was looking for such literature. Schofield also conceded that the distinction in the Virginia statute "between the tendency of principles and overt acts arising from principles had special reference to the subject of religion and to nonconformists in the Christian religion." He maintained, however, that this distinction "applies equally to any matter of public concern within the sphere of the right of liberty of the press."[74]

Consistent with his claim that the First Amendment abolished the English common-law crime of seditious libel, Schofield asserted that the Sedition Act of 1798 was clearly unconstitutional. Although the Sedition Act referred to the "intent to defame" the government, Schofield pointed out that judges interpreting it essentially equated intent and tendency by inferring unlawful intent from the bad tendency of antigovernment publications. Lower court judges refused to hold the Sedition Act unconstitutional, and no defendant challenged these decisions in the Supreme Court. Schofield maintained, however, that the destruction of the Federalist Party for its role in passing this law demonstrated the popular understanding of its unconstitutionality. He emphasized that there had been no subsequent seditious libel cases in the United States until the 1908 prosecutions that led to the Supreme Court's decision in *Press Publishing.* The publications that criticized President Roosevelt for misleading the American people about the purchase of the Panama Canal, Schofield insisted, "were not seditious, and could not be, because the crime of sedition and liberty of the press as declared in the First Amendment cannot co-exist."[75]

Schofield, however, did not maintain that the American constitutional provisions on freedom of speech and press abolished the bad tendency test in all circumstances. These provisions, he argued, precluded the English common-law crimes of sedition and blasphemy, but allowed punishment based on the tendency of speech for obscenity and for libels based on falsehood. Schofield had no constitutional objections to the American adoption of the English definition of obscenity in the *Hicklin* case. He acknowledged that this definition, by focusing on the tendency of a publi-

---

[74] Schofield, supra note 4, at 77–78.   [75] Id. at 86–87.

cation to corrupt anyone who might read it, could fairly be criticized as being too subjective and "offensive to Americans devoted
to equality." He maintained without citing cases, however, that the
judges who applied the *Hicklin* test generally examined "whether
the publication in question has a tendency to shock the moral
sense of the average, normal head of a family," a formulation close
to the one Hand suggested in *Kennerley* while admitting that judges
had construed the *Hicklin* test more restrictively. Schofield
acknowledged that even his understanding of the existing test of
obscenity might prevent "truthful and useful publications of educational value on sex hygiene, commercialized vice, and other subjects, heretofore tabooed, but now thought by many fit topics for
public discussion." While he indicated that he would support legislative efforts to change the common law of obscenity, however,
he reiterated his view that the *Hicklin* test did not violate the constitutional protection for speech.[76]

The American constitutions, Schofield added, modified but did
not abolish the law of defamation. They precluded the punishment of truth about matters of public concern, wiping out the
English concept, "the greater the truth the greater the libel." He
did not believe, however, that the American constitutional provisions on free expression either applied to matters of private concern, or abolished the punishment of falsehood on matters of
public concern having "a tendency to defame personal or professional reputation or to cast suspicion on the title or quality of
property." Even nondefamatory falsehoods "having a tendency to
mislead the people on matters of public concern," Schofield
emphasized, could clearly be punished without violating constitutional guarantees of free expression.[77]

Cooley shared many of Schofield's views about the ways in
which the American constitutional protection of free speech limited the bad tendency test of the English common law. Under the
common law, Cooley observed, publications could be punished
because of their "tendency . . . to excite disaffection with the government, and thus induce a revolutionary spirit." This principle,
he asserted, was "unsuited to the condition and circumstances of
the people of America" and was never adopted in the United
States. "Repression of full and free discussion," Cooley emphasized, "is dangerous in any government resting upon the will of the
people." Thus, just as Schofield maintained that the American
conception of popular sovereignty precluded Blackstone's limitation of free speech to the absence of prior restraints, Cooley relied

[76] Id. at 82.   [77] Id. at 79, 81.

on popular sovereignty to reject the application of the English common law of bad tendency to speech on matters of public affairs. Cooley attributed the Sedition Act of 1798 to a period "when the fabric of government was still new and untried." Even at the time, he pointed out, many questioned its constitutionality. Cooley did not explicitly state his own opinion about the constitutionality of the Sedition Act, but he maintained that "its impolicy was beyond question" and that the passage of a similar statute "is impossible to conceive."[78]

Cooley, like Schofield, seemed to acknowledge that the English common law of bad tendency survived in the United States for certain categories of expression that did not pertain to public affairs. The American constitutional provisions guaranteeing freedom of speech and press, he believed, did not apply to expression on private topics unless there was a "reason in public policy demanding protection to the communication." In "cases of publications injurious to private character, or public morals or safety," punishment would not violate the federal or state constitutions.[79] Somewhat more specifically, Cooley wrote that the English common law remained in effect after the adoption of American constitutions for publications that are blasphemous, obscene, scandalous, or libelous based on falsehood and malice.[80]

Freund did not agree with Cooley and Schofield that the American constitutions repudiated the English common law of seditious libel and its reliance on the bad tendency of speech attacking the government.[81] He did not view the Sedition Act of 1798 as an unconstitutional departure from the First Amendment or as a false step by an inexperienced government, but as evidence that "the principle of freedom of the press was not believed to be contrary to the punishment of seditious libel." Freund added, however, that the American understanding of the constitutional protection for expression had changed since 1800. He pointed out that the last prosecution for seditious libel had occurred in 1805 and that American codifications of the criminal law generally did not cover sedition. "The most ample freedom of discussion of public affairs," he stressed, "is now generally understood to be guaranteed by the freedom of speech and of the press, and the long continued practice of toleration may be accepted as sufficient warrant for modifying the interpretation of the express constitutional guaranty to that effect."[82]

---

[78] Cooley, supra note 2, at 528–31.   [79] Id. at 531.
[80] Id. at 521.   [81] Freund, supra note 3, at 506–7.
[82] Id. at 508–9.

For example, Freund opposed as "inconsistent with the freedom of speech and press" the punishment of anarchists for maintaining that "all established government is wrongful and pernicious and should be destroyed." Just as freedom of religion would be meaningless if people could not attack all religion, Freund believed, freedom of speech would have no content if such anarchist views were unprotected. "It is of the essence of political liberty," he maintained, "that it may create disaffection or other inconvenience to the existing government, otherwise there would be no merit in tolerating it."[83] Under English common law, the creation of disaffection with existing government was proof of the bad tendency of speech. Freund clearly believed that in the early twentieth century, if not in 1798, the American constitutional protection for free expression precluded punishment for the bad tendency of speech about public affairs. On the other hand, Freund, like Schofield and Cooley, accepted the punishment of obscenity for its "natural and probable consequences"[84] and emphasized that American constitutions did not abolish the common law of slander and libel.[85]

Alone among the prewar scholars, Schroeder rejected application of the bad tendency test to expression on any topic. Reflecting his libertarian radicalism, Schroeder did not differentiate between obscenity and seditious libel in opposing the bad tendency test. In fact, he concentrated on the law of obscenity to illustrate his general criticisms of prevailing constitutional interpretations of free expression. The title of his major collection of essays on free speech, "Obscene" Literature and Constitutional Law, captured this focus.

Schroeder understood the First Amendment to require that "no form of speech (including printing) can be penalized merely on the basis of a jury speculation about the prospective psychological tendency of the idea upon a hypothetical future reader."[86] Punishing expression for its "supposed bad tendency," in Schroeder's view, violated the First Amendment.[87] The Articles of Incorporation of the Free Speech League reflected Schroeder's position by stating that one of the League's principle objects was "to preclude punishment of any mere psychological offense."[88] According to Schroeder, "the agitation for more freedom of speech and press" that culminated in the First Amendment opposed "mere psycho-

[83] Id. at 509–10.   [84] Id. at 223.
[85] Id. at 506.
[86] Schroeder-Free Speech, supra note 1, at 93.
[87] Schroeder-"Obscene" Literature, supra note 1, at 207.
[88] Schroeder-Free Speech, supra note 1, at frontispiece.

logical crimes" such as constructive treason, seditious libel, and heresy.[89] The "demand for certainty in the criteria of guilt," he observed, was a significant part of this agitation and reflected the understanding that the bad tendency test based punishment on unprovable assumptions about the evil influences of opinions.[90] Obscenity, Schroeder maintained, resembled these other crimes because "the unrealized psychological tendency by which a particular book is judged 'obscene' has no demonstrable existence except as a belief about a doubtful future possibility."[91]

For Schroeder, the power to suppress expression based on a bad tendency that "is only speculatively, prospectively, and imaginatively ascertained, is the admission of a power to enslave the mind of all, and upon all subjects." The Constitution, he stressed, "makes no distinction" based on the content of speech.[92] Schroeder developed this point in opposing the suppression of alleged obscenity. The congressional power to regulate the mail, he protested, did not give it discretion to determine "the psychologic tendencies of ideas expressed upon the transmitted matter."[93] In a series of rhetorical questions, Schroeder made clear that he considered alleged obscenity to be an expression of ideas deserving the same protection as all other views.

> Can the literature of Catholics, free-lovers, theists, agnostics be excluded as unapproved by the law-making power, while the literature of evangelicals, polygamists and Christian scientists is transmitted because approved? May the literature of trades unionism be excluded and that of the employer's association transmitted? May literature favoring the single tax, free trade, or state ownership of railroads be excluded, and those favoring an income tax, protective tariff and the repeal of anti-trust laws, be transmitted? Has congress the power to so regulate the mails as to transmit all literature "tending" to a centralization of power, progressive tyranny, moralization by force and that which "tends" to foster the ascetic ideal of sexual life, while it excludes all matter which "tends" toward decentralization and personal liberty, or 'tends' to foster unconventional ideas of sex-life, all other conditions being the same? May the literature of prohibitionists be excluded, while that of their opponents is transmitted?[94]

---

[89] Schroeder-"Obscene" Literature, supra note 1, at 237, 408.
[90] Id. at 237–38.   [91] Id. at 362.
[92] Schroeder-Free Speech, supra note 1, at 64; see id. at 47–48.
[93] Schroeder-"Obscene" Literature, supra note 1, at 133; see id. at 137.
[94] Id. at 132.

These questions covered many of the most contentious issues of Schroeder's time and, in libertarian radical fashion, linked a general commitment to personal liberty with unconventional views about sex that others frequently deemed obscene. Schroeder reiterated that Congress had no power to suppress speech on any of these issues.[95] "Books once condemned for their supposed evil tendencies," Schroeder observed, "are now believed to have been good and useful." He maintained that continued use of the bad tendency test presented the danger of "a repetition of such error."[96]

Although Schroeder relied primarily on the First Amendment in rejecting any punishment based on the bad tendency of speech, he also invoked the inherent uncertainty of the bad tendency test to allege connections between the First Amendment and other constitutional rights. The due process clauses of the Fifth and Fourteenth Amendments, Schroeder pointed out, require "absolute certainty in the criteria of guilt" as a check against "arbitrary power." He asserted that his conception of the First Amendment was the only way to "coordinate" freedom of expression with due process of law.[97] "It goes without saying," he added, "that so long as an *ex post facto* judicial guess as to the psychologic tendency of a speech, book, or picture is the test of guilt, there can be no such thing as liberty under the law."[98] Uncertainty, Schroeder also maintained, is inconsistent with the Sixth Amendment's assurance that the defendant in all criminal prosecutions "shall be informed of the nature and cause of the accusation."[99]

ALTERNATIVE STANDARDS FOR
ANALYZING FREE SPEECH CLAIMS

The prewar legal scholars did not simply argue against survivals of the English common law that they deemed inconsistent with the American constitutional protection for free speech. In addition to rejecting Blackstone's conception of free speech as merely the absence of prior restraints and to advocating significant limits on the punishment of speech for its alleged bad tendency, these scholars proposed alternative standards for analyzing free speech claims. Some of these standards emerged from reflection about a discrete

---

[95] Id.   [96] Id. at 236.

[97] Schroeder-Free Speech, supra note 1, at 92–93; see Schroeder-"Obscene" Literature, supra note 1, at 359–60, 364, 408.

[98] Schroeder-"Obscene" Literature, supra note 1, at 237; see id. at 363; Schroeder-Free Speech, supra note 1, at 96.

[99] Schroeder-Free Speech, supra note 1, at 95–96.

free speech issue. Others applied to a broader range of topics and occasionally derived from social theories beyond the law.

Many of the prewar scholars, with varying degrees of emphasis and explicitness, distinguished "public" from "private" speech and advocated substantially more protection for speech on matters of public concern. This distinction, which scholars often traced to the historical origins of the First Amendment and the state constitutions, lay behind their approaches to a variety of free speech issues. Analysis of the bad tendency of speech frequently reflected this distinction by opposing the law of seditious libel and other tests of bad tendency for "public" speech while accepting some form of the bad tendency test for "private" speech such as libel and obscenity.

In addition to his rejection of the bad tendency test for speech on public affairs, Cooley advocated more protection for public than for private speech while supporting a privilege for publishers of news. He stressed that the newspaper "is one of the chief means for the education of the people," especially about politics, and urged in his treatise, as in his judicial opinions, that the law should protect all publications on matters of public concern as long as they have not "been inspired by malice." On the other hand, Cooley objected to protection for articles in which "private character is dragged before the public for detraction and abuse, to pander to a depraved appetite for scandal." He also cautioned that "there is a difference between the mere publication of items of news in which the public may take an interest, as news merely, and the discussion of matters which concern the public because they are their own affairs." However interested the public may be in the conduct of a private individual, Cooley maintained, that conduct becomes a matter of public concern, justifying a privilege for publishers, only when "it threatens to be injurious to others."[100]

The conduct of public officials, Cooley emphasized by contrast, is a legitimate subject of public concern. It is impossible to discuss public affairs, Cooley believed, without making some derogatory comments about individuals.[101] In defending a general privilege for criticism of public officials and candidates for office, Cooley rejected the common judicial "assumption that the private character of a public official is something aside from, and not entering into or influencing, his public conduct." A person who is dishonest in private life, Cooley observed, is likely to be corrupt in office.[102] Matters of public concern, he added, extend beyond the activities of government and include "all schemes, projects, enter-

---

[100] Cooley, supra note 2, at 557, 559, 562–63.
[101] Id. at 560.   [102] Id. at 542–43.

prises and organizations of a semi-public nature, which invite the public favor, and depend for their success on public confidence." As examples, he mentioned the management and integrity of institutions such as banks, insurance companies, private asylums, boards of trade, and public fairs.[103]

Schofield was the prewar legal scholar who relied most heavily on the distinction between private and public speech. He applied this distinction not just in his discussion of the bad tendency test, but throughout his discussion of legal doctrine. Schofield emphasized the constitutional protection of the press "as a public-education right" while rejecting Schroeder's claim that statutes excluding obscene publications from the mails violated the First Amendment. Under the assumption that obscene publications lacked educational value, Schofield characterized them as private rather than public speech. Schofield similarly accepted the constitutionality of laws that created boards of censors for the emerging film industry. While acknowledging that plays and movies are protected by freedom of the press if they deal with matters of public concern, a concession not made by the Supreme Court in the *Mutual Film* case, Schofield maintained that no such protection exists for obscene performances for private profit. Rejecting the argument that the possibility of administrative mistakes in categorizing the subject matter of films as private or public made the underlying statutory scheme unconstitutional, Schofield emphasized the availability of judicial review to correct any errors.[104]

Advertising, like obscenity, struck Schofield as private speech unprotected by the First Amendment. For Schofield, advertising included both publications promoting lotteries "and other devices to make easy and quick money"[105] as well as "Unfair" and "We don't patronize" lists such as the ones enjoined by the Supreme Court in the *Gompers* case. Those lists, he wrote, were simply advertisements "to make a strike or boycott more effective" and "are not exercises of the right of liberty of the press any more than 'U-Need-a-Biscuit' or 'Drink Schlitz, the beer that made Milwaukee famous,' are exercises of the right." Schofield stressed the crucial difference between mere advertisements "to promote the private welfare" and "educational publications to promote the general welfare."[106]

In discussing Alexander Hamilton's definition of freedom of the press, Schofield further elaborated his distinction between public and private speech. Representing a defendant in an 1804 libel

---

[103] Id. at 562–63.
[104] Schofield, supra note 4, at 82–83, and at 82 n.1.
[105] Id. at 83.   [106] Id. at 105.

case, Hamilton formulated a definition that many states incorporated into their constitutional provisions on free expression. "The liberty of the press," Hamilton asserted, "consists in the right to publish, with impunity, truth, with good motives, for justifiable ends, though reflecting on government, magistracy, or individuals." Schofield reported that no court had ever analyzed the meaning of Hamilton's definition.[107] Schofield himself rejected its application to speech on public affairs, warning that bad motives and unjustifiable ends "almost inevitably will come down in practice to a fiction inferred from the supposed bad tendency of the publication."[108]

Schofield, however, did approve Hamilton's test as a judicial limitation whenever liberty of the press is extended to matters of private concern. This additional but properly confined protection, Schofield believed, would safeguard desirable private speech without unfairly exposing individuals to invasions of privacy and other potential abuses of totally unrestrained freedom of expression.[109] Schofield mentioned labor publications in support of a strike or boycott as examples of private speech that should be protected under the Hamiltonian state constitutions.[110] On the other hand, he claimed that advertisements for "getting rich quick without work" are not made for good motives or justifiable ends.[111] Despite his libertarian concerns, even Schroeder seemed to agree with Schofield's analysis of the Hamiltonian state constitutions.[112] In an article published the year after Schofield's, Schroeder accepted Hamilton's test as "sufficient liberty" for publications about the private affairs of private citizens while rejecting its application to "matters of public concern."

Although he emphasized the special constitutional protection for public speech, Schofield did not advocate absolute immunity. The centrality of speech on matters of public concern to a democracy based on popular sovereignty, Schofield observed, justifies regulation as well as protection. He agreed with the Supreme Court's decision in the *Lewis* case, which upheld the required publication of information about ownership as a condition for receiving low mailing rates. The statutory obligation to disclose this information, Schofield believed, promoted rather than restricted liberty of the press. He reasoned that because newspapers and magazines "educate the public on matters of public concern,"

---

[107] Id. at 95.

[108] Id. at 92 n.2.

[109] Id. at 92–94.

[110] Id. at 106.

[111] Id. at 83.

[112] Theodore Schroeder, Presumptions and Burden of Proof as to Malice in Criminal Libel, 49 Am. L. Rev. 199, 208–9 (1915).

readers have a right to know who owns these "public educational institutions." Cases that allowed a privilege for publications "of defamatory falsehood on matters of public concern," Schofield added, constituted "unauthorized judicial legislation destructive of men's reputation and property." Although he stressed the fundamental constitutional protection for all truthful publications about public affairs, Schofield did not want publishers "to found their educational power on falsehood."[113] This concern probably also accounts for Schofield's openness to laws punishing even non-defamatory falsehoods "having a tendency to mislead the people on matters of public concern."[114]

Schofield, like other prewar scholars, carefully distinguished speech about matters of public concern from advocacy of crime and violence. He agreed with the New York court that convicted Johann Most for publishing an article advising the murder of public officials, riot, and arson. Schofield maintained that such speech constituted "an overt act against peace and good order" and could not properly be compared with the kind of criticism that was unconstitutionally punished as defamation of government under the Sedition Act of 1798.[115] In discussing the constitutionality of President Jackson's attempts in the 1830s to prohibit mailing abolitionist literature into the slave states, Schofield made a similar distinction. While arguing that the First Amendment right "to publish truth on all matters of *national* public concern" demonstrated the unconstitutionality of a total prohibition of such literature, he maintained that Jackson was on constitutionally sound ground if his "message was limited to abolitionist literature teaching the use of force."[116]

Freund defined incitement more specifically as beyond the protection of free speech. He concluded that "a statute may validly forbid all speaking and writing the object of which is to incite directly to the commission of violence and crime." Incitement may be punished, Freund emphasized, even if the "end is never accomplished or even undertaken."[117] On the other hand, Freund considered it "contrary to constitutional liberty in a free state to exercise compulsory control over public opinion and agitation, which refrains from the practice or incitement of violence and from injury to private rights." The First Amendment and state constitutional provisions that guaranteed free speech, press, assembly, and petition, Freund maintained, withdrew such control from the police power.[118]

---

[113] Schofield, supra note 4, at 114–15.   [114] Id. at 81.

[115] Id. at 88.   [116] Id. at 113.

[117] Freund, supra note 3, at 510.   [118] Id. at 10–11.

Cases that involved anarchists, Freund acknowledged, raised difficult problems in drawing the line between constitutionally protected agitation and criminal incitement. He defined incitement to include the "glorification" of previous crimes and words not addressed to or aimed at a specific person. Freund, however, did not view an assertion that crime could be justified under certain stated circumstances as an incitement. Reasoning that "it is impossible to strike at anarchism as a doctrine without jeopardising valuable constitutional rights," Freund opposed much of the antianarchy legislation passed after the assassination of President McKinley. The commission of a crime by an adherent of a doctrine, he also observed, does not necessarily make an advocate of that doctrine guilty of incitement. Freund believed that underlying "morbid brooding" over social conditions, rather than speech, was frequently responsible for criminal conduct by anarchists. Freund, however, did accept the controversial finding of the Supreme Court of Illinois that the Haymarket anarchists had incited to violence, and he raised no objections to the convictions of Johann Most in New York.[119]

Cooley's earlier treatise lent implicit support to the more developed positions of Freund and Schofield. Cooley advocated punishment for criticisms of government only "when they are made in furtherance of conspiracy with the evident intent and purpose to excite rebellion and civil war." All other political speech, he believed, is free under American constitutions, "however sharp, unreasonable and intemperate it might be." Cooley justified this position by a frank acknowledgment of social and economic differences. He maintained that classes excluded from participating in government are often the most vigorous in criticizing it. Judges and juries, Cooley observed, generally belong "to the very classes who have established the exclusion" under attack, and will have preconceived views that the criticism is unreasonable. Furthermore, they can only evaluate it after "the heat of the occasion has passed away" and therefore cannot appreciate the magnitude of the evil the critic perceived. The danger of repression, Cooley added, is increased "in times of high party excitement." For all these reasons, he reiterated, even "violent discussion" of public affairs beyond "all the proper bounds of moderation" is protected by American constitutional provisions.[120]

For Schroeder, the libertarian radical, even an incitement standard was insufficient to protect speech. He maintained that the First Amendment and the free speech provisions of state constitu-

---

[119] Id. at 510–13.   [120] Cooley, supra note 2, at 529–31.

tions guaranteed "the right of every man to advocate the moral righteousness of anything, even though such conduct has been denounced by the statute as a crime." According to Schroeder, "every such advocacy was intended to be protected against punishment, excepting only the one condition, that a criminal act follows, as a direct and designed result of his utterances; and, in that event, he is to be punished for the subsequent crime and his intentional participation in it, and not merely for his utterances, as such."[121] Utterances, Schroeder concluded, "may be evidence tending to show his responsibility for the *actual injury* which is penalized, but the penalty attaches on account of that injury, and can never be predicated merely upon the sentiments uttered" without violating the constitutional protection for speech.[122]

In applying this standard, Schroeder pointed out that a speaker could be punished as an accessory to murder, arson, or any other crime that had already occurred, and that his speech could be used as evidence of his responsibility for the resulting injury.[123] Schroeder asserted, however, that even the advocacy of treason and assassination is protected by the constitutional right of free speech "so long as no one was actually injured thereby."[124] Schroeder similarly distinguished between using the mail to accomplish an actual crime and using it to express ideas, including "incendiary" opinions that might advocate crime. "There is all the difference in the world," Schroeder maintained, "between punishing the use of the mails for disseminating opinions advocating the morality of gambling and punishing the use of mails to accomplish the crime of gambling." Based on this reasoning, he conceded that Congress could prohibit lotteries that constitute gambling and publications that are part of a fraud from the mail.[125] Schroeder, however, vigorously rejected the Supreme Court's position that the same congressional power to regulate the mail also justified the exclusion of obscenity. Unlike gambling and fraud, he tartly observed, "fornication and adultery cannot be committed by mail."[126] From the admitted authority of Congress to punish "certain sexual misconduct," Schroeder emphasized, "it does not follow that it may punish purely intellectual crimes predicated merely upon sex discussions through the mails."[127] According to Schroeder, laws against "obscene" literature derived from the same

---

[121] Schroeder-Free Speech, supra note 1, at 34.

[122] Schroeder-"Obscene" Literature, supra note 1, at 151.

[123] Schroeder-Free Speech, supra note 1, at 40; Schroeder-"Obscene" Literature, supra note 1, at 151.

[124] Schroeder-Free Speech, supra note 1, at 41.

[125] Schroeder-"Obscene" Literature, supra note 1, at 21–22.

[126] Id. at 134.   [127] Id. at 22.

unfortunate and irrational moral passion that had previously produced legal crusades against witchcraft.[128] On the other hand, he acknowledged that personal libel can produce a material injury and can thus be punished without violating constitutional guarantees of free speech.[129]

At times, Schroeder backed off his strict standard, which precluded the punishment of speech unless a criminal act had occurred. Speech that directly leads to an attempt, he occasionally conceded, might constitutionally be punished even if the completed crime never takes place.[130] Schroeder seemed to give additional ground when he acknowledged the possibility that a legislature, consistent with the First Amendment, might "regulate the imminent danger of actual and material injury."[131] Speech could conceivably create "imminent danger" without producing an actual attempt.

Schroeder made clear, however, that this language, which bears a linguistic similarity to Holmes's "clear and present danger" phrase in *Schenck,* should not be considered a restatement of the bad tendency test that Schroeder repeatedly condemned. The "imminent danger," Schroeder stressed, can only be ascertained according to "the known laws of the physical universe."[132] Connecting his requirement of known physical laws to his rejection of the bad tendency test, Schroeder protested that the crime of obscenity depends upon jury "speculation about the psychologic tendency of a particular book upon a future hypothetical reader, which tendency has not yet become actualized at the time of indictment or trial, and which psychologic tendency is not known to us to be controlled by any exact known law having the immutability of the physical laws of our material universe." By contrast, he indicated that he would not object to a definition of obscenity that identified specific "sense-perceived qualities" by which a book could produce illegal sexual behavior.[133]

Schroeder also attacked the courts, as Justice Harlan criticized his colleagues in *Patterson,* for restricting freedom of discussion to "whatever a legislature of mediocre attainments" considers in the "interest of the public welfare." Indeed, Schroeder maintained that this limitation on free speech would make inexplicable the enactment of the First Amendment "because no other opinions than such as had been deemed contrary to the public welfare ever

---

[128] Id. at 25.   [129] Id. at 408.

[130] Id. at 207; Schroeder-Free Speech, supra note 1, at 100.

[131] Schroeder-"Obscene" Literature, supra note 1, at 238; Schroeder, Free Speech, supra note 1, at 113.

[132] Schroeder-"Obscene" Literature, supra note 1, at 238; see id. at 160, 350; Schroeder-Free Speech, supra note 1, at 113.

[133] Schroeder-"Obscene" Literature, supra note 1, at 362–63.

had been suppressed anywhere." Schroeder pointed out that the language of the First Amendment makes no exception for "the interest of the public welfare," and insisted that courts could not properly read such a restriction into it.[134]

In comparison to the other major scholars before World War I, Pound's writings on freedom of expression were both more firmly grounded in his general jurisprudence and less comprehensive in treating the range of free speech issues. Pound only focused on free speech in portions of several articles, but he applied to his analysis of this subject the balancing of competing social interests at the heart of his sociological jurisprudence. Unlike Schroeder, Pound recognized the public welfare as a legitimate social interest in the balance even as he criticized the courts for giving insufficient weight to competing interests in free speech. Citing political opposition to the federal government during the Civil War, Pound maintained that in certain circumstances free speech "may so affect the activities of the state necessary to its preservation as to outweigh the individual interest or even the social interest in free belief and free speech."[135] Pound believed that the public welfare outweighed interests in expression in a variety of less threatening contexts. A revealing footnote listed a number of cases that restricted free speech, identified the social interest in general security or morals at stake, and apparently approved the results in all of the cases cited. Pound did not differentiate among Most's publications, a public meeting led by a socialist, the distribution of handbills causing a threat of fire, newspaper reports of crime, and Salvation Army parades.[136] Consistent with his rejection of Blackstone's prohibition against prior restraints as a formalistic application of "mechanical jurisprudence" insensitive to social realities, Pound maintained that a balancing approach should be used to determine the merits of injunctive relief against defamation.[137]

The nature of the audience, Pound added, should be considered in the balance when determining the protection for expression. The same social and economic differences that led Cooley to propose wide latitude for free speech were, in Pound's opinion, grounds for restrictions. In a classic expression of progressive elitism, Pound worried about "the danger of mobs, which are controlled by suggestion," in the large and congested cities populated by the poor and ignorant. As a result, he approved restrictions on

[134] Id. at 210, 212.
[135] Pound-Personality, supra note 5, at 456.
[136] Id. at 455, n.99.
[137] Pound-Equitable Relief, supra note 5, at 682.

the time and place of political speech in order to avoid "grave danger of violence and disorder."[138]

In addition to developing standards of analysis that cut across a variety of free speech issues, the prewar scholars commented on discrete doctrinal subjects, often disagreeing with prevailing judicial analysis. For example, Schofield vigorously attacked judges for extending the doctrine of contempt of court to publications that criticized their conduct. He called this approach "intolerable in a land of equality before the law where judges are not more important to the universe than executives and legislators."[139] Schofield complained that judges hypocritically tried to insulate themselves from criticism they allowed against other public officials.[140] For Schofield, Justice Holmes's opinion for the Supreme Court majority that upheld the contempt conviction of Senator Patterson was "far from satisfactory," and he expressed confidence that it would not be "the last word on the subject." Using stronger language, Schofield added that the "practice of dealing with publications scandalizing judges under the criminal process of contempt of court ought to be stopped, voluntarily by the judges or under the compulsion of impeachment." Addressing another issue raised by the *Patterson* case, Schofield maintained that the First Amendment should apply to the states through the privileges and immunities clause of the Fourteenth Amendment.[141]

Freund's treatise on *The Police Power* covered other discrete free speech issues, often without referring directly to the First Amendment or analogous provisions in state constitutions. Public use of the streets, he declared, is essential to "the full enjoyment of individual liberty and property."[142] Freund explicitly rejected the reasoning by Holmes in the *Davis* case, which asserted that a legislature could control access to public streets as completely as a private home owner controls access to his house. To concede this analogy, Freund maintained, would be inconsistent with a democratic system of government, for it "would be equivalent to the recognition of a despotic power over every act which may be done in the public streets without regard even to the requirement of due process and equality." Rather, he asserted that restrictions on the common use of the streets must be justified in each instance rather than through an "uncontrolled exercise of proprietary discretion."[143] Freund conceded that a public park is legitimately subject to more restrictions than a street[144] and that even street meetings can be regulated on

---

[138] Pound-Personality, supra note 5, at 455.
[139] Schofield, supra note 4, at 115.   [140] Id. at 108.
[141] Id. at 111–13.   [142] Freund, supra note 3, at 150.

the basis of time, place, number, and duration. He insisted, however, that constitutional guarantees of assembly and petition preclude "the restraint or punishment of the mere act of meeting" on public streets "for the purpose of debate, discussion or cooperation."[145]

On the issue of obscenity, by contrast, Freund supported the common law while indicating concern about its possible extension to "legitimate purposes," such as science, social reform, art, and literature. He apparently reasoned that "legitimate purposes" determine the effects of publications and thereby shield them from charges of obscenity. A scientist, Freund assumed, does not have the purpose "of arousing impure emotions," an author "may depict immorality for a moral purpose," and an artist, even in creating nudes, is interested in beauty rather than the "grossness" that is an essential element of obscenity. Freund seemed uncomfortable in recognizing that the publication of true facts could constitute obscenity. "The interest of public decency," he nevertheless conceded, "demands that even in the legitimate pursuit of truth the channels selected for the spreading of truth be those least harmful to the community."[146]

THE HERITAGE OF PREWAR SCHOLARSHIP

The work of these five authors illustrates the chasm that existed before World War I between the world of legal scholarship and the judiciary. The restrictive results and the analytic poverty of the prewar decisions reflected the pervasive judicial hostility to the value of free speech. Those cases bear little resemblance to more recent First Amendment adjudication. Much of the legal scholarship of that period, on the other hand, hardly seems the product of an earlier age. Scholars identified and addressed many of the issues that continue to generate judicial and scholarly commentary. From historical and functional analyses of the purposes of the First Amendment, they derived practical tests for determining its scope.

The prewar scholarship on free speech, which judges of the period generally ignored, is largely forgotten today. Chafee is now considered the seminal scholar of the First Amendment. Chafee himself, however, relied on his scholarly predecessors, and Holmes and Brandeis in turn relied on Chafee in creating more protective standards of First Amendment interpretation in their dissenting opinions in the 1920s. As a result, prewar scholarship exerted belated yet significant influence on the development of First Amendment theory in a more receptive era.

[143] Id. at 151.
[145] Id. at 514–15.

[144] Id. at 155.
[146] Id. at 223–25.

5

Free Speech in Progressive Social Thought

Although important legal scholars devoted substantial attention to the meaning of free speech between the Civil War and World War I, American intellectuals in other fields rarely wrote directly about freedom of expression. For example, no major American philosopher of this period published a sustained analysis of free speech comparable to John Stuart Mill's nineteenth-century classic, *On Liberty*.[1] In the years immediately preceding World War I, however, progressive social thinkers attacked American traditions of individualism, represented in very different forms by libertarian radicalism and by Supreme Court decisions protecting constitutional rights to liberty against infringement by the state. The progressive attack against individualism, which Pound applied directly to legal analysis through his sociological jurisprudence, contained important implications for constitutional theory in general and free speech in particular.

Leading progressive intellectuals before the war, despite many significant differences among them, attributed the social problems produced by industrial capitalism to excessive individualism. They challenged the idea of natural, prepolitical rights held by autonomous individuals in isolation from society, associated law and constitutions with this erroneous conception of human nature, and rejected the related position that a laissez-faire government should do little more than protect individual rights. The legalistic formal rights of individualism, progressive intellectuals complained, had created a materialistic and immoral society divided by inequality and class conflict. Individual rights, intended by the framers of the Constitution to provide equal opportunity for all, had become the legal justification for protecting the selfish and irresponsible rich against government efforts on behalf of the entire society.

Progressive intellectuals developed alternative social theories in opposition to individualism. They viewed individuals as interde-

---

[1] John Stuart Mill, On Liberty (Penguin Classics ed. 1985) (1859).

pendent social beings whose own interests could be harmonized with broader community interests. They were confident that individuality could best be realized in a cooperative society sharing common values that transcended the materialism of capitalism. Government, rather than being a threat to individuals, could promote the public welfare and help create a consensual community by providing the resources needed for the actual exercise of positive and not merely formal rights. The prevailing legal conception of individual constitutional rights as absolute protections against the state, many progressives believed, posed significant barriers to their programs of social reform. They maintained instead that individual rights are derived from, and defined by, shifting social interests, as Pound elaborated in his sociological jurisprudence.

In attacking individual constitutional rights, progressives focused on Supreme Court decisions that invoked economic rights, especially property and liberty of contract, to invalidate reform legislation enacted in the public interest. *Lochner v. New York,* the 1905 decision in which the Supreme Court majority relied on liberty of contract to declare a law limiting working hours unconstitutional, became the infamous symbol of misplaced individualism for many progressives.[2] For legal scholars such as Cooley and Freund, the individual rights protected by the Constitution against the state extended as least as much to freedom of speech as to liberty of contract. By contrast, the Supreme Court's overwhelming hostility to free speech claims revealed a much more limited conception of constitutionally protected rights. As a result, when progressives attacked the Supreme Court for relying on individual constitutional rights to protect economic interests against legislative regulation, they were not forced to confront the relationship between economic and expressive rights. Progressive social thought, however, had significant implications for free speech. The progressive position that individual rights should be recognized only to the extent that they contribute to social interests applied in principle to speech as well as to liberty of contract. Pound explicitly acknowledged this point when he justified balancing social interests in free speech against competing social interests in the security of state institutions. The commitment of progressives to the creation of a harmonious community also limited their conception of free speech. While often recognizing the social value of criticism, progressives ignored and occasionally condemned dissent that did not contribute to the community.

Libertarian radicals agreed with much of the progressive critique

[2] 198 U.S. 45 (1905).

of industrial capitalism. Yet in contrast to the progressives, who believed that the excesses of capitalism derived from American traditions of individualism, the libertarian radicals tried to rescue meaningful conceptions of individual rights from their debasement under industrial capitalism to economic self-interest and justifications for inequality. Throughout the nineteenth century, libertarian radicals protested the loss of worker independence under developing capitalism. They linked labor reform with sex reform and the defense of free speech as coordinated efforts to preserve and extend individual autonomy. Much of the work of the Free Speech League, whose activities coincided with the rise of the progressive movement in the years before World War I, involved the defense of sex and labor radicals who attacked capitalism. The League's repeated assistance to Margaret Sanger, who perceived the birth control movement as a weapon against capitalism as well as part of the fight for free speech, provides the best, but far from the only, example. Progressive intellectuals ignored the libertarian radical tradition, but they made clear throughout their writings that all varieties of individualism, however historically valuable they once might have been, were powerless to combat the evils of industrial capitalism at the turn of the twentieth century. In their own era, progressives believed, the promise of American democracy could only be realized by replacing an outmoded attachment to individualism with a commitment to an activist state dedicated to the shared social interests of a democratic community.

The dual commitment of progressives to critical inquiry and community harmony created a tension at the core of their attitudes about free speech. Critical inquiry depends on free speech, but free speech can also undermine community harmony. Many progressive intellectuals emphasized the importance of broadly dispersed powers of critical inquiry throughout society. Consistent with their rejection of individualism, they developed a radical theory of knowledge that considered the verification of truth to be a social rather than an individual activity. They believed that social life changes over time, and that knowledge is therefore contingent, provisional, and subject to the unending tests of new inquiry. This theory of knowledge, with its emphasis on uncertainty, experimentation, and change, often lent itself to a reformist approach to politics.[3]

Progressive intellectuals frequently invoked the value of critical

---

[3] See James T. Kloppenberg, Uncertain Victory: Social Democracy and Progressivism in European and American Thought, 1870–1920, at 65, 98, 101, 113–14, 159, 413 (1986).

inquiry in science as a model for democratic life. Just as scientists form a community of inquirers who depend on mutual critical inquiry to formulate and test new ideas, society as a whole depends on critical inquiry to address social issues. Some progressive intellectuals believed that only exceptionally intelligent and specially trained experts, the counterparts of scientists, had the ability to apply the techniques of critical inquiry to social life. Much writing on academic freedom, a favorite theme of progressives and their major contact with actual free speech issues, reflected this view, as did the growth of administrative regulatory agencies during the early twentieth century. Many others believed, however, that in a democracy the community of inquirers must extend to the entire population, which requires educating citizens in the skills of critical inquiry. These progressives did not object to the growth of administrative agencies, but they emphasized that the public in a democracy must retain the ultimate power to determine social policy.[4]

The tension between critical inquiry and community harmony, evident even in the limited realm of scientific theory, became exacerbated as progressives extended the model of science to social issues and had enormous implications for the role of free speech in a democracy. Charles Peirce, who developed the view that scientific truth depends on the consensus of a community of inquirers, maintained that the "irritation of doubt" about existing beliefs motivates the critical inquiry that leads to the progress of knowledge.[5] The initial irritation may begin with individuals and is essential to the continual process of inquiry, but new truth is achieved only when the community of inquirers reaches consensus. Moreover, Peirce viewed the community of inquirers, even while disagreeing about particular hypotheses, as engaged in a cooperative search for truth, a spirit he contrasted favorably to the competitive individualism of the broader capitalist society. Thus, for Peirce, individual criticism has a vital but limited role. It usefully provokes the growth of knowledge, but it is pursued within a spirit of cooperation and resolved in a new consensus.[6] Although this new consensus may itself be challenged by additional irrita-

---

[4] See John Patrick Diggins, The Promise of Pragmatism: Modernism and the Crisis of Knowledge and Authority 236–40 (1994); David A. Hollinger, In the American Province: Studies in the History and Historiography of Ideas 34–35 (1985); Kloppenberg, supra note 3, at 380, 383–86; Dorothy Ross, The Origins of American Social Science 253 (1991).

[5] For references to the "irritation of doubt," see, e.g., Charles Peirce, The Fixation of Belief, in 5 Collected Papers: Pragmatism and Pragmaticism 231 (Charles Hartshorne and Paul Weiss, eds. 1934); Charles Peirce, How to Make Our Ideas Clear, in id. at 252, 255.

tions of doubt, solitary dissenters, who disdain the opinion of the broader community while defending their own conception of truth, did not play a role in Peirce's conception of science.[7] At some ambiguous point, valuable individual doubt becomes antisocial disruptive dissent. Many progressive intellectuals, without resolving this ambiguity, saw science as the model for viewing individual criticism of existing social life as a useful spur to reconstructing society on a new, consensual basis.[8]

A number of important intellectuals, especially John Dewey and his colleagues at the University of Chicago in the years around 1900, relied more specifically on new ideas in the field of individual psychology as the model for social theory. Rejecting traditional dualisms between different mental functions, such as stimulus and response, innovative psychologists understood the human mind as an organic unity that coordinated these functions. They believed that when new perceptions conflict with preexisting habits, the mind adjusts, resulting in a new coordination. For example, when a child used to reaching for bright lights is exposed for the first time to a burning flame, the child resolves the conflict between pleasant habit and painful new experience by learning the difference between flames and other bright lights and in the future responds accordingly. The Chicago pragmatists reasoned that society must similarly resolve social conflict by new forms of coordination in a reconstructed and improved community. They viewed settlement houses and schools, institutions to which they often devoted substantial energy, as agencies of social coordination and as solutions to class conflict.[9]

In their confident optimism that individual criticism and social conflict could be resolved in a harmoniously reconstructed society, progressive intellectuals neglected the problem of persistent and irreconcilable dissent. They seemed impervious to the possibility that the rational and cooperative methods they attributed to scientific inquiry might not apply to social issues, even though

---

[6] "The opinion which is fated to be ultimately agreed to by all who investigate," Peirce maintained, "is what we mean by the truth, and the object represented in this opinion is the real." Peirce, How We Make Our Ideas Clear, supra note 5, at 268.

[7] See Diggins, supra note 4, at 163–64, 189, 192–94, 198, 201.

[8] Hollinger, supra note 4, at 45, 50–53, makes this point extremely effectively in analyzing Walter Lippmann's Drift and Mastery: An Attempt to Diagnose the Current Unrest (reprint 1985) (1914).

[9] See Andrew Feffer, The Chicago Pragmatists and American Progressivism 147–53, 156–58, 161, 166–68, 227, 244–45 (1993); Kloppenberg, supra note 3, at 67–70, 380, 402.

Peirce himself made no such claim and tried instead to insulate the autonomy of the scientific community from the corrupting influences of the broader society.[10] They were unwilling to concede that some problems, including the antagonisms of class conflict, may be rooted in values and interests whose differences cannot rationally be bridged, even with the best intentions.[11] Despite their genuine belief in the social value of individual criticism, many progressive intellectuals could not accommodate views incompatible with their own confidence that conflict and disagreement could ultimately be reconciled through good faith and rational cooperation.[12] They saw no value in, and occasionally expressed hostility toward, dissent that was not directed at positive social reconstruction.

In examining the relation between the social thought of progressive intellectuals and free speech, I will focus particularly on John Dewey and Herbert Croly.[13] In the years before World War I, Dewey was a leading, and perhaps the preeminent, figure in American social thought. He played a decisive role both in the philosophical challenge to individualism and in the application of these new philosophical ideas to social problems.[14] Dewey himself emphasized the practical implications of his philosophical work. In addition, while sharing many characteristic views of progressive intellectuals, Dewey was more committed than most of them to a radical vision of the potential of democratic life.[15] Dewey repeatedly emphasized the importance of retaining individuality in a participatory democracy. The general insensitivity of progressive intellectuals to dissenting speech is underlined by the extent to which even Dewey, the radical democrat, shared this trait. Perhaps most importantly, the latent implications of progressive social thought for free speech emerged explicitly in essays Dewey wrote for *The*

---

[10] See Diggins, supra note 4, at 236–39.

[11] See Alfonso J. Damico, Individuality and Community: The Social and Political Thought of John Dewey 61–62, 95–96 (1978); Ross, supra note 4, at 254; Robert B. Westbrook, John Dewey and American Democracy 82, 214 (1991).

[12] See Feffer, supra note 9, at 268–69.

[13] Other important progressive intellectuals included Charles Horton Cooley (the son of Thomas M. Cooley, the author of Constitutional Limitations), Mary Parker Follett, Walter Lippmann, George Herbert Mead, E. A. Ross, E.R.A. Seligman, Albion W. Small, and J. Allen Smith.

[14] See especially Kloppenberg, supra note 3, at 9–10, 146.

[15] Casey Nelson Blake, Beloved Community: The Cultural Criticism of Randolph Bourne, Van Wyck Brooks, Waldo Frank, & Lewis Mumford 3, 5 (1990); Henry F. May, The End of American Innocence: A Study of the First Years of Our Own Time 1912–1917 at 148 (reprint 1964) (1959); Ross, supra note 4, at 162; Westbrook, supra note 11, at xiv–xv, xvi, 189.

New Republic soon after the United States entered World War I in 1917. His criticism of pacifist opposition to the war as a failure to seize its democratic possibilities reflected his impatience with dissent he did not deem constructive. Moreover, by ridiculing reliance on the First Amendment to combat the repression of antiwar speech, Dewey simply extended his general aversion to individual constitutional rights to free speech.

Croly, who became the founding editor of *The New Republic* in 1914, was the leading popularizer of progressive thought. In the years before the war, he went beyond Dewey in elaborating the relationship between the legal system and the excessive individualism of American life. More than any other theorist, Croly applied the progressive belief in a "socialized democracy" to the specific issue of free speech. Key passages in his prewar work contain remarkable linguistic similarities to the opinion Justice Holmes wrote in *Schenck v. United States* while explaining the Supreme Court's unanimous decision to reject the First Amendment arguments of socialists convicted for antiwar speech under the Espionage Act of 1917. Moreover, under Croly's editorship *The New Republic* became a major barometer of changing views about free speech by progressives during and immediately after World War I, views that arguably influenced Justice Holmes to develop a more protective construction of the First Amendment.

Only a few progressives, such as Jane Addams and Randolph Bourne, opposed American intervention in World War I. But the failure of the war "to make the world safe for democracy," combined with the widespread repression of speech during and after the war, forced many progressives to reconsider their prewar faith in a benevolent state. Some of them became active civil libertarians following the war and recognized government as a constant threat to civil liberties. In dramatic contrast to their prewar attacks on constitutional rights as barriers to social reform, they emphasized the centrality of constitutional free speech to the democratic themes they had elaborated before the war. This transformation in social thought created the modern civil liberties movement and anticipated the ideology of the New Deal.

JOHN DEWEY

In the years immediately preceding World War I, John Dewey produced popular articles for a general audience in addition to prolific scholarship that reinforced his standing as a major American philosopher and public intellectual. This combination of popular and scholarly writings was particularly appropriate for Dewey, who believed that the major task of philosophy was to identify and solve "the needs of democracy in America."[16] Although Dewey became the first president of the American Association of University Professors (AAUP) in 1915 and a founding member of the American Civil Liberties Union (ACLU) in 1920, his voluminous work before World War I rarely identified free speech as a distinctive topic.[17] Moreover, as many critics have observed, Dewey's writing is extremely difficult to penetrate. Justice Holmes, who expressed this view most memorably, quipped that Dewey wrote as "God would have spoken had he been inarticulate but keenly desirous to tell you how it was."[18] Substantial implications for free speech, however, do emerge from Dewey's argument that traditional American individualism rooted in autonomy from the state should be replaced by a "generalized individualism" that acknowledges the interdependence of the individual and society. Dewey appreciated free speech, and even dissent, as qualities that contribute to, and should be nurtured by, a progressive democratic society. But Dewey had no patience for dissent that did not contribute to his ideal progressive society. He was insensitive to the possibility of persistent dissent by people who did not share his optimistic vision of a benevolent state leading the nation to a cooperative participatory democracy. While he was confident that society, particularly through its schools, could induce individuals voluntarily to accept social interests as their own, he justified placing social pressure on individuals who refused to conform to legitimate community values. Moreover, like Pound and other progressives, Dewey main-

---

[16] John Dewey, Philosophy and American National Life (1905), in 3 John Dewey, The Middle Works, 1899–1924, at 73, 74 (1977).

[17] For examples of rare occasions when Dewey directly addressed free speech issues, see John Dewey and James H. Tufts, Ethics 399–400 (1908), in 5 John Dewey, The Middle Works, 1899–1924 (1983) (section entitled "Freedom of Thought and Affection") [hereinafter Dewey-Ethics]; John Dewey, Academic Freedom (1902), in 2 John Dewey, The Middle Works, 1899–1924, at 53 (1976) [hereinafter Dewey-Academic Freedom]. Dewey and Tufts identified the portions of Ethics written by each. Dewey-Ethics, supra at 6. All citations to Ethics are to material written by Dewey.

[18] Letter from Oliver Wendell Holmes, Jr., to Sir Frederick Pollock (May 15, 1931), in 2 Holmes-Pollock Letters 287 (Mark DeWolfe Howe, ed. 1941). See also Richard J. Bernstein, John Dewey 171 (1966) ("Dewey lacked the technical skill and patience to develop and establish his insights in systematic detail"); Kloppenberg, supra note 3, at 375 ("Dewey's own woolly style is at least partly responsible for the distortions of his meaning by self-styled progressive educators"; Dewey's thought often "hidden in the thickets of his prose"); Westbrook, supra note 11, at xiii ("precision and clarity often escaped" Dewey); Charles L. Stevenson, Introduction to Dewey-Ethics, supra note 17, at xxix (Dewey "was a rich but often unclear thinker").

John Dewey, 1902. (Morris Library,
Southern Illinois University)

tained that social interests must determine the extent to which
society recognizes individual rights.

Although Dewey condemned the destructive individualism of
the United States in the early twentieth century, he viewed earlier
forms of individualism as historically valuable. In contrast to "the
prejudice and artificial restraints of church and state," to doctrines
based only on "tradition and class interest," and to government
action that was "despotic in intention and stupid in execution,"
individualism was an impetus toward a broader, freer, and more
democratic society committed to progress.[19] Dewey especially
appreciated "intellectual individualism," the emphasis on "the
rights and responsibilities of the individual in gaining knowledge
and personally testing beliefs, no matter by what authorities they
were vouched for." In contrast to the "'authority' theory" that "sets

---

[19] Dewey-Ethics, supra note 17, at 425; John Dewey, Democracy and Education
91–92, 298–99 (reprint 1966) (1916) [hereinafter Dewey-Democracy and
Education].

apart a sacred domain of truth which must be protected from the inroads of variation of beliefs," intellectual individualism valued "freedom of inquiry" and believed that "the possibilities of human good are widened and made more secure by trusting to a responsibility built up within the very process of inquiry."[20]

Unfortunately, Dewey lamented, a "legitimate intellectual individualism, the attitude of critical revision of former beliefs which is indispensable to progress," became associated with "philosophic subjectivism," a philosophy that perpetuated existing inequalities while inhibiting the development of shared commitment to the common good. "The reaction against authority in all spheres of life," Dewey observed, "and the intensity of the struggle, against great odds, for freedom of action and inquiry, led to such an emphasis upon personal observation and ideas as in effect to isolate mind, and set it apart from the world to be known." Dewey believed that philosophic subjectivism presented both theoretical problems for epistemology and practical problems for society. As an epistemological matter, it questioned "the possibility of any cognitive relationship of the individual to the world." As a practical matter, it questioned "the possibility of a purely individual consciousness acting on behalf of general or social interests." Individualism, which for Dewey had the laudable potential of developing agencies for healthy social reconstruction, instead became reduced to the "assertion that each individual's mind was complete in isolation from everything else."[21]

Dewey vigorously opposed subjectivism as part of his broader attack against philosophical dualisms. Throughout his writings, he tried to demonstrate the irrelevance or meaninglessness of many topics that had dominated Western philosophical analysis. He considered especially pernicious the focus by previous philosophers on presumed dualisms reflecting "a radical existential cleavage in the nature of things."[22] In a short encyclopedia article, Dewey gave as examples of dualisms "those between spirit and matter, mind and body, logic and psychology." Dewey himself regarded such distinctions of antithetical terms "as relative and working, not fixed and absolute, so that they are capable of coming together in functional unity."[23]

---

[20] Dewey-Democracy and Education, supra note 19, at 295, 298; see id. at 293–94.

[21] Id. at 293, 297, 305.

[22] John Dewey, The Realism of Pragmatism, in 3 John Dewey, The Middle Works, 1899–1924, at 153, 155 (1977).

[23] John Dewey, Dualism, in Contribution to A Cyclopedia of Education (1911), Volumes 1 and 2 [hereinafter Cyclopedia of Education], in 6 John Dewey, The Middle Works, 1899–1924 (1978), at 424.

Much of Dewey's social philosophy responded to his perception of a false dualism between the individual and society. He repeatedly attacked the widespread assumption that people are instinctively or naturally selfish and individualistic, and are therefore anti-social and uncooperative. He rejected as "pure fiction" the supposition that individuals are so focused on the satisfaction of "private pleasure" that they consider the good of others only when forced to do so. "Any individual," Dewey maintained, "is *naturally* an erratic mixture of fierce insistence upon his own welfare and of profound susceptibility to the happiness of others – different individuals varying much in the respective intensities and proportions of the two tendencies." Many individual capacities, he added, can be fully realized only in association with others.[24]

Dewey elaborated the unfortunate political impact of individualist traditions in various countries,[25] but as a self-consciously American philosopher he devoted most attention to the United States. Dewey readily acknowledged that individualism had brought about many benefits in his country, including personal initiative, generosity, self-reliance, the demand for equality of opportunity, and the development of multiple voluntary agencies devoted to education and other means of human improvement. The distrust of government associated with American individualism, he added, made sense at the time of the American Revolution against the British monarch. Unfortunately, however, aversion to government became encrusted in popular culture and fundamental law. Government became nothing more than "a benevolently neutral umpire" to resolve conflicts between individuals and could not play a constructive role in promoting the common interests of all citizens. Moreover, the moral duty of citizens became mere obedience to law because American society lost sight of any conception of morality as an obligation to make "the legal order a more adequate expression of the common good."[26]

In the United States, Dewey worried, rights had become abstract and formal rather than effective. As a result, people invoked "indi-

---

[24] Dewey-Democracy and Education, supra note 19, at 23–24, 302; Dewey-Ethics, supra note 17, at 325–26, 347.

[25] Dewey maintained, for example, that French rationalism, though helpful in encouraging freedom of discussion to destroy "old falsities," did not aid "the construction of new ties and associations among men." Dewey-Democracy and Education, supra note 19, at 299. He added that British utilitarianism, despite its contribution to individual equality, similarly ignored "the constructive work that needs to be done by the state" to generate "an equal chance to count in the common good." John Dewey, Intelligence and Morals (1908), in 4 John Dewey, The Middle Works, 1899–1924, at 31, 41 (1977).

[26] Dewey-Ethics, supra note 17, at 417–19, 422, 426.

vidual liberties and rights" to defend "privileges based on inequality." They correspondingly opposed attempts to provide "equality of opportunity to *all*" through constructive social legislation as an invasion of these rights. When the state acts only as an umpire between contentious individuals, Dewey asserted, the "ignorant, the poor, the foreign, and the *merely* honest are almost inevitably at a discount." The excesses of American individualism, Dewey stressed, had worsened as the country became more industrialized, congested, and complex in ways earlier generations could not have foreseen.[27] He observed that the "every-man-for himself" ethos of isolated, pioneer America developed in a "society which ceased to exist a hundred years ago."[28] The anachronistic survival of this ethos into the twentieth century, Dewey believed, posed an unfortunate barrier to effective government responses to contemporary social problems, such as public health, poverty, and unemployment.[29]

In contrast to the "partial individualism" of previous philosophies, Dewey proposed a "generalized individualism" that would recognize the interdependence of the individual and society. Generalized individualism would permit a benevolent government to participate actively in creating a society in which all citizens have the resources to exercise effective freedom and to develop their individual capacities for the common good. While overcoming the excesses and inequalities of partial individualism, generalized individualism would also avoid the "collectivist formula" that "tends to set up a static social whole and to prevent the variations of individual initiative which are necessary to human progress." Generalized individualism, Dewey maintained, would not magnify state power at the expense of individuals, but would make "individual liberty a more extensive and equitable matter."[30]

---

[27] Id. at 416–17, 428, 430.

[28] John Dewey, Schools of To-Morrow (1915), in 8 John Dewey, The Middle Works, 1899–1924, at 205, 314 (1979).

[29] Dewey-Ethics, supra note 17, at 421–22.

[30] Id. at 422, 430, 433. While recognizing the contribution of German idealism to "rescuing philosophy" from the "isolated individualism" that had predominated in France and England, Dewey rejected its overemphasis on the state at the expense of the individual. German idealism, he observed, sought to achieve "individual freedom through developing individual convictions in accord with the universal law found in the organization of the state as objective Reason." Dewey-Democracy and Education, supra note 19, at 300. Dewey identified many benefits from this philosophical orientation. It gave the state a legitimate role in advancing public concerns rather than leaving them to the fortuitous play of selfish private interests. It also promoted freedom of inquiry in various technical subjects. For Dewey, however, German idealism had the fatal flaw of reinstating the authority of the state "in all ultimate moral matters." Id. at 301. Dewey preferred political democracy, "with its belief in the right of individual desire and purpose to take part in readapting even the fundamental constitution of society." Id.

Dewey emphasized that through the "unconscious influence of the environment," particularly the schools, individuals would voluntarily identify their own interests with the interests of society. The assumptions and habits that unconsciously determine people's thinking and conclusions, he felt, are "formed in the constant give and take of relationship with others." For example, adults can influence the moral and mental development of students by controlling the environment of the school. The educator can "modify stimuli so that response will as surely as is possible result in the formation of desirable intellectual and emotional dispositions."[31]

The laudable goal of developing individuals who have "a benevolent interest in others," Dewey warned, "may be but an unwitting mask for an attempt to dictate to them what their good shall be, instead of an endeavor to free them so that they may seek and find the good of their own choice."[32] He observed that even the best intentioned leaders and reformers frequently make the mistake of seeking "ends which promote the social welfare in ways which fail to engage the active interest and cooperation of others." As a result, they provoke "antagonisms and resentment" among the very people they are trying to help. The "common good," Dewey insisted, cannot be attained "by methods which forbid its being either common or a good."[33] He remained confident, however, that the unconscious influence of a properly controlled environment could create "conditions which will enable an individual to make his own special contribution to a group interest, and to partake of its activities in such ways that social guidance shall be a matter of his own mental attitude, and not a mere authoritative dictation of his acts."[34]

Dewey's conception of generalized individualism in a true democracy explicitly recognized the positive value of free speech. He emphasized that "democracy means freeing intelligence for

[31] Dewey-Democracy and Education, supra note 19, at 17–19, 180. See also John Dewey, Environment and Organism, in Cyclopedia of Education, supra note 23, at 437, 439.

    Dewey supported his conception of education by analogy to the process of learning to speak. Speech begins with the instinctual babblings of infants, but communication requires "sounds which are *mutually intelligible*" and thus "depends upon connection with a shared experience." Dewey-Democracy and Education, supra note 19, at 15. Adults do not simply mimic what infants say; rather, they direct the development of speech through example and selective reinforcement. Id. at 113–15. Similarly, education both draws upon and shapes the instincts of children, ideally providing "an environment in which native powers will be put to better uses." Id. at 118.

[32] Dewey-Democracy and Education, supra note 19, at 121.

[33] Dewey-Ethics, supra note 17, at 276–77.

[34] Dewey-Democracy and Education, supra note 19, at 301; see id. at 123.

independent effectiveness"[35] and highlighted "freedom of action and thought" as an essential personal quality for democratic citizens.[36] Consistent with his general position that formal rights are meaningless without basic economic resources, Dewey asserted that preoccupation with maintaining a life that does not fall below the level of subsistence can limit free speech as fully as the more obvious danger of despotism.[37]

Beyond simply encouraging free speech, Dewey recognized the social value of dissent. He maintained that individuals who dissent from conventional thinking themselves benefit the community by promoting reconstruction and progress. Dewey believed that as social conditions change, judgments and values that were correct under prior circumstances have to be reevaluated and readjusted. Particularly in periods of rapid economic, political, and scientific transformation, as in the United States during the early twentieth century, "ideas once true" may become "unfit, and therefore wrong." Even the same concept may develop different meanings. For example, courage, which "in one society may consist almost wholly in willingness to face physical danger and death in voluntary devotion to one's community," in another "may be willingness to support an unpopular cause in the face of ridicule."[38]

Dewey observed that lags typically exist between a society's conventional thinking and its current situation. Views that accurately fit the past no longer apply to the present and the emerging future. Thus, prevailing tradition, "while on the whole a mainstay of moral guidance and instruction, is also a menace to moral growth." People too often confuse the conventional with the moral and equate what is customarily done with what ought to be done. They mistakenly perceive "mere conformity to custom" as a virtue, and censure "the individual who deviates from custom in the interest of wider and deeper good."[39]

By contrast, Dewey asserted that the good person is never smugly satisfied with existing standards, but is instead constantly open to revising them. Individuals who react against custom and develop new ideas "are necessary if there is to be progress in society." Dewey bemoaned the failure of many to realize that individuals who challenge prevailing norms are of great value to society because they provide "the means of *social* reconstruction."

---

[35] John Dewey, Democracy in Education (1903), in 3 John Dewey, Middle Works, 1899–1924, at 229 (1977).

[36] John Dewey, Democracy and Education, in Cyclopedia of Education, supra note 23, at 417, 418; Dewey, Education, in id. at 430; Dewey, supra note 28, at 398.

[37] Dewey-Ethics, supra note 17, at 401.

[38] Id. at 291, 361.　　　　　　　　　　[39] Id. at 361, 387.

Although he valued optimism, Dewey warned against reducing it to a mere "cheerful animal buoyancy" that can blind people to the existence of evil and create "a brutality bathed in the atmosphere of sentimentality and flourishing the catchwords of idealism." He maintained that "a certain intellectual pessimism, in the sense of a steadfast willingness to uncover sore points, to acknowledge and search for abuses, to note how presumed good often serves as a cloak for actual bad, is a necessary part of the moral optimism which actively devotes itself to making the right prevail."[40]

Diversity within a society, Dewey added, produces the individual variation that stimulates socially necessary challenges to custom. A progressive, democratic society "counts individual variations as precious since it finds in them the means of its own growth."[41] Although variations may produce opposition to existing values, they "may be the sole means by which the existing State is to progress." "Minorities may not always be right," Dewey conceded, "but every advance in right begins in a minority of one, when some individual conceives a project which is at variance with the social good as it *has* been established."[42]

A just society, Dewey therefore concluded, "does not aim at intellectual and moral subordination." Rather, it recognizes that all communities contain "survivals of the past which need to be reorganized" and encourages both criticism of existing ideas and experimentation in new ones. "The struggle of some individuals *against* the subordination of their good to the good of the whole," he maintained, "is the method of the reorganization of the whole in the direction of a more generally distributed good."[43]

Dewey identified "intellectual freedom"[44] not just as "the method of graduated and steady reconstruction," but as the "chief safeguard against explosive change and intermittent blind action and reaction." He defined intellectual freedom to include free speech, freedom of the press, freedom of assembly, religious freedom, and the right to education. "Looked at as a mere expedient," Dewey observed, "liberty of thought and expression is the most successful device ever hit upon for reconciling tranquillity with progress, so that peace is not sacrificed to reform nor improvement to stagnant conservatism." In one of his few references to contemporary free speech controversies before his articles in *The New Republic* during World War I, Dewey noted police suppression of

[40] Id. at 371, 379, 387.
[41] Dewey-Democracy and Education, supra note 19, at 305.
[42] Dewey-Ethics, supra note 17, at 433.
[43] Id.
[44] Dewey-Democracy and Education, supra note 19, at 395.

public meetings held to discuss unemployment "or other matters deemed by some dangerous to vested interests." This suppression, Dewey lamented, demonstrated how many people still had to learn the value of free speech as a "safety-valve." It also impressed on him that "the victories of freedom in the past have to be fought and won over again under new conditions, if they are to be kept alive."[45]

Consistent with his basic position that schooling should provide training for democratic citizenship, Dewey related his views about the social value of dissent to the educational process. He emphasized that a progressive democracy should have "different standards and methods of education" from a society that "aims simply at the perpetuation of its own customs." Dewey acknowledged that in much of his writing he had simplified his general treatment of education by portraying it as a process that conveys to children the values of the adult society to which they belong. Yet he added that this model, while descriptive of "static societies," did not fully convey the role of education in "progressive communities" committed to democratic values. These communities "endeavor to shape the experiences of the young so that instead of reproducing current habits, better habits shall be formed, and thus the future adult society be an improvement on their own."[46]

Dewey believed that education should do more than simply elicit the desirable traits of existing society from the young. Education should also teach how to use these traits "to criticize undesirable features and suggest improvement." In a progressive society, he maintained, individual virtues are more "reflective" and "critical" than in "customary society."[47] Dewey vigorously denied that this position in any way undermined his broader claim that individual traits are socially conditioned. "*The very habits of individual moral initiative, of personal criticism of the existent order, and of private projection of a better order, to which moral individualists point as proofs of the purely 'inner' nature of morality,*" he proclaimed, "*are themselves effects of a variable and complex social order.*"[48]

Dewey stressed more specifically that education must encourage "openness of mind." Intellectual and social growth, he maintained, require "an active disposition to welcome points of view hitherto alien; an active desire to entertain considerations which modify existing purposes." "The teacher who does not permit and encourage diversity of operation in dealing with questions,"

---

[45] Dewey-Ethics, supra note 17, at 399–400, 400 n.7.
[46] Dewey-Democracy and Education, supra note 19, at 78–81.
[47] Id. at 83, 389.
[48] Dewey-Ethics, supra note 17, at 389.

Dewey complained, "is imposing intellectual blinders upon pupils" and thereby inhibiting the development and improvement of a democratic society.[49]

Dewey used his discussion of education to rebut the claim that free speech could promote dangerous ideas. He maintained that freedom of expression, in the classroom as well as in political life generally, generates a wide range of views that allows for "mutual offsetting and supplementing of erroneous ideas by one another." Opponents of free speech, Dewey asserted, fail "to realize the extent to which an atmosphere of free discussion carries with it its own protection against unbalanced propagandism."[50]

In discussing the social value of criticism, Dewey often invoked the model of scientific inquiry. He urged "a larger application of the scientific method to the problems of human welfare and progress," including the intelligent administration of government.[51] Dewey emphasized that science frees the present from the past by substituting "effectively directed reflection" for the authority of tradition. As a result, it opens "intellectual vistas unobscured by the accidents of personal habit and predilection." He defined science as "an intelligent and persistent endeavor to revise current beliefs so as to weed out what is erroneous, to add to their accuracy, and, above all, to give them such shape that the dependencies of the various facts upon one another may be as obvious as possible."[52] Applied to social life, the scientific method allows "the transformation of a society whose purpose is to repeat its own past – to be 'true' or loyal to what is already established – into a society whose purpose is that its future shall be a variation of its past, a society whose interest is in fostering and subjecting novelty." According to Dewey, "the conditions of a progressive society and of the experimental formation of beliefs fit each other as if by pre-established harmony."[53]

Dewey directly connected the rise of experimental science with the development of social progress and political liberty. "Only when experimental science broke the bondage of man to his animal past (embodied in his sense perceptions) and to his human past (embodied in his political and religious institutions)," Dewey wrote,

---

49 Dewey-Democracy and Education, supra note 19, at 175.
50 John Dewey, Freedom, Academic, in Cyclopedia of Education, supra note 23, at 460, 463.
51 Dewey-Ethics, supra note 17, at 5, 425–26.
52 Dewey-Democracy and Education, supra note 19, at 189, 219, 230.
53 John Dewey, The Problem of Truth (1911), in 6 John Dewey, The Middle Works, 1899–1924, at 12, 57, 59–60 (1978).

"did progress become at once an idea and an ideal."[54] The struggle of science against inherited beliefs, he maintained, promoted "the political struggle for the right to free speech and publication" and the related conception of academic freedom.[55] The experimental methods of science, Dewey emphasized, must constantly be applied to prevent people from allowing "the crutch of dogma, of beliefs fixed by authority, to relieve them of the trouble of thinking and the responsibility of directing their activity by thought."[56]

Dewey never explicitly opposed free speech or even specified limitations on its exercise. In elaborating his social thought, however, he revealed substantial hostility to behavior that did not ultimately contribute to a harmonious community. Although Dewey was confident that in a genuinely democratic society individuals would voluntarily identify personal fulfillment with community interests, he advocated extensive social pressure on people whose values or characteristics did not benefit society. Dewey essentially ignored the possibility that significant numbers of people might not agree with his vision of a good society or with his optimism that it could be achieved. His commitment to consensus and harmony offered scant protection for dissent that did not contribute to social reconstruction. Irreconcilable, persistent dissent found no place in Dewey's defense of free speech. His conception of rights as socially defined and subject to revision further jeopardized dissenting speech by weakening the protection against state interference afforded by prior theories of individual rights.

A society, Dewey believed, must develop a "public point of view, with its extensive common purposes and with a general will for maintaining them." Otherwise, "society and hence morality would remain sectional, jealous, suspicious, unfraternal." A diverse and complex community unable to achieve harmony, Dewey warned, "would dissolve in anarchy and confusion." Just as cooperation liberates individuals, social "maladjustment" creates "loss and friction" in personal relations and "introduces defect, division, and restriction into the various powers which constitute an individual."[57] Dewey observed that the variety of classes, nationalities, races, religions, and other groups in the United States afforded the opportunity for a broader common environment, but also the danger of social isolation.[58] Isolated groups, Dewey wor-

---

[54] Id. at 61.   [55] Dewey, supra note 50, at 461.

[56] Dewey-Democracy and Education, supra note 19, at 339.

[57] Dewey-Ethics, supra note 17, at 386, 390.

[58] See id. at 402; Dewey-Democracy and Education, supra note 19, at 21, 249; John Dewey, Custom, in Cyclopedia of Education, supra note 23, at 413, 414 [hereinafter Dewey-Custom].

ried, develop an "antisocial spirit" devoted to "selfish ideals within the group" rather than to "reorganization and progress through wider relationships."[59] He declared that "it is the business of education in a democratic social group to struggle against this isolation in order that the various interests may reinforce and play into one another."[60] Schools should be an "assimilative force" in which a shared environment "accustoms all to a unity of outlook upon a broader horizon than is visible to the members of any group while it is isolated."[61] Effective education "must select and propagate that which is common and hence typical in the social values that form its resources, leaving the eccentric, the partial, and exclusive gradually to dwindle."[62]

Despite his careful distinction between subordination to coercive authority and benevolent social control that induces voluntary identification of personal and social interests, Dewey could be quite forceful in justifying social pressure on individuals to meet legitimate community expectations. An ideal democracy, Dewey believed, will expect a "social return" from all citizens as the price for providing to each the "opportunity for development of distinctive capacities."[63] When a society "liberates powers otherwise torpid and latent," it understandably "exacts that they be employed in ways consistent with its own interests."[64] Through social interaction, an individual is forced continually *"to meet the expectations and requirements of others"* and to differentiate tendencies *"which are socially harmful or useless"* from those that are helpful to the community. When these tendencies conflict, Dewey maintained, an individual has a moral duty to act in the community interest.[65] Society naturally "'makes it hot' for any one who disturbs its values," and this "disagreeable attention" inhibits individual characteristics "of the socially disliked kind."[66]

Concern that "maladjustment" would cause "loss and friction" and even "anarchy," advocacy of a "unity of outlook" that would eliminate "the eccentric, the partial, and exclusive," identification of a moral duty to inhibit individual tendencies that "are socially harmful or useless," and approval of social pressure that "makes it hot" for individuals who disturb community values did not suggest solicitude for dissenting speech. Dewey remained confident, however, that conflict and dissent would ultimately produce desirable

[59] Dewey-Democracy and Education, supra note 19, at 85–86.
[60] Id. at 249.   [61] Id. at 21.
[62] Dewey-Ethics, supra note 17, at 402.
[63] Dewey-Democracy and Education, supra note 19, at 122.
[64] Dewey-Ethics, supra note 17, at 385–86.
[65] Id. at 326–27.   [66] Id. at 360.

social reconstruction and orderly progress.[67] The "conflict of stimuli, impulses, and habits," Dewey maintained, promotes thought and reconciliation. "When one stimulus tends to evoke one response, while another stimulus is acting in another and incomplete direction, or when inconsistent aims present themselves simultaneously, reflective thought is demanded in order to discover a new single stimulus which will coordinate the conflicting ones, or to project a comprehensive aim which will reconcile those opposing each other."[68]

Dewey generalized the process of conflict and reconciliation to broad social issues. He was confident that "when the scientific interest conflicts with, say, the religious, or the economic with the scientific or aesthetic, or when the conservative concern for order is at odds with the progressive interest in freedom, or when institutionalism clashes with individuality, there is a stimulus to discover some more comprehensive point of view from which the divergencies may be brought together, and consistency or continuity of experience recovered." Dewey assumed that the application of his pragmatic philosophy would bring about "a harmonious readjustment of the opposed tendencies" and a "better balance of interests."[69] The number of people who would "be anti-social enough deliberately to sacrifice the welfare of others," he speculated, "is probably small."[70]

Dewey's confidence in the constructive role of conflict in producing a broader social harmony exhibited the idealistic optimism he occasionally decried. His discussion of academic freedom, the free speech issue with which he was personally most familiar, provided specific evidence of his misplaced optimism and eerily foreshadowed his treatment of threats to pacifist speech in 1917. Dewey wrote frequently in support of academic freedom before World War I. In an essay published in 1902, he dissented "most thoroughly from the opinion sometimes expressed that there is a growing danger threatening academic freedom." He cited advances in scientific inquiry, the growing community among university professors, public opinion, and "the active willingness of a large part of the public press to seize upon and even to exaggerate anything squinting towards an infringement upon the rights of free inquiry and free speech" as support for his position.[71] Thir-

---

[67] Id. at 387, 433.
[68] John Dewey, Conflict, in Cyclopedia of Education, supra note 23, at 392–93.
[69] Dewey-Democracy and Education, supra note 19, at 326, 332.
[70] Dewey-Ethics, supra note 17, at 234.
[71] Dewey-Academic Freedom, supra note 17, at 61.

teen years later, after serving as the first president of the AAUP,
Dewey expressed surprise at the unanticipated number of academic freedom cases that "overwhelmed" the new organization,
yet this realization did not prompt him to reevaluate his prior optimism. Rather, he emphasized that he did not regard the initial
experience of the AAUP "as typical or even as wholly normal."[72]

On occasion, however, Dewey tempered his optimism and
acknowledged that social harmony might be difficult to attain. "It
is hard," he once recognized, "to learn to accommodate one's
ends to those of others; to adjust, to give way here, and fit in there
with respect to our aims." It is even harder, he added, to accommodate in ways that "are helpful to others as will call out and make
effective their activities."[73] Dewey placed on the public school
responsibility for solving the admittedly "delicate" and "crucial"
problem of adjusting "social habit and individualistic departures,"
of "promoting genuine individuality and at the same time conserv-
ing the factors of continuity and coherence of action and belief
that are supplied by custom."[74] Beyond his general faith in the
unconscious influence of a controlled environment, Dewey never
really addressed the "delicate" problem of adjustment at the core
of his social philosophy. He gave even less attention to the possibility that the problem might be too difficult to solve. Dewey never
speculated about how society should handle conflict and dissent if
his optimistic assumptions about reconciliation and progress failed
his own scientific standards of experimental verification.

In addition to ignoring the possibility of persistent dissent that
did not ultimately lead to harmony, Dewey briefly set forth a concept of rights that offered relatively weak protection to speech.
Despite assurances that he did not advocate increasing the power
of the state at the expense of individuals,[75] Dewey challenged prevailing views of individual rights. Conceding that rights are "individual in residence," he emphasized that they are "social in origin
and intent." Dewey denied the existence of absolute rights, "if we
mean by absolute those not relative to any social order and hence
exempt from any social restriction." Such a view "regards rights as
private monopolies" and is the most fundamental form of anarchy.
Rather, rights are activities defined by conditions that create corre-

---

[72] American Association of University Professors, 1915 Declaration of Principles,
in Academic Freedom and Tenure 155, 156 (Louis Joughin, ed. 1969). Reports
of academic freedom cases in AAUP publications during the last eighty years
indicate Dewey's misplaced optimism.

[73] Dewey-Ethics, supra note 17, at 275–76.

[74] Dewey-Custom, supra note 58, at 414.

[75] Dewey-Ethics, supra note 17, at 430.

sponding obligations,[76] and the state "fixes the fundamental terms and conditions on which at any given time rights are exercised and remedies secured."[77]

Dewey did not use free speech as an example of his concept of rights. His illustrations involved property and transportation. He observed that the right to property coexists with the obligation to pay taxes and that the right to use public roads requires obedience to traffic signals.[78] Dewey, however, did include a short discussion of the right of "freedom of thought and affection" and predictably emphasized the social benefits derived from the gradual recognition of individual rights to free speech. He focused especially on the contribution of free speech to healthy social reconstruction and on its function as a "safety-valve" for potential unrest.[79] At no point did he identify significant individual interests in free speech.

Dewey's naïve optimism about the creation of a harmonious democratic society might explain both his insensitivity to persistent dissent and his social definition of rights. Dewey seemed unable to conceive that individuals would seriously dissent from the attractive community he envisaged or that such a community would define rights in unfairly restrictive ways. World War I exposed the dangers of Dewey's optimism and the negative consequences of his prewar social thought for free speech. His confidence that the war would facilitate democratic transformation led him to treat the antiwar speech of pacifists as lacking social value and to dismiss their First Amendment arguments as silly political platitudes.

HERBERT CROLY

Herbert Croly, like Dewey, criticized traditional American individualism and advocated a positive role for the state in creating a more equal and harmonious society. He also shared many of Dewey's views about both the values and limits of free speech. Croly believed that society properly defines and revises the scope of individual rights, and he assumed that dissent would dissolve into harmony in a progressive democracy. Moreover, both Dewey and Croly perceived a direct link between the destructive individualism of American life and the legal system established by the Constitution. But while Dewey only briefly addressed the pernicious influence of the law as part of his broader attack on American individualism, Croly devoted substantial attention to the ways in which the American legal system, particularly the constitutional system of

[76] Id. at 394–95.
[78] Id. at 394.

[77] Id. at 404.
[79] Id. at 399–400.

individual rights, obstructed the development of a progressive democracy.

The book he published in 1909, *The Promise of American Life*,[80] established Croly as a major figure in progressive social thought. His book was widely and favorably reviewed and was praised by other progressive intellectuals, including Felix Frankfurter, Learned Hand, and Walter Lippmann. Reading *The Promise of American Life* prompted Willard and Dorothy Straight to finance a weekly journal of opinion, which became *The New Republic*, and to hire Croly as its editor.[81] Croly and his book derived their greatest visibility from close association with Theodore Roosevelt. Much of the educated public believed, perhaps erroneously, that Croly's book formed the intellectual basis for Roosevelt's "New Nationalism."[82]

The Promise of American Life exhibited some of the most elitist strains in progressive thought, especially by urging in its closing pages that "the few exceptional leaders" must lead "the many 'plain people'." Croly believed that patriotic but inferior people "can be made willing prisoners by able and aggressive leaders whose achievements have given them personal authority and whose practical programme is based upon a sound knowledge of the necessary limits of immediate national action."[83] Under the continuing influence of John Dewey, Croly's thought became significantly more democratic by the time he published *Progressive Democracy*[84] in 1914.[85] Croly's two books, however, revealed substantial thematic continuity in their treatment of law and free speech.

Croly maintained that the Constitution reflected views that combined mistrust of a powerful state with belief in personal freedom, defined largely as "the unlimited popular enjoyment of all

[80] Herbert Croly, The Promise of American Life (reprint 1989) (1909) [hereinafter Croly-Promise].

[81] See Charles Forcey, The Crossroads of Liberalism: Croly, Weyl, Lippmann, and the Progressive Era, 1900–25, at 5–6, 121–22, 170–74, 184 (reprint 1972) (1961); Kloppenberg, supra note 3, at 313–14; David W. Levy, Herbert Croly of the New Republic: The Life and Thought of an American Progressive 132–35 (1985); Ronald Steel, Walter Lippmann and the American Century 47, 58–60, 78–79 (1981); Edward A. Stettner, Shaping Modern Liberalism: Herbert Croly and Progressive Thought 33, 77 (1993).

[82] Scholars since the 1960s have reiterated the public perception of Croly's influence on Roosevelt while challenging its accuracy. Forcey, supra note 81, at 123–30, 139; Kloppenberg, supra note 3, at 314; Levy, supra note 81, at 136; Stettner, supra note 81, at 4, 82.

[83] Croly-Promise, supra note 80, at 441, 449; see generally id. at 427–54.

[84] Herbert Croly, Progressive Democracy (1914) [hereinafter Croly-Democracy].

[85] Forcey, supra note 81, at 155; Levy, supra note 81, at 176; Kloppenberg, supra note 3, at 189 n.45, 193, 315; Stettner, supra note 81, at 94–99.

available economic opportunities."[86] The Constitution established an "individualist democracy," which "considered social and political organization chiefly as an instrument for the promotion of individual interests."[87] Identifying democracy with various political and civil rights, the Constitution assumed that "democratic consummation was merely a matter of exercising and preserving those rights."[88] In order to protect individual rights and "to prevent the people from being betrayed," the Constitution limited the role of government to "temporary police supervision."[89]

This "negative formulation of the democratic purpose," Croly emphasized, depended on the theory that the constitutional scheme of individual rights and a weak government itself embodied the popular will. Ongoing popular control of government was unnecessary because the Constitution deprived the government of the power to harm.[90] "The American democracy," Croly wrote, "accepted in the beginning an inaccessible body of Law and an uncontrollable mechanism of government, because the Law promised property to all, and because a government organized to perform such negative functions did not need to be rigidly controlled."[91]

Croly supported his view of the Constitution by demonstrating how the Bill of Rights both incorporated and transformed traditional English liberties. In England, the liberties eventually recognized in the American Bill of Rights constituted a valuable national heritage, but they had always remained subject to modification or even abolition by ordinary legal process. By contrast, the Bill of Rights elevated these traditional English liberties into a higher law. Government, even when supported by a popular majority, could not interfere with these individual rights without breaking the underlying social contract and justifying revolution.[92] By grounding individual rights in natural law, Croly observed, the Constitution reflected the general rationalism of the eighteenth century. Nineteenth-century economic theory, he added, reinforced eighteenth-century rationalism because both assumed a natural harmony between individual and social interests. Thus, the American legal system "was willing to trust the social welfare to the free expression of individual and class economic interests."[93]

The location of the popular will in the constitutional structure,

---

[86] Croly-Promise, supra 80, at 409.
[87] Croly-Democracy, supra note 84, at 58–59.
[88] Croly-Promise, supra note 80, at 281.
[89] Croly-Democracy, supra note 84, at 213, 270.
[90] Id. at 214, 270–71.   [91] Id. at 125.
[92] Id. at 37.   [93] Id. at 175.

Croly emphasized, gave enormous power to the legal interpreta-tions of judges. He described American democracy as paternalis-tic, guided by "the monarchy of the Law and an aristocracy of the robe, but without any effective consultation with public opinion."[94] The role of the law as "a permanent and righteous expression of the sovereign will," he observed, "tends to convert questions of political policy into cases to be decided by a court according to its interpretation of the meaning of the supreme Word." Describing judicial review of legislation, Croly wrote, "The angel of due process of law hovered over the dragon of the police power and prevented him from becoming the scourge of the land."[95]

Just as Dewey acknowledged that American individualism made sense at the time of the American Revolution against the British monarchy, Croly frequently conceded that the Constitution and its "monarchy of the Law" had served important historical purposes. "Legalism," he recognized, "was an enormous improvement on the official tyranny of a class or an individual."[96] The legal restric-tions in the Bill of Rights, he added, provided important guaran-tees of liberty that had enormous value in expressing "an essential element in the composition and the ideal of the American nation."[97] The Bill of Rights also supported a "positive national economic policy."[98] Croly therefore urged his fellow progressives to admit that the traditional constitutional system, while not "a permanently valuable formulation of the principles of right and a perfect mechanism of government," embodied "a useful working compromise between democracy, the common law and the eigh-teenth-century ideal of social justice."[99]

While acknowledging the historical value of the constitutional system, Croly emphasized that it had become outmoded and even destructive for the United States in the twentieth century. In the opening chapter of *The Promise of American Life*, Croly declared that the original promise of the Constitution had been betrayed. Indi-vidual freedom, which was supposed to guarantee unlimited eco-nomic opportunity for all Americans, had instead produced "a morally and socially undesirable distribution of wealth" that deprived most Americans of real freedom. "The individuals consti-tuting a democracy," Croly observed, "lack the first essential of individual freedom when they cannot escape from a condition of economic dependence." Like Dewey, he protested that the con-centration of wealth and power in a small group of socially irre-

---

[94] Id. at 215.
[95] Id. at 136, 140.
[96] Id. at 418.
[97] Croly-Promise, supra note 80, at 35.
[98] Croly-Democracy, supra note 84, at 218.
[99] Id. at 145.

sponsible people "is inimical to democracy, because it tends to erect political abuses and social inequalities into a system."[100]

In *The Promise of American Life,* Croly attributed the troubled state of American society to "the inevitable outcome of the chaotic individualism of our political and economic organization."[101] By the time he wrote *Progressive Democracy,* he had developed a historical explanation. During the last two decades of the nineteenth century, Croly asserted, economic scarcity became a serious problem in the United States. Prior economic activity had helped to socialize the American people into a unified nation. In conditions of scarcity, however, the distribution of wealth had become so unequal that irreconcilable class antagonisms divided Americans from each other and undermined the prior harmony between economic and social interests.[102]

Croly insisted that the original constitutional structure, whatever its past successes, could not effectively address these changed circumstances.[103] Rather than a system of individual rights protected by the Constitution from a weak government, the United States in the twentieth century needed a strong and active government to promote the public welfare as defined by popular majorities. Only by removing existing constitutional barriers to such a government could "the promise of American life" become a reality.

Just as Dewey advocated a "generalized individualism," Croly urged "a more highly socialized democracy" to replace "the excessively individualized democracy" that had broken down by the end of the nineteenth century.[104] "American political organization," he maintained, "will have to be adapted to the accomplishment of affirmative rather than of negative public purposes."[105] Croly therefore applauded the political philosophy of Alexander Hamilton. In contrast to Thomas Jefferson, Hamilton "realized that genuine liberty was not merely a matter of a constitutional declaration of rights," but "could be protected only by an energetic and clear-sighted central government."[106] A democratic government, Croly believed, should have the power to take any action desired by a majority of the people. Yet the individual rights embedded in the Constitution as natural law deprived the

---

[100] Croly-Promise, supra note 80, at 22–23, 205.
[101] Id. at 23.
[102] Croly-Democracy, supra note 84, at 97–98.
[103] See id. at 173.
[104] Croly-Promise, supra note 80, at 25.
[105] Croly-Democracy, supra note 84, at 122.
[106] Croly-Promise, supra note 80, at 44

people of this power, in violation of any reasonable theory of popular sovereignty.[107]

Croly lamented that the Constitution "was democratic, not by virtue of the powers which the electorate were permitted to exercise through the agency of government, but through the powers that the Law reserved to the people" through the amendment process. The Constitution, however, made this process extremely difficult and thereby "converted its democracy into a golden hoard, to which access could be obtained only at rare intervals and after an heroic effort." Croly understood the theory behind this constitutional structure. The easier it is to amend the Constitution, the easier it is to impair the rights the Constitution secures. But at the beginning of the twentieth century, Croly was less concerned about individual rights than he was about the abuse of these rights to support inequality. He wanted a strong government to create "a genuine democratic community" based on interdependence and cooperation.[108] "The revision of the amending clause of the Constitution," Croly emphasized, "is the indispensable effective method of giving to the American democracy a chance to be nationalized, and of giving American nationality the chance to be democratized."[109] Amending the Constitution, Croly enthusiastically proclaimed, would emancipate "popular political power from the overruling authority of the Law and the courts"[110] and allow the American people to seek social justice through collective action.[111] The "monarchy of the people" would finally replace the "monarchy of the Law."[112]

The American tendency to view the Constitution with a reverence approaching "superstitious awe," Croly realized, might prompt many "to shrink with horror from modifying it even in the smallest detail." Bemoaning the prevalence of the "abject worship of legal precedent for its own sake," Croly worried that the law would rule the American spirit just as it had ruled the Jews at the time of Jesus.[113] The "tenacious devotion to legalism" by Americans, he maintained, had undermined their ability to meet their "deeper responsibilities" to a democratic community. Croly tried to convince his readers that "democracy and legalism are incompatible."[114] The continuing failure to provide true popular sover-

---

[107] Id. at 35–36.
[108] Croly-Democracy, supra note 84, at 237–38.
[109] Id. at 243.   [110] Id. at 220.
[111] Id. at 210.   [112] Id. at 55.
[113] Croly-Promise, supra note 80, at 278–79.
[114] Croly-Democracy, supra note 84, at 225, 253.

eignty, he also warned, could prompt illegal and even revolutionary activity.[115]

By emphasizing the centrality of popular sovereignty, Croly intended to reassure potential critics who feared a strong state as a threat to individual liberty. He maintained that increased legislative and administrative power, though desirable, must always be subject to popular control.[116] Croly anticipated the further criticism that his proposed revision of the Constitution's amending clause would place individual liberties "at the mercy of a capricious or headstrong majority." Croly conceded this danger. "A free man," he observed, "can always commit suicide." Croly added, however, that a democratic community must trust the majority. He tried to offer some reassurance by suggesting that the majority is more likely to be trustworthy when it has meaningful responsibility for the public welfare. A capricious majority, he also suggested, is unlikely to remain a majority for long. "It remains to be seen," Croly nevertheless acknowledged, "what kind of community the American people will choose to be."[117]

Croly devoted substantial attention to the role of free speech in the progressive democracy he advocated. He made clear that he did not intend his attack on the Constitution and the Bill of Rights to deprecate the value of speech. On the contrary, Croly believed that Americans needed to translate their formal constitutional right of free speech into meaningful intellectual independence. Yet Croly also accepted significant constraints on speech. Like Dewey, he valued free speech as long as it ultimately contributed to social unity. Moreover, in his more specific analysis of legal issues Croly emphasized that the balance between individual liberty and government authority must vary pragmatically with social circumstances.

Croly stressed that his criticism of the individualistic democracy sustained by the constitutional system should not be understood as a rejection of individual rights. Although Croly disagreed with the traditional view that government should do no more than protect these rights, he maintained that a democracy "must give individual liberty abundant scope." Moreover, a democracy "has the deepest interest in the development of a higher quality of individual self-expression."[118] Croly identified "the individuality which may reside in the gallant and exclusive devotion to some disinterested, and

---

[115] Croly-Promise, supra note 80, at 36; see Croly-Democracy, supra note 84, at 233.
[116] Croly-Democracy, supra note 84, at 212–13, 271–72.
[117] Id. at 244.
[118] Croly-Promise, supra note 80, at 207, 209.

perhaps unpopular moral, intellectual, or technical purpose" as "indispensable to the fullness and intensity of American national life."[119] Rejecting both "dogmatic individualism" and "dogmatic socialism,"[120] Croly, like Dewey, insisted that "qualitative self-expression" depended on the "improved distribution of wealth" that could only be achieved by an active state.[121]

Croly made clear that his call for increased government regulation did not extend to speech. In the economic and political spheres, "constructive regulation" required "certain fruitful limitations upon traditional economic freedom." By contrast, the intellectual development and moral unity of the United States depended on greater individual freedom of thought. According to Croly, "American intelligence has still to issue its Declaration of Independence."[122]

Croly linked the sorry state of intellectual life in the United States to the country's traditional belief, which he associated especially with Thomas Jefferson, that economic individualism would promote material opportunity while preserving equality. Americans, in Croly's view, mistakenly assumed that a broadly shared prosperity would result from the sacrifice of intellectual liberty to social conformity and homogeneity. As a result, Americans enjoyed freedom of speech only as a formal constitutional right. Croly acknowledged that the law neither favored nor punished the expression of any particular ideas. The United States had not suffered from the repression of speech by a despotic government, but from a more insidious tradition of national self-censorship and conformity. In practice, Croly claimed, Americans had no more free speech than did domestic animals or prisoners.[123]

"The freedom of opinion of which we boast," Croly maintained, "has consisted for the most part in uttering acceptable commonplaces with as much defiant conviction as if we were uttering the most daring and sublimest heresies." Croly conceded that the typical American is not hypocritical in proclaiming his right to free speech. "He is prepared to do battle for his convictions, but his really fundamental convictions he shares with everybody else." Undoubtedly thinking of his own work, Croly concluded that the desirable "adoption of a nationalized economic and political system" needed "the assertion of intellectual independence or moral individuality."[124]

---

[119] Id. at 65.
[120] Croly-Democracy, supra note 84, at 217. For other rejections of socialism by Croly, see, e.g., id. at 176; Croly-Promise, supra note 80, at 209–11.
[121] Croly-Promise, supra note 80, at 209.
[122] Id. at 421.   [123] Id. at 44–45, 187, 420–22.
[124] Id. at 420, 422.

While stressing that a progressive democracy depended on the exercise of meaningful free speech rights, Croly also justified some restrictions on speech. Unfortunately, he was extremely vague about the relationship between the public welfare and free speech. He never specified how free speech contributes to democratic life, or when it exceeds legitimate boundaries.

Croly's discussion of free speech reflected the general confidence of progressives that conflict, if properly addressed, can lead to social unity. He believed that progressives could "convert civil and political liberty into a socially desirable consummation."[125] "Loyal and fruitful association," rather than requiring uniformity of conviction, "gains enormously from a wide variety of individual differences."[126] Just as the United States had absorbed huge numbers of diverse immigrants into its economy, so the country should be able to "assimilate" intellectual diversity.[127] The last sentence of *Progressive Democracy* envisioned a society that "would be bathed in eager, good-humored and tireless criticism, and the bath would purify as well as cleanse."[128]

Croly gave occasional hints of how dissent would dissolve in social harmony. He believed in "some machinery of mutual consultation, which may help to remedy grievances and whose decisions shall determine the political action taken in the name of the whole community."[129] Somewhat more specifically, Croly advocated effective minority representation in legislatures. The resulting "battleground of opinion" would elevate political discussion and would convince minorities that their good ideas have a reasonable chance of becoming part of an eventual majority. Instead of being hostile, majorities and minorities "would become supplementary" and "would interpenetrate one with another." Through this process, "obstacles to social unity" would be "gradually eradicated" and all people would share "an effective desire for a genuinely social consummation."[130]

Croly's confidence in the harmonious resolution of disagreement diverted him, as similar confidence had diverted Dewey, from examining the limits of dissent. In the course of discussing the value of democratic debate, however, he observed that differences of opinion cannot be resolved if opponents "become fac-

---

[125] Croly-Democracy, supra note 84, at 215.
[126] Croly-Promise, supra note 80, at 229.
[127] Id. at 425.
[128] Croly-Democracy, supra note 84, at 430.
[129] Croly-Promise, supra note 80, at 229.
[130] Croly-Democracy, supra note 84, at 319, 321, 323.

tious in spirit."[131] A long passage in *The Promise of American Life* is the closest Croly came to addressing when protest goes too far.

> National policies and acts will be welcome to some citizens and obnoxious to others, according to their special interests and opinions; and the citizens whose interests and ideas are prejudiced thereby have every right and should be permitted every opportunity to protest in the most vigorous and persistent manner. The nation may, however, on its part demand that these protests, in order to be heeded and respected, must conform to certain conditions. They must not be carried to the point of refusing obedience to the law. When private interests are injured by the national policy, the protestants must be able to show either that such injuries are unnecessary, or else they involve harm to an essential public interest. All such protest must find an ultimate sanction in a group of constructive democratic ideas. Finally, the protest must never be made the excuse for personal injustice or national disloyalty. Even if the national policy should betray indifference to the fundamental interests of a democratic nation, as did that of the United States from 1820 to 1860, the obligation of patient good faith on the part of the protestants is not diminished. Their protests may be as vivacious and as persistent as the error demands. The supporters of the erroneous policy may be made the object of most drastic criticism and the uncompromising exposure. No effort should be spared to secure the adoption of a more genuinely national policy. But beyond all this there remains a still deeper responsibility – that of dealing towards one's fellow-countrymen in good faith, so that differences of interest, of conviction, and of moral purpose can be made the agency of a better understanding and a firmer loyalty.[132]

The ambiguity of this passage fails to address many important questions. What if the majority believes that the views of protesters are not "constructive democratic ideas"? Can a majority determine when "vivacious" and "persistent" protests, "drastic criticism," and "uncompromising exposure" are only the "excuse for personal injustice or national disloyalty"? Does the First Amendment impose any limitations on the laws protesters must obey? All of these questions soon arose under the Espionage Act of 1917, but this passage provides no answers, or even routes to answers, for any of them.

---

[131] Croly-Promise, supra note 80, at 229.   [132] Id. at 285–86.

Moreover, by tying his concept of a progressive democracy to a pragmatic understanding of law, Croly could not give much assurance about how he would answer these questions. Social laws, he wrote, have "merely temporary and instrumental value." They are useful "for a while and under certain conditions."[133] He criticized attempts to "sanctify" for eternity specific formulations of individual rights. He maintained instead, as had Dewey, that "the amount of liberty which can be left to the individual without endangering the social interest will vary at different times."[134]

Justice Holmes used very similar language five years later in *Schenck v. United States,* which is the case most commentators still regard as the first important Supreme Court decision construing the First Amendment. Writing for a unanimous Court, Holmes upheld the convictions under the Espionage Act of socialists who had sent antiwar circulars to men accepted for military service. Holmes acknowledged that "in many places and in ordinary times" the circulars would be protected by the First Amendment. He added, however, that "the character of every act depends upon the circumstances in which it is done." "When a nation is at war," Holmes reasoned, "many things that might be said in time of peace are such a hindrance to its effort that their utterance will not be endured so long as men fight and that no Court could regard them as protected by any constitutional right."[135] Translated into Croly's analogous language, the "social interest" in winning a war justifies more restrictions on individual liberty than would be permissible in other, less threatening circumstances.

Although Holmes had written Croly a long letter about *Progressive Democracy* soon after the book was published, it is difficult to speculate about how much direct influence Croly's book had on Holmes's language in *Schenck.* Holmes in *Schenck* was clearly relying on his own earlier legal writings, and his letter criticized Croly for a tendency to "over-emphasize the importance of the particular Club we call nation or State."[136] The linguistic parallels between Croly and Holmes, however, reveal the shared view that the legal protection of speech varies with the threat it poses to social interests in particular circumstances.

---

[133] Croly-Democracy, supra note 84, at 177.

[134] Id. at 240.

[135] Schenck v. United States, 249 U.S. 47, 52 (1919), discussed infra, Chapter 6, at text accompanying notes 148–53.

[136] Letter from Oliver Wendell Holmes to Herbert Croly (Nov. 22, 1914) (Herbert Croly Papers, Autograph File, Houghton Library, Harvard University).

CONTINUITIES IN DEWEY'S CRITICISM OF
PACIFIST DISSENT DURING WORLD WAR I

In a series of four essays in *The New Republic* only months after the American entry into World War I in 1917, John Dewey made explicit the limited protection for free speech implicit in progressive social thought before the war. In these essays, Dewey criticized pacifists for failing to recognize the democratic potential of the war. By condemning pacifists for continuing to oppose the war when the only realistic option was to influence the purposes of American intervention, Dewey revealed the hostility to nonconstructive dissent contained within his prewar scholarship. And by attacking pacifists for relying on discredited conceptions of individual constitutional rights even as he increasingly opposed the suppression of their speech as harmful to American social interests, Dewey clearly extended his prewar analysis of legal rights to the specific issue of free speech.

"Conscience and Compulsion," the first of the four Dewey essays, addressed the "perplexity of conscience from which idealistic youth has suffered" in the wake of American participation in World War I. Dewey expressed sympathy for the many young Americans who had committed themselves to the peace movement before the war and who subsequently became upset when prevailing opinion, led by President Wilson, shifted so rapidly from neutrality to war. These idealistic and morally serious young people, Dewey asserted, "deserve something better than accusations, varying from pro-Germanism and the crime of Socialism to traitorous disloyalty." Dewey attempted to provide a better response himself while urging legal authorities that youthful conscientious objectors, instead of being punished, should be assigned useful tasks.[137]

Dewey observed that Americans generally "are not an over-agile people morally." He attributed this deficiency to inadequate moral training, rooted in evangelical Protestantism and reinforced by a legal system focused more on rules than on social conditions. Such training "emphasizes the emotions rather than intelligence, ideals rather than specific purposes, the nurture of personal motives rather than the creation of social agencies and environments." Conscientious objectors, in Dewey's opinion, were at worst innocent victims of unfortunate American moral traditions.[138]

---

[137] John Dewey, Conscience and Compulsion (1917), in 10 John Dewey, The Middle Works, 1899–1924, Essays on Philosophy and Education 1916–1917, at 260, 261–62 (1985).

[138] Id. at 261–62.

Dewey suggested that "a more social and less personal and evangelical" approach to moral issues would have enabled conscientious objectors to take the war issue "out of the emotional urgencies and inhibitions of inner consciousness into the light of objective fact." According to Dewey, the "merely good" and the "merely conscientious" are inevitably the victims in periods of social crisis. He viewed such stances not simply as "moral futility," but as "largely self-conceit." "If at a critical juncture the moving force of events is always too much for conscience," Dewey maintained, then "the remedy is not to deplore the wickedness of those who manipulate events," but to "connect conscience with the forces that are moving in another direction." Only through such connection "will conscience itself have compulsive power instead of being forever the martyred and the coerced."[139]

In subsequent essays, Dewey indicated his view of "the forces that are moving in another direction." He stressed "the immense impetus to reorganization afforded by this war," particularly the promise of "new agencies of international control."[140] Winning the war, Dewey reiterated, held "the prospect of a world organization and the beginnings of a public control which crosses nationalistic boundaries and interests." Dewey was convinced that these "genuine possibilities" were not "mere idealistic glosses, sugar-coatings of the bitter pill of war," even though they had yet to become "immediate actualities."[141]

Dewey expressed respect for his old friend Jane Addams, whose pacifism did not reduce to laissez-faire isolationism, but who maintained that international reorganization could be achieved without war. Dewey believed, however, that "the force of circumstances" made even the Addams version of pacifism unrealistic. He felt that "the pacifists wasted rather than invested their potentialities when they turned so vigorously to opposing entrance into a war which was already all but universal, instead of using their energies to form, at a plastic juncture, the conditions and objects of our entrance." For pacifists "to direct attention to stopping the war rather than to determining the terms upon which it shall be stopped" was, in Dewey's view, a colossal "stupidity."[142]

Dewey urged pacifists to submit their idealism to a course in

---

[139] Id. at 263–64.
[140] John Dewey, The Future of Pacifism (1917), in 10 John Dewey, supra note 137, at 265, 267–68.
[141] John Dewey, What America Will Fight For (1917), in 10 John Dewey, supra note 137, at 271, 275.
[142] Dewey, supra note 140, at 267–68.

"severe realism"[143] and to join his "genuine vision of a world some-
how made permanently different by our participation in a task
which taken by itself is intensely disliked."[144] Dewey even claimed
that he and the majority of the American people "still think of
themselves as fundamentally pacifists" despite their belief that the
United States had to enter the war. Dewey accepted the responsibility of "pacifists" like himself to make certain that the ideals of an
international community expressed by President Wilson "are
forced upon our allies."[145]

Throughout his essays, Dewey differentiated his conception of
the war as a force for international reconstruction from appeals
that were merely militaristic and patriotic. He opposed attempts by
political leaders and newspapers to manipulate the public through
posters, poetry, and other tributes to the glory and honor of war.
Just as pacifists failed "to connect conscience with the forces that
are moving in another direction,"[146] militaristic appeals to patriotism operated "against the tide of events" and virtually invited failure in a country where many people believed that an excess of
"nationalistic patriotism was chiefly responsible for the outbreak of
war." Dewey recognized that his vision of the war lacked "the glam-
our and impetuous rush of traditional war psychology." Yet precisely for this reason, it allowed "infinitely more potential for intelligence" and more closely reflected the American "national
psychology – the psychology of a businesslike people."[147] Dewey
seemed to believe that advocates of "traditional war psychology,"
like pacifists who continued to oppose the war after American
intervention, acted unrealistically by letting their emotional
responses blind them to the possibilities of intelligent control over
the force of events.

Dewey opposed the suppression of antiwar speech as part of his
general attack on the excesses of militaristic patriotism. In "Conscription of Thought," the last of the four essays, he commented
that the most striking effect of American participation in the war
"has been a morbid sensitiveness at any exhibition of diversity of
opinion."[148] Consistent with the general thrust of his essays, Dewey
stressed the irrationality and inefficiency of suppression rather
than the rights of dissenters or the value of their speech.

---

[143] Id. at 270.   [144] Dewey, supra note 141, at 274.
[145] Dewey, supra note 140, at 268.
[146] See supra text accompanying note 139 (quoting this phrase).
[147] Dewey, supra note 141, at 273–74.
[148] John Dewey, Conscription of Thought (1917), in 10 John Dewey, supra note
    137, at 276.

Dewey conceded that "intellectual and emotional unity" contributes vitally to the "social solidarity" and "union of action" required by war. "Without a certain sweep of undivided beliefs and sentiments," he maintained, "unity of outer action is likely to be mechanical and simulated." But he denied that force could effectively "remove disunion of thought and feeling." Rationalizing suppression of dissent on the ground that it produces social cohesion, Dewey protested, "is a piece of self-inflicted camouflage," a lesson that should become apparent by recalling "the inefficiency of all prior attempts to dragoon thought and feeling."[149]

History demonstrated to Dewey that suppression of thought only dignified "the unpopular cause with persecution" and increased "the vitality of obnoxious beliefs." If left unmolested, unpopular ideas generally "burn themselves out or die of inanition." Dewey lamented that during the passion of war many Americans, who generally realized that toleration would have been the best response to previous heresies, could not apply similar reasoning to pacifists.[150]

Dewey tried to teach this historical lesson in his essay. Governmental and public suppression of antiwar speech did not persuade dissenters or create national unity, but made these views seem important while forcing them underground where they would "breed and fester." He emphasized "the historically demonstrated inefficiency of the conscription of mind as a means of promoting social solidarity, and the gratuitous stupidity of measures that defeat their own ends." By maintaining that the dissenters did not pose any real threat to the American war effort, Dewey presented another argument against repression.[151]

At no point in his essay did Dewey express any concern for the dissenters themselves. He could not "arouse any genuine distress" that free speech would suffer in any lasting way, in part because it had survived substantially greater repression in the past. He suggested that many radicals who professed shock and resentment at the hostility directed toward them probably had their tongues in their cheeks and actually were grateful that their views would reach a much greater audience through persecution than they ever could have managed on their own. Dewey indicated his disdain for antiwar views while protesting their suppression. In opposing censorship, he maintained that radical ideas should be rendered "innocuous by humor and polite indifference." Dewey even ridiculed the "ultra-socialists" and other radicals who protested the

[149] Id. at 277.   [150] Id.
[151] Id. at 278–79.

suppression of their antiwar views by invoking "all the early Victorian political platitudes," including "the sanctity of individual rights and constitutional guaranties."[152]

Further deprecating the dissenters, Dewey provocatively asserted that the damage from "the conscription of mind" was not to the dissenters themselves, but to the freedom of thought "of those who do the attacking or who sympathize, even passively, with the attack." Suppression caused intellectual apathy, which might prevent Americans from taking advantage of the main opportunity presented by the war: "the great experience of discovering the significance of American national life by seeing it reflected into a remaking of the life of the world." This experience, Dewey felt, would in turn contribute "to the creation of a united America." He worried that repression of "stop-the-war" speech would be extended to all discussions about the purposes of the war and the shape of the ensuing peace.[153] Dewey did not recognize any rights of "stop-the-war" speakers or any value in their speech. Rather, he wanted to make sure that ideas of value to society would not be lost through attempts to suppress speech that made no social contribution.

Dewey demonstrated continuities with his prewar thought in 1917. It is most revealing that he emphasized the social value of free speech while castigating pacifists for relying on outmoded notions of individual constitutional rights to protest the suppression of their futile and counterproductive dissent. The reaction of federal judges to prosecutions of antiwar speech under the Espionage Act of 1917 demonstrated parallel continuities in their approach to free speech. In jury instructions and appellate decisions, most judges relied on the bad tendency test and on other restrictive doctrines that they had used to deny a wide variety of free speech claims before the war. Although operating within distinctive and largely incompatible intellectual universes, both progressive social thinkers and the judges they frequently criticized retained their shared prewar insensitivity to individuals asserting free speech rights. Under the pressure of the war and its aftermath, however, important progressive social thinkers and key judges transformed their views about free speech in ways that ultimately produced significant convergence in their thought. This convergence, which recognized individual rights to free speech as a socially valuable limitation on an activist state, became a fundamental feature of twentieth-century liberalism.

---

[152] Id. at 278–79.   [153] Id. at 279–80.

6

The Espionage Act

Ever since Chafee, scholars have assumed that judicial interpretation of free speech began with decisions construing the Espionage Act of 1917. Judicial decisions on a huge range of free speech issues between the Civil War and World War I demonstrate that this assumption is incorrect. The prewar cases also make clear that the Espionage Act decisions extended the longstanding judicial hostility toward free speech claims.

During public hearings held by the House Committee on the Judiciary on the bill that became the Espionage Act, many witnesses warned that the proposed legislation would stifle legitimate democratic debate about American war policy. The most effective testimony came from Gilbert Roe, who appeared as the representative of the Free Speech League. Based on his previous experience litigating free speech cases, Roe highlighted the danger that the legislation would allow juries to punish speakers for the supposed bad tendency of their speech. Congress essentially ignored the objections of Roe and others, whose fears were soon confirmed by scores of jury instructions and judicial decisions.

In deciding Espionage Act cases, lower court judges overwhelmingly invoked prewar doctrines and holdings. *Schenck, Frohwerk,* and *Debs,* the initial Supreme Court decisions that construed the Espionage Act, continued this trend. Writing for a unanimous Court in all three cases, Justice Holmes rejected the elaborate First Amendment arguments of socialists convicted for antiwar speech. Counsel for the defendants, especially Gilbert Roe in an amicus brief for Eugene Debs, challenged the bad tendency test as inconsistent with the First Amendment. In each of his three opinions, however, Holmes relied heavily on the bad tendency of speech to uphold the convictions, just as he had in his prewar opinions involving free speech claims. He used the phrase *clear and present danger* in *Schenck* as an expression of bad tendency and not, as Chafee soon claimed, to establish an alternative protective standard of First Amendment interpretation.

As Holmes himself acknowledged in correspondence, he treated the defendants' First Amendment arguments rather summarily in *Schenck, Frohwerk,* and *Debs.* Throughout these opinions, and especially in his discussion of clear and present danger in *Schenck,* Holmes relied on general principles that emphasized the role of law in enforcing community will through external and objective standards. He first announced these principles in his 1881 volume, *The Common Law,* and employed them for decades as a judge in a wide variety of cases, including many that did not implicate the meaning of free speech. Holmes emphasized his adherence to his longstanding jurisprudential principles in dismissing penetrating criticisms of his decision in *Debs* by Ernst Freund, who had written thoughtfully about free speech issues in his prewar treatise. Revealing increasingly overlapping intellectual and personal connections, Holmes made this point in a letter to Herbert Croly, the editor of *The New Republic,* in which Freund's critique of Holmes appeared.

Some rare lower court decisions construed the Espionage Act in ways that precluded the punishment of antiwar speech. Like the few prewar cases that deviated from the general judicial hostility to free speech claims, they revealed that judges as well as scholars could conceive of more legal protection for speech than did most of the judiciary, including the justices of the United States Supreme Court.

THE LEGISLATIVE HISTORY OF THE ESPIONAGE ACT

As the likelihood of American participation in World War I increased, lawyers in the Department of Justice became concerned that existing federal laws would be insufficient "to regulate the conduct of the individual during war time."[1] These lawyers wanted to repress "political agitation . . . of a character directly affecting the safety of the state," particularly "disloyal propaganda" threatening the formation and maintenance of the armed forces.[2] They assumed that the provisions of the existing federal penal code would be of only limited use.[3] The eminent legal scholar Charles Warren, who was an assistant attorney general during this period, maintained that speech "[a]dvising, inciting and persuading others to give aid and comfort to the enemy" might itself constitute

---

[1] O'Brian, Civil Liberty in War Time, 42 Rep. N.Y. St. Bar Ass'n 275, 299 (1919); see also id. at 277; Gregory, Suggestions of Attorney-General Gregory to Executive Committee in Relation to the Department of Justice, 4 A.B.A. J. 305, 305–6 (1918).

[2] O'Brian, supra note 1, at 277, 300.

[3] 1918 Att'y Gen. Ann. Rep. 16–17, 45; letter from Charles Warren to F. A. O'Connor (May 15, 1916) (National Archives File RG 60, 9-4-25).

treason.[4] The Department concluded, however, that the strict constitutional provision defining treason and its proof, as well as the
absence of any convictions under a federal treason statute over
one hundred years old, made the law of treason a fragile instrument "for suppressing or punishing disloyal and hostile acts and
utterances." Convinced that new federal legislation was needed,
the Department drafted the Espionage bill and submitted it to
Congress.[5] Charles Warren was its chief author.[6]

Congress debated the Espionage bill at length during April and
May 1917. Much of the debate focused on the history and meaning of the First Amendment. It is ironic that the section of the bill
that ultimately provided the basis for most of the prosecutions
hardly received any attention. Discussion of other proposed provisions, however, gives some indication of congressional views on
free speech issues that would soon reach the courts. Contrary to
the confident but uninformed subsequent assertions of Learned
Hand and Zechariah Chafee, these debates reveal that the majority of Congress intended the Espionage Act to encourage the
restrictive decisions that resulted.

A provision of the bill that would have allowed the president to
censor the press dominated congressional discussion and was
eventually eliminated by the conference committee.[7] Some congressmen protested that the First Amendment precludes prior
restraints,[8] and objected to delegating vast and unconfined "legislative" power over publications to the president and his subordi-

---

[4] Warren, What Is Giving Aid and Comfort to the Enemy?, 27 Yale L.J. 331,
340–43 (1918); memorandum for the Attorney General by Mr. Warren (Jan. 16,
1918) (National Archives File RG 60, 9-12-86).

[5] 1918 Att'y Gen. Ann. Rep. 41.

[6] The Chairman of the House Committee on the Judiciary stated that Warren
"drew practically all" the statutes that became the Espionage Act. 2 Hearings on
H.R. 291 Before the House Comm. on the Judiciary, 65th Cong., 1st Sess. 55
(1917) (statement of Rep. Webb) [hereinafter cited as Hearings on H.R. 291].
Attorney General Gregory also referred to Warren's "active part in the framing
of the Espionage Act." Letter from T.W.G. to Mr. Warren (Dec. 12, 1917)
(National Archives File RG 60, 189676).

[7] H.R. 291, 65th Cong., 1st Sess. § 2(c) (1917). A similar provision was included
in S. 2, 65th Cong., 1st Sess. § 4 (1917). For discussions of the legislative history
of this provision, see Thomas F. Carroll, Freedom of Speech and of the Press in
War Time: The Espionage Act, 17 Mich. L. Rev. 621, 622–29, 636 (1919);
Harold Edgar & Benno C. Schmidt, The Espionage Statutes and Publication of
Defense Information, 73 Colum. L. Rev. 929, 946–66 (1973). Both articles focus
on the defeated "censorship" provision.

[8] See, e.g., 55 Cong. Rec. 779, 2118–19 (1917) (statements of Sen. Borah),
2004–5 (statement of Sen. Ashurst).

nates.[9] More particularly, they pointed out that the government officials most likely to enforce this provision would naturally be inclined to censor legitimate public criticism as seditious.[10] The existing law of treason, several congressmen also suggested, would be sufficient to punish newspapers that published information aiding an enemy – the danger the censorship provision was designed to prevent.[11] A proviso that precluded restrictions on "any discussion, comment, or criticism of the acts or policies of the Government and its representatives, or the publication of the same"[12] did not allay concern about the potential abuse of official discretion.[13] Nor did an early conference report, which modified the original language of the bill by specifically defining the categories of nonpublishable information and by allowing the president to permit publication of otherwise illegal material deemed "not useful to the enemy."[14] The House instructed the conferees to strike the entire censorship provision,[15] and Congress passed the Espionage Act without it.

Congressmen raised similar concerns while debating a provision that proposed to expand the authority of postmasters to declare objectionable publications "nonmailable." Since the Comstock Act already allowed postmasters to exclude "obscene" and "indecent" publications, the initial version of the Espionage bill proposed to add to the nonmailable list publications of "treasonable or anarchistic character"[16] as well as those in violation of the bill's other provisions.[17] Congressmen protested that these provisions would confer unprecedented and unreviewable "autocratic power" upon the postmaster general and could be used to ban "perfectly inof-

---

[9] See, e.g., id. at 1751 (statement of Rep. Chandler); see also id. at 784 (statement of Sen. Brandegee), 1712 (statement of Rep. Dillon).

[10] See, e.g., id. at 2119 (statement of Sen. Borah), 781–82 (statement of Sen. Lodge).

[11] See id. at 1766 (statement of Rep. Thomas); see also id. at 781 (statement of Sen. Lodge), 2008 (statement of Sen. Walsh).

[12] Both the Senate and House bills contained this proviso. Id. at 2109 (Senate bill), 1813 (House bill). The House Committee on the Judiciary acknowledged the "broad powers" given to the president, but stressed its confidence that he "will not abuse this authority." The Committee added that the proviso, although "hardly necessary," was included to calm "the public and the newspaper fraternity." H.R. Rep. No. 30, 65th Cong., 1st Sess. 10 (1917).

[13] See, e.g., 55 Cong. Rec. 1813 (1917) (statement of Rep. Chandler).

[14] H.R. Rep. No. 65, 65th Cong., 1st Sess. 3 (1917) [hereinafter cited as Report No. 65]; see id. at 19 ("statement of the managers" on modification of § 4).

[15] H.R. Rep. No. 69, 65th Cong., 1st Sess. 19 (1917).

[16] H.R. Rep. No. 30, 65th Cong., 1st Sess. 9 (1917).

[17] H.R. 291, 65th Cong., 1st Sess. § 1101, 55 Cong. Rec. 1820 (1917).

fensive and harmless" publications on virtually any subject of "political, social, and industrial life."[18] Many stressed that the prohibition against "anarchistic" publications, which was inserted after the Post Office Department sent the members of the House Committee on the Judiciary some "horrible" samples, would be especially subject to administrative abuse because it could be interpreted so broadly.[19] The term *treasonable*, however, also caused concern. "A whole lot of people here and elsewhere," warned one representative, "seem to think that if a man does not agree with you he is a traitor and is guilty of treasonable utterances."[20]

Even vociferous opponents of the nonmailability provision conceded throughout the lengthy congressional debates that a variety of publications should not be circulated. For example, they agreed that it would be desirable to exclude socialist and IWW publications advocating opposition to the war and mass resistance to the draft from the mails. But they believed that no statute could be so limited. Any nonmailability provision, they feared, would allow postmasters to exclude "legitimate" publications as well, thereby producing "a far greater evil than the evil which is sought to be prevented."[21] Senator Borah made this point concretely. He shared Senator Overman's hostility to a publication that called every national flag a symbol of bondage and oppression, and characterized a recruitment publication as a device to obtain "food for the cannon." But he countered this example with "another from the opposite extreme," pointing out that a New York official had censored the fourth verse of "The Star-Spangled Banner" because it might offend England, an ally during the war. Borah complained that the proposed statute would not force postmasters to distinguish between these very different publications.[22] Yet even such limited objections failed to convince a majority of Congress. The Senate easily defeated two motions to strike the nonmailability provision,[23] and neither house limited the discretion of the Post Office Department.

Why did Congress, despite several similar objections to both provisions, grant broad authority to the Post Office Department while denying it to the president of the United States? To a certain extent this anomaly can be attributed to legal and historical fac-

---

[18] 55 Cong. Rec. 1836 (1917) (statement of Rep. Stafford), id. at 3138 (statement of Rep. Crosser), id. at 1871 (statement of Sen. Cummins).

[19] Id. at 1595, 1821; see generally id. at 1820–24.

[20] Id. at 1822 (statement of Rep. Mann).

[21] Id. at 2062 (statement of Sen. Thomas).

[22] Id. at 1869; see id. at 2062 (statement of Sen. Borah).

[23] Id. at 2072 (motion defeated 39–28), 2269–70 (motion defeated 52–29).

tors. Although the exclusion of publications from the mail could effectively prevent circulation, it did not constitute an actual prior restraint. By contrast, the censorship provision expressly prohibited publication. This distinction may have more formal than practical significance, but the debates reveal that many congressmen considered the Blackstonian prohibition against prior restraints the cornerstone of First Amendment protection.[24] Moreover, as defenders of the nonmailability provision pointed out to its critics, Congress had already given the Post Office Department power to exclude obscene and other "indecent" matter from the mail.[25] Several Supreme Court decisions had upheld this statute against First Amendment challenges.[26] Extending the list of nonmailable publications could have seemed a much less threatening departure than a law permitting censorship.

These explanations, however convincing, do not fully account for the contrasting votes. As the debates on the nonmailability provision indicate, a more pragmatic consideration motivated Congress. Although many were concerned about protecting the free speech of most citizens and newspapers, almost all appeared willing, and often eager, to restrict and punish the more extreme antiwar statements by radicals. The censorship provision would have allowed the president to forbid the publication of information on matters relating to the military and to national defense. The prohibition would have attached to the information, not to the style or tone of its presentation. Although the president's discretion to determine what information would be "useful to the enemy" might have allowed some selectivity in enforcement,[27] the focus on specified subjects endangered all publications. This provision could have prevented a major daily newspaper from publishing a thorough factual report on the armed forces, but could not have restrained a general socialist attack on the war as an imperialist adventure by capitalists that workers should resist. By contrast, the nonmailability provision referred to the language of the publication rather than to the information published. Despite the faults identified by its opponents, it was a more suitable tool to reach those antiwar statements that had few defenders in Congress. Under this provision, a heated socialist or IWW publication could

[24] See supra note 8.
[25] See, e.g., 55 Cong. Rec. 1836 (1917) (statement of Rep. Mann), 2057 (statement of Sen. Sterling).
[26] See, e.g., In re Rapier, 143 U.S. 110, 133–35 (1892); Ex parte Jackson, 96 U.S. 727, 736–37 (1877), discussed supra, Chapter 3, at text accompanying notes 22–23, 57–63.
[27] See 55 Cong. Rec. 2094–95 (1917) (statement of Sen. Husting).

be interpreted as advocating treason or resistance to law even if it contained no sensitive facts about the military.

Federal officials invoked the nonmailability provision in several prosecutions, most notably in *Masses Publishing Co. v. Patten*,[28] an early and particularly important case. The overwhelming majority of Espionage Act cases, however, arose under title I, section 3. Between 1917 and 1919, hundreds of jury instructions and federal court decisions interpreted its language:

> Whoever, when the United States is at war, shall willfully make or convey false reports or false statements with intent to interfere with the operation or success of the military or naval forces of the United States or to promote the success of its enemies and whoever, when the United States is at war, shall willfully cause or attempt to cause insubordination, disloyalty, mutiny, or refusal of duty, in the military or naval forces of the United States, or shall willfully obstruct the recruiting or enlistment service of the United States, to the injury of the service or of the United States, shall be punished by a fine of not more than $10,000 or imprisonment for not more than twenty years, or both.[29]

Almost every clause in this provision turned out to have crucial significance in subsequent litigation, but just a few congressmen referred to it during the entire debate about the Espionage bill.

One change from an earlier version reflected congressional concern about protecting free speech. The Senate bill had included language that allowed punishment for statements made "with intent to cause disaffection" with military operations. Senator Cummins moved to delete this language, explaining that the term *disaffection* could be invoked to punish exposure of military mismanagement and criticism of official policies and acts.[30] The Senate defeated Cummins's amendment,[31] but the House Committee on the Judiciary, perhaps in response to the vigorous criticisms of the proposed legislation at the Committee's public hearings, subsequently deleted the word *disaffection* from a later version of the Espionage bill. Chairman Webb explained that *disaffection* was overly "broad," "elastic," and "indefinite," and "might ofttimes subject a perfectly innocent person to punishment," such as a mother who might create disaffection in her soldier son by describing "sad conditions back home."[32]

---

[28] 244 F. 535 (S.D.N.Y.), rev'd, 246 F. 24 (2d Cir. 1917).
[29] Tit. I, § 3.   [30] 54 Cong. Rec. 3606–7.
[31] Id. at 3613.   [32] Id. at 1594–95.

The deletion of the word *disaffection* did not respond to the full range of criticism expressed at the public hearings. The majority of speakers at these hearings were lawyers, professors, and ministers appearing for themselves or on behalf of organizations such as the American Federation of Labor, the American Union Against Militarism, the Emergency Peace Foundation, the Free Speech League, and the Women's Peace Party of America. Jane Addams, John Reed, and Norman Thomas were some of the most prominent participants. Given his substantial experience with the Free Speech League, it is not surprising that Gilbert Roe made the most trenchant and prescient criticisms of the bill.

Appearing on behalf of the League, Roe maintained that by restricting the offenses of title I, section 3, to false reports and interference with the success of the armed forces, the legitimate purposes of the Espionage Act could be met without jeopardizing free speech. Roe warned especially about the dangers of the proposed intent requirement. Under standard definitions of intent, Roe stressed, "you are presumed to intend what are the natural consequences of your act." The determination of intent, he added, is a matter for the jury, and during a war "you are going to get a conviction any time any United States district attorney asks for it." Having represented the anarchist editor, Jay Fox, before the Supreme Court on behalf of the Free Speech League, Roe was able to cite Justice Holmes's opinion in *Fox v. Washington* as an illustration of the unfortunate results that can occur when judges allow juries to determine the consequences of speech.[33] Congress, however, retained the language of intent throughout the Espionage Act.

ESPIONAGE ACT LITIGATION
IN THE LOWER FEDERAL COURTS

Government attorneys began to prosecute antiwar speech soon after the United States entered World War I. At first, they used various provisions of the federal penal code to reach agitation that seemed to advocate disobedience to the Selective Draft Law, passed by Congress one month before the Espionage Act. Most of these prosecutions resulted in convictions.[34] As one federal judge bluntly pointed out, the Selective Draft Law created a different situation: Speech that previously would have been considered "merely . . . general discussion" could now be viewed as "inducing

---

[33] Hearings on H.R. 291, supra note 6, at 63. See supra, Chapter 3, text accompanying notes 24–29 (discussing Fox).
[34] 1918 Att'y Gen. Ann. Rep. 46–47; 1917 Att'y Gen. Ann. Rep. 74.

persons to violate the law."[35] The government also instituted several prosecutions of antiwar speech under the treason statute, despite reservations about its utility.[36] An early decision substantiated these doubts. In a case against a German-language newspaper, the *Philadelphia Tageblatt*, the court held that "mere words, no matter how vilely disloyal . . . , if accompanied by no other overt act than their utterance or publication, cannot be made the basis of a charge of treason." "Seditious utterances" that do not constitute treason, the opinion quickly added, may nevertheless be punished as misdemeanors at common law.[37]

As soon as Congress passed the Espionage Act, the Department of Justice viewed the new law as the most effective method of suppressing unwanted "propaganda" and of dealing with "disturbing malcontents."[38] The Department of Justice urged the United States attorney who had tried and lost the treason case against the *Philadelphia Tageblatt* to prosecute it under the Espionage Act "when you believe that the accumulation distinctly shows a pro-German or antiwar propaganda."[39] The government ultimately obtained convictions of the paper's officers, which the Supreme Court affirmed in *Schaefer v. United States*,[40] the 1920 decision that produced the first dissent written by Justice Brandeis in an Espionage Act case. Of the approximately two thousand Espionage Act prosecutions, the overwhelming majority were brought and won under title I, section 3.[41]

Espionage Act cases in the lower federal courts extended the prewar tradition of hostility to free speech, often by the familiar technique of relying on the alleged bad tendency of language. The lower court decisions foreshadowed the construction of the Espionage Act by the Supreme Court, beginning in 1919 with the unanimous opinions by Justice Holmes in *Schenck, Frohwerk,* and *Debs.* By contrast, the few protective opinions, like their predecessors before the war, highlighted the restrictiveness of the typical

---

[35] United States v. Phillips 5 (S.D.N.Y. 1917) (Interp. of War Stat. Bulletin 14). The Justice Department's Interpretation of War Statutes Bulletins are pamphlets containing opinions, rulings, and jury instructions by federal judges in response to prosecutions, during World War I, under the various war statutes. The bulletins are on file at the Library of Congress.

[36] 1918 Att'y Gen. Ann. Rep. 41–42.

[37] United States v. Werner, 247 F. 708, 710 (E.D. Pa. 1918).

[38] 1918 Att'y Gen. Ann. Rep. 45; 1917 Att'y Gen. Ann. Rep. 75.

[39] Letter from John Lord O'Brian to Francis Fisher Kane (April 9, 1918) (National Archives File No. 9-12-86-65).

[40] 251 U.S. 466 (1920).

[41] 1919 Atty. Gen. Ann. Rep. 22; 1918 Att'y Gen. Ann. Rep. 47.

decision. Despite the mythology subsequently created by Chafee, lower court decisions make clear that Holmes's first Espionage Act opinions, resembling his prewar decisions, were in the repressive mainstream, not the libertarian vanguard, of judicial interpretation of free speech claims.

Federal district judges generally let juries decide as a question of fact whether a defendant's language violated the law. Whatever the offending language, surrounding circumstances, or jury instructions, almost all prosecutions led to guilty verdicts. Some defendants appealed these verdicts, usually without success. Most circuit courts affirmed simply by relying on the general principle that judges in criminal appeals should not overrule jury findings of fact.

As Gilbert Roe had warned the House Committee on the Judiciary, juries instructed on the law of intent and tendency typically convicted defendants. The majority of federal district judges carefully reviewed the law of intent. Based on the traditional principle that intent must be inferred from external manifestations, they repeatedly announced the basic rule that one is presumed to intend the natural and usual consequences of his acts and that all relevant surrounding circumstances should be taken into account.[42] Like their prewar counterparts, judges often made this point by telling juries to weigh the "tendency" of language in determining its legality.[43] Judges also encouraged a loose construction of the tendency of language by observing that an indictment under the Espionage Act need not allege the illegal effects of language,[44]

---

[42] See, e.g., United States v. Nearing 16 (S.D.N.Y. 1919) (Interp. of War Stat. Bulletin 192); United States v. Weist 4–5 (E.D. Mo. 1918) (Interp. of War Stat. Bulletin 169); United States v. Bunyard 9 (E.D. Mo. 1918) (Interp. of War Stat. Bulletin 168); United States v. Prieth 12 (D.N.J. 1918) (Interp. of War Stat. Bulletin 156); United States v. Rhuberg 5 (D. Or. 1918) (Interp. of War Stat. Bulletin 94); United States v. Zittel 4 (W.D. Wash. 1918) (Interp. of War Stat. Bulletin 90); United States v. Henricksen 2 (D. Neb. 1918) (Interp. of War Stat. Bulletin 86); United States v. Mackley 3 (D. Vt. 1918) (Interp. of War Stat. Bulletin 83); United States v. Foster 3, 5–6 (W.D. Wash. 1918) (Interp. of War Stat. Bulletin 78); United States v. Ramp 6 (D. Or. 1918) (Interp. of War Stat. Bulletin 66); United States v. Huhn 5 (D. Wyo. 1918) (Interp. of War Stat. Bulletin 58); United States v. Baltzer 8–9 (D.S.D. 1918) (Interp. of War Stat. Bulletin 3); United States v. Doll 3 (D.S.D. 1917) (Interp. of War Stat. Bulletin 5).

[43] See, e.g., United States v. Bold 8–9 (D. Or. 1919) (Interp. of War Stat. Bulletin 183); United States v. Equi 23 (D. Or. 1918) (Interp. of War Stat. Bulletin 172); United States v. Wishek 5 (D.N.D. 1918) (Interp. of War Stat. Bulletin 153); United States v. Fontana 6–7 (D.N.D. 1918) (Interp. of War Stat. Bulletin 148); United States v. Pierce 35, 37 (N.D.N.Y. 1918) (Interp. of War Stat. Bulletin 52); United States v. Doll 4 (D.S.D. 1917) (Interp. of War Stat. Bulletin 5).

[44] Doe v. United States, 253 F. 903, 904–5 (8th Cir. 1918).

that the relationship between language and the statutory prohibitions need not be direct,[45] and that the offending speech need not be made in the presence of soldiers.[46] "Can a man who contaminates the spring at its source," one judge asked in a vivid formulation of the bad tendency test, "avoid responsibility because the resulting damage occurs at the mouth of the stream?"[47] Another judge upheld the seizure by the government of a film about the Revolutionary War because it portrayed "unspeakable atrocities committed by British soldiers," which might "tend . . . to make us a little bit slack in our loyalty to Great Britain."[48]

Judges and juries interpreted specific clauses of title I, section 3 in ways that facilitated convictions. In a prosecution against a man accused of "false statements" under the first clause for maintaining that the war was designed to produce slavery to financial barons, the judge instructed the jury to accept the congressional war resolution as reciting well-known historical facts and as "correctly stating the causes" of American participation.[49] Even without such explicit instructions, many juries construed as "false statements" claims by defendants that the financial interests of capitalists were responsible for American participation in the war.[50]

Moreover, judges observed that statements need not be false to violate the insubordination and obstruction clauses.[51] "A presentation of historic facts," one judge emphasized, if "marshalled so as to extol and glorify Germany, and so as to hold up to criticism and

---

45 See, e.g., United States v. Equi 11 (D. Or. 1918) (Interp. of War Stat. Bulletin 172); United States v. Stephens 7 (D. Del. 1918) (Interp. of War Stat. Bulletin 116).

46 See, e.g., Goldstein v. United States, 258 F. 908, 911 (9th Cir. 1919); Coldwell v. United States, 256 F. 805, 809 (1st Cir. 1919); Kirchner v. United States, 255 F. 301, 302–4 (4th Cir. 1918) (citing for support many jury instructions from Interpretation of War Statutes Bulletins); United States v. Weinsberg 7 (E.D. Mo. 1918) (Interp. of War Stat. Bulletin 123); United States v. Miller 4 (D. Colo. 1918) (Interp. of War Stat. Bulletin 104).

47 United States v. Nagler, 252 F. 217, 222 (W.D. Wis. 1918).

48 United States v. Motion Picture Film "The Spirit of '76," 252 F. 946, 947–48 (S.D. Cal. 1917), aff'd sub nom. Goldstein v. United States, 258 F. 908 (9th Cir. 1919).

49 United States v. Harper 3 (W.D. La. 1918) (Interp. of War Stat. Bulletin 76).

50 See, e.g., United States v. Kirchner 2 (N.D.W. Va. 1918) (Interp. of War Stat. Bulletin 69); United States v. Pierce 2 (N.D.N.Y. 1918) (Interp. of War Stat. Bulletin 52).

51 See, e.g., Goldstein v. United States, 258 F. 908, 910 (9th Cir. 1919); United States v. Equi 12 (D. Or. 1918) (Interp. of War Stat. Bulletin 172); United States v. Wishek 5 (D.N.D. 1918) (Interp. of War Stat. Bulletin 153); United States v. Binder 5 (E.D.N.Y. 1918) (Interp. of War Stat. Bulletin 126).

reproach Great Britain, with whom our soldiers were to fight and wage this war, might accomplish the results forbidden by the law."[52] Judges also construed *obstruct* loosely.[53] One judge acknowledged that the obstruction clause, unlike the insubordination clause, did not expressly punish attempts, yet he concluded that the enlistment and recruitment service could be obstructed without actually being stopped. He therefore told the jury, using a phrase commonly adopted in other instructions, "that obstruction in its broad sense means to hinder, to impede, to embarrass, to retard, to check, to slacken, to prevent, in whole or in part" and even "to render more burdensome or difficult the enforcement and execution of the law."[54] Some judges instructed juries that a defendant's opinions or prophesies could cause insubordination or obstruction,[55] although others pointed out that these clauses of the Espionage Act did not prevent Americans from expressing their opinions about the war.[56]

Defendants occasionally used fairly strong language. For example, a jury found a man guilty of attempting to cause insubordination because he told people subject to the draft that he hoped Germany would win the war and that "the best thing they . . . could do when in battle would be to put up their hands and let the Germans

---

[52] United States v. Wishek 5 (D.N.D. 1918) (Interp. of War Stat. Bulletin 153). The judge did concede that the truth of a statement is relevant to determining the intent of a speaker. Id.

[53] See, e.g., Deason v. United States, 254 F. 259, 261 (5th Cir. 1918); Doe v. United States, 253 F. 903, 906 (8th Cir. 1918); O'Hare v. United States, 253 F. 538, 540 (8th Cir. 1918); United States v. Rhuberg 4 (D. Or. 1918) (Interp. of War Stat. Bulletin 94); United States v. Frerichs 4 (D. Neb. 1918) (Interp. of War Stat. Bulletin 85); United States v. Wolf 5–6 (D.S.D. 1918) (Interp. of War Stat. Bulletin 81); United States v. Hitt 6 (D. Colo. 1918) (Interp. of War Stat. Bulletin 53).

[54] United States v. Hitt 6 (D. Colo. 1918) (Interp. of War Stat. Bulletin 53). The decision by the Second Circuit in Masses Publishing Co. v. Patten, 246 F. 24, 38 (1917), may have been the original source of this phrase.

[55] See, e.g., United States v. Binder 5 (E.D.N.Y. 1918) (Interp. of War Stat. Bulletin 126); United States v. Weinsberg 6–7 (E.D. Mo. 1918) (Interp. of War Stat. Bulletin 123); United States v. Frerichs 9 (D. Neb. 1918) (Interp. of War Stat. Bulletin 85).

[56] See, e.g., United States v. Nearing 14 (S.D.N.Y. 1919) (Interp. of War Stat. Bulletin 192); United States v. Albers 17 (D. Or. 1919) (Interp. of War Stat. Bulletin 191) (interpreting language of 1918 amendment); United States v. Berger 8–9 (N.D. Ill. 1919) (Interp. of War Stat. Bulletin 186); United States v. Bold 7–8 (D. Or. 1919) (Interp. of War Stat. Bulletin 183) (interpreting language of 1918 amendment); United States v. Elmer 3 (E.D. Mo. 1918) (Interp. of War Stat. Bulletin 171); United States v. Debs 12 (N.D. Ohio 1918) (Interp. of War Stat. Bulletin 155) (interpreting language of 1918 amendment).

take them prisoners."[57] Another jury convicted an IWW speaker, indicted on similar charges, for advising conscripted men that they "better have a pick and shovel laboring for the working men instead of carrying a gun for the capitalists."[58] Yet juries convicted defendants for much more innocuous speech. A jury found a minister guilty of an attempt to cause insubordination because he distributed a pamphlet teaching that Christians should not kill in wars.[59] Another jury convicted twenty-seven "German" farmers in South Dakota, who belonged to the Socialist Party, for conspiring to obstruct the recruitment service because they petitioned the governor to change his decision exempting entire counties from the draft.[60] One judge, in the case of a defendant accused of interfering with the fundraising efforts of the Red Cross and the YMCA, instructed the jury that the statutory definition of "military and naval forces of the United States" included these two organizations.[61]

Judges hearing Espionage Act cases, like their predecessors faced with free speech claims before the war, often did not refer to the First Amendment. Those who cited it generally stressed that the Constitution does not provide absolute protection for speech. They listed the traditional exceptions for libel, slander, blasphemy, and obscenity, and emphasized, as had the Supreme Court in its *Turner* decision of 1904, that the government's right of "self-preservation" supersedes an individual's freedom of expression. For example, in the case of a defendant who claimed that the capitalists' war would make Liberty Bonds worthless, the judge instructed the jury that the First Amendment "can not be successfully invoked as a protection where the honor and safety of the Nation is involved."[62] Judges also observed that free speech is but one of many equally important rights protected by the Constitution. As a jury instruction pointed out, the same Constitution that forbids Congress from abridging free speech also grants it power to declare war and raise armies. Neither provision, the judge asserted, could "destroy or break down" the other. He concluded that the Espionage Act, by punishing interference with the war effort without reaching "the proper advocacy of principle within

---

57 United States v. Rhuberg 2 (D. Or. 1918) (Interp. of War Stat. Bulletin 94).

58 United States v. Ramp 2 (D. Or. 1918) (Interp. of War Stat. Bulletin 66).

59 United States v. Waidron 3–4 (D. Vt. 1918) (Interp. of War Stat. Bulletin 79).

60 United States v. Baltzer 1 (D.S.D. 1918) (Interp. of War Stat. Bulletin 3).

61 United States v. Wallace 5 (S.D. Iowa 1917) (Interp. of War Stat. Bulletin 4).

62 United States v. Tanner 3 (D. Colo. 1918) (Interp. of War Stat. Bulletin 56).

the limitations of the law," appropriately balanced these two constitutional provisions.[63] Another judge bluntly stated that speech "which in ordinary times might be clearly permissible, or even commendable, in this hour of national emergency, effort, and peril, may be as clearly treasonable, and therefore properly subject to review and repression."[64]

A few decisions demonstrated that it was possible to construe the Espionage Act in ways that protected antiwar speech. A handful of district judges withheld cases from juries, and an equally small number of their colleagues on the circuit courts reversed convictions on appeal. Judge Learned Hand's opinion in *Masses Publishing Co. v. Patten*,[65] decided the month after Congress passed the Espionage Act, merits special attention.[66] Hand thoughtfully rejected the prevailing bad tendency test and interpreted the Espionage Act in ways that would have precluded most subsequent convictions had other judges adopted his approach.

The New York Postmaster precipitated the case by invoking the Espionage Act to declare *The Masses* "nonmailable." *The Masses* described itself as a "revolutionary and not a reform magazine." Max Eastman, its editor, wrote his dissertation in philosophy under John Dewey. In addition to Eastman, contributors included IWW leader Bill Haywood, John Reed, Carl Sandburg, Louis Untermeyer, and Art Young.[67] According to the postmaster, antiwar articles and cartoons in *The Masses* "tended to produce a violation" of all three clauses of title I, section 3.[68] Gilbert Roe represented the editors, who were threatened with the same dangers to free speech that Roe had highlighted in his testimony before the House Committee on the Judiciary.

Hand granted the injunction Roe sought against the postmaster. He treated the clauses of the Espionage Act in order, and

---

[63] United States v. Equi 21 (D. Or. 1918) (Interp. of War Stat. Bulletin 172); see also Doe v. United States, 253 F. 903, 906 (8th Cir. 1918) (stressing war power as constitutional justification for Espionage Act).

[64] United States v. Motion Picture Film "The Spirit of '76," 252 F. 946, 948 (S.D. Cal. 1917), aff'd sub nom. Goldstein v. United States, 258 F. 908 (9th Cir. 1919).

[65] 244 F. 535 (S.D.N.Y.), rev'd, 246 F. 24 (2d Cir. 1917).

[66] Gerald Gunther, Hand's biographer, uncovered the importance of this case. Gerald Gunther, Learned Hand and the Origins of Modern First Amendment Doctrine: Some Fragments of History, 27 Stan. L. Rev. 719 (1975).

[67] Gerald Gunther, Learned Hand: The Man and the Judge 153 (1994). See generally Leslie Fishbein, Rebels in Bohemia – The Radicals of "The Masses" (1982).

[68] 244 F. at 536.

Drawn by H. J. Glintenkamp.

Cartoons by H. J. Glintenkamp in the August 1917 issue of *The Masses*. According to the New York Postmaster, these cartoons "tended to produce a violation" of the Espionage Act.

Conscription

H. J. Glintenkamp.

began his opinion by reasoning that the "false statements" punished by the first clause referred only to "the spreading of false rumors which may embarrass the military." The government's application of this clause to *The Masses,* Hand reasoned, constituted an impermissible attempt "to raise it into a means of suppressing intemperate and inflammatory public discussion, which was surely not its purpose." Hand conceded as "unhappily true" that the contents of the magazine might "enervate public feeling at home" and cause "mischievous effects" on the war effort. But he insisted that these tendencies were beside the point in construing the falsity clause.[69]

Hand's discussion of the remainder of the Espionage Act made clear that his objection to judging speech by its tendencies did not depend on the limitation of the first clause to "false statements." While conceding the postmaster's position that "to arouse discontent and disaffection among the people with the prosecution of the war and with the draft tends to promote a mutinous and insubordinate temper among the troops," Hand refused to find a violation of the insubordination clause.[70] He also granted that praise of convicted opponents of the draft has "a tendency to arouse emulation in others."[71] Yet such tendencies, he concluded, did not constitute obstruction.

Hand worried that evaluating the legality of speech by its tendency would make it difficult if not impossible for defendants to disprove the charges against them and would create an imprecision in standards and a discretion in administration inconsistent with "the normal assumption that law shall be embodied in general propositions capable of some measure of definition." "The tradition of English-speaking freedom," Hand reasoned, "has depended in no small part upon the merely procedural requirement that the state point with exactness to just that conduct which violates the law."[72] Hand was sensitive to the problems of vagueness emphasized before the war by Gilbert Roe and Theodore Schroeder of the Free Speech League, which Roe may have stressed to him in oral argument.

In contrast to the bad tendency test, Hand asserted that language should be declared illegal under the insubordination and obstruction clauses only if it could "be thought directly to counsel or advise insubordination" or to constitute "direct advocacy of resistance to the recruitment and enlistment service."[73] Hand

[69] Id. at 539.
[71] Id. at 541
[73] Id. at 541.

[70] Id.
[72] Id. at 543.

acknowledged that "words are to be taken, not literally, but according to their full import." He insisted, however, that "the literal meaning is the starting point for interpretation."[74] Hand reasoned that words "which have no purport but to counsel the violation of law" are themselves illegal. Yet he warned that "to assimilate agitation, legitimate as such, with direct incitement to violent resistance, is to disregard the tolerance of all methods of political agitation which in normal times is a safeguard of free government." Hand feared that such an interpretation would render illegal all political speech "apt to create a seditious temper," and he concluded that in passing the Espionage Act "Congress had no such revolutionary purpose in view." Although Hand readily conceded that illegal counseling "may be accomplished as well by indirection as expressly," he did not indicate in his decision when it was necessary to look beyond the "literal meaning" of words.[75] In *Masses*, at least, he saw no reason to do so.

Hand made clear throughout his opinion that he was construing the Espionage Act rather than interpreting the Constitution. He granted the possibility "that Congress may forbid the mails to any matter which tends to discourage the successful prosecution of the war." "It may be," he added, "that the fundamental personal rights of the individual must stand in abeyance, even including the right of the freedom of the press."[76] He assumed that Congress could repress hostile criticism "in the throes of a struggle for the very existence of the state."[77] He also reiterated that he was not questioning "the power of Congress to establish a personal censorship of the press under the war power."[78] Hand, however, accompanied each of these caveats with the confident assertion that Congress had not chosen to invoke such power in passing the Espionage Act. Indeed, he concluded that "its exercise is so contrary to the use and wont of our people that only the clearest expression . . . justifies the conclusion that it was intended."[79] Yet the legislative history of the Espionage Act, which Hand never cited in his opinion, demonstrates the congressional intent to punish the very kind of antiwar material that prompted the postmaster to declare *The Masses* "nonmailable."

Hand's decision in *Masses* did not take hold. A circuit court judge wrote an opinion disapproving Hand's test while staying the injunction,[80] and a full panel of the Second Circuit soon reversed

---

[74] Id. at 542.
[76] Id. at 538.
[78] Id. at 543.
[75] Id. at 540.
[77] Id. at 540.
[79] Id. at 540.
[80] Masses Publishing Co. v. Patten, 245 F. 102 (2d Cir. 1917).

Hand's order. After quoting Hand's statement that anything less than urging resistance to law is protected, the panel simply announced its disagreement. The Second Circuit expressed the familiar bad tendency approach by evaluating "the natural and reasonable effect of what is said" and held that an incitement to crime may be indirect.[81]

Other judges, while following the traditional tests of intent and bad tendency, were nevertheless able to place some restraints on the government's use of title I, section 3 as a dragnet to secure convictions for antiwar speech. Judge Bourquin's directed verdict in *United States v. Hall* was the earliest of these decisions. The defendant, in the presence of men registered for the draft, used harsher language than most convicted speakers. In addition to typical comments about President Wilson being a "Wall Street tool," he stated that "he would flee to avoid going to the war." Judge Bourquin pointed out, however, that these statements were made, in "badinage," at picnics, and during saloon arguments in a small village in Montana, sixty miles from the nearest railroad, and apparently hundreds of miles from the nearest army base. He cited the standard interpretation of intent, but maintained that the natural consequences and surrounding circumstances in this case made the inference of intent to interfere with the operation and success of the military "absurd."[82]

Bourquin added that many of the substantive offenses defined by the Espionage Act "are of the nature of attempts," which require "proximity to the object of their operation." By defining military forces to include only men actually in service, rather than all registered men, Bourquin found insufficient "proximity to constitute attempts." He maintained that the final clause, by creating the crime of obstruction rather than "mere attempts to obstruct," could not be violated without a showing of actual "injury to the service." Like Hand in *Masses,* Bourquin also observed that the false statements punished by the Espionage Act did not include "opinions, beliefs, intentions, and arguments." The "public impression" that the Espionage Act could punish "mere disloyal utterances" and slander or libel of public officials, he concluded, was a "mistake." While conceding that such expressions could vio-

---

[81] Masses Publishing Co. v. Patten, 246 F. 24, 38 (2d Cir. 1917). In a concurring opinion, Judge Ward emphasized that not every publication may be punished for its "indirect effect" to obstruct recruitment. "In addition to the natural effect of the language on the reader, " he maintained, "the intention to discourage is essential." Id. at 39. Judge Ward did not indicate what would constitute evidence of such an intention.

[82] United States v. Hall, 248 F. 150, 152–53 (D. Mont. 1918).

late state law when tending to breach the peace, he emphasized that since the Sedition Act of 1798 Congress, perhaps reflecting "the genius of democracy," had not made them federal crimes.[83]

Judge Bourquin's opinion in *Hall* so disturbed the Department of Justice that its lawyers sought an amendment of the Espionage Act. In an address to the executive committee of the American Bar Association while Congress was considering such an amendment, Attorney General Gregory cited this "celebrated case" as an example of the "ineffectiveness" of the Espionage Act "when applied by a judge not in accord with its purposes." Gregory observed that most district judges "properly left to the jury the duty of determining the intention of the accused from the language used and the circumstances under which it was used," but he expressed confidence that "a much more drastic" amendment being considered by Congress "will form the basis for convictions in all federal districts."[84] Gregory got what he wanted in the 1918 "Sedition Act," which amended the Espionage Act by expressly prohibiting "unpatriotic or disloyal" language.[85]

A few circuit court reversals of guilty verdicts also interpreted the Espionage Act in ways that limited its restrictions on speech. These protective decisions, often echoing Judge Bourquin's reasoning in *Hall*, addressed many of the same issues of statutory construction as their restrictive counterparts while reaching opposite results. Several courts carefully distinguished unpopular but legal opinions from the "false statements" prohibited by the Espionage Act. For example, Judge Munger dismissed charges of falsity against statements alleging that Jesus Christ was the only person better than the Kaiser, that "Germany can't be whipped,"[86] and that the Red Cross "are a lot of thieves and grafters." He came to the same conclusion about the claim that President Wilson and the munitions makers were responsible for the war. According to Munger, no consensus existed about the causes of the war; indeed, historians could probably cite one hundred. "[T]o charge a man with making a false statement because he undertakes to single out one thing as the cause of the war," he reasoned, "is placing a construction upon the law that was not contemplated."[87]

Other protective decisions stressed that there must be some

---

[83] Id. at 152–54.

[84] Suggestions of Attorney-General Gregory, 4 A.B.A. J. 305, 306–7 (1918).

[85] Act of May 16, 1918, ch. 75, 40 Stat. 553; see 1918 Att'y Gen. Ann. Rep. 18.

[86] United States v. Frerichs 2 (D. Neb. 1918) (Interp. of War Stat. Bulletin 85).

[87] United States v. Koenig 2 (E.D. Mo. 1918) (Interp. of War Stat. Bulletin 166); see also Kammann v. United States, 259 F. 192, 193 (7th Cir. 1919); Sandberg v. United States, 257 F. 643, 646, 648 (9th Cir. 1919).

proximity between language and the crimes defined by the Espionage Act; intent could not be inferred from the secondary, remote, or indirect effects of language. However unfair, unjust, unpatriotic, or disloyal, speech could not be punished without some substantial evidence of its impact.[88] The protective decisions conceded that the effect of speech can be inferred from its surrounding circumstances, but they emphasized that these circumstances must be examined carefully. As a result, several judges maintained that the failure to specify them in the pleadings or indictment precluded a conviction. Where "circumstances are an element of a crime," Judge Amidon observed, they "cannot be left to speculation or inference, but must be clearly and directly charged." Simply to identify the challenged language and assert illegal intent would be insufficient.[89] A pleading lacking such specificity, one circuit court held, violated the Sixth Amendment because it failed to inform the defendants of the charges against them.[90]

The kind of surrounding circumstances that prompted most judges and juries to find violations of the Espionage Act did not satisfy some judges. Focusing on the nature of the audience, judges held that speech to a women's club,[91] or in private conversations,[92] could not be punished under the Espionage Act. Some courts explicitly held that speech must reach men in the military before provisions of the Espionage Act could apply.[93] Another judge added that the identification of a soldier in the audience was not itself sufficient to constitute an attempt to cause insubordination.[94] In the case of a defendant charged with obstruction for his statement that the sons of farmers, not of merchants and

---

[88] See, e.g., United States v. Mills 2, 4 (D.N.D. 1919) (Interp. of War Stat. Bulletin 204); United States v. Henning 15 (E.D. Wis. 1919) (Interp. of War Stat. Bulletin 184); United States v. Koenig 3–4 (E.D. Mo. 1918) (Interp. of War Stat. Bulletin 166); United States v. Schutte, 252 F. 212, 213, 215 (D.N.D. 1918).

[89] United States v. Schutte, 252 F. 212, 214 (D.N.D. 1918); see also Grubl v. United States, 264 F. 44, 46 (8th Cir. 1920); Fontana v. United States, 262 F. 283, 286–87 (8th Cir. 1919); Shilter v. United States, 257 F. 724, 725–26 (9th Cir. 1919); United States v. Koenig 1, 3 (E.D. Mo. 1918) (Interp. of War Stat. Bulletin 166).

[90] Foster v. United States, 253 F. 481, 482 (9th Cir. 1918).

[91] United States v. Schutte, 252 F. 212, 214 (D.N.D. 1918).

[92] See, e.g., Fontana v. United States, 262 F. 283, 288 (8th Cir. 1919); Harshfield v. United States, 260 F. 659, 660 (8th Cir. 1919); Wolf v. United States, 259 F. 388, 393 (8th Cir. 1919); Sandberg v. United States, 257 F. 643, 648 (9th Cir. 1919).

[93] See, e.g., Grubl v. United States, 264 F. 44, 46–48 (8th Cir. 1920); Kammann v. United States, 259 F. 192, 194 (7th Cir. 1919); Shilter v. United States, 257 F. 724, 725–26 (9th Cir. 1919).

[94] United States v. Henning 16 (E.D. Wis. 1919) (Interp. of War Stat. Bulletin 184).

bankers, were fighting in France, Judge Amidon identified a variety of extenuating circumstances. Amidon pointed out that the speaker had been harassed with accusations of disloyalty, and that the speech was extemporaneous, constantly interrupted, and delivered at the end of a heated political campaign.[95]

Several of the protective decisions emphasized that Congress did not intend the Espionage Act to punish unpatriotic or disloyal language. "Such a perversion of law," one judge concluded, "would itself be a supreme act of disloyalty."[96] Another judge observed that if Congress had wanted to pass a sedition law, it could have modeled one after the Sedition Act of 1798. He construed the provisions of the Espionage Act as evidence that Congress "industriously sought to keep away" from this ancient precedent.[97]

A few remarkable circuit court reversals, decided after the Armistice and after most Espionage Act decisions, recognized the difficulty of reaching fair verdicts during war – the problem identified by Gilbert Roe during the hearings on the Espionage bill. The courts pointed out that patriotic citizens had become "particularly impatient" and "to a certain extent [had] lost their mental poise."[98] Only two months after the Supreme Court unanimously upheld convictions in its first Espionage Act cases, one circuit court observed:

> It is natural, in time of war, when patriotic sentiment is high, that it is particularly difficult to secure a fair trial for men accused of crimes connected with the war. At such times the task of the court becomes especially difficult and requires great care to prevent miscarriage of justice. These are practical considerations, which must be constantly borne in mind, or the verdicts of juries in such cases will mistakenly become expressions of their hatred for unpatriotic acts in general, instead of their careful judgment on the facts shown by the evidence in the particular case. Patriotism must not become, even innocently, a cloak for injustice. The right of an accused in the courts of this nation to a fair trial must not vary with the character of the crime.[99]

This judicial perception came too late and too infrequently to make any difference in most cases.

---

[95] United States v. Mills 3–4 (D.N.D. 1919) (Interp. of War Stat. Bulletin 204).

[96] United States v. Schutte, 252 F. 212, 213 (D.N.D. 1918).

[97] United States v. Henning 17 (E.D. Wis. 1919) (Interp. of War Stat. Bulletin 184).

[98] Stokes v. United States, 264 F. 18, 25 (8th Cir. 1920).

[99] Wolf v. United States, 259 F. 388, 394 (8th Cir. 1919).

THE SELECTIVE DRAFT LAW CASES

Ten appeals of convictions under the 1917 Selective Draft Law reached the Supreme Court one year before the first group of Espionage Act cases. All concentrated on attacking the constitutionality of the draft. The Supreme Court, prompted by the solicitor general,[100] consolidated six of them and, in the *Selective Draft Law Cases,* upheld the draft as a legitimate exercise by Congress of its constitutional power "to declare war" and "to raise and support armies."[101] The Court issued additional opinions in the four remaining cases to deal with "other questions"[102] left unresolved by its consolidated opinion. In three of these four cases – *Ruthenberg v. United States, Kramer v. United States,* and *Goldman v. United States* – the government claimed that an antiwar speaker had violated the criminal code by inducing or conspiring to induce an eligible person not to register for the draft.[103]

Like many cases that implicated freedom of speech before World War I, neither the briefs nor the decisions in *Ruthenberg, Kramer,* and *Goldman* explicitly addressed the meaning of the First Amendment or concentrated on free speech issues. The attorneys for the convicted speakers, however, did challenge the punishment for speech. Protesting that the indictment failed to show how the defendants' "multifarious political activities" aided a man not to register, the lawyers in *Ruthenberg* claimed that it was unconstitutionally vague and a "legal ambush." They pointed out that their clients had never met the man they allegedly aided. Was this man, the attorneys asked, "influenced by printed leaflets, form, letter, speech, song, public exhortation, private appeal? And when? Where?" According to the attorneys, all their clients "could know till the moment of trial was, they were charged with 'aiding' a man unknown to them, somewhere in Cleveland, sometime before the registration, not to register."[104] The government responded by asserting that the defendants "knew the speeches that caused their arrests,"[105] and the Supreme

---

[100] Motion by the United States to Advance, Ruthenberg v. United States, 245 U.S. 480 (1918).

[101] Selective Draft Law Cases, 245 U.S. 366, 377 (1918).

[102] Goldman v. United States, 245 U.S. 474, 476 (1918).

[103] Ruthenberg v. United States, 245 U.S. 480, 481 (1918) (inducement); Kramer v. United States, 245 U.S. 478, 479 (1918) (conspiracy); Goldman v. United States, 245 U.S. 474, 475 (1918) (conspiracy). The fourth case, Jones v. Perkins, 245 U.S. 390 (1918), affirmed the denial of a petition for a writ of habeas corpus from a man arrested for failing to register as required by the Selective Draft Law.

[104] Brief for Plaintiffs in Error at 23, 25.

[105] Brief for the United States at 104–5.

Court dismissed the defendants' objections as "so unsubstantial as not to require even statement."[106]

Harry Weinberger, who had worked closely with the Free Speech League in the years immediately before the war, represented the defendants in *Goldman* and *Kramer*. He maintained in his brief for codefendants Emma Goldman and Alexander Berkman that nothing either defendant ever said or wrote could be construed as an overt act in a conspiracy to urge men not to register. The government, he pointed out, had produced "no evidence that they advised people to disobey the law." Nor had it submitted any proof that anything Goldman or Berkman said or wrote had even reached men subject to the draft. Weinberger acknowledged that Goldman and Berkman strongly disapproved of the draft, but he stressed that "no one was ever convicted before of the crime of disapproving of laws." In Weinberger's view, a jury under the influence of the prevailing "war hysteria" had convicted his clients simply for expressing their views on a "public question."[107] Conceding that Goldman and Berkman distinguished between opposition to conscription and advice not to register, the government's brief supported the jury verdict because "the result reasonably deduced from advice not to be conscripted is to refuse to take the first step."[108]

The Supreme Court emphasized that its opinion sustaining the draft in the *Selective Draft Law Cases* disposed of all the constitutional questions in *Goldman*. It rejected Weinberger's arguments about the sufficiency of the evidence by attributing them to the erroneous "assumption that the power to review embraces the right to invade the province of the jury by determining questions of credibility and weight of evidence." Despite this disclaimer, the Court did review the record and "without recapitulating the evidence" – indeed, without referring to any of it – concluded in a summary sentence that "the proposition that there was no evidence whatever of guilt to go to the jury is absolutely devoid of merit."[109] The Court reached the same determination in *Kramer*. As long as there was "evidence tending to show guilt," the case could not be taken from the jury. Once again, the Court, without identifying such evidence, claimed to have found it.[110]

---

[106] 245 U.S. at 483.

[107] Brief on Behalf of the Plaintiffs-in-Error at 18–21.

[108] Brief for the United States at 120. In fact, Goldman and Berkman indicated that they would not have registered had the law applied to them. Id. at 117–19 (quoting speeches by Berkman and Goldman).

[109] 245 U.S. at 476–77.

[110] Kramer v. United States, 245 U.S. 478, 479 (1918).

SUPREME COURT BRIEFS IN THE FIRST ESPIONAGE ACT CASES

The first four Espionage Act cases reached the Supreme Court the following term. In all of them, the government charged that anti-war articles and speeches caused or attempted to cause insubordination in the armed forces or obstruction of recruitment or enlistment. The case involving Eugene V. Debs, the Socialist Party's perennial candidate for president, was the most thoroughly briefed, probably because Debs was the most prominent defendant in an Espionage Act prosecution. Seymour Stedman, who defended many socialists in Espionage Act cases, devoted his main effort to the *Debs* case, as did Alfred Bettman and John Lord O'Brian, who wrote the government's briefs in all four of these cases before the Supreme Court. Gilbert Roe, who represented a defendant in another Espionage Act case awaiting argument, also selected *Debs* as the one initial Espionage Act case in which to file an amicus brief.

Stedman repeated the objections that lawyers for the defendants in *Goldman, Kramer*, and *Ruthenberg* had raised to their indictments under the Selective Draft Law.[111] He went on, however, to make a quantum leap beyond his predecessors by translating these objections into constitutional arguments for *Debs*. Stedman called the First Amendment "the vital issue of this case." To emphasize the importance of the First Amendment, and perhaps as a warning to the Court that it should resist its frequent inclination to avoid free speech claims, Stedman introduced his constitutional argument by citing the public reaction to the government's prosecution of Debs. "The millions in many countries who respond to the idealism of Eugene V. Debs," Stedman reminded the Court, "will bluntly speak of the *Debs* case as a free speech fight."[112]

Because the indictment itself presented "no theory of the pleader as to the pertinence of defendant's words to move others to action," Stedman claimed, any relationship between Debs's speech and the prohibitions of the Espionage Act was "left for conjecture of judge and jury." According to Stedman, these deficiencies "led to a sedition conviction under a thin disguise of a charge of actual military obstruction by means of words." The First Amendment, Stedman added, does not permit convictions simply because a jury concludes that a defendant has a "seditious temper." Stedman borrowed the phrase *seditious temper* from Hand's opinion in

---

[111] Brief of Plaintiff in Error at 8–16, Sugarman v. United States; Brief for Plaintiff in Error at 38, Debs v. United States [hereinafter Stedman Brief for Debs].

[112] Stedman Brief for Debs, supra note 111, at 61–62.

Masses, which he quoted at length, identifying it incorrectly, although understandably given its reasoning and result, as the only case "leading to anything in the nature of a rule as to when the Espionage Act, applied to speech and press, might pass the bounds of constitutional validity." He asserted without citation that Hand's requirement of "purposeful incitement to specific unlawfulness" was simply a restatement of an accessory's liability at common law, and claimed that it provided the only constitutionally permissible basis for "Congress to make public utterances criminal."[113]

Stedman simultaneously criticized the bad tendency approach as inconsistent with the First Amendment. He objected to any reliance on the "indirect effect" or "the reasonable and natural consequences" of speech to find specific criminal intent under the Espionage Act. According to Stedman, affirmance of Debs's conviction by the Supreme Court would distort the literal meaning of the statute and suppress the discussion and advocacy of socialist opposition to war. "Antiwar politics," he protested, "would be confined to times of peace, when the issue has not the vitality of national immediacy." As a result, discussion of war – the most crucial subject of public policy – would become the exclusive concern of high government officials, and restrictions on free speech would arise in direct proportion to the importance of the issues at stake. Stedman urged the Court not to allow such a "caricature" of the First Amendment through a "preposterous perversion of the established precedents of our own history."[114]

Gilbert Roe's amicus brief in *Debs* reinforced Stedman's arguments by demonstrating in a particularly effective manner the First Amendment implications of the technical and evidentiary objections others had raised. Reiterating the basic theme of his testimony while Congress was considering the Espionage bill, Roe underlined the danger of the bad tendency test to evaluate the legality of speech and claimed that this approach violated the First Amendment. The conviction of Debs, and the similar plight of many other Espionage Act defendants in federal district courts, demonstrated to Roe that a judge or jury could punish a speaker for a speech or article "in the absence of any evidence that it produced a particular effect" simply because they believed "it would have a tendency to produce the results complained of." If the Court upheld this approach in *Debs,* Roe pointed out, Congress could proscribe the use of unidentified language subsequently found to have had a tendency to cause a prohibited effect, or spe-

---

[113] Id. at 63–64, 71, 77.   [114] Id. at 80, 84.

cific language deemed in itself to have a bad tendency.[115] Roe added that the Espionage Act decisions by the lower federal courts suppressed "substantially all hostile criticism of every measure even remotely connected with the war."[116]

By raising First Amendment challenges to the bad tendency test, Stedman and Roe attacked the heart of the traditional judicial approach to free speech issues. The briefs for the defendants in these cases, however, did not limit their discussions of the First Amendment to this central point. Relying on prewar scholars such as Cooley and Freund, several briefs made the historical argument that the First Amendment superseded the law of seditious libel and expanded the protection for free speech beyond Blackstone's mere prohibition against prior restraints.[117] In an argument that closely resembled Schroeder's scholarship, Roe devoted particular attention to refuting Blackstone. He emphasized that Blackstone's discussion of free speech was written a generation before the adoption of the First Amendment and simply reflected the effect on English law of the repeal of the Licensing Act in 1694. Blackstone's conservative views on speech, Roe pointed out, were opposed by many of his English contemporaries.[118] In the passage most reminiscent of Schroeder, Roe added that "Blackstone's belief in the fortunate condition of the English press after the repeal of the licensing acts in 1694, like his belief in witchcraft, have a historical interest, but there is no more reason for accepting his beliefs about one than about the other as a measure of liberty and freedom in this country today."[119] Roe also observed that Professor St. George Tucker, in his 1803 American edition of Blackstone's *Commentaries,* stated that freedom of the press protects against subsequent penalties as well as precludes prior restraints.[120]

Other briefs presented broad policy arguments in support of a generous construction of the First Amendment. One stressed that free speech, including the "scrutiny and condemnation" of government officials, promotes the exercise of responsible citizenship

---

[115] Brief of Gilbert E. Roe, as Amicus Curiae, at 16, Debs v. United States [hereinafter Roe Amicus Brief in Debs].

[116] Id. at 10.

[117] Stedman Brief for Debs, supra note 111, at 74–76, 85–86; Roe Amicus Brief in Debs, supra note 115, at 23–26, 32–42; Statement, Brief and Argument for Plaintiff in Error by Frans E. Lindquist at 28–31, Frohwerk v. United States [hereinafter Lindquist Brief for Frohwerk]; Brief of Plaintiffs in Error at 5–6, Schenck v. United States [hereinafter Brief for Schenck].

[118] Roe Amicus Brief in Debs, supra note 115, at 23, 25–26. See supra, Chapter 4, at text accompanying notes 59–64, for Schroeder's treatment of Blackstone.

[119] Id. at 24.   [120] Id. at 44.

and the "spread of truth in matters of general concern" that "is essential to the stability of a republic."[121] Some emphasized the importance of allowing "honest criticism of the majority by the minority"[122] and claimed that the "degree of tolerance of minority sentiments" is the traditional test of political freedom.[123] More specifically, another brief suggested that the First Amendment prohibits the punishment of any criticisms of government policy that do not meet the Constitution's definition of treason.[124] Without making such a bold assertion, Stedman rejected the "possible" theory that the Espionage Act could punish "instigation to treason." "Congress has no power," Stedman asserted, "to amend or enlarge the definition of treason written into the Constitution."[125]

In their briefs for Debs, Stedman and Roe denied that Congress could rely on the war power to restrict speech, an issue Learned Hand explicitly left undecided in his statutory construction of the Espionage Act in *Masses*. If the war power could limit the scope of the First Amendment, Stedman argued, public officials would be too eager to discover grave dangers to the state in any "agitation desired to be suppressed." He vigorously maintained that the First Amendment's protection of public discussion could not be "swept aside" merely "as an incident of the war power."[126] Roe claimed that the First Amendment is an absolute prohibition against all exercises of congressional power affecting speech. Just as Congress cannot abridge free speech to borrow money or collect taxes, he reasoned, it cannot abridge free speech to wage war. Roe maintained that the First Amendment is the constitutional provision "most calculated to preserve our free institutions to ourselves and to posterity." Unless the "breach already made in the wall of constitutional liberty" by the lower courts' interpretation of the Espionage Act is "speedily and permanently repaired," he warned, "it will certainly be enlarged as one exigency after another seems to make it necessary, until the whole structure will give way before the assaults of real enemies of constitutional and democratic government."[127]

The government's reply briefs, submitted by O'Brian and Bettman, made explicit much of the reasoning that, although not clearly articulated, seemed to provide the basis for the Supreme Court decisions in *Goldman, Kramer,* and *Ruthenberg*. These briefs

[121] Brief for Schenck, supra note 117, at 6.
[122] Id. at 8.
[123] Stedman Brief for Debs, supra note 111, at 62.
[124] Lindquist Brief for Frohwerk, supra note 117, at 28–29.
[125] Stedman Brief for Debs, supra note 111, at 85.
[126] Id. at 71, 74.
[127] Roe Amicus Brief in Debs, supra note 115, at 19–21, 48.

vigorously disagreed with the defendants' objections to the form of the indictments and to the sufficiency of the evidence. "When the tendency of the words used, rather than the particular words themselves, constitute the gist of the offense," the government argued, "it is sufficient for the indictment to charge this general tendency, without detailing the particular words." The precise words that constitute an attempt are "the evidentiary details of the method by which the unlawful purpose was carried out" and to identify them specifically "would be pleading evidence."[128] According to O'Brian and Bettman, their adversaries were incorrectly trying to transform a challenge to the sufficiency of evidence, a question trial judges properly left to juries, into a First Amendment case.[129] The Supreme Court's decisions in *Goldman, Kramer,* and *Ruthenberg,* O'Brian and Bettman maintained, foreclosed the defendants' First Amendment arguments in the Espionage Act cases, which involved the same relation between speech and crime.[130]

In *Debs,* probably because Stedman and Roe raised First Amendment issues so explicitly, O'Brian and Bettman did not belittle the constitutional dimensions of the case, as they had in the government's other Espionage Act briefs. Although they suggested that no constitutional question was "necessarily involved"[131] in *Debs,* O'Brian and Bettman did respond to their adversaries' First Amendment claims. Even Stedman, they observed, accepted "intentional incitement to violations of law" as beyond the constitutional protection for free speech, and they insisted that this was precisely the standard under which Debs had been charged and convicted. Debs, they claimed, "seems to contend that as he did not express this unlawful advice in words so direct, plain, and unmistakable as to leave no room whatever for the slightest thought or intellectual process on the part of the jury, no need of any process of inference whatever, the constitutional immunity applies to his speech." O'Brian and Bettman protested that acceptance of this position would put the government in the impossible position of being "powerless to punish any incitement to lawlessness, however intentional and however effective, so long as it is concealed in veiled, indirect, or rhetorical language."[132]

---

[128] Brief for the United States at 10–11, Sugarman v. United States [hereinafter Brief for the United States in Sugarman].

[129] Brief for the United States at 77–78, Debs v. United States [hereinafter Brief for the United States in Debs].

[130] Brief for the United States in Sugarman, supra note 128, at 36–37.

[131] Brief for the United States in Debs, supra note 129, at 69, 78.

[132] Id. at 72.

O'Brian and Bettman emphasized that Hand's decision in *Masses,* so heavily relied upon by Stedman, had been reversed by the Second Circuit. The trial court's charge to the jury in *Debs,* they added, was a model of fairness consistent with the proper standard established by the Second Circuit in *Masses.*[133] Like many of his district court colleagues, the judge had told the jury that the Espionage Act did not forbid a citizen to "discuss, criticize, or disapprove" of any proposed or existing law or policy. To convict Debs, the judge concluded, the jury would have to find that he had a "specific, willful, criminal intent" and that he used language having "a natural and reasonably probable tendency to cause the results which have been forbidden by these provisions of the espionage law."[134] In emphasizing this jury charge and the Second Circuit decision in *Masses,* O'Brian and Bettman reiterated the government's position that a conviction for an unlawful attempt under the Espionage Act could properly be based on a jury determination of the bad tendency of language.

In their reply to Roe, O'Brian and Bettman stated in conclusory language that Debs was not punished for his beliefs or opinions, which they acknowledged would have been unconstitutional, but for a willful attempt, through the use of language, to obstruct recruitment. Yet O'Brian and Bettman did address Roe's basic concerns. "Mr. Roe claims," they correctly paraphrased, "that by reason of the temper of the public during a war, a law directed at obstruction of the war will inevitably be applied so as to suppress all critical discussion of the war, and that the Espionage Act, as applied by the courts and juries, has produced that effect." Without disputing Roe's analysis, O'Brian and Bettman contended that his position, in its "zeal for free speech," would subvert the jury system and the separation of powers. They construed his "plea" as an appeal to the Supreme Court "to ignore the constitutional limitations of its functions and correct what he conceives to be a mistaken legislative policy or mistaken, though lawful, verdicts."[135]

O'Brian and Bettman responded to most of the defendants' additional First Amendment arguments, especially in their main brief in *Debs.* Despite Holmes's decision in *Patterson v. Colorado,* they conceded that the First Amendment might be broader than Blackstone's rule against prior restraints and might restrict legislative power over speech to traditional common-law crimes.[136] They

---

[133] Id. at 73–75.   [134] Id. at 76–77.

[135] Brief for the United States, in Reply to Brief of Gilbert E. Roe, As Amicus Curiae, at 2–4 [hereinafter Reply to Roe].

[136] Brief for the United States in Debs, supra note 129, at 81.

agreed that the First Amendment protects "legitimate political agitation"[137] and "hostile criticism of the war,"[138] but stressed that the speeches and articles for which the defendants in the Espionage Act cases were prosecuted and convicted went well beyond these bounds. Contrary to the conclusions of the scholars cited in the defendants' briefs, they insisted that seditious speech could be punished at common law in the United States as well as in England.[139] In response to Roe's lengthy attack on the Sedition Act of 1798, they maintained that the authorities he cited were "partisan documents put forth in the heat of a bitter political contest" during which future Chief Justice John Marshall had written a substantial defense of the Sedition Act's constitutionality.[140]

Even while defending the right of Congress to punish seditious libel, O'Brian and Bettman took pains to distinguish the 1917 Espionage Act from the "objectionable features" of the 1798 Sedition Act, which "sought to punish libelous attacks on the Government." The Espionage Act, they asserted, "carefully avoids that pitfall" by limiting its prohibitions to "interference with the process of raising armies," a valid exercise of the war power vested in Congress by the Constitution. They maintained that the war power "includes the power to punish willful obstruction of that process, whether that obstruction be by spoken or written word or by other means."[141] O'Brian and Bettman also invoked the war power to refute the argument that the constitutional clause on treason defines the limits of prohibited speech. The Constitution, they observed, defined treason explicitly, but it "has left to Congress the definition of other offenses which may interfere with the conduct of a war."[142]

O'Brian and Bettman ended the government's main brief in *Debs* by relying on recent Supreme Court decisions. If the war power allows Congress to deprive someone of liberty or even life in order to raise an army, as the Supreme Court held in *The Selective Draft Cases,* they reasoned that it must also allow Congress to punish obstruction of recruitment. They maintained that the "right of self-preservation," identified by the Supreme Court in *Turner,* further supported the validity of the Espionage Act. To sup-

---

[137] Brief for the United States at 13, Schenck v. United States.

[138] Reply to Roe, supra note 135, at 2.

[139] Brief for the United States in Debs, supra note 129, at 81.

[140] Reply to Roe, supra note 135, at 9, 11. O'Brian and Bettman quoted at length from Marshall's pamphlet. Id. at 12–16.

[141] Brief for the United States in Debs, supra note 129, at 80, 83. Accord, Brief for the United States at 22–23, Frohwerk v. United States [hereinafter Brief for the United States in Frohwerk]; Reply to Roe, supra note 135, at 8–9.

[142] Brief for the United States in Frohwerk, supra note 141, at 22.

port the proposition that obstruction by speech or press is not entitled to special protection, they cited the Supreme Court's decision only months earlier in *Toledo Newspaper Co. v. United States*, which, like so many lower court cases before the war, relied on the bad tendency theory to sustain a newspaper's contempt conviction for criticizing judicial conduct during a trial.[143] O'Brian and Bettman maintained that the war power of Congress can limit free speech as readily as the contempt power of a court. "No authority," they concluded, "can be adduced for the defendant's contention that there is a constitutional right to obstruct by speech the exercise of the power to raise armies so long as the speaker does not urge a violation of law."[144]

THE SUPREME COURT DECISIONS

The Supreme Court decided its first four Espionage Act cases in March 1919. In *Sugarman,* a unanimous opinion written by Justice Brandeis, the Court granted the government's request to dismiss the case for lack of jurisdiction because the defendant did not present any substantial constitutional question.[145] The government had also contended that the First Amendment should not, or need not, be addressed in the other three cases, *Schenck, Frohwerk,* and *Debs.* Although the Court refused to accept this contention, it only briefly discussed First Amendment issues while upholding the convictions of antiwar socialists.

Justice Holmes wrote for a unanimous Court in all three cases. He discussed the First Amendment in one paragraph in *Schenck,*[146] and then relied on *Schenck* in dismissing similar claims in *Frohwerk* and *Debs.*[147] He never mentioned the *Masses* litigation or other protective precedents and legal authorities cited in the defendants' briefs. Instead, Holmes concentrated on issues of criminal law and accepted most of the positions advocated by the government. Holmes approved punishment based on the indirect tendency of speech, upheld substantial judicial deference to jury evaluations of evidence, and supported greater restrictions on speech during times of war. In all three cases, his analysis bore a remarkable similarity to his prewar decisions, particularly his opinion in *Fox v. Washington*.

---

[143] 247 U.S. 402, 419 (1918).
[144] Brief for the United States in Debs, supra note 129, at 89–90.
[145] Sugarman v. United States, 249 U.S. 182, 185 (1919).
[146] Schenck v. United States, 249 U.S. 47, 51–52 (1919).
[147] Frohwerk v. United States, 249 U.S. 204, 206–7 (1919); Debs v. United States, 249 U.S. 211, 215 (1919).

Although *Debs* was the most thoroughly briefed of the three cases, Holmes chose *Schenck* as the vehicle for discussing First Amendment issues, perhaps because the defendants in *Schenck,* unlike those in *Frohwerk* or *Debs,* had sent antiwar circulars to men accepted for military service, a somewhat more sympathetic factual context for affirmance. Holmes maintained that the defendants would not have mailed such a document "unless it had been intended to have some effect, and we do not see what effect it could be expected to have upon persons subject to the draft except to influence them to obstruct the carrying of it out."[148] Holmes then wrote a paragraph on the First Amendment emphasizing his continued adherence to the bad tendency approach.[149]

The briefs in *Schenck,* unlike those in *Debs,* did not attack this approach as being inconsistent with the First Amendment, but Holmes assumed that Schenck claimed First Amendment protection even if the circulars did tend to obstruct the draft. Holmes spent the remainder of the paragraph emphasizing his disagreement. He observed that *Goldman* could be considered to dispose of *Schenck,* but he "thought fit to add a few words" on the First Amendment because the defendants raised this constitutional concern and *Goldman* did not specifically refer to it. Perhaps influenced by the government's concession in its *Debs* brief, Holmes retreated from his position in *Patterson* equating the First Amendment with Blackstone's prohibition against prior restraints. Holmes admitted as well that "in many places and in ordinary times" the publications punished in *Schenck* would be protected by the First Amendment. He pointed out, however, that "the character of every act depends upon the circumstances in which it is done." Holmes illustrated this point in language that has since become famous: "The most stringent protection of free speech would not protect a man in falsely shouting fire in a theatre and causing a panic." He also cited his prewar opinion in *Gompers,* presumably to indicate that in the circumstances of a labor boycott free speech "does not even protect a man from an injunction against uttering words that may have all the effect of force."[150]

Holmes then wrote the two sentences that Chafee soon identified as the clear and present danger standard: "The question in every case is whether the words used are used in such circumstances and are of such a nature as to create a clear and present danger that they will bring about the substantive evils that Congress has a right to prevent. It is a question of proximity and

---

[148] Schenck v. United States, 249 U.S. 47, 51 (1919).
[149] Id. at 51–52.   [150] Id.

The Justices of the Supreme Court, 1916–21. Standing from left: Associate Justices Louis Dembitz Brandeis, Mahlon Pitney, James Clark McReynolds, John Hessin Clarke. Seated from left: Associate Justices William Rufus Day, Joseph McKenna, Chief Justice Edward Douglas White, Associate Justices Oliver Wendell Holmes, Willis Van Devanter. (Photograph by Clinedin Street, 1916, Collection of the Supreme Court of the United States)

degree."[151] Though the words *clear and present danger,* as Chafee immediately recognized, had protective overtones, in its context this passage did not appear to announce a novel standard of First Amendment interpretation. In the sentence immediately following, Holmes apparently concluded that the war power can override the First Amendment, addressing the issue left open by Hand in *Masses* and debated in the briefs in *Debs.* "When a nation is at war," Holmes reasoned, "many things that might be said in time of peace are such a hindrance to its effort that their utterance will not be endured so long as men fight and that no Court could regard them as protected by any constitutional right."[152]

[151] Id. at 52.   [152] Id.

The "circumstances" of war, Holmes seemed to be saying, are themselves likely "to create a clear and present danger" that speech will hinder the nation's effort, thereby producing one of "the substantive evils Congress has a right to prevent."

Moreover, in his very next sentence Holmes turned to the familiar bad tendency doctrine. Citing *Goldman,* he concluded: "If the act (speaking, or circulating a paper), its tendency and the intent with which it is done are the same, we perceive no ground for saying that success alone warrants making the act a crime."[153] Like the lower federal courts in Espionage Act cases, Holmes in *Schenck* inferred intent from the probable consequences and surrounding circumstances of speech. Contrary to the subsequent assertions of Chafee and others, this sequence strongly suggests that Holmes did not consider clear and present danger a protective replacement for the bad tendency doctrine he himself had often invoked in prior decisions. It seems inconceivable that Holmes would use the word *tendency,* stress the unimportance of a successful act, rely on cases that did not demonstrate any sensitivity to free speech, and uphold the convictions of antiwar socialists in order to elaborate a protective test designed as a constitutional bar to convictions based on predicting the tendency of speech.

Holmes's decisions in *Frohwerk* and *Debs* relied on *Schenck* and provide further proof that he did not regard any of these opinions as a significant departure from his restrictive prewar analysis of speech. Neither *Frohwerk* nor *Debs* contained the phrase *clear and present danger* and both, on weaker facts than *Schenck,* sustained convictions under the Espionage Act by relying on the bad tendency theory.

In discussing the First Amendment in *Frohwerk,* Holmes considered it necessary to add only slightly to what he had already said in *Schenck.* He cited one prewar case[154] for the proposition that the First Amendment did not provide "immunity for every possible use of language." No "competent person," Holmes commented, would consider a law against counseling murder "an unconstitutional interference with free speech." After citing *Schenck* to support his statement "that a person may be convicted of a conspiracy to obstruct recruiting by words of persuasion," he treated the *Frohwerk* case as a matter of criminal law. As Holmes observed, Frohwerk's publications consisted of "the usual repetition that we went to war to protect the loans of Wall Street." Even though Frohwerk had deplored draft riots, Holmes did not find "much to choose"[155]

---

[153] Id.
[154] Robertson v. Baldwin, 165 U.S. 275 (1897).
[155] Frohwerk v. United States, 249 U.S. 204, 206–7 (1919).

between his article and Schenck's "impassioned language"[156] against the draft, evidently because Frohwerk used words "that might be taken to convey an innuendo of a different sort."[157] Holmes's reliance on possible innuendo and his metaphor that "a little breath would be enough to kindle a flame" demonstrated his continued use of the bad tendency theory to punish speech, as did his acknowledgment that Frohwerk, unlike Schenck, had not made any special effort to contact men eligible for the draft.[158]

As in *Goldman*, which he did not cite, Holmes also gave great deference to the factual determinations by the jury. Holmes suggested that the record in *Frohwerk* was inadequate and that a more complete one might have provided grounds for reversing "the very severe penalty imposed." Holmes, however, felt obligated to reach his decision "on the record as it is." Because he did "not know how strong the Government's evidence may have been," he found it impossible to say "that the articles could not furnish a basis for a conviction." Holmes, as the government had urged in its briefs, proceeded to reject attacks on the lack of specificity in the indictment[159] even though, as Stedman effectively argued in his brief for Debs, this very vagueness encourages unsatisfactory records.[160] Holmes also dismissed the suggestion that the treason clause limits the punishment for speech by claiming that it "need no more than to be stated" to be refuted.[161] Holmes did acknowledge in *Frohwerk* that even during war some speech cannot be penalized. "We do not lose our right to condemn either measures or men," he reasoned, "because the Country is at war."[162] He negated the potential value of his one protective concession, however, by refusing to limit jury determinations of the possible consequences of speech.

Even more clearly than *Frohwerk*, *Debs* demonstrated Holmes's continued reliance on the tendency of speech as the test for its legality and his willingness, bordering on eagerness, to sustain jury findings of fact. Despite the excellence and thoroughness of the analysis in the briefs, Holmes stated in a peremptory sentence that any First Amendment issues in *Debs* were "disposed of" in *Schenck*.[163] As O'Brian and Bettman had urged in their brief for the government, Holmes treated *Debs* as if it presented evidentiary rather than consti-

---

[156] Schenck v. United States, 249 U.S. at 51.
[157] Frohwerk v. United States, 249 U.S. at 207.
[158] Id. at 208–9.   [159] Id. at 208–10.
[160] See Stedman Brief for Debs, supra note 111, at 38.
[161] Frohwerk v. United States, 249 U.S. at 210.
[162] Id. at 208.
[163] Debs v. United States, 249 U.S. 211, 212 (1919).

tutional questions. But at least Holmes in *Debs*, in contrast to Chief Justice White in *Goldman*, *Kramer*, and *Ruthenberg*, explained the basis for his conclusion that the evidence supported the guilty verdict.

In reviewing the speech for which Debs was indicted, Holmes acknowledged that its "main theme" was "socialism, its growth, and a prophecy of its ultimate success," topics that could not be punished under the Espionage Act. Holmes added, however, that "if a part or the manifest intent of the more general utterances was to encourage those present to obstruct the recruiting service and if in such passages such encouragement was directly given, the immunity of the general theme may not be enough to protect the speech." Later in his opinion, Holmes suggested that the encouragement contained in a part of the speech need not be direct. Much of Debs's speech, he pointed out, "had only the indirect though not necessarily ineffective bearing on the offences alleged." The fact that Debs told his audience that prudence required him not to disclose the full force of his opposition to the war was, for Holmes, an intimation that they "might infer that he meant more" rather than an indication, to be counted in Debs's favor, that he had tried to avoid the prohibitions of the Espionage Act. Based on these observations, Holmes concluded that the speech contained sufficient evidence "to warrant the jury in finding that one purpose of the speech, whether incidental or not does not matter, was to oppose not only war in general but this war, and that the opposition was so expressed that its natural and intended effect would be to obstruct recruiting."[164]

Consistent with the approach of all judges except Learned Hand in *Masses*, Holmes stated that evaluating the tendency of language as evidence of the speaker's intent is a principle "too well established and too manifestly good sense to need citation of the books." Following the government's lead in praising the trial judge's charge to the jury, Holmes apparently approved the common practice whereby judges, after giving juries essentially neutral instructions, allowed them to consider virtually any speech that the government considered objectionable. He also rejected Stedman's objection to the admissibility at trial of the "Anti-war Proclamation and Program" of the Socialist Party, which, according to Holmes, "contained the usual suggestion that capitalism was the cause of the war." Holmes reasoned that Debs's acceptance of this program would be evidence of his intent to obstruct the recruitment service. In *Debs*, as in *Frohwerk*, Holmes deferred to jury findings of intent based on the indirect tendency of speech.[165]

---

[164] Id. at 212–15.   [165] Id. at 214–16.

Holmes thus continued the prewar judicial tradition of hostility to First Amendment values by using the bad tendency theory to reject free speech claims in *Schenck, Frohwerk,* and *Debs.* Even within this framework, he did not take as his model the few decisions by district and circuit judges, some of which had been brought to his attention in the defendants' briefs, that protected some antiwar speech by requiring specificity in indictments and a direct relationship between speech and potential effects. Instead, Holmes adopted the looser construction of the Espionage Act that had prevailed in the lower federal courts.

THE ORIGINS OF CLEAR AND PRESENT DANGER

Chafee wrote Holmes in 1922 to ask for "[a]ny light that you can give me on the background of your opinion in the Schenck case." In particular, Chafee wondered if "your test of clear and present danger . . . was at all suggested to you by any writers on the subject or was the result entirely of your reflections." Chafee also mentioned his hope that this test would "drive out the old notion of bad tendency."[166]

In a brief response, Holmes made clear that he did not perceive any tension between "clear and present danger" and the "old notion of bad tendency." His letter to Chafee confirms the analysis suggested by the texts of *Schenck, Frohwerk,* and *Debs,* and provides fascinating insights into the phrase that would assume crucial importance in First Amendment interpretation. Apologizing for having to "make a hurried answer" based on "ancient memory," Holmes wrote:

> The expression that you refer to was not helped by any book that I know of. I think it came without doubt after the later cases (and probably you – I do not remember exactly) had taught me that in the earlier Paterson [sic] case, if that was the name of it, I had taken Blackstone and Parker of Mass. as unrefuted, wrongly. I simply was ignorant. But I did think hard on this matter of attempts in my Common Law and a Mass. case – later in the Swift case (U.S.) – and I thought it out unhelped.[167]

---

[166] Letter from Zechariah Chafee, Jr., to Oliver Wendell Holmes, Jr. (June 9, 1922) (Zechariah Chafee, Jr., Papers, Box 14, Folder 12, Harvard Law School Library) [hereinafter Chafee Papers].

[167] Letter from Oliver Wendell Holmes, Jr., to Zechariah Chafee, Jr. (June 12, 1922) (Chafee Papers, supra note 166, Box 14, Folder 12).

"Parker of Mass." is Isaac Parker, the former chief justice of the Massachusetts Supreme Judicial Court, whose 1825 decision in *Commonwealth v. Blanding* approved Blackstone's rule against prior restraints. Holmes's reference to the "later cases" is unclear; the Supreme Court did not modify its approval of Blackstone in *Patterson v. Colorado* until Holmes's own opinion in *Schenck*. Perhaps Holmes was thinking of *Toledo Newspaper Co. v. United States,* in which he, joined by Justice Brandeis just months before *Schenck,* dissented in a contempt case similar to *Patterson*.[168] In any event, Holmes's letter to Chafee, in language understandably more explicit than that of a judicial decision, underlined the retreat from his statement in *Patterson* limiting the First Amendment to the prohibition against prior restraints, a retreat he signaled in the text of his *Schenck* opinion.

Holmes's reliance on his earlier thinking about the law of criminal attempts, particularly on his book, *The Common Law,*[169] is even more revealing. It provides convincing additional support for the conclusion, suggested by the language of his first Espionage Act opinions, that he did not use the words *clear and present danger* as a protective alternative to the bad tendency test. Holmes's discussion of attempts, in this book and in his subsequent opinions, is part of a cohesive framework of analysis that informed his approach to all legal questions. A review of the key doctrines of *The Common Law* helps relate his Espionage Act decisions to the totality of his work and demonstrates that both clear and present danger and bad tendency were roughly equivalent measures of proximity used by Holmes to determine whether an act should be punished as a criminal attempt.

Holmes completed *The Common Law* in 1881, the week before his fortieth birthday. This milestone was particularly important to Holmes, who believed that "if a man was to do anything he must do it before 40."[170] Holmes tried to reduce the common law to fundamental principles of broad applicability. For the remaining fifty years of his long life, he relied on these principles, and often on the precise language of *The Common Law,* even in constitutional adjudication. "Both as an aphorist and as a judge," Yosal Rogat has pointed out, "Holmes rarely changed his mind." As Brandeis observed of

---

168 Commonwealth v. Blanding, 20 Mass. (3 Pick.) 304, 313 (1825); Toledo Newspaper Co. v. United States, 247 U.S. 402 (1918).

169 Oliver Wendell Holmes, Jr., The Common Law (1938 ed.).

170 Letter from Oliver Wendell Holmes, Jr., to Mrs. Charles S. Hamlin (Oct. 12, 1930), quoted in Mark DeWolfe Howe, Justice Oliver Wendell Holmes: The Proving Years, 1870–1882, at 135 (1963). The Common Law, according to Howe, was the "achievement by which he wanted to be judged at the age of forty." Id.

Holmes: "He has said many things in their ultimate terms, and as new instances arise they just fit in."[171]

Two fundamental themes pervade *The Common Law*. Holmes maintained that legal development necessarily replaces internal and moral standards with external and objective ones and that the law must enforce the community's will against individual claims. Near the beginning of his book, Holmes promised that he would demonstrate that the law, although rooted in primitive desires for revenge against blameworthy conduct and often retaining the language of morals, "is continually transmuting those moral standards into external or objective ones, from which the actual guilt of the party concerned is wholly eliminated." A few pages later, he announced his other major theme: "The first requirement of a sound body of law is, that it should correspond with the actual feelings and demands of the community, whether right or wrong." Holmes assumed that communities, like individuals, are ultimately motivated by "justifiable self-preference." "If a man is on a plank in the deep sea which will only float one," he elaborated, "and a stranger lays hold of it, he will thrust him off if he can. When the state finds itself in a similar position, it does the same thing."[172]

With obvious disdain, Holmes quickly dismissed the Kantian argument that the harshness of this position denies men their inherent natural rights to equality and reduces them to things. "If man lives in society," Holmes observed sardonically, "he is liable to find himself so treated." Kant's moralistic "dogma of equality" might be a laudable ideal, but, Holmes maintained, rules of law should be based on tougher, more realistic views about human nature.[173] Holmes's views were distinctly those of a Social Darwinist. In dramatic contrast to Dewey and other progressive social theorists, he rejected the "tacit assumption of the solidarity of the interests of society," and claimed instead that the "struggle for life" that "is constantly putting the interests of men at variance with those of the lower animals . . . is equally the law of human existence."[174] The law appropriately expresses the community's self-preference, he reiterated, by treating "the individual as a means to an end, and uses him as a tool to increase the general welfare at his own expense."[175]

---

[171] Yosal Rogat, The Judge as Spectator, 31 U. Chi. L. Rev. 213, 214, 247 (1963) (quoting Brandeis).

[172] Holmes, supra note 169, at 38, 41, 44.

[173] Id. at 42–44.

[174] 7 Am. L. Rev. 583, 583–84, quoted in part in Howe, supra note 170, at 43–44.

[175] Holmes, supra note 169, at 46–47.

In his typically cryptic manner, Holmes did not explain the full meaning of his often brilliant prose. He gave the clear impression that his two fundamental themes of objective standards and community will were related, but he never stated precisely how. He did, however, leave enough hints to allow a plausible reconstruction.

Holmes apparently believed that the general welfare is achieved when the community deters actions it deems dangerous or harmful. The law is thus primarily designed "only to induce external conformity to rule," and prevention of deviance becomes "the chief and only universal purpose of punishment." In this scheme, a theory of retribution that posits a "mystic bond between wrong and punishment" has no function and may even interfere with the realization of social goals.[176] Holmes attributed the retributive theory of justice to the idealism he discredited as unrealistic.[177]

Holmes also seemed to deny that punishing or rewarding individual motives has any bearing on the desired social results. He entirely divorced individual blameworthiness from liability. Holmes acknowledged that the modern legal system includes the concept of culpability, which he considered a psychological necessity whose "denial would shock the moral sense of any civilized community." But culpability is retained, he observed, only by imposing liability for conduct that the community considers blameworthy in an idealized average person. Holmes reasoned that "a law which punished conduct which would not be blameworthy in the average member of the community would be too severe for that community to bear." However, the conduct of this average man "of ordinary intelligence and reasonable prudence," often represented by the jury, "is an external or objective standard when applied to any given individual." Someone "morally without stain" may nevertheless be punished if he lacks the qualities of the average man.[178]

The origins of Holmes's attachment to externality may have been more psychological than logical, rooted in his desire for certainty[179] or in his fundamental detachment from life.[180] The connection he posited between community will and "external conformity to rule" does not entail his conclusion that attention to individual motives is unrelated to achieving this conformity. An individual's internal state may affect his likelihood of obeying a given rule, as Holmes himself recognized in extreme cases such as infancy and madness.[181]

---

[176] Id. at 42, 46, 49.

[177] See id. at 42–47.

[178] Id. at 49–51.

[179] Howe, supra note 170, at 197.

[180] Rogat, supra note 171, at 221–22.

[181] Holmes, supra note 169, at 50; see H.L.A. Hart, Holmes's Common Law, N.Y. Rev. of Books, Oct. 17, 1963, at 15–16.

Whatever the source of Holmes's views, he spent much of *The Common Law* "reducing" various forms of modern legal liability to external standards. He observed that "acts, taken apart from their surrounding circumstances, are indifferent to the law,"[182] and concluded that most "acts are rendered criminal because they are done under circumstances in which they will probably cause some harm which the law seeks to prevent."[183] Holmes reiterated that the foresight of probable harm on which liability depends must be determined by reference to the "prudent man, that is, by general experience," and not by investigating the consciousness of a particular defendant.[184]

Holmes devoted much of *The Common Law* to applying his fundamental themes to different substantive areas of the law. His belief in the priority of community will is apparent throughout the book, but he emphasized the centrality of external and objective standards. His analysis of criminal attempts most directly foreshadowed his opinions almost forty years later in *Schenck, Frohwerk,* and *Debs.* Holmes's discussion of the law of criminal attempts, the specific portion of *The Common Law* he mentioned in his letter to Chafee, is particularly interesting and important because the speeches at issue in *Schenck, Frohwerk,* and *Debs* were punished as attempts to violate the Espionage Act. Holmes defined an *attempt* as an overt act that "has failed to bring about the result which would have given it the character of the principal crime." The act is punished as an attempt "if, supposing it to have produced its natural and probable effect, it would have amounted to a substantive crime." The failure of an act to produce its natural consequences, while properly mitigating the severity of punishment, should not remove liability entirely if the preventive purpose of law is maintained. Thus, in the law of attempts, as in the criminal law generally, "[a]cts should be judged by their tendency under the known circumstances, not by the actual intent which accompanies them." The common "statement that a man is presumed to intend the natural consequences of his acts," a frequent assertion of federal judges in Espionage Act decisions, was, for Holmes, "a mere fiction disguising the true theory," another vestige of moral terminology in a mature legal system actually based on external and objective standards.[185]

Holmes recognized that actual intent is an element of many crimes, yet he cleverly assimilated even these crimes into his general theory. For Holmes, the main purpose for punishing an act is

---

[182] Holmes, supra note 169, at 54.   [183] Id. at 75.
[184] Id. at 56; see id. at 53–57.   [185] Id. at 65–66 and 66 n.2.

"to prevent some harm which is foreseen as likely to follow that act under the circumstances in which it is done." Prediction is typically based on "the common working of natural causes as shown by experience," but an otherwise innocent act is sometimes rendered dangerous because the accompanying actual intent "raises a probability that it will be followed by such other acts and events as will all together result in harm." Salvaging his preference for objective over moral standards, Holmes emphasized that actual intent is important "not to show that the act was wicked, but to show that it was likely to be followed by hurtful consequences" that the law properly seeks to prevent.[186]

Holmes pointed out that bad intent does not necessarily entail liability for a criminal attempt and alluded to judges' prior difficulty in deciding when actual intent is relevant. His proposed solution reiterated his emphasis on the primacy of community demands. "Public policy, that is to say, legislative considerations, are at the bottom of the matter." The specific considerations identified by Holmes in *The Common Law* – "the nearness of the danger, the greatness of the harm," the "degree of apprehension," and "the degree of probability that the crime will be accomplished"[187] – foreshadowed his formulation of clear and present danger in *Schenck.*

Holmes's prewar decisions in cases involving attempts connect *The Common Law* with his first Espionage Act decisions and demonstrate the essential consistency of his analysis through almost four decades. In *Swift & Co. v. United States,*[188] the Supreme Court case he identified in his letter to Chafee, Holmes twice cited his decision in *Commonwealth v. Peaslee,*[189] probably the "Mass. case" to which he also referred. In *Peaslee,* Holmes relied on the opinion he wrote in *Commonwealth v. Kennedy.*[190] In all three cases, Holmes drew heavily on his discussion of attempts in *The Common Law.*

In *Kennedy,* Holmes repeated his underlying emphasis on externality and foreseeability. "As the aim of the law is not to punish sins, but is to prevent certain external results, the act done must come pretty near to accomplishing that result before the law will notice it." He pointed out that determinations of proximity depend on surrounding circumstances and alluded to additional bases of liability, including "the gravity of the crime, the uncertainty of the result, and the seriousness of the apprehension."

---

[186] Id. at 67–68.   [187] Id. at 68–69.
[188] 196 U.S. 375 (1905).
[189] 177 Mass. 267, 59 N.E. 55 (1901), cited in Swift, 196 U.S. at 396, 406.
[190] 170 Mass. 18, 48 N.E. 770 (1897), cited in Peaslee, 177 Mass. at 272, 59 N.E. at 56.

Affirming a conviction for attempted murder by poison, Holmes stated that even a nonlethal dose is an evil that "would warrant holding the liability for an attempt to begin at a point more remote from the possibility of accomplishing what is expected than might be the case with lighter crimes."[191]

Peaslee was an appeal of a conviction for an unsuccessful attempt to burn a building by soliciting a servant to light combustibles arranged by the defendant. Holmes, relying on *Kennedy*, again observed that the "degree of proximity" necessary to constitute an attempt "may vary with circumstances." He added that an overt act normally does not constitute an attempt as long as "further acts are contemplated as needful" to bring about the crime. Evidence of bad intent, however, may so increase the probability of an actual crime that an otherwise innocent act may be considered an attempt.[192] *Swift*, a case brought under the Sherman Act alleging an attempted monopoly, raised analogous issues. "Not every act that may be done . . . to produce an unlawful result," Holmes observed, "is unlawful, or constitutes an attempt. It is a question of proximity and degree." The Sherman Act, Holmes emphasized, simply adopted these principles from the common law.[193]

The borrowing so evident in his prewar attempt opinions is equally apparent in *Schenck, Frohwerk,* and *Debs.* In *The Common Law,* Holmes maintained that "acts, taken apart from their surrounding circumstances, are indifferent to the law."[194] In *Schenck,* he claimed that "the character of every act depends upon the circumstances in which it was done."[195] In *The Common Law,* Holmes concluded that most "acts are rendered criminal because they are done under circumstances in which they will probably cause some harm which the law seeks to prevent."[196] In *Schenck,* he based liability on "whether the words used are used in such circumstances and are of such a nature as to create a clear and present danger that they will bring about the substantive evils that Congress has a right to prevent."[197] In *The Common Law,* Holmes asserted that intent should be evaluated by the tendency of acts, including utterances, to harm.[198] In *Schenck, Frohwerk,* and *Debs,* he judged the intent requirement of the Espionage Act by the tendency of words rather than through an effort to uncover the defendants' actual states of mind. In *Schenck,* he observed that "the document would not have been sent unless it

---

[191] 170 Mass. at 20, 22, 48 N.E. at 770–71.   [192] 177 Mass. at 272, 59 N.E. at 56.
[193] 196 U.S. at 396, 402.   [194] Holmes, supra note 169, at 54.
[195] Schenck v. United States, 249 U.S. 47, 52 (1919).
[196] Holmes, supra note 169, at 75.   [197] 249 U.S. at 52.
[198] Holmes, supra note 169, at 66, 138.

had been intended to have some effect,"[199] and in *Debs,* more pointedly, he emphasized that the use of words "tending to obstruct the
recruiting service" was evidence that Debs "meant that they should
have that effect." Holmes thought this point too obvious "to need
citation of the books,"[200] but *The Common Law* could have provided
excellent authority. For Holmes, the phrase *clear and present danger,*
like the word *tendency,* was a way of evaluating whether the proximity between an act and a forbidden crime justified punishing the
act as a criminal attempt.

Without explicitly so stating, Holmes apparently considered the
speeches and articles punished in the Espionage Act cases as
attempts requiring additional acts to cause the substantive evil.
The lawyers for Debs had emphasized that the connection
between the indicted speech and an actual obstruction of the war
effort was far from direct. But Holmes had a familiar method of
dealing with this problem: He applied the variables he had identified in *The Common Law* and had employed in the prewar attempt
cases. Immediately following the sentence in *Schenck* containing
the words *clear and present danger,* Holmes added the phrase he had
used in discussing attempts in *Swift:* "It is a question of proximity
and degree."[201] In the Espionage Act cases, as in *Kennedy,* Holmes
was particularly concerned about the seriousness and the degree
of apprehension by the community of the potential danger.
Obstruction of the war effort, like the "great harm likely to result
from poison,"[202] justified the imposition of liability for an attempt
at a point more remote than usual from the actual crime. As
Holmes observed in *Schenck,* even though the defendants "in many
places and in ordinary times" might have been "within their constitutional rights," "many things that might be said in time of peace"
lose this constitutional protection "[w]hen a nation is at war."[203]

Views rooted in his earliest and most sustained thinking about
the law best account for Holmes's insensitivity to the claim that the
bad tendency theory could not support the democratic values protected by the First Amendment, the position articulated by prewar
scholars, by Hand in *Masses,* and by Stedman and Roe in their
briefs in *Debs.* Holmes's contempt for "the dogma of equality" and
his belief that law should sacrifice individual rights to the community's will did not predispose him to accept this view. On the con-

[199] 249 U.S. at 51.
[200] Debs v. United States, 249 U.S. 211, 216 (1919).
[201] Compare Schenck, 249 U.S. at 52 with Swift, 196 U.S. at 402.
[202] Commonwealth v. Kennedy, 170 Mass. 18, 22, 48 N.E. 770–71 (1897).
[203] 249 U.S. at 52.

trary, the *clear and present danger* phrase in *Schenck*, like bad tendency and other external measures of liability, translated the deference to community will Holmes derived from his Social Darwinism into legal standards. It is ironic that a test considered for decades to be a protective standard of First Amendment interpretation originated in the view that the will of the majority, whether right or wrong, could limit individual freedom by imposing external standards of liability. Holmes did not seem to regard the wartime speeches and writings against the draft and the war as significantly different from the solicitation to light a fire in *Peaslee*.

Holmes's correspondence in 1918 and 1919 vividly confirms that the views he expressed in *The Common Law* directly influenced his approach to the Espionage Act cases. In June 1918 – one year after *Masses* and nine months before *Schenck, Frohwerk,* and *Debs* – Hand and Holmes met by chance on a train and talked about "tolerance." Hand regretted that he "gave up" too easily during this conversation and wrote Holmes three days later to "take my stand." Hand advocated tolerance of dissent because opinions are "never absolutes"; they are "at best provisional hypotheses, incompletely tested."[204] Free speech, Holmes replied, "stands no differently than freedom from vaccination," which the Supreme Court, in a decision joined by Holmes, had permitted a legislature to restrict through a law requiring compulsory vaccinations.[205] Although people usually would not "care enough" to suppress speech, "if for any reason you did care enough you wouldn't care a damn for the suggestion that you were acting on a provisional hypothesis and might be wrong." Holmes closed his letter to Hand by saying that he "used to define the truth as the majority vote of that nation that can lick all others. So we may define the present war as an inquiry concerning truth."[206]

In the wake of his Espionage Act decisions less than one year after this exchange of letters with Hand, Holmes had a flurry of correspondence about free speech. He expressed serious reservations about the wisdom of the prosecutions under the Espionage

---

[204] Letter from Learned Hand to Oliver Wendell Holmes, Jr. (June 22, 1918) (Oliver Wendell Holmes, Jr., Papers, Box 43, Folder 30, Harvard Law School Library) [hereinafter cited as Holmes Papers], reprinted in Gerald Gunther, supra note 66, at 755–56, and in 1 Holmes-Laski Letters 159 n.2 (M. Howe ed. 1953).

[205] Jacobson v. Massachusetts, 197 U.S. 11 (1905).

[206] Letter from Oliver Wendell Holmes, Jr., to Learned Hand (June 24, 1918) (Learned Hand Papers, Box 103, Folder 24, Harvard Law School Library) [hereinafter Hand Papers], reprinted in Gunther, supra note 66, at 756–57.

Act. He "greatly regretted[207] his "misfortune"[208] in having the "disagreeable task"[209] of writing the opinions, and he suspected that the chief justice had assigned them to him in part because he favored free speech more than any of his colleagues.[210] In fact, Holmes had drafted a dissent in an Espionage Act case in which the government confessed error before the Supreme Court issued a decision. The defendants had been convicted for sending a petition to the governor of South Dakota and two other officials protesting the exemption of certain counties from the draft, demanding a referendum on the draft, insisting that the war effort be financed in cash, and advocating the repudiation of existing war debt. The defendants had not circulated their petition publicly. Displaying more hostility to antiwar speech than the government prosecutors, the Supreme Court majority was prepared to sustain the conviction. By contrast, in his draft dissent Holmes maintained that "the emergency would have to be very great before I could be persuaded that an appeal for political action through legal channels" was outside the protection of the First Amendment.[211]

Holmes was surprised that the government pursued the *Debs* case to the Supreme Court, particularly after the war had ended, "as the inevitable result was that fools, knaves, and ignorant persons were bound to say he was convicted because he was a dangerous agitator and that obstructing the draft was a pretence."[212] He

---

[207] Letter from Oliver Wendell Holmes, Jr., to Harold Laski (March 19, 1919), reprinted in 1 Holmes-Laski Letters, supra note 204, at 189–90.

[208] Letter from Oliver Wendell Holmes, Jr., to Sir Frederick Pollock (June 17, 1919), reprinted in 2 Holmes-Pollock Letters 14–15 (M. Howe ed. 1941).

[209] Letter from Oliver Wendell Holmes, Jr., to Baroness Moncheur (April 4, 1919) (Holmes Papers, supra note 204, Box 36, Folder 4).

[210] Letter from Oliver Wendell Holmes, Jr., to Sir Frederick Pollock (April 5, 1919), reprinted in 2 Holmes-Pollock Letters, supra note 208, at 7–8.

[211] Baltzer v. United States (Holmes dissenting), memorandum distributed to the Justices on Dec. 3, 1918, Holmes Papers, supra note 204, reprinted in Sheldon M. Novick, The Unrevised Holmes and Freedom of Expression, 1991 Sup. Ct. Rev. 303, 388–90, at 390. See supra text accompanying note 60 (jury conviction of Baltzer). Novick deserves great credit for discovering the draft dissent by Holmes in Baltzer, which provides independent confirmation for Holmes's position in private correspondence that he favored free speech more than the other justices. For reasons I explore in Chapter 8, I disagree with Novick's extrapolation from the Baltzer dissent that "Holmes did not change his position" about free speech between his opinion for a unanimous Court in Schenck and his dissent the next fall in Abrams v. United States, 250 U.S. 616, 624 (1919). Novick, supra, at 358 and generally at 350–61. G. Edward White also disagrees with Novick's reading of Baltzer. G. Edward White, Justice Oliver Wendell Holmes: Law and the Inner Self 414, 429 (1993).

[212] Letter from Holmes to Pollock, supra note 210; see letter from Holmes to Laski, supra note 207; letter from Holmes to Moncheur, supra note 209.

thought the federal judiciary had become "hysterical about the war," and he hoped that President Wilson would pardon many of those convicted.[213] As to the legal questions before the Supreme Court in *Schenck, Frohwerk,* and *Debs,* however, Holmes repeatedly emphasized that he had no doubts.[214] Holmes maintained that the Espionage Act itself was constitutional, and even wise policy during the war,[215] although he acknowledged that he had dealt "somewhat summarily" with the First Amendment in the Espionage Act cases.[216] He declared himself generally "for aeration of all effervescing opinions – there is no way so quick for letting them get flat." During a war, however, he did not "think it unreasonable to say we won't have obstacles intentionally put in the way of raising troops – by persuasion any more than by force."[217]

Holmes gave conflicting indications about how he would have voted had he been a member of the jury in *Debs.* Holmes seems to have told people what he thought they wanted to hear.[218] Holmes did make clear, however, that his vote as a hypothetical juror was irrelevant to his role as a judge. As long as there was any evidence to support the jury findings, Holmes did not believe a judge could overturn them. Even when he conceded that the jury may have based its conviction of Debs on impermissible considerations, Holmes emphasized that he could not go behind the verdict.[219] Holmes was also unmoved by complaints that jury determinations of probable consequences undermined free speech. Stedman's

---

[213] Letter from Holmes to Laski, supra note 207; see letter from Oliver Wendell Holmes, Jr., to Sir Frederick Pollock (April 27, 1919), reprinted in 2 Holmes-Pollock Letters, supra note 208, at 10–11.

[214] See letter from Oliver Wendell Holmes, Jr., to Herbert Croly (May 12, 1919) (not mailed to Croly but enclosed with letter to Laski), reprinted in 1 Holmes-Laski Letters, supra note 204, at 202–4; letter from Holmes to Laski, supra note 207; letter from Holmes to Moncheur, supra note 209; letter from Holmes to Pollock, supra note 213; letter from Oliver Wendell Holmes, Jr., to John P. Wigmore (June 7, 1919) (Holmes Papers, supra note 204, Box 36, Folder 4).

[215] Letter from Holmes to Croly, supra note 214; see Letter from Holmes to Pollock, supra note 213 (Espionage Act constitutional).

[216] Letter from Holmes to Pollock, supra note 210.

[217] Letter from Holmes to Croly, supra note 214.

[218] Holmes wrote or left the impression with liberals that as a juror he would have voted to acquit Debs. See letter from Zechariah Chafee, Jr., to Judge Charles F. Amidon (Sept. 30, 1919) (Chafee Papers, supra note 166, Box 4, Folder 1); letter from Holmes to Croly, supra note 214; letter from Holmes to Laski, supra note 207. In a letter to Dean Wigmore, however, Holmes gave his opinion that the jury finding was correct. Letter from Holmes to Wigmore, supra note 214.

[219] See, e.g., letter from Holmes to Croly, supra note 214; letter from Holmes to Pollock, supra note 210.

petition for rehearing in *Debs,*[220] which again advanced this argument, was unsuccessful, as were similar criticisms by Learned
Hand and Ernst Freund.

Within weeks of the Espionage Act decisions, Hand wrote
Holmes again. Promising that his letter would be "positively my
last appearance in the role of liberator," Hand expanded on the
letter he had sent the previous summer. Hand did not agree that
speech might be punished simply because "the result is known as
likely to follow"; even a "reasonable forecast" of the effect of
speech should not make the speaker liable. Hand observed that
free speech "cases actually occur when men are excited" and that
"juries are especially clannish groups," which "won't much regard
the difference between the probable result of the words and the
purposes of the utterer." As a matter of historical fact, Hand
emphasized, the test of motive sanctioned by Holmes allowed
juries to "intimidate" and "scare" many people who might have
"moderate[d] the storms of popular feeling" in 1918. Although he
doubted its future, Hand adhered instead to the test he set forth
in *Masses:* that liability for speech begins when words are "directly
an incitement."[221]

Ernst Freund, whose prewar treatise, *The Police Power,* proposed a
direct incitement standard that anticipated Hand's approach in
Masses, wrote a more extensive critique of *Debs* in the May 3, 1919,
issue of *The New Republic.* Freund accused Holmes of taking "the very
essentials of the entire problem for granted." According to Freund,
"to be permitted to agitate at your own peril, subject to a jury's guessing at motive, tendency and possible effect, makes the right of free
speech a precarious gift." Freund indicated that the Espionage Act
itself was unconstitutional because it insulated from judicial review
jury findings "of a conceivable psychological nexus between words
and deeds." This comment bears a striking resemblance to
Theodore Schroeder's criticism of prewar judges who punished
speech because of its speculative psychological tendency. Freund's
subsequent commendation of Schroeder's writings to Chafee suggests that Freund's thinking on the subject had been influenced by
Schroeder.[222] In any event, Freund added that the "checking func-

---

220 Defendant's Petition for Rehearing at 2–4, Debs v. United States, 249 U.S. 211
    (1919).
221 Letter from Learned Hand to Oliver Wendell Holmes, Jr. (late Mar. 1919)
    (Holmes Papers, supra note 204, Box 43, Folder 30), reprinted in Gunther,
    supra note 66, at 758–59.
222 Letter from Ernst Freund to Zechariah Chafee, Jr. (Aug. 13, 1919) (Chafee
    Papers, supra note 166, Box 14, Folder 10).

tion" of the jury, which may protect the people from unpopular exercises of governmental power, "fails where government policies are supported by majority opinion." He was horrified that Holmes could not distinguish between shouting "fire" in a crowded theater and "political offenses." Freund concluded that Holmes's analysis of free speech must consist of "unsafe doctrine if it has to be made plausible by a parallel so manifestly inappropriate."[223]

Holmes responded to Hand with a puzzled letter in which he stated on three separate occasions that he did not see how Hand's direct incitement standard differed from his own test in *Schenck*.[224] Holmes had no such difficulties, however, in recognizing Freund's pointed objections to his opinion in *Debs*. When Harold Laski asked if he had been "at all influenced"[225] by Freund's article on *Debs* in *The New Republic*, Holmes replied that he "thought it rather poor stuff." He elaborated by enclosing with his response to Laski a letter he had drafted to Herbert Croly, the editor of *The New Republic*, but had decided not to send "as some themes may become burning."[226] Holmes wrote in his draft to Croly that "Freund's objection to a jury 'guessing at motive, tendency and possible effect' is an objection to pretty much the whole body of law, which for thirty years I have made my brethren smile by insisting to be everywhere a matter of degree." Holmes cited earlier antitrust and criminal cases for support and quoted his previous statement that "the law is full of instances where a man's fate depends on his estimating rightly, that is, as the jury subsequently estimates it, from matters of degree."[227]

This correspondence reinforces Holmes's subsequent letter to Chafee about the origins of the *clear and present danger* test. Even in the face of criticism from Hand and Freund, Holmes continued to rely on the fundamental principles he had set forth in *The Common Law* and had applied during four decades as a judge to all areas of the law. The very example in *Schenck* that Freund perceptively found so inappropriate underscores Holmes's consistency. Indeed, Holmes may well have been thinking of the solicitation to light a

---

[223] Ernst Freund, The Debs Case and Freedom of Speech, 19 New Republic 13, 14 (1919), reprinted in 40 U. Chi. L. Rev. 239, 240–41 (1973).

[224] Letter from Oliver Wendell Holmes, Jr., to Learned Hand (April 3, 1919) (Hand Papers, supra note 206, Box 103, Folder 24), reprinted in Gunther, supra note 66, at 759–60.

[225] Letter from Harold Laski to Oliver Wendell Holmes, Jr. (March 18, 1919), reprinted in 1 Holmes-Laski Letters, supra note 204, at 201–2.

[226] Letter from Oliver Wendell Holmes, Jr., to Harold Laski (May 13, 1919), reprinted in 1 Holmes-Laski Letters, supra note 204, at 202.

[227] Letter from Holmes to Croly, supra note 214.

fire in *Peaslee* when he wrote in *Schenck* that the First Amendment would not protect "falsely shouting fire in a theatre."[228] Just a few months after his decisions in *Schenck, Frohwerk,* and *Debs,* however, Holmes joined the postwar civil libertarians, who were rapidly becoming more sensitive to the importance of free speech in a democracy. With a substantial assist from Chafee, Holmes soon revised his analysis of clear and present danger in ways that transformed the phrase into a protective standard of First Amendment interpretation.

[228] 249 U.S. at 52.

7

World War I and the Creation of the Modern Civil Liberties Movement

The modern civil liberties movement emerged during and after World War I. The war and the ensuing "Red Scare" created a broader and more powerful constituency prepared to support freedom of expression, a development the founders of the Free Speech League mistakenly had predicted during the period of intensified government attacks on anarchist speech following the assassination of President McKinley in 1901. Most of the new civil libertarians had been progressives before the war. They opposed traditional American individualism, which they associated with constitutional protection for individual rights. They maintained that judicial enforcement of individual constitutional rights to property and "liberty of contract" had produced socially disruptive economic inequalities and prevented benevolent government regulation that could produce a more equal and harmonious society. Even though it was focused on the economic sphere, this skepticism about individual rights did not predispose progressives to consider the legal meaning of free speech or the right of dissent. Moreover, prewar progressives often seemed to assume that dissent would not be a problem in the rational new order they were confidently creating, and they were impatient with people who did not share their vision of community. On a personal level, many prewar progressives enjoyed lives of privilege and power far removed from the iconoclasts in the Free Speech League, and even more distant from the workers and radicals who most often suffered from the repression of speech before the war.

The transformation of consciousness that created the postwar civil liberties movement did not occur at the same time or in the same manner for all its future leaders. Some of them opposed the war, and threats to the free speech of pacifists and conscientious objectors alerted them to First Amendment problems relatively early, just as threats to radicals under antiobscenity and antianarchy legislation had previously alerted the founders of the Free Speech

299

League. It is significant that the ACLU developed from a Civil Liberties Bureau within the American Union Against Militarism, an organization founded in 1916 by prominent social workers to campaign against President Wilson's drive for military preparedness and to advocate a mediated settlement of the war. Most of the founders of the ACLU, including Roger Baldwin, were pacifists and conscientious objectors before they became civil libertarians.[1] Randolph Bourne, a pacifist who had been an ardent disciple of John Dewey, vigorously criticized Dewey's early wartime essays in *The New Republic* for their condescending impatience with pacifist dissent and for their insensitivity to the threat of repression. A philosopher "who senses so little the sinister forces of war" and "who can feel only amusement at the idea that any one should try to conscript thought," Bourne wrote, "is speaking to another element of the younger intelligentsia than that to which I belong." For Bourne, hope for the future rested with the new ideas and free speculation of the skeptical "malcontents" disparaged by Dewey.[2]

The extensive official and unofficial repression of even the most innocuous antiwar speech shocked some supporters of the war into concern for free speech rights. The wartime attacks against unpopular speech were in many respects no worse in degree than were those suffered by many radicals before the war – for example, by the IWW and its supporters during the 1912 San Diego free speech fight – but they were more widespread. Instead of a temporary and localized outbreak against supposedly dangerous radicals, there was sustained, nationwide repression of even the mildest and most respectable dissenters. This repression prompted protests from prowar liberals, perhaps most visibly from John Dewey, Herbert Croly, and others associated with *The New Republic*, who sometimes even criticized their own prior insensitivity to infringements on speech.

In November 1917, only two months after the last of his essays criticized by Bourne, Dewey wrote another piece in *The New Republic* contritely entitled "In Explanation of Our Lapse." He acknowledged that "the increase of intolerance to the point of religious

[1] See, e.g., Donald Johnson, The Challenge to American Freedoms: World War I and the Rise of the American Civil Liberties Union 1–25, 197; C. Roland Marchand, The American Peace Movement and Social Reform, 1898–1918, at 240–61 (1972); David M. Kennedy, Over Here: The First World War and American Society 33–36 (1980); Paul L. Murphy, World War I and the Origin of Civil Liberties in the United States 153–73 (1979); Samuel Walker, In Defense of American Liberties: A History of the ACLU 16–20 (1990); Roger Baldwin, Recollections of a Life in Civil Liberties – I, 2 Civ. Lib. Rev., Spring 1975, at 39, 51–55.

[2] Randolph Bourne, Twilight of Idols (1917), in Randolph Bourne, The Radical Will: Selected Writings 1911–1918, at 336, 346 (Olaf Hansen ed. 1977).

bigotry" during the intervening period made his earlier writing seem "strangely remote and pallid." Dewey forcefully condemned the practice of defining as treason "every belief which irritates the majority of loyal citizens."[3] Perhaps thinking of his own "lapse," Dewey warned that the prowar "liberal who for expediency's sake would passively tolerate invasions of free speech" may be "preparing the way for a later victory of domestic Toryism."[4] *The New Republic,* under Croly's leadership and frequent authorship, began publishing many other articles and editorials that criticized government repression of speech.[5] These articles eventually included Chafee's essay on free speech that grew into his seminal article in the *Harvard Law Review* and Freund's blistering critique of Holmes's decision in *Debs.*[6]

Most supporters of the war who became civil libertarians, however, did not do so until after the Armistice in November 1918. They were often too involved in the war effort to focus on the domestic abuse of power. The failure of the Versailles Peace Conference "to make the world safe for democracy," along with the extensive violations of the right to free speech and other civil liberties during the Red Scare of 1919, led many to reevaluate the views they had held during the war. A large number discovered that they had come to share positions for which opponents of the war had been prosecuted under the Espionage Act.

Others, who did not change their opinions about the war itself, were nevertheless outraged by the repression that followed. Official participation or acquiescence in this repression challenged their prewar confidence in the promise of benevolent state action. It also made them recognize that constitutional rights, which they had previously attacked as trumps against reform legislation, could also serve as socially valuable checks against the government. While retaining their prewar hostility to constitutional rights based on property and liberty of contract, they lauded the constitutional right of free speech and protested infringements against it for the

---

[3] John Dewey, In Explanation of Our Lapse (1917), in 10 John Dewey, The Middle Works, 1899–1924, Essays on Philosophy and Education 1916–1017, at 292 (1985).

[4] Id. at 295.

[5] David W. Levy, Herbert Croly of the New Republic 275 and n. 46 (1985); Edward A. Stettner, Shaping Modern Liberalism: Herbert Croly and Progressive Thought 136–38 (1993).

[6] Zechariah Chafee, Jr., Freedom of Speech, 17 New Republic 66 (1918) [hereinafter Chafee-New Republic]; Zechariah Chafee, Jr., Freedom of Speech in War Time, 32 Harv. L. Rev. 932 (1919) [hereinafter Chafee-Harvard]; Ernst Freund, The Debs Case and Freedom of Speech, 19 New Republic 13 (1919), reprinted in 40 U. Chi. L. Rev. 235 (1973).

first time. Many progressive publicists, who had eagerly joined the Wilson administration and supported the war effort, became increasingly concerned about the repression of speech during and especially after the war.[7] For some people, the defense of free speech became an active, and often a primary, concern. Several worked hard to protect the rights of the IWW and other radicals whose suppression before the war they had largely ignored. In January 1920, Roger Baldwin was finally able to overcome the taint of the pacifist origins of the Civil Liberties Bureau and convince a significant number of previously reluctant prowar liberals to join him in establishing the ACLU.[8] Later that year, Harvard law professors Zechariah Chafee, Jr., Roscoe Pound, and Felix Frankfurter joined other eminent lawyers in a report detailing "Illegal Practices of the United States Department of Justice" and signed a petition for the pardon of people imprisoned under the Espionage Act.[9]

The emergence of modern First Amendment doctrine reflected this transformation of consciousness in the language of the law. Chafee, who had not been interested in free speech before World War I, took the first major step by obscuring the restrictive prewar judicial tradition while advancing unfounded protective interpretations of legal history and of the *clear and present danger* phrase Holmes used in the *Schenck* case. As Holmes and Brandeis rapidly became more sensitive to free speech concerns, they faced the difficult problem of dealing with the judicial hostility to free speech before the war and its continuation in the initial Espionage Act cases, including *Schenck*. Trapped in a tradition from which they wanted to escape, but reluctant to acknowledge that tradition or their own role in it, they followed the lead provided by Chafee's article. Beginning with the dissent Holmes wrote in the *Abrams* case, just six months after he had composed the Court's unanimous opinion in *Schenck*, Holmes and Brandeis incorporated Chafee's erroneous interpretations into their own opinions. By the 1930s, the Supreme Court majority began to accept many of the free speech values expressed in the previous dissents by Holmes and Brandeis.

The free speech views of the new civil libertarians reflected the continuing influence of progressive ideology and the debate over antiwar speech during which they developed. It is most striking that the postwar civil libertarians essentially limited the protection

---

[7] John A. Thompson, Reformers and War: American Progressive Publicists and the First World War 177–286 (1987).

[8] See Johnson, supra note 1, at 147.

[9] Paul L. Murphy, The Meaning of Freedom of Speech: First Amendment Freedoms from Wilson to FDR 95–96 (1972).

of the First Amendment to political expression. They simultaneously obscured the deep commitment to individual rights that lay behind the much more comprehensive prewar understandings of free speech by liberal individualists such as Cooley and especially by libertarian radicals such as Schroeder and his colleagues in the Free Speech League. The ACLU focused on protecting political speech while ignoring other problems of censorship. Its early agenda, as Samuel Walker's comprehensive history makes clear, was "extremely limited" and "grew slowly and haltingly."[10]

Chafee, who frequently worked with the ACLU founders, similarly emphasized the importance of political expression in a democracy, a reflection of progressive concern about social interests in the public welfare and a reminder of the kind of speech repressed under the Espionage Act. Chafee borrowed extensively from Pound's sociological jurisprudence, stressing that law must balance competing social interests. As a new civil libertarian, however, Chafee insisted, as Pound had not before the war, that the democratic purpose of the First Amendment requires added weight to free speech in any balance. Just as the ACLU obscured the Free Speech League, Chafee largely ignored Schroeder's voluminous prewar scholarship on free speech while denying that laws prohibiting obscenity violate the First Amendment. Chafee's first major article on free speech did not cite Schroeder at all. When sending a reprint to Schroeder, Chafee apologized for failing to acknowledge receipt of Schroeder's books and for not citing them.[11] "I am hoping in your future publications," Schroeder wrote Chafee in response, "you will be interested in covering the whole subject of speech."[12] Ernst Freund had a similar reaction to Chafee's article, underlining that contemporary scholars viewed Chafee as narrowing the concept of free speech. "If you consider Freedom of Speech socially as well as politically," Freund wrote Chafee, "Theodore Schroeder deserves a place in your bibliography."[13]

---

[10] Walker, supra note 1, at 86.

[11] Letter from Zechariah Chafee, Jr., to Theodore Schroeder (Sept. 29, 1919) (Zechariah Chafee, Jr., Papers, Box 14, Folder 26, Harvard Law School Library) [hereinafter Chafee Papers].

[12] Letter from Theodore Schroeder to Zechariah Chafee, Jr. (Oct. 1, 1919) (Chafee Papers, supra note 11, Box 14, Folder 26).

[13] Letter from Ernst Freund to Zechariah Chafee, Jr. (Aug. 19, 1919) (Chafee Papers, supra note 11, Box 14, Folder 26). Chafee followed Freund's advice in the bibliography of his 1920 book, Freedom of Speech. "Much useful material," Chafee wrote, "is collected in the writings of Theodore Schroeder." Chafee added references to a bibliography of Schroeder's work and to two of Schroeder's recent articles. Id. at 378.

John Dewey's postwar writings reiterated many of the central themes of his prewar thought, especially his focus on democratic citizenship. Yet he emphasized for the first time after the war the role of free speech in democratic political life. While continuing to oppose traditional individualism and to stress the relationship between the individual and the state, Dewey moderated his prewar confidence in benevolent government and identified state power as a danger to civil liberties. When Dewey referred to the "unexpected difficulties which democracy has had to meet" in protecting free speech, he was almost certainly thinking about his own "lapse" in not anticipating the extent of repression during World War I and the postwar Red Scare.[14]

THE NEW CIVIL LIBERTARIANS OF THE ACLU
AND THE DEMISE OF THE FREE SPEECH LEAGUE

The declining relationship between the Free Speech League and the ACLU most clearly illustrates the different and narrower views of the postwar civil libertarians. The Free Speech League remained active through the American intervention in World War I. Threats to free speech during the war, while creating a broader constituency committed to First Amendment values, represented to members of the Free Speech League an extension of their traditional concerns. League members, however, recognized the additional dangers posed by the overwhelming national hostility to expressions of antiwar opinions, and particularly by the widespread prosecution of such speech under the Espionage Act. "We are passing through a veritable reign of terror, psychologically," Abbott wrote Schroeder in 1918. "Expressions of opinion that, a year ago, were innocent, have now become criminal."[15] Schroeder agreed. "In my opinion," he replied, "we are only at the beginning of a psychological terrorism which will increase as the war progresses. I hope the Kaiser will be licked before this emotional debauch goes much further."[16]

Even before he testified in Congress or participated in *Masses, Debs,* and other Espionage Act cases, Gilbert Roe drew on his close personal relationship with Senator La Follette to warn about the dangers to freedom of expression posed by the Espionage bill.

[14] John Dewey and James H. Tufts, Ethics 398–99 (1932) [hereinafter Dewey-Ethics II].
[15] Letter from Leonard Abbott to Theodore Schroeder (Apr. 23, 1918) (Theodore Schroeder Papers, Box 12, Southern Illinois University Library) [hereinafter Schroeder Papers].
[16] Letter from Theodore Schroeder to Leonard Abbott (April 25, 1918) (Schroeder Papers, supra note 15, Box 12).

"There are worse calamities," Roe advised La Follette, "even than war. One of them would be the destruction of free speech and of free press – both of which have been much restricted even in times of peace." Roe urged public hearings on the bill, pointing out that he heard of its existence only through his participation in the Free Speech League. "I do not suppose," Roe added, "that there is one person in a million outside of official life who knows that a measure of this sort is under consideration." He worried that "[u]nless public hearings are held and some information given the public about it, we may have our most cherished and fundamental right swept away over night."[17]

Roe followed up this letter to La Follette with additional personal correspondence regarding the legislation. In one letter, Roe enclosed an editorial from the Hearst papers announcing that Hearst intended to disobey any provisions of the proposed Espionage Act he deemed objectionable. Roe told La Follette that the Hearst chain, "with its power and influence and with the wealth that he has back of it, will not be stopped," but accurately predicted that "[i]f any small Socialist or radical paper would make the same announcement, that would be sufficient reason for shutting it out of the mail."[18] In a subsequent letter, he cautioned that the most dangerous provision of the proposed act was the discretion it gave the postmaster general to exclude publications "containing any matter of a seditious, anarchistic or treasonable character" from the mails. He stressed that even though the definition of treason in the Constitution requires an overt act, "[n]o one can appeal to the Courts from a decision of the Post Office Inspector who may declare anything to be anarchistic or treasonable or seditious that he pleases." Based on his prewar experience with free speech issues under the Comstock Act, Roe was able to warn La Follette: "I have been through this with other publications which the Post Office Officials suppressed on the ground that they were obnoxious to other portions of the Statute and I know what a tremendous instrument of tyranny this rather innocent looking provision of the bill will become."[19]

Roe subsequently represented Senator La Follette before a Senate committee conducting hearings on a motion to expel him

---

[17] Letter from Gilbert E. Roe to Robert M. La Follette (Apr. 7, 1917) (La Follette Family Collection, Series H, Manuscript Division, Library of Congress) [hereinafter Roe Papers].

[18] Letter from Gilbert E. Roe to Robert M. La Follette (Apr. 30, 1917) (Roe Papers, supra note 17, Container H7).

[19] Letter from Gilbert E. Roe to Robert M. La Follette (May 8, 1917) (Roe Papers, supra note 17, Container H7).

from the Senate for a September 1917 address to the Nonpartisan League, a political movement of populist farmers in the upper Midwest who overwhelmingly opposed the war.[20] La Follette's speech urged that high taxes be levied against potential war profiteers. In January 1919, over one year after charges were brought and two months after the war ended, the Senate finally voted to take no action against La Follette.[21]

Following their prewar pattern, Schroeder remained further in the background than did Roe. Yet Schroeder, like Roe, opposed the Espionage bill. He wrote Senator William E. Borah, one of the six senators who ultimately voted against the legislation, offering to confer in Washington. Borah, while declining this offer, informed Schroeder that "I have been reading your articles in some of the law journals upon this subject and have found them immensely instructive."[22] Harry Weinberger consulted with Schroeder when Weinberger represented Emma Goldman in 1917 and Jacob Abrams in 1919 before the Supreme Court.[23] Schroeder also continued to publicize free speech, sending reprints of his articles to each justice on the Supreme Court in the fall of 1917.[24]

As Roe and Schroeder extended their free speech activities in 1917, Roger Baldwin began his. After the American Union Against Militarism (AUAM) failed to prevent American intervention in World War I, it established a Civil Liberties Bureau to defend the free speech rights of conscientious objectors, and named Baldwin its executive.[25] The work of the Bureau soon expanded to defending other opponents of the war, such as socialists and IWW members.[26]

---

[20] See Kennedy, supra note 1, at 23; William E. Leuchtenburg, The Perils of Prosperity, 1914–32, at 128–29 (1958).

[21] 2 Belle Case La Follette & Fola La Follette, Robert M. La Follette (1953), at 761–62, 928; see generally id. at 731–931 for a discussion of La Follette's ordeal before the Senate.

[22] Letter from William E. Borah to Theodore Schroeder (Apr. 17, 1917) (Schroeder Papers, supra note 15, Box 12).

[23] Letter from Harry Weinberger to Theodore Schroeder (Dec. 3, 1917) (Harry Weinberger Papers, Box 30, Sterling Memorial Library Collection, Yale University) [hereinafter Weinberger Papers]; Letter from Theodore Schroeder to Harry Weinberger (Dec. 4, 1917) (Weinberger Papers, supra, Box 30); Letter from Harry Weinberger to Theodore Schroeder (Sept. 20, 1919) (Weinberger Papers, supra, Box 30).

[24] Letter from Theodore Schroeder to Harry Weinberger (Nov. 1917) (Weinberger Papers, supra note 23, Box 30).

[25] The Reminiscences of Roger Baldwin 54 (1954) (Oral History Collection, Butler Library, Columbia University) [hereinafter Baldwin Reminiscences]. Johnson, supra note 1, at 21; Marchand, supra note 1, at 254.

[26] Murphy, supra note 1, at 157; Walker, supra note 1, at 25.

Roger Baldwin, 1917. (Roger N. Baldwin
Papers, Department of Rare Books and Special
Collections, Princeton University Libraries)

The Bureau's increasing association with radical groups upset many
leaders of the AUAM. In October 1917, the bureau separated from
the AUAM and became an independent organization, the National
Civil Liberties Bureau (NCLB).[27]

Largely because they lacked prior involvement in free speech
issues, Baldwin and his colleagues in the NCLB relied heavily on
the Free Speech League, particularly on Schroeder and Roe. The
minutes of an early meeting of the original Bureau's Lawyers Advi-
sory Committee reported that Schroeder had furnished it with
background material on freedom of expression.[28] Soon after, Baldwin requested that Schroeder send him a complete set of the pamphlets published by the Free Speech League, which Baldwin found

[27] Johnson, supra note 1, at 24; Murphy, supra note 1, at 155–57; Walker, supra
note 1, at 20.
[28] Minutes of National Civil Liberties Bureau (July 20, 1917) (Amos Pinchot
Papers 1, Container 90, Manuscript Division, Library of Congress).

extremely useful.[29] In 1918, Leon Whipple, an NCLB employee
assigned "to collect historical and current data on American Liberties for a book to be printed after the War," wrote Schroeder for
his advice and help. "All the trails on the free speech section,"
Whipple informed Schroeder, "lead to you."[30]

Roe maintained connections with the NCLB and subsequently
with the ACLU until his death in 1929. Baldwin later reported
that Roe had been one of a small group who provided valuable
assistance to the ACLU.[31] Baldwin's relations with Schroeder, however, soon became strained. Like many others, Schroeder suspected that Baldwin and the NCLB had greater interest in pacifism than in free speech. Consistent with his prewar policy of
preserving the Free Speech League from "entangling alliances"
with groups that had special interests, Schroeder, supported by the
League's directors, refused in late 1917 to associate the League or
himself with Baldwin's new organization.[32] Baldwin vigorously
attempted to change Schroeder's mind, but after several unsuccessful efforts,[33] he soon turned to others, including Roscoe
Pound.[34] Baldwin later recalled that Schroeder was never asked to

---

[29] Letter from Roger Baldwin to Theodore Schroeder (Aug. 4, 1917) (Schroeder
Papers, supra note 15, Box 12); Letter from Theodore Schroeder to Roger
Baldwin (Nov. 9, 1917) (3 ACLU Papers 118, Microfilm Collection, Mudd
Manuscript Library, University of Pennsylvania) [hereinafter ACLU Papers];
Letter from Roger Baldwin to Theodore Schroeder (Nov. 15, 1917) (3 ACLU
Papers, supra at 166).

[30] Letter from Leon R. Whipple to Theodore Schroeder (Apr. 5, 1918)
(Schroeder Papers, supra note 15, Box 12). Whipple eventually completed his
book. Leon Whipple, The Story of Civil Liberty in the United States (1927),
which Whipple himself accurately described to Chafee as "a useful book, but
not a very good one." Whipple hoped that others would eventually write a "real
social history" of civil liberties in American history. Letter from Leon Whipple
to Zechariah Chafee, Jr. (Jan. 21, 1928) (Chafee Papers, supra note 11, Box 3,
Folder 22).

[31] Baldwin Reminiscences, supra note 25, at 134, 137.

[32] Letter from Theodore Schroeder to Roger Baldwin (Nov. 27, 1917) (3 ACLU
Papers, supra note 29, at 171). Schroeder had previously complained about a
meeting Baldwin had organized. "While it was called to discuss liberty of the
press," Schroeder observed, "the discussion was mainly pacifism." Schroeder
protested that this change of emphasis, in which freedom of speech became
"incidental," was "not a fair way to play the game and it should not be
repeated." Letter from Theodore Schroeder to Roger Baldwin (Oct. 26, 1917)
(3 ACLU Papers, supra note 29, at 115).

[33] See Letter from Roger Baldwin to Theodore Schroeder (Nov. 23, 1917) (3
ACLU Papers, supra note 29, at 170); Letter from Roger Baldwin to Theodore
Schroeder (Dec. 1, 1917) (3 ACLU Papers, supra note 29, at 172).

[34] Letter from Louis P. Lochner to Theodore Schroeder (Aug. 6, 1918) (Schroeder
Papers, supra note 15, Box 42).

aid the Civil Liberties Bureau because many thought he could not be "detached from his prejudices and notions."[35]

Schroeder himself did not seem particularly upset that he and the Free Speech League lost influence just when wartime repression made free speech a substantial concern of a broader and more influential group of Americans. In fact, he acknowledged without bitterness that the League did not retain a meaningful role "since Roger Baldwin could then do the same work more efficiently."[36] Schroeder's equanimity probably reflected the shift in his own concerns. He had always been interested in psychology, but after undergoing psychoanalysis in 1914–1915, this subject began to take precedence over his free speech work. He came to believe that the problems he was trying to solve "by logic and intellect alone" were essentially "matters of impulse and emotion."[37] Schroeder informed Abbott that he was "putting less and less emphasis upon defending views of free speech and much more emphasis upon making psychological explanations of the view of opponents."[38] Beginning with this period, the bulk of Schroeder's always voluminous publications focused on psychology. Schroeder became a prolific contributor to the *Psychoanalytic Review*, a journal co-founded by William Alanson White, an eminent psychiatrist and Schroeder's own analyst. In fact, during the *Review's* first fourteen years, only the editor published more articles in it than did Schroeder.[39]

Moreover, Schroeder's shifting interests reflected his own complicated personality. Regarded by many as isolated and eccentric, Schroeder appeared eager to cultivate this image. As his transformation of views about Mormonism had indicated, Schroeder seemed to lose interest when a previously unpopular cause attracted broader support. Psychoanalysis remained controversial long after the reaction against wartime and postwar repression made freedom of speech a respectable concern for many leading citizens.

Without Schroeder's active involvement, the Free Speech League essentially disintegrated. Its collapse had significant conse-

---

[35] Baldwin Reminiscences, supra note 25, at 114–15.
[36] Maynard Shipley, A Maverick Psychologist, The New Humanist, Mar.–Apr. 1933, reprinted in Joseph Ishill, Theodore Schroeder: An Evolutionary Psychologist 1, 25 (quoting Schroeder).
[37] Theodore Schroeder, Autobiographical Notes, Varieties of Autobiographical Technique 11 (Schroeder Papers, supra note 15, Box 3).
[38] Letter from Theodore Schroeder to Leonard Abbott (Dec. 8, 1919) (Schroeder Papers, supra note 15, Box 12).
[39] Shipley, supra note 36, at 21; see David Brudnoy, Liberty's Bugler: The Seven Ages of Theodore Schroeder 281–82 (1971) (unpublished Ph.D. dissertation, Brandeis University).

quences. Cut off from the tradition of libertarian radicalism that informed the work of the Free Speech League, the ACLU took a more restrictive view of free speech. Chafee, who supplanted Schroeder as the leading scholar of the subject, similarly narrowed Schroeder's libertarian analysis of the First Amendment.

The exchange of correspondence between Baldwin and Schroeder in late 1917, which probably ended the possibility of a close working relationship between the ACLU and the Free Speech League, revealed a fundamental disagreement over the concept of civil liberties that implicated the more specific issue of free speech. Schroeder complained that a list of individuals Baldwin proposed inviting to a conference on civil liberties indicated a "possible narrowing of the issues to economic liberty with a maximum Pacifist leaning," and would result in "neglect of the more personal liberties which are being very much invaded."[40] When Baldwin asked Schroeder to identify more precisely those personal liberties,[41] however, Schroeder responded with a self-defeating letter that would have intrigued the psychoanalysts in whom he was becoming increasingly interested, but which also reflected the libertarian radical background of the Free Speech League. Schroeder cited as endangered personal liberties Sunday regulations against ball games and motion pictures, the suppression of freethought lecturers, expenditures of public funds for religious institutions, laws that restricted unlicensed medical activities, antiliquor and antitobacco laws, and penalties against women "for riding horseback astride and for wearing heels that are too high."[42] Baldwin responded curtly that such personal liberties "are not an issue before the country just now, and are hardly involved in the wider political question which we are discussing."[43]

Given Baldwin's understandable preoccupation with the immediate crisis posed by widespread prosecutions under the Espionage Act, Schroeder's letter was clearly inadequate. Schroeder seemed almost deliberate in choosing examples of personal liberties that he knew Baldwin would consider minor or irrelevant. Yet Schroeder could have effectively criticized Baldwin for limiting his attention to pressing political questions. Schroeder could have informed Baldwin, as he had many others who sought League assistance before the war, that the League was committed to free

[40] Letter from Schroeder to Baldwin (Nov. 27, 1917), supra note 32.
[41] Letter from Baldwin to Schroeder (Dec. 1, 1917), supra note 33.
[42] Letter from Theodore Schroeder to Roger Baldwin (Dec. 4, 1917) (3 ACLU Papers, supra note 29, at 173).
[43] Letter from Roger Baldwin to Theodore Schroeder (Dec. 7, 1917) (3 ACLU Papers, supra note 29, at 174).

speech regardless of the identity or ideology of the speaker. Drawing on the League's extensive knowledge and experience, Schroeder could have demonstrated that postal censorship of allegedly obscene material, the use of contempt proceedings to punish newspaper articles critical of courts, labor injunctions, prohibitions of public meetings, libel suits, restrictions on the speech of anarchists, socialists, advocates of birth control, and religious minorities, and many other incidents – including the repression of pacifists and others opposed to American participation in World War I – all raised significant and interrelated free speech issues. Schroeder could even have invoked the examples of personal liberties he did cite to demonstrate to Baldwin the connection between contemporary free speech controversies and the libertarian radical tradition. Many of Schroeder's examples illustrated his commitment to protecting personal autonomy and freedom from government control, values derived from the individualist anarchists who were active before the Civil War. Schroeder's letter to Baldwin could have been far more effective had Schroeder explicitly stated that freedom of expression, historically and theoretically, related to issues at the core of the relationship between the individual and the state. On the other hand, the traditional progressive focus on social over individual interests might have made it difficult for Baldwin and other emerging civil libertarians to appreciate even the best defense of free speech as a right of individual autonomy.

The ACLU's narrower conception of free speech emerged more clearly several years later, when Baldwin and many of his associates had difficulty perceiving censorship of allegedly obscene material as a First Amendment issue. In 1923, Harry Weinberger became the manager of a production of *The God of Vengeance*, a play about prostitution written by Sholom Asch, the most popular Yiddish American writer of his day.[44] Officials in New York City prosecuted Weinberger and the entire cast under a local obscenity law.[45] Weinberger wrote Schroeder that the prosecution was based upon the "objection of certain Jews" that the play "showed the Jews in a bad light . . . just as some Christians object to the 'Scarlet Letter' as showing the Minister in a bad light."[46]

After Weinberger and the cast were convicted and the produc-

---

[44] See Irving Howe, World of Our Fathers 96, 449 (1976) (discussing The God of Vengeance).

[45] Letter from Harry Weinberger to Roger Baldwin 1 (Aug. 21, 1925) (Weinberger Papers, supra note 23, Box 24).

[46] Letter from Harry Weinberger to Theodore Schroeder (Oct. 1 1924) (Weinberger Papers, supra note 23, Box 25).

tion shut down, Weinberger asked the ACLU to support an appeal. Roger Baldwin, writing on behalf of the ACLU, refused to assist them, although he had previously agreed with Weinberger that the case implicated free speech.[47] "The issue in the case," Baldwin maintained, "is not primarily one of freedom of opinion – it is one of censorship on the ground of morality," a right that "has been accepted for several centuries" and could not be questioned. The ACLU saw no "clear-cut" constitutional issue at stake, little chance of success on appeal, and no point in "agitating, irrespective of result."[48]

Weinberger disagreed with Baldwin's assessment and tried to persuade him to reconsider. Invoking a basic theme from Schroeder's prewar writings, Weinberger maintained that "the uncertainty of the law and its interference with free drama and free books" rendered it unconstitutional. He acknowledged that a court would probably not accept his constitutional argument, but added "that is no reason why the contention should not be made nor why the contention is not correct." Weinberger observed that although he had a feeling of "absolute hopelessness" when he argued the *Abrams* case before the Supreme Court, Justice Holmes, who had written for the unanimous majority in the initial Espionage Act cases, wrote the dissenting opinion in *Abrams*. A challenge to the New York obscenity law, he implied, might produce a similar result. Weinberger also tried to persuade Baldwin by pointing out that Schroeder, an expert on free speech issues, had helped him write his brief challenging the censorship of *The God of Vengeance*.[49]

Schroeder himself wrote Baldwin to criticize his decision and ask for reconsideration. In a more effective letter than his 1917 correspondence with Baldwin, Schroeder emphasized the connections between the censorship of alleged obscenity and free discussion of social problems.

> The censorship of the theatre began before reading became a general accomplishment, and when the theatre was the conspicuous mode of propaganda. The opposition to the theatre came primarily from the church, because the plays so often undermined the religious morality and respect for religion and its promoters within the church and state. . . . In our modern times, every play has an influence upon the thought

[47] See id. (reproducing note from Baldwin).
[48] Letter from Roger Baldwin to Harry Weinberger (Oct. 1, 1924) (Weinberger Papers, supra note 23, Box 24).
[49] Letter from Harry Weinberger to Roger Baldwin (Sept. 16, 1924) (Weinberger Papers, supra note 23, Box 24).

and feelings of the audience, concerning some social problems. Every worthwhile play is consciously a piece of propaganda, to put across some kind of message of social consequence. Whether that message is spoken in the ordinary way
of a sermon or lecture, or is accompanied by a theatrical stage
setting and stage clothing, surely must be immaterial to its
classification as raising a free speech issue when censored.

Schroeder warned that the eventual decision about *The God of
Vengeance* would not only serve as a precedent for future cases
involving censorship of plays, but would also be used by analogy
"in every other kind of free speech issue."[50]

The ACLU's board of directors, although sympathetic to the
case, ultimately decided that it was not "significant enough to warrant an investment."[51] It is ironic that board member Morris Ernst,
who by the end of the decade persuaded the ACLU to challenge
literary censorship and won the important 1933 case overturning
the ban on James Joyce's *Ulysses*,[52] supported the refusal to assist
Weinberger.[53]

The lingering elitism and respectability of the new civil libertarians in the ACLU provided as revealing a contrast with the Free
Speech League as did the substantive disagreements between the
two organizations. Even Roger Baldwin, the ACLU leader most
attracted to radicals, sought to distance himself and the ACLU
from the anarchists with whom he increasingly identified. Despite
sharing the anarchists' opposition to the draft, the war, and the
wartime suppression of civil liberties, Baldwin – with the unanimous support of his colleagues – rejected collaboration. As Baldwin

---

[50] Letter from Theodore Schroeder to Roger Baldwin (Oct. 3, 1924) (Schroeder
Papers, supra note 15, Box 14).

[51] Letter from Roger Baldwin to Harry Weinberger (Nov. 28, 1924) (Weinberger
Papers, supra note 23, Box 24).

[52] Walker, supra note 1, at 66, 68, 83.

[53] Letter from Morris L. Ernst to Harry Weinberger (Apr. 8, 1925) (Weinberger
Papers, supra note 23, Box 24); Letter from Morris L. Ernst to Harry Weinberger
(Apr. 24, 1925) (Weinberger Papers, supra note 23, Box 24). These letters from
Ernst to Weinberger, in contrast to the earlier correspondence from Baldwin to
Weinberger, suggested that the financial interest of Weinberger in the play was
the key factor in a second decision against providing funds. Weinberger found
this argument unconvincing. He reiterated that he had spent all the money he
had made from the play in the fight against censorship and added that Ernst and
his colleagues would not have inquired into financial matters had socialists such
as Norman Thomas or Scott Nearing been arrested while lecturing for pay. Letter
from Harry Weinberger to Morris L. Ernst (Apr. 14, 1925) (Weinberger Papers,
supra note 23, Box 24). Ernst rejected this analogy as unfair without explaining
why. Letter from Ernst to Weinberger (Apr. 24, 1925), supra.

himself recollected, "I believed that their support compromised the rest of us, who carried no such heavy burden of public hostility, and I found myself in the unhappy position of rejecting the cooperation of my old friends," including Emma Goldman. Baldwin later regretted not attending Goldman's trial when she was prosecuted, convicted, and eventually deported for antiwar speech alleged to have violated the Selective Draft Law. Indeed, Baldwin and his colleagues were not even asked to assist her defense, "so separate was the anarchist group from us more reputable folk."[54] Instead, Harry Weinberger, who frequently worked with the Free Speech League, represented Goldman through her final and unsuccessful appeal to the Supreme Court.

Chafee, like Baldwin, went out of his way to dissociate himself from the radicals whose free speech rights he had begun to defend during the war. "I have no sympathy myself," he wrote in the opening pages of the book on free speech he published in 1920, "with the views of most of the men who have been imprisoned since the war began for speaking out."[55] Chafee reiterated his traditional political and economic views throughout the text, and constantly reviewed it before publication to make sure his position was sufficiently clear "to show thoughtful progressive readers that my own place was with them and not with the persecuted radicals."[56] When defending his work before a special committee of the Harvard Overseers, Chafee again stressed his conservative family background. "My sympathies and all my associations," he stated, "are with the men who save, who manage and produce. But I want my side to fight fair."[57] In responding to a friend who had expressed concern over Chafee's apparent preoccupation with the IWW after the war, Chafee put his interest in perspective.

> [T]he thought that these wrecks of our industrial system are shut up by your courts for five or ten years out of the fields and sunlight because they join the one organization that has ever taken any interest in them makes me anxious to do a little to procure them fairer treatment. I hope that you are not entirely indifferent to the bad policy of trying to cure discontent by creating more of it without attacking its causes.

---

[54] Baldwin Reminiscences, supra note 25, at 66–67.

[55] Chafee, supra note 13, at 2.

[56] Letter from Zechariah Chafee, Jr. to Richard Hooker 1 (Aug. 29, 1921) (Chafee Papers, supra note 11, Box 14, Folder 12).

[57] Jerold S. Auerbach, The Patrician as Libertarian: Zechariah Chafee, Jr. and Freedom of Speech, 42 New Eng. Q. 511, 525 (1969) (quoting Chafee).

Chafee added, however,

> Don't suppose that the agitators take all my attention. . . .
> [B]ut when I am loafing around on my boat, or taking an
> inordinately large number of strokes on the golf course, I
> occasionally think of these poor devils who won't be out for
> five or ten years and want to do a bit to make the weight of
> society less heavy upon them.[58]

The early leaders of the ACLU participated happily in the elite
institutions of American society. To Albert DeSilver, one of Baldwin's closest colleagues in the ACLU, the Skull-and-Bones Society
at Yale College represented "the most perfect institution of any
sort yet devised by man," whose "ideal [was] tolerance" and whose
qualifications for membership were "distinctly democratic."[59] To
Felix Frankfurter, an early member of the ACLU's executive committee, "the *Harvard Law Review* in particular and the Harvard Law
School in general" were "the most complete practices in democracy that I have ever known anything about" because they based
decisions on academic excellence rather than on influence or
prejudice.[60] By contrast, the members of the Free Speech League
were inheritors of a long American tradition of libertarian radicalism that challenged dominant values. Rooted in the perfectionism
of individualist anarchism and radical abolitionism, they had very
different notions of ideal societies than did Skull-and-Bones and
the *Harvard Law Review.*

The connections to mainstream thought and culture that shel-
tered the postwar civil libertarians from the prewar repression of
radical speech ultimately made them more successful advocates
once they were aroused by the widespread attacks on expression
during and after World War I. These same connections, however,
prevented the founders of the ACLU from appreciating the tradition of libertarian radicalism that underlay the Free Speech
League's commitment to constitutional protection for a wide variety of expression. Neither the status of the postwar civil libertarians nor their belated attention to the value of free speech should
overshadow their courage and achievements. Many were ostracized by former friends. Chafee was threatened with dismissal from

---

[58] Letter from Zechariah Chafee, Jr., to Sayre Macneil 2 (Oct. 9, 1923) (Chafee
Papers, supra note 11, Box 14, Folder 17).
[59] Walter Nelles, A Liberal in Wartime 55 (1940).
[60] Felix Frankfurter Reminisces: Recorded in Talks with Dr. Harlan B. Phillips 27
(1960).

the Harvard faculty.[61] The newly organized ACLU fought against enormous odds, including an unsympathetic Supreme Court majority from which Justices Brandeis and Holmes, beginning in the fall of 1919, repeatedly dissented. The successes of the postwar civil libertarians, however, should not obscure the achievements of earlier activists, who defended broader conceptions of free speech and who fought against even greater odds, including the indifference and occasional hostility of those who later formed the ACLU.

ZECHARIAH CHAFEE, JR.: THE SCHOLAR AS ADVOCATE

Zechariah Chafee, Jr., was a crucial figure in the attempt by the new civil libertarians to translate their recent interest in protecting political dissent into legal doctrine. Like most postwar civil libertarians, Chafee had not been involved in the defense of free speech before World War I. He reminisced at the end of his career that before beginning to teach at Harvard Law School in 1916, he had "no enthusiasm or even interest in the importance of free speech." In fact, he had supported efforts to close down a play called *The Easiest Way* in his home town of Providence, Rhode Island. According to Chafee, the play "depicted a young woman escaping from the rigors and low wages of a department store into an expensive life of sin." Chafee worried that real salesgirls who saw the play might be persuaded "to follow the heroine's example."[62]

Chafee described his interest in free speech as the result of two accidents. Joining the Harvard faculty the year Pound became Dean, Chafee replaced Pound in a course that dealt with injunctions against torts. To enliven what Chafee called the traditionally "humdrum" subject matter, Pound had prepared a casebook that included the issue of enjoining libels. Chafee decided that in addition to learning the law of libel, he should study more generally about freedom of speech. The following year, his reading started turning up the many prosecutions under the Espionage Act against antiwar speeches and articles.[63]

An encounter with Harold Laski, a tutor at Harvard College and a contributor to *The New Republic*, was the second accident. Laski became the intermediary between *The New Republic* and Chafee, who later claimed that the $75 promised by the magazine

---

[61] See Peter H. Irons, "Fighting Fair": Zechariah Chafee, Jr., the Department of Justice, and the "Trial at the Harvard Club," 94 Harv. L. Rev. 1205 (1981).

[62] Zechariah Chafee, Jr., Thirty-Five Years with Freedom of Speech, 1 Kan. L. Rev. 1, 2 (1952).

[63] Id. at 2–3.

Zechariah Chafee, Jr., 1920. (Courtesy of Art
Collection, Harvard Law School)

for an article on the Espionage Act cases "was a sharp spur to an
assistant professor" who had never previously earned money by
writing. Chafee developed his short piece in *The New Republic* in
1918 into a longer and more technical article that became "Freedom of Speech in War Time." At the urging of Walter Lippmann,
who had become an adviser to a new publishing company, Chafee
expanded his work on free speech into a book, *Freedom of Speech*,
which appeared in 1920.[64] His article and book became the starting point for all subsequent legal analysis of free speech.

Chafee made clear at the beginning of "Freedom of Speech in
War Time" that he would not "confine" himself to a technical
analysis of "whether a given form of federal or state action against
pacifist and similar utterances is void under the constitutions." He
set as his "main task" an explanation of "the nature and scope of
the policy which finds expression in the First Amendment,"[65] a
subject he had begun to explore in his *New Republic* essay four
months before Holmes decided *Schenck*, *Frohwerk*, and *Debs*. To

---

[64] Id. at 3.
[65] Chafee-Harvard, supra note 6, at 934–35.

accomplish this task, Chafee often found it "worth while to forsake
the purely judicial discussion of free speech, and obtain light upon
its meaning from the history of the constitutional clauses and from
the purpose free speech serves in social and political life."[66]

Chafee had good strategic reasons to look beyond the law. His
newly formulated views about free speech conflicted with the
restrictive judicial tradition. Chafee, however, did not simply
develop an alternative interpretation of the First Amendment. He
allowed his ideological purposes to distort his discussion of history
and judicial precedent. Unlike Ernst Freund, who directly
attacked Holmes's decision in *Debs* as inconsistent with a proper
understanding of the policies embodied in the First Amendment,
and unlike several prewar scholars, who vociferously criticized
restrictive decisions by their judicial contemporaries, Chafee tried
within the limits of plausibility to conform history and precedent
to his own interpretation of what the First Amendment should
mean. To do so, he often sacrificed scholarly accuracy. Written
under the guise of scholarship, "Freedom of Speech in War Time"
was essentially a work of propaganda.

Chafee considered the First Amendment "a declaration of
national policy in favor of the public discussion of all public questions."[67] He elaborated on that theme in a paragraph he privately
described as "key"[68] and included in his *New Republic* essay, his *Harvard Law Review* article, and his book.

> The true meaning of freedom of speech seems to be this. One
> of the most important purposes of society and government is
> the discovery and spread of truth on subjects of general con-
> cern. This is possible only through absolutely unlimited discus-
> sion, for . . . once force is thrown into the argument, it
> becomes a matter of chance whether it is thrown on the false
> side or the true, and truth loses all its natural advantage in the
> contest. Nevertheless, there are other purposes of govern-
> ment, such as order, the training of the young, protection
> against external aggression. Unlimited discussion sometimes
> interferes with these purposes, which must then be balanced
> against freedom of speech, but freedom of speech ought to
> weigh very heavily in the scale. The First Amendment gives
> binding force to this principle of political wisdom.[69]

[66] Id. at 945.   [67] Id. at 934.
[68] Statement of Zechariah Chafee, Jr., about his work on freedom of speech
(Chafee Papers, supra note 11, Box 29, Folder 22).
[69] Chafee-Harvard, supra note 6, at 956–57; Chafee-New Republic, supra note 6,
at 67; Chafee, supra note 13, at 34.

As Chafee insisted in subsequent correspondence with Alfred Bettman, the primary author of the government's briefs in *Schenck, Frohwerk,* and *Debs,* "a policy of sifting out truth" justifies the inevitable risk that speech may interfere with proper objectives. Following the approach of Hand in *Masses,* Chafee acknowledged that "all discussion opposed to the government is bound to have some effect in delaying the progress of the war, however slight." Chafee, like Hand before him, concluded that "the first amendment was designed to insure that risk should be taken."[70]

Chafee also argued that the repression of speech during World War I provided excellent empirical support for his position. He asserted that "an opponent makes the best cross-examiner" in public affairs as well as in legal proceedings. Recent history proved that it was a "disastrous mistake to limit criticism to those who favor[ed] the war."[71] Anyone who discussed secret treaties during the war, Chafee pointed out, ran the risk of a jail term, but "[o]pen discussion would have made it impossible for the President to be ignorant of them until he went to Paris."[72] War objectives, he added, often change completely, as the fluctuating government positions during World War I amply illustrated. Chafee considered such reevaluations and reformulations of national policy healthy, and he maintained that they should be influenced by the freest possible expression of all divergent views.[73]

Chafee translated his general interpretation of the First Amendment into "technical language" by relying on Pound's prewar balancing approach while reaching results that provided substantially more protection to interests in speech. Citing Pound and using similar language, Chafee identified individual and social interests in free speech. Chafee described the individual interest as "the need of many men to express their opinions on matters vital to them if life is to be worth living," and the social interest as "the attainment of truth, so that the country may not only adopt the wisest course of action but carry it out in the wisest way." Chafee also seemed to accept Pound's sociological jurisprudence. "To find the boundary line of any right," he maintained, "we must get behind rules of law to human facts." He stressed that "balancing cannot be properly done unless all the interests involved are adequately ascertained, and the great evil of all this

---

[70] Letter from Zechariah Chafee, Jr., to Alfred Bettman (Oct. 16, 1919) (Chafee Papers, supra note 11, Box 14, Folder 3).

[71] Chafee-Harvard, supra note 6, at 958.

[72] Letter from Chafee to Bettman, supra note 70.

[73] Chafee-Harvard, supra note 6, at 958–59.

talk about rights is that each side is so busy denying the other's claim to rights that it entirely overlooks the human desires and needs behind that claim."[74]

While closely following Pound's general approach, however, Chafee believed in the relative value of speech much more strongly than Pound had before the war. Chafee insisted, as Pound had not, that in balancing interests "freedom of speech ought to weigh very heavily in the scale." According to Chafee, "the great interest in free speech should be sacrificed only when the interest in public safety is really imperiled, and not, as most men believe, when it is barely conceivable that it may be slightly affected." Whereas Pound justified repression of speech during the Civil War by emphasizing that the social interest of the state in its preservation outweighed individual and social interests in free speech, Chafee stressed that the social interest in free speech "is especially important in war time." Chafee alluded without details to "the national value of the opposition in former wars" and criticized judicial construction of the Espionage Act for ignoring this social interest while regarding free speech "as merely an individual interest, which must readily give way like other personal desires the moment it interferes with the social interest in the national safety."[75]

Even during a war, Chafee concluded, speech should not be censored or punished "unless it is clearly liable to cause direct and dangerous interference with the conduct of the war." While acknowledging that the process of balancing cannot be reduced to a simple legal rule, Chafee maintained that speech should be protected by the First Amendment until it comes "close to the point where words will give rise to unlawful acts." He also declared "with certitude" that "the First Amendment forbids the punishment of words merely for their injurious tendencies."[76] Chafee believed that "the most essential element of free speech is the rejection of bad tendency as the test of a criminal utterance."[77] He observed that application of the bad tendency test by a jury rather than a judge protects popular attacks on government but has relatively little value for dissidents "in times of war or threatened disorder when the herd instinct runs strong." For Chafee, the test of criminality was more important than the locus of decision. "The real issue in every free-speech controversy," Chafee stressed, is "whether the state can punish all words which have some tendency, however remote, to bring about acts in violation of law, or

---

[74] Id. at 957–58.
[76] Id. at 960.

[75] Id. at 957–60.
[77] Id. at 953.

only words which directly incite to acts in violation of law."[78] Chafee made clear throughout his work that he preferred the direct incitement standard.

Chafee relied on history and precedent to support his interpretation of the First Amendment. Frequently citing the prewar scholarship of Cooley and Schofield, Chafee maintained that the framers of the First Amendment intended to overthrow the English common law of free speech as formulated by Blackstone earlier in the eighteenth century. He quoted at length from Cooley's "unanswerable" argument that the American constitutions rejected Blackstone's limitation of free speech to the absence of prior restraints. Without direct citation, Chafee also accepted the view of Pound and Schofield that Blackstone went "altogether too far in restricting state action" and gave "very inadequate protection to the freedom of expression."[79] Like the prewar scholars, Chafee emphasized the historical connection between the First Amendment and the American conception of popular sovereignty secured by the Revolution and the Constitution. "It must not be forgotten," he stressed, "that the controversy over liberty of the press was a conflict between two views of government, that the law of sedition was a product of the view that the government was the master, and that the American Revolution transformed into a working reality the second view that the government was servant, and therefore subjected to blame from its master, the people." According to Chafee, the framers of the First Amendment "intended to wipe out the common-law of sedition, and make further prosecutions for criticism of the government, without any incitement to law-breaking, forever impossible in the United States of America."[80]

Chafee added that the adoption of the free speech clauses in American constitutions eliminated two pernicious doctrines based on the bad tendency of speech.[81] The doctrine of indirect causation provided that "words can be punished for a supposed bad tendency long before there is any probability that they will break out into unlawful acts." The doctrine of constructive intent established a defendant's "violent intent from the bad tendency of the words on the ground that a man is presumed to intend the consequences of his acts."[82] Chafee recognized that the "bitterly resented" Sedition Act of 1798 "revived" these doctrines; however, he agreed with Thomas Jefferson that the Sedition Act was uncon-

[78] Id. at 948–49.
[80] Id. at 947.
[82] Id. at 949.
[79] Id. at 939–40.
[81] Id. at 951.

stitutional and emphasized that it "surely defeated the fundamental policy of the First Amendment, the open discussion of public affairs." Experience under the Sedition Act, Chafee concluded, demonstrated that "the most essential element of free speech is the rejection of bad tendency as the test of a criminal utterance."[83]

In 1960, Leonard Levy raised substantial doubts about Chafee's understanding of the original meaning of the First Amendment.[84] Without resuscitating all of Chafee's claims about the framers' intent, subsequent scholarship has provided renewed support for the claim by Chafee and the prewar scholars that the ideology of popular sovereignty secured by the American Revolution and the Constitution included an understanding of the First Amendment that repudiated Blackstone's views about free speech.[85] By contrast, Chafee's treatment of judicial interpretation of free speech before World War I was clearly wrong, as Chafee himself must have known. Before writing his article, Chafee had read every free speech case decided before 1916.[86] Many of these cases used the bad tendency test to reject free speech claims. The prewar scholars he cited to support his analysis of the original meaning of the First Amendment themselves criticized the reliance by their judicial contemporaries on the bad tendency test. Yet Chafee made the incredible assertion that, over the entire course of American history following the Revolution, the "disastrous" prosecutions under the Sedition Act of 1798 constituted the only attempt to apply the bad tendency test before the cases brought under the Espionage Act.[87]

Chafee peremptorily dismissed recent prewar decisions incompatible with his personal views. He rarely mentioned those cases and never discussed any in detail. Instead, he lamented that prior free speech cases lacked sufficient rigor and were "too few, too varied in their character, and often too easily solved to develop any definite boundary between lawful and unlawful speech."[88] Chafee promoted the historical fiction that the "failure" of prior courts "to formulate any principle for drawing a boundary line around the right of free speech" left the judges who decided the Espionage

---

[83] Id. at 952–53.

[84] Leonard W. Levy, Legacy of Suppression: Freedom of Speech and Press in Early American History (1960).

[85] See David M. Rabban, The Ahistorical Historian: Leonard Levy on Freedom of Expression in Early American History, 37 Stan. L. Rev. 795 (1985).

[86] Chafee, supra note 62, at 2; Chafee, supra note 68. In a notebook entitled "Freedom of Speech," Chafee kept lists of state and federal cases decided before he wrote his article. Chafee Papers, supra note 11, Box 30, Folder 8.

[87] Chafee-Harvard, supra note 6, at 952.

[88] Id. at 944.

Act cases without any guidance. As a result, he lamented, judges were able "to impose standards of their own"[89] and create a "revival of the doctrines of indirect causation and constructive intent" based on the bad tendency theory.[90]

According to Chafee, Hand's opinion in *Masses* gave "the fullest attention to the meaning of free speech during the war"[91] while applying the "normal" and "ordinary" test for punishing speech.[92] He complained that the Second Circuit, by reversing Hand, rejected the "common-law test of incitement" and "deprived us of the only standard of criminal speech there was, since there had been no well-considered discussion of the meaning of free speech in the First Amendment." In Chafee's opinion, the Second Circuit, perhaps unwittingly, thereby established the "old-time doctrine of indirect causation in the minds of district judges throughout the country."[93] In most subsequent Espionage Act decisions, Chafee unhappily reported, "bad tendency has been the test of criminality."[94] A few judges "stemmed the tide,"[95] but Chafee found "astounding" the "large number of cases which ignore the clear meaning of the statute" as interpreted by Hand.[96] Judicial misconstruction of the Espionage Act, Chafee complained, made its application worse than the Sedition Act of 1798, which at least allowed truth as a defense.[97]

Chafee never acknowledged that the Espionage Act decisions he attacked were consistent with the prewar cases he largely ignored and his scholarly predecessors heavily criticized. He did not point out that the prewar cases actually drew a tight boundary line that excluded, through the use of the bad tendency test, much speech he thought should be protected. Such concessions would have weakened, perhaps irreparably, the protective interpretation of the First Amendment he was trying to construct, particularly because the prewar decisions could not be attributed to the excesses of wartime excitement. It was Chafee, not the judges he criticized, who tried to impose a standard of his own. In his discussion of the crucial bad tendency test, Chafee allowed the passion of his newly discovered belief in the democratic value of political dissent to compromise his scholarly integrity.

After freeing himself from the burdens of history and precedent, Chafee, with even more ingenuity and disingenuousness,

---

[89] Id. at 959.
[90] Id. at 965.
[91] Id. at 961.
[92] Id. at 961, 963.
[93] Id. at 964.
[94] Id. at 968.
[95] Id. at 965.
[96] Id. at 961 n. 93.
[97] Id. at 965.

developed his clever and erroneous interpretation of clear and present danger. Chafee opened his analysis of the four Espionage Act cases decided by the Supreme Court in March 1919 with the shockingly inaccurate statement that *Sugarman, Schenck,* and *Frohwerk* "were clear cases of incitement to resist the draft, so that no real question of free speech arose." He did not discuss the facts of any of these cases; to have done so would have undermined this crucial conclusion. Chafee then focused on *Schenck,* which on its facts presented the weakest free speech claim, because it contained Holmes's "fullest discussion" of the First Amendment.[98]

Chafee quoted extensively from the paragraph in *Schenck* that included the phrase *clear and present danger* and italicized the sentence containing this phrase: "The question in every case is whether the words used are used in such circumstances and are of such a nature as to create a clear and present danger that they will bring about the substantive evils that Congress has a right to prevent." Chafee maintained that the entire passage "substantially agrees" with Schofield's prewar scholarship, with Hand's opinions in *Masses,* and with Chafee's own "investigation of the history and political purpose of the First Amendment." "It is unfortunate," Chafee admitted, "that 'the substantive evils' are not more specifically defined, but if they mean overt acts of interference with the war, then Justice Holmes draws the boundary line very close to the test of incitement at common law and clearly makes the punishment of words for their bad tendency impossible."[99]

Chafee did not explain why the definition of substantive evils as overt acts of interference with the war entailed the substitution of an incitement test for the bad tendency approach. Moreover, for the remainder of his analysis Chafee neglected his provisional "if" and assumed that Holmes did conceive of clear and present danger as a protective alternative to bad tendency. Chafee provided no support for his assumption that Holmes actually meant what Chafee said he might have meant, except to cite *Peaslee.* Chafee asserted that in using the words *proximity and degree* in *Schenck* as well as in *Peaslee,* Holmes recognized "the close relation between free speech and criminal attempts."[100] In Chafee's view, *Peaslee* held that attempts "must come dangerously near success" to be punished.[101] The *Peaslee* opinion itself, however, stated only that the issue is whether they "come near enough to the accomplishment of the substantive offense," a determination which "may vary

---

[98] Id. at 967.
[100] Id.

[99] Id.
[101] Id. at 963.

with circumstances."[102] Holmes also made clear throughout all his discussions of criminal attempts that the seriousness of the threatened crime, whether a fire, a murder, or an obstruction of the war effort, is a crucial circumstance.

After reading an unjustifiable libertarian meaning into clear and present danger and identifying it as the "Supreme Court test," Chafee characterized *Debs* as a deviation from this proper standard. If Holmes had applied the clear and present danger test in *Debs,* Chafee maintained, "it is hard to see how he could have been held guilty." Chafee also recognized that Holmes, by accepting "the verdict as proof that actual interference with the war was intended and was the proximate effect of the words used," had allowed Debs to be convicted "merely because the jury thought his speech had a tendency to bring about resistance to the draft." "If the Supreme Court test is to mean anything more than a passing observation," Chafee concluded, "it must be used to upset convictions for words when the trial judge did not insist that they must create 'a clear and present danger' of overt acts."[103]

Chafee did not analyze *Frohwerk* at all, perhaps to avoid having to explain away another embarrassing deviation from the clear and present danger standard that Holmes used in only one of his three Espionage Act decisions. Any attention to *Frohwerk* would have made it even harder for Chafee to maintain that clear and present danger was "anything more than a passing observation" in elaboration of the bad tendency test Holmes allegedly had rejected by using this phrase. Throughout his article, Chafee never wavered from his adherence to clear and present danger as a protective alternative to the restrictive bad tendency test. Despite the generally "inconclusive" nature of the Supreme Court's Espionage Act decisions, he confidently asserted that "they lay down a good test for future free speech cases, 'clear and present danger.'"[104] Chafee proclaimed that if this standard had been announced in the summer of 1917, rather than in the spring of 1919, many more Espionage Act prosecutions in the lower federal courts would have resulted in acquittals.[105]

In attempting to assimilate his misconstruction of clear and present danger to the incitement standard Hand used in *Masses,* Chafee seemed to have genuine difficulty recognizing that Hand's

---

[102] Commonwealth v. Peaslee, 177 Mass. 267, 271–72, 59 N.E. 55, 56 (1901), discussed infra, Chapter 6, at text accompanying note 192.

[103] Chafee-Harvard, supra note 6, at 967–68.

[104] Id. at 969.   [105] Id. at 968.

focus on the objective content of language was very different from Holmes's emphasis on the degree of proximity between speech and crime. At one point in his article, Chafee accurately concluded that Hand's test in *Masses* "places outside the limits of free speech one who counsels or advises others to violate existing laws."[106] Chafee, however, incorrectly stated at another point that this test would punish speech where there is "strong danger that it will cause injurious acts."[107] In a confusing combination of these two approaches, Chafee claimed that within "a range of circumstances is the point where direct causation begins and speech becomes punishable as incitement under the ordinary standards of statutory construction and the ordinary policy of free speech, which Judge Hand applied."[108]

Charles Amidon, the federal district judge in North Dakota who wrote several of the few protective Espionage Act decisions in the lower courts, criticized this passage in an otherwise congratulatory letter to Chafee. Amidon called Chafee's "remarkable" article "the ablest discussion of the First amendment to the Federal Constitution which has been made and will, I trust, challenge sufficient thought to right the public opinion of the nation on this important matter." Amidon agreed that Chafee drew "the line where it ought to be drawn, namely, that language, either written or spoken, which directly advises men to resist or violate laws, may be made a crime and prosecuted, notwithstanding the First Amendment." Yet he believed that Chafee had made a mistake by indicating that the relationship between language and speech is "simply a matter of degree to be determined by a jury, or of a tendency."[109] It is fascinating that Amidon equated degree with tendency despite Chafee's repeated objections to the bad tendency test and his strenuous efforts to characterize clear and present danger as requiring a much closer proximity between speech and crime. Amidon's reaction is understandable, however, because even Chafee's construction of clear and present danger, like the bad tendency test, examines the probable consequences of words rather than their objective meaning.

Chafee remained confused about the difference between incitement and clear and present danger while defending his own distinction between clear and present danger and bad tendency. Several people responded to Chafee's article by identifying bad

---

[106] Id. at 962.   [107] Id. at 961.
[108] Id. at 963.
[109] Letter from Judge Charles F. Amidon to Zechariah Chafee, Jr. 1, 4 (Aug. 29, 1919) (Chafee Papers, supra note 11, Box 4, Folder 1).

tendency as the ordinary test of criminality and defending its use by judges construing the Espionage Act. Professor Edward S. Corwin of Princeton University made this point in correspondence with Chafee,[110] as did a student note in the *Harvard Law Review,* which Chafee generously characterized as "able and thoughtful"[111] despite its criticism of his article. The most remarkable response, however, came from Alfred Bettman, who identified himself to Chafee as having written the government's briefs in *Schenck* and *Debs* "and other Espionage Act cases in the Supreme Court (subject, of course, to some touching up by my immediate chief, Mr. O'Brian)."[112]

Bettman wrote Chafee in September 1919 to congratulate him on the publication of "Freedom of Speech in War Time" and "to state that I agree most heartily with all that you say, subject to a few points." Bettman was quite defensive about the role of the Department of Justice in enforcing the Espionage Act. He felt it was unfair for critics to portray the Department as "the main offender in creating a system and atmosphere of intolerance, which in effect, if not technically, may have violated the First Amendment and which all must agree was one of the shadows in our conduct of the war." Bettman absolved Chafee of this portrayal, but he claimed that articles in *The New Republic* and other unspecified periodicals had at least hinted at it. Bettman responded that he and his colleagues "were more constantly engaged in preventing, discouraging and avoiding prosecutions, than in instituting or encouraging them." "The major part of our energies," he maintained, "went in stemming the tide of intolerance."[113] Government confessions of error in Espionage Act appeals, as in the *Baltzer* case that produced Holmes's draft dissent, provides some support for Bettman's perhaps overstated defense of his office.

Writing from private practice in 1919, Bettman agreed with many prowar liberals that the "present continuation of wartime intolerance of discussions of radical political and economic theories is a deplorable product of the war." "Much as I was troubled during the war by some of the manifestations of this intolerance," he added, "the post-war manifestations have been a source of fearful anxiety."

---

[110] See letter from Zechariah Chafee, Jr., to Edward S. Corwin (Jan. 3, 1921) (Chafee Papers, supra note 11, Box 14, Folder 7).

[111] Note, The Espionage Act and the Limits of Legal Toleration, 33 Harv. L. Rev. 442, 443 (1920); Zechariah Chafee, Jr., A Contemporary State Trial – The United States Versus Jacob Abrams et al., 33 Harv. L. Rev. 747, 771 (1920).

[112] Letter from Alfred Bettman to Zechariah Chafee, Jr. 1 (Sept. 20, 1919) (Chafee Papers, supra note 11, Box 14, Folder 3).

[113] Id. at 1, 2.

Bettman closed his letter by expressing his gratitude to Chafee and others "who, instead of joining in the mob attacks on Socialism, Bolshevism etc., or remaining supinely silent in the face of official lawlessness now prevalent against so-called radicals, bravely take the field for the preservation of our precious civil liberties."[114]

Despite this extraordinary praise, Bettman identified as a "doubtful point" a conclusion he considered implicit in Chafee's article and had already rebutted in his reply brief to Roe in *Debs*. Bettman understood Chafee to maintain that the likelihood of guilty verdicts by juries in Espionage Act prosecutions rendered unconstitutional an otherwise constitutional law. Bettman vigorously disagreed. He defined the doctrines of indirect causation and presumptive intent as basic principles of criminal law. "I do not see," he wrote Chafee, "how the First Amendment can be construed as eliminating, without express legislative decree, those accepted general principles of the criminal law in cases based upon verbal or written utterances." Bettman also did not detect any flaw in the trial judge's reliance on the bad tendency test in his charge to the jury in the *Debs* case. Bettman acknowledged the greater likelihood of jury verdicts against unpopular speakers during a war, but he denied that even the probability of erroneous verdicts made the bad tendency test unconstitutional. Whether such a probability should create an exception to the basic principles of criminal law for "a particular class of cases," he reasoned, "is a question of legislative policy and not constitutional law."[115]

In a subsequent letter, Bettman further conceded that a constitutional provision restraining jury discretion might be needed, but he denied that the First Amendment could be interpreted to serve this function. "That the individual needed protection against the jury," he added, "was a thought which could hardly have occurred to the framers of the amendment." Bettman believed that the constitutional guarantee of free speech should "unquestionably" prevent any legislative attempt "to suppress the absolutely free discussion of past, present and future governmental policies" and officials, and admitted that many Espionage Act convictions violated this conception of the First Amendment.[116] He criticized federal judges in some of these cases for having "lost their heads," for giving "unfair charges," and for not exercising sufficient "control over the juries."[117] He hoped that the Supreme Court would hand down a decision in at least one of the Espionage Act cases still

---

[114] Id. at 3.   [115] Id. at 2.

[116] Letter from Alfred Bettman to Zechariah Chafee, Jr. 3 (Oct. 27, 1919) (Chafee Papers, supra note 11, Box 14, Folder 3).

[117] Id. at 2

pending that "will assist the Department of Justice during the next war in counteracting the pressure of public intolerance."[118] Bettman, however, maintained that neither criminal nor constitutional law mandated restrictions on jury determinations of presumptive intent based on the bad tendency of speech.

Bettman included a comment about *Frohwerk* that indirectly underlined Chafee's devious neglect of this case as part of his misconstruction of clear and present danger. Bettman believed that "Frohwerk is one of the clearest examples of the political prisoner." Frohwerk's articles, Bettman wrote Chafee, were clearly "an advocacy of a change in governmental policy as distinguished from advocacy of obstruction of existing governmental policy, and seemed to me therefore to fall within the protection of the constitutional guaranty of free speech and press." Bettman was puzzled that Chafee cited *Frohwerk* as a case in which the First Amendment was not involved, "in other words, as one of the justified convictions."[119]

Chafee wrote a lengthy and respectful response to Bettman's first letter in which he restated his confused conflation of *Masses* and *Schenck*. Chafee disagreed with Bettman's view that "the principle of indirect causation is part of the criminal common law relating to utterance." He recognized that "there is always a chain of possible events between an utterance and actual interference with the activities of government," and added that the test of criminality is "just a question of degree how short that chain must be." Chafee concluded that the "common law has fixed that point with reasonable certainty at the place where the utterance furnishes a clear and present danger of a criminal act, to use the language of Justice Holmes in the Schenck case." Chafee then cited Hand to support his position.[120] In his response to Bettman, as in his article, Chafee failed to recognize that Hand's direct incitement test, by focusing on words rather than on probable effects, differed significantly from clear and present danger.

Hand himself brought this difference to Chafee's attention several months later. He compared his approach in *Masses,* which provided "an absolute and objective test to language," with Holmes's requirement in *Abrams v. United States* that "the connection between the words used and the evil aimed at should be immediate and direct."[121] Chafee replied by reiterating his attempt

---

[118] Id. at 5.   [119] Id. at 2.

[120] Letter from Chafee to Bettman, supra note 70.

[121] Letter from Learned Hand to Zechariah Chafee (Dec. 3, 1919) (Chafee Papers, supra note 11, Box 4, Folder 20), reprinted in Gerald Gunther, Learned Hand and the Origins of Modern First Amendment Doctrine: Some Fragments of History, 27 Stan. L. Rev. 719, 762, 763 (1975).

to "embrace" both approaches "in defining the constitutional limits of speech." He suggested that "incitement to resistance to law or violation of law," Hand's standard, "can be punished only if it satisfies the danger test," Holmes's standard.[122] Without referring specifically to this suggestion, Hand restated his preference for his test "based upon the nature of the utterance itself" over Holmes's "test of immediacy and directness."[123]

In *Freedom of Speech*, the book he published in 1920, Chafee inserted additional material in his discussion of clear and present danger that seemed to respond to some of the comments by Hand and Bettman. Chafee clearly recognized a difference between Hand and Holmes. Holmes, Chafee remarked, "interprets the Espionage Act more widely than Judge Hand, in making the nature of the words only one element of danger, and in not requiring that the utterances shall in themselves satisfy an objective standard." Chafee acknowledged that Holmes thereby "loses the great administrative advantages of Judge Hand's test" and "allows conviction for expressions of opinion uttered with a bad intention."[124] Chafee also included in his book, as he had not in his article, a discussion of *Frohwerk*, the case Bettman criticized as an unjustified conviction. Chafee admitted that *Frohwerk* was a "more difficult" case than *Schenck*. "Even in the Department of Justice," Chafee wrote while closely paraphrasing but not citing Bettman's letter, "there was considerable question whether" the articles under review "were not an advocacy of a change in governmental policy as distinguished from advocacy of obstruction of such policy, and it did not appear that there was any special effort to reach men who were subject to the draft."[125]

Despite these concessions, Chafee reiterated his interpretation of clear and present danger as a protective alternative to the bad tendency test. While recognizing advantages to Hand's approach, Chafee asserted that Holmes's interpretation of the Espionage Act had benefits of its own. Holmes's insistence that the relation of speech and crime "must be so close that the words constitute 'a clear and present danger' of injury," Chafee emphasized, meant that "[w]ords and intentions are not punishable for their own

---

[122] Letter from Zechariah Chafee, Jr., to Learned Hand (Jan. 6, 1920) (Hand Papers, Box 15, Folder 26, Harvard Law School Library) [hereinafter Hand Papers], reprinted in Gunther, supra note 121, at 764.

[123] Letter from Learned Hand to Zechariah Chafee, Jr. (Jan. 8, 1920) (Chafee Papers, supra note 11, Box 4, Folder 20), reprinted in Gunther, supra note 121, at 764, 765.

[124] Chafee, supra note 13, at 89.   [125] Id. at 90.

sake, or merely for their tendency to discourage citizens at war."[126] Chafee also rescued the clear and present danger test while acknowledging the weaknesses of *Frohwerk*. He ascribed to Holmes the position that "on the record as it was the evidence might conceivably have been sufficient to sustain a conviction, since the circumstances and the intention, though not the words *per se,* might satisfy the danger-test."[127] Chafee ignored the inconvenient fact that Holmes, while using the language of bad tendency throughout *Frohwerk,* nowhere mentioned "the danger-test."

Chafee's attempt to construct a protective interpretation of the First Amendment made much of his writing seem more like a legal brief, or even a sermon, than legal scholarship. In the last paragraph of "Freedom of Speech in War Time," the appearance of scholarly restraint that Chafee had tried, with varying degrees of success, to maintain gave way to a moving statement of the strong commitment to freedom of political expression he developed during World War I.

> Those who gave their lives for freedom would be the last to thank us for throwing aside so lightly the great traditions of our race. Not satisfied to have justice and almost all the people with our cause, we insisted on an artificial unanimity of opinion behind the war. Keen intellectual grasp of the President's aims by the nation at large was very difficult when the opponents of his idealism ranged unchecked while the men who urged greater idealism went to prison. In our efforts to silence those who advocated peace without victory we prevented at the very start that vigorous threshing out of fundamentals which might to-day have saved us from a victory without peace.[128]

These words captured the disillusion and second thoughts of many progressive intellectuals.

Perhaps because he found himself writing more as an advocate than as a scholar, Chafee emphasized his reliance on policy as well as on law throughout his article. Probably for the same reason, he often left ambiguous the extent to which any particular argument was based on either. At times, Chafee seemed to equate the two. In his "key" paragraph, Chafee claimed that the First Amendment gives "binding force" to "political wisdom."[129] Later, in declaring that the First Amendment precludes the bad tendency test, Chafee

---

[126] Id. at 89.
[128] Chafee-Harvard, supra note 6, at 973.

[127] Id. at 90.
[129] Id. at 957.

confidently maintained that the "history of the Amendment and the political function of free speech corroborate each other and make this conclusion plain."[130] Chafee more frequently resorted to independent arguments from policy to reinforce his legal analysis. Near the beginning of his article, he stated his intention to look beyond purely constitutional issues. The First Amendment, he suggested, not only establishes the constitutional boundaries of free speech, but also serves as "an exhortation and a guide for the action of Congress inside that boundary." The fundamental policies embodied in the First Amendment "should make Congress reluctant and careful in the enactment of all restrictions upon utterance, even though the courts will not refuse to enforce them as unconstitutional."[131]

As Jerold Auerbach has observed, Chafee tried "to cover his bet on the intention of the framers."[132] Chafee maintained that "the meaning of the First Amendment did not crystallize in 1791," but had developed over time. "The framers," he acknowledged, "would probably have been horrified at the thought of protecting books by Darwin or Bernard Shaw, but 'liberty of speech' is no more confined to the speech they thought permissible than 'commerce' in another clause is limited to the sailing vessels and horse-drawn vehicles of 1787."[133] "Whether or not the Sedition Act was unconstitutional," Chafee also asserted (while making clear his own view that it was), "it surely defeated the fundamental policy of the First Amendment, the open discussion of public affairs."[134] Similarly, after minimizing the importance of prewar free speech cases, Chafee warned that many of them "seem to ignore so seriously the economic and political facts of our time, that they are precedents of very dubious value."[135] In discussing the Espionage Act, he emphasized that "freedom of speech is not only a limit on Congressional power, but a policy to be observed by the courts in applying constitutional statutes to utterance."[136]

Chafee also did not think that current understandings should limit the meaning of the First Amendment. In response to Edward S. Corwin's defense of jury determinations of "bad tendency," he argued that "to give the Constitution a real meaning, it is necessary to look at the functional value of freedom of speech and not merely at contemporary practice."[137] Indeed, Chafee confided to

---

[130] Id. at 960.   [131] Id. at 934.

[132] Auerbach, supra note 57, at 522.

[133] Chafee-Harvard, supra note 6, at 594–95.

[134] Id. at 953.   [135] Id. at 944–45.

[136] Id. at 960.

[137] Letter from Chafee to Corwin, supra note 110.

Learned Hand that even the "best test we can find . . . will some-times break down," making "channels outside the law" the ulti-mate safeguard for free speech. Chafee's goal, he informed Hand, was "to produce greater tolerance in Judges and jurors and the public at large, so that when the next emergency arises we shall be better prepared."[138] "Freedom of Speech in War Time" is better understood as an effort toward that goal than as a work of conven-tional scholarship.

Chafee's erroneous interpretation of clear and present danger is the most important and dramatic evidence of his willingness to sacrifice scholarship for advocacy. Chafee apparently made a con-scious and pragmatic decision to become a propagandist for the most protective construction he could derive from Justice Holmes's Espionage Act decisions. In a letter to Corwin, Chafee even referred to "my danger test."[139] There is substantial evidence, however, that Chafee personally favored Hand's incitement stan-dard. In "Freedom of Speech in War Time," Chafee gave Hand lav-ish praise for his decision in *Masses*. After analyzing *Masses* at length, Chafee concluded that "[t]here is no finer judicial state-ment of the right of free speech."[140] He later dedicated *Freedom of Speech* to Learned Hand.[141]

Despite his awkward attempts to reconcile the differing approaches of Hand and Holmes, Chafee acknowledged through-out his career both that Holmes's clear and present danger lan-guage could not be entirely reconciled with Hand's incitement standard and that Hand's approach was better as well as different. Hand wrote Chafee just after he finished reading *Freedom of Speech* to clarify the difference Hand had always recognized between him-self and Holmes.

> I am not wholly in love with Holmes's test and the reason is this. Once you admit that the matter is one of degree, while you may put it where it genuinely belongs, you so obviously make it a matter of administration, i.e., you give to Tomdickandharry, D.J., so much latitude [Hand here wrote and struck out "as his own fears may require"] that the jig is

138 Letter from Zechariah Chafee, Jr., to Learned Hand (March 28, 1921) (Hand Papers, supra note 122, Box 15, Folder 26), reprinted in Gunther, supra note 121, at 773.

139 Letter from Chafee to Corwin, supra note 110.

140 Chafee-Harvard, supra note 6, at 962.

141 Chafee, supra note 13, at iii. See letter from Zechariah Chafee to Learned Hand (Oct. 25, 1920) (Hand Papers, supra note 122, Box 15, Folder 26), reprinted in Gunther, supra note 121, at 766–67 (asking Hand for permission to dedicate book to him).

at once up. Besides their Ineffabilities, the Nine Elder Statesmen, have not shown themselves wholly immune from the
"herd instinct" and what seems "immediate and direct" today may seem very remote next year even though the circumstances surrounding the utterance be unchanged. I own I
should prefer a qualitative formula, hard, conventional, difficult to evade.[142]

"I agree with you," Chafee wrote in response, "that Holmes' distinction would prove unworkable in many cases. The Jury would
go over it rough shod." Hand's test, Chafee added, "is surely easier
to apply."[143] In a letter written almost thirty years later to Alexander Meiklejohn, Chafee acknowledged the importance and dis-
tinctiveness of Hand's approach in *Masses,* and indicated his continuing preference for the incitement standard over Holmes's
clear and present danger test.[144] Chafee was even more direct in
his reminiscences in 1952, writing that "I still like better Judge
Learned Hand's phrase . . . 'direct incitement to violent
resistance.'"[145] Chafee must have decided that the best chance of
obtaining judicial support for a more protective interpretation of
the First Amendment was to argue from language already
accepted by a unanimous Supreme Court rather than to promote
a better standard, which, as its author himself realized, had "met
with almost unanimous disapproval by other Federal judges,"[146]
including the justices of the Supreme Court.

Hand indicated his own approval of Chafee's approach after reading *Freedom of Speech:* "You have, I dare say, done well to take what has
fallen from Heaven and insist that it is manna rather than to set up
any independent solution."[147] Chafee acknowledged his pragmatic
motivation in less explicit terms by replying that "we ought to take
the best test we can find even though it will sometimes break
down."[148] A generation later Chafee seemed to suggest that Holmes
himself had made a similar pragmatic compromise in writing
Schenck, Frohwerk, and *Debs.* Alluding to the relationship between bad

---

[142] Letter from Learned Hand to Zechariah Chafee, Jr. (Jan. 2, 1921) (Chafee
    Papers, supra note 11, Box 4, Folder 20), reprinted in Gunther, supra note
    121, at 769, 770.
[143] Letter from Chafee to Hand, supra note 138.
[144] Letter from Zechariah Chafee, Jr. to Alexander Meiklejohn 2 (Nov. 23, 1948)
    (Chafee Papers, supra note 11, Box 2, Folder 16), quoted in part in Gunther,
    supra note 121, at 747 n.153.
[145] Chafee, supra note 62, at 8–9.
[146] Letter from Hand to Chafee, supra note 123.
[147] Letter from Hand to Chafee, supra note 142.
[148] Letter from Chafee to Hand, supra note 138.

tendency and clear and present danger he rejected in his original article, Chafee wrote Meiklejohn in 1948 that "Holmes could not possibly have convinced his colleagues that all speech which tended to produce evasion of the draft was immune." In any event, Chafee remained certain that these decisions, whether an expression of Holmes's personal views or the best he could get his colleagues to accept, had subsequently "saved" the United States from the horrible lower court interpretations of the Espionage Act and had "kept down suppression during World War II."[149] Chafee's strenuous and effective public support for a standard whose weaknesses he acknowledged in private is the most striking manifestation of the pragmatism that lay behind his entire approach to the First Amendment.

Chafee's transformation of clear and present danger was adopted almost immediately by Justices Holmes and Brandeis. By the time Holmes wrote his *Abrams* dissent in November 1919, just eight months after *Schenck, Frohwerk,* and *Debs,* and five months after Chafee's article in the *Harvard Law Review,* Holmes had accepted as his own the "manna" into which Chafee had converted this phrase. Brandeis relied even more explicitly on Chafee's interpretation of clear and present danger in the First Amendment opinions he began to write in 1920.

DEWEY'S REVISED ANALYSIS OF FREE SPEECH

Of the major prewar progressive thinkers, only Dewey addressed free speech issues in his postwar writings. Like Chafee, Dewey retained the progressive emphasis on social over individual rights while recognizing substantial social interests in free speech he had not perceived before the war. Dewey helped form the ACLU in 1920, and he objected to various forms of political repression

---

[149] Letter from Chafee to Meiklejohn, supra note 144, at 2, 3. Chafee elaborated this point in his review of Meiklejohn's book, Free Speech and its Relation to Self-Government (1948). Chafee, the lawyer, condescended to Meiklejohn, the philosopher:

> Even if Holmes had agreed with Mr. Meiklejohn's view of the First Amendment, his insistence on such absolutism would not have persuaded a single colleague, and scores of men would have gone to prison who have been speaking freely for three decades. After all, a judge who is trying to establish a doctrine which the Supreme Court will promulgate as law cannot write like a solitary philosopher. He has to convince at least four men in a specific group and convince them very soon. The true alternative to Holmes's view of the First Amendment was not at all the perfect immunity for public discussion which Mr. Meiklejohn desires. It was no immunity at all in the face of legislation.

Zechariah Chafee, Jr., Book Review, 62 Harv. L. Rev. 891, 900–901 (1949).

throughout the 1920s. But he did not become actively involved in the work of the ACLU or write extensively about free speech until the 1930s.[150]

Perhaps the best evidence of the increased importance Dewey placed on free speech can be found in his heavily revised 1932 edition of *Ethics*,[151] the book he first published in 1908. In the 1908 edition, Dewey included a single paragraph under the heading "freedom of thought and affection."[152] In the 1932 edition, Dewey wrote more than ten pages under the heading "liberty of thought and expression."[153] These ten pages applied many of the major themes of Dewey's work, such as the fulfillment of the individual through society and the fundamental importance of education in a democracy, to the specific issue of free speech. These pages also emphasized, as Dewey's prewar writings had not, that free speech is a fundamental right protected by the Constitution and threatened by economic and political power.

Free speech, Dewey proclaimed, is the central right in a democracy because the essential democratic principle is persuasion rather than coercion.[154] The relationship of free speech to the proper functioning of a democracy also prompted Dewey to recognize the expressive rights of minorities. All new ideas, Dewey maintained, begin with a minority, often a very small one. A "genuine democracy," therefore, "will always secure to every individual a maximum of liberty of expression and will establish the conditions which will enable the minority by use of communication and persuasion to become a majority."[155]

In addition to stressing the role of free speech in democratic political life, Dewey viewed freedom of expression as providing an opportunity for personal growth that simultaneously benefits society. Dewey conceded the legitimacy of the frequent defense of free speech as a safety-valve for discontent,[156] the defense he himself

---

[150] Robert B. Westbrook, John Dewey and American Democracy 278 (1991); Paul L. Murphy, The Meaning of Free Speech: First Amendment Freedoms from Wilson to FDR 127 (1972).

[151] Dewey-Ethics-II, supra note 14. Professor Westbrook describes the 1932 edition of Ethics as "heavily revised." Westbrook, supra note 150, at 413. See also John Dewey, Philosophies of Freedom (1928), in 3 John Dewey, The Later Works, 1925–53, at 92 (Jo Ann Boydston ed., 1984) [hereinafter Later Works].

[152] John Dewey and James H. Tufts, Ethics, reprinted in 5 John Dewey, The Middle Works 1899–1924, at 399–400 (Jo Ann Boydston ed., 1980).

[153] Dewey-Ethics II, supra note 14, at 398–409.

[154] Id. at 398–99.   [155] Id. at 404.

[156] Id. at 402.

had highlighted in his earlier edition of *Ethics*.[157] By his revised edition, however, Dewey maintained that this defense based on expediency valued speech only at its "lowest level."[158] Dewey wanted to emphasize the "positive values involved" in protecting speech.[159] He maintained that "public expression," by allowing people to learn from each other's ideas, "gives opportunity for growth" to all but "those who are most completely hardened in their own opinion and conceit."[160]

The opportunity for growth through discussion, Dewey emphasized, benefits society as well as the individual. He called free speech "the best method humanity has discovered for combining conservation of attained values with progress toward new goods."[161] By contrast, repression of speech dooms the intellectual life of a society to mediocrity. "It is not merely the liberty of the individual that suffers" from repression, he concluded, "but the health of society and the development of its culture."[162]

Dewey related the democratic and developmental functions of free speech by invoking the central themes of his prewar thought. He maintained that "the cause of democracy is bound up with development of the intellectual capacities of each member of society."[163] According to Dewey, the commitment of Americans to public education reflected the widespread recognition that schools play a crucial role in supporting democracy by fostering the intellectual growth of students.[164] Dewey added that law and legal institutions, by protecting free speech, can themselves contribute to education in a democracy.[165] Dewey also observed, as he had in other contexts before World War I, that economic inequalities prevented many, if not most, Americans from "effective access to the means of real cultivation of their capacities."[166]

In one crucial respect, however, Dewey departed dramatically from his prewar writings, which repeatedly emphasized the state as a force for good. By contrast, his postwar discussion of free speech identified state power as a danger to civil liberties. Rather than portraying the threat of government to individual liberties as legitimate at the time of the American Revolution but as a barrier to progress in the twentieth century, as he had before the war, Dewey observed "the fact that it is much more of a task to maintain intel-

---

[157] Dewey, supra note 152, at 399–400.
[158] Dewey-Ethics II, supra note 14, at 402.
[159] Id.   [160] Id.
[161] Id.   [162] Id. at 403.
[163] Id. at 406.   [164] Id.
[165] Id. at 405–6.   [166] Id. at 408.

lectual courage and energy than the founders of the [constitutional] system contemplated."[167]

Dewey wrote in 1932 about repression of speech in words that could have been used to describe the actual situation during and after World War I. In the United States, he believed, the

> attack on freedom comes from those who are already entrenched in power, economic and political, and who fear that general exercise of civil rights, such as freedom of speech, writing, press, assembling, although guaranteed by the Constitution, will disturb the existing order. Accordingly, they claim that every such expression, when it takes the form of criticisms of the *status quo* and of proposal of significant change, is a dangerous radicalism, seditious, subversive of law and order. They believe in freedom of thought and communication as long as it repeats their own convictions, but only under this condition. . . . Those who strive to sustain even the rights nominally guaranteed by the bill of rights of the Constitution find themselves attacked as dangerous enemies of the nation and its Constitution.[168]

Dewey added that direct attacks on free speech by police and vigilantes, even though they were serious, had been less significant than the "more insidious means" of manipulating public opinion by propaganda consisting of half-truths and falsehood distributed "under the guise of disinterested publicity" by people representing "hidden interests."[169]

In other postwar writings, Dewey made clear that he retained his prewar opposition to individualism even as he increasingly addressed threats to free speech.[170] His 1936 essay, "Liberalism and Civil Liberties," captured most succinctly the relationship between his fundamental rejection of individualism and his

---

[167] Id. at 400.   [168] Id. at 400–1.

[169] Id. at 401–2.

[170] John Dewey, Liberalism and Civil Liberties (1936), reprinted in 11 Later Works, supra note 151, at 372 (1987) [hereinafter Dewey, Liberalism and Civil Liberties]; see also John Dewey, Individualism, Old and New (1929), reprinted in 5 Later Works, supra note 151, at 41 (1984) (containing a collection of essays originally published in The New Republic in 1929 and 1930). In these essays, Dewey reiterated his longstanding criticism of American "rugged – or is it ragged? – individualism." Id. at 45. He emphasized the need to create "a new individualism" suitable for the modern "collective age." Id. at 55–56. Dewey asserted his inability to depict the new individualism "until more progress has been made in its production." Id. at 89. He nevertheless described it as "an integrated individuality," id. at 122, that would find expression "through personal participation in the development of a shared culture," id. at 57.

belated attention to free speech. In this essay, Dewey attributed "the present confused and precarious condition of civil liberties" in the United States to the unresolved tension between individualistic and social justifications for protecting them.[171]

As in his earlier work, Dewey stressed the historical origins of liberalism in the battle against political authoritarianism. This battle, he maintained, led to a conception of government as inherently antagonistic to individual liberties and to a theory of natural rights "that inhere in individuals prior to political organization and independent of political authority." Most unfortunately from Dewey's perspective, freedom to engage in business activity became included in the rights guaranteed against government intervention. He illustrated this point by mentioning the Supreme Court's recent decision that invalidated a key piece of New Deal legislation, the Agricultural Adjustment Act, on constitutional grounds. Although Dewey himself saw no relationship between "regulation of agriculture and the right, say, of free speech," he stressed that "the two things have been brought together in the theory that there is an inherent opposition between political power and individual liberty."[172]

The individualistic justification for civil liberties, Dewey observed, had become increasingly ineffective as more complicated social relations made it harder to maintain public order. In such circumstances, "*merely* individual claims will be forced to give way in practice to social claims." As proof, Dewey cited the ease with which courts rejected First Amendment claims whenever judges believed that the exercise of free speech endangered the public welfare. "It is a commonplace," Dewey elaborated, that civil liberties nominally protected by the Constitution "go into the discard when a nation is engaged in war."[173] Yet this "commonplace" was not obvious to Dewey in 1917, when he minimized the threat to pacifist speech. Nor had Dewey recognized the many judicial decisions before World War I that cited the public welfare as the basis for denying free speech claims.

In addition to emphasizing the weakness of the individualistic justification for civil liberties in the modern age, Dewey accused laissez-faire liberals of bad faith. "They constantly protest against any 'interference' on the part of government with freedom of business enterprise," he protested, "but are almost uniformly silent in the case of even flagrant violations of civil liberties – in spite of

---

[171] Dewey, Liberalism and Civil Liberties, supra note 170, at 373.

[172] Id. at 373.

[173] Id. at 374.

lip service to liberal ideas and professed adulation of the Constitution."[174] Dewey had a simple explanation for this inconsistency: "Business interests have been and still are socially and politically dominant."[175]

While rejecting individualism and laissez faire, Dewey emphasized his own commitment to civil liberties based on their contribution to the public welfare. He distinguished "civil" liberties from "natural" and "political" liberties, pointing out that the "term *civil* is directly connected with the idea of citizenship." Dewey closed his essay by urging liberals to abandon "the doctrine that liberty is a full-fledged ready-made possession of individuals independent of social institutions and arrangements, and to realize that social control, especially of economic forces, is necessary in order to render secure the liberties of the individual, including civil liberties."[176]

Even though he attacked the contradiction in laissez-faire liberalism between support for economic liberties and indifference to civil liberties, Dewey never acknowledged that he and other prewar progressives had themselves displayed substantial indifference to civil liberties while advocating increased regulation of economic liberties. Moreover, in stressing that social control over economic forces is necessary to secure individual liberties, Dewey left ambiguous the extent to which other forms of social control, perhaps including control of free speech itself, might occasionally be needed to secure these liberties. Dewey's postwar writings, however, did make clear that World War I had made him much more sensitive to both political and economic threats to freedom of expression. Dewey extended his prewar emphasis on the social basis of rights to the defense of free speech, especially in "Liberalism and Civil Liberties." Just as Chafee's 1919 article had relied on Pound's prewar analysis of rights as social interests while placing more weight on the relative social value of free speech, Dewey relied on his own prewar social definition of rights while justifying his new postwar commitment to free speech in the 1930s.

Justices Holmes and Brandeis also became committed to the defense of free speech in the aftermath of World War I. In mostly dissenting opinions beginning in the fall of 1919, they made forceful arguments for protecting free speech through the First Amend-

---

[174] Id.

[175] Id. Making a similar point in Individualism, Old and New, supra note 170, at 85, Dewey stressed the "irony of the gospel of 'individualism' in business conjoined with suppression of individuality in thought and speech."

[176] Dewey, Liberalism and Civil Liberties, supra note 170, at 373, 375.

ment. Chafee's creative misreading of clear and present danger provided the most important technical vehicle for Holmes and Brandeis to express their transformed interpretation of the First Amendment, for it allowed them to finesse their complicity in the traditional judicial rejection of free speech claims that extended through their own initial decisions in Espionage Act cases. As Brandeis developed his distinctive First Amendment jurisprudence in the 1920s, the similarities between his and Dewey's postwar views became clear, especially to Dewey himself. The process of transformation that began in 1917 with Roger Baldwin's organization of a Civil Liberties Bureau within the AUAM, and included Chafee and Dewey, reached the Supreme Court in November 1919, when Justices Holmes and Brandeis dissented in *Abrams v. United States*.[177]

[177] 250 U.S. 616 (1919).

8

Holmes, Brandeis,
and the Judicial Transformation
of the First Amendment after World War I

Justices Holmes and Brandeis joined the postwar civil libertarians between March and November 1919. As discussed in Chapter 6, in four related cases in March – *Schenck, Sugarman, Frohwerk,* and *Debs* – the Supreme Court unanimously rejected First Amendment challenges by socialists convicted for antiwar speech under the Espionage Act.[1] Brandeis wrote the Court's opinion in *Sugarman;* Holmes wrote the other three. In November, Holmes, joined by Brandeis, dissented on First Amendment grounds in *Abrams,* the Court's next Espionage Act decision.[2] The same factors that transformed many progressives into civil libertarians probably influenced Holmes and Brandeis as well. During the period between March and November, debate over the Versailles Peace Treaty prompted many Americans to realize that the war had failed to achieve the idealistic goals that justified their initial support of American intervention. These same months also marked the height of the postwar repression of radical speech, which horrified many people previously uninterested in free speech issues. Moreover, in June 1919, the *Harvard Law Review* published Chafee's "Freedom of Speech in War Time,"[3] which Holmes and Chafee discussed in July.

The dissent by Justice Holmes in *Abrams* relied heavily on Chafee's article. Holmes recognized the strategic possibilities of Chafee's misconstruction of Holmes's original use of the phrase *clear and present danger* in *Schenck.* He accepted as his own the pro-

---

[1] Schenck v. United States, 249 U.S. 47; Sugarman v. United States, 249 U.S. 182 (1919); Frohwerk v. United States, 249 U.S. 204 (1919); Debs v. United States, 249 U.S. 211 (1919).
[2] Abrams v. United States, 250 U.S. 616 (1919).
[3] Zechariah Chafee, Jr., Freedom of Speech in War Time, 32 Harv. L. Rev. 932 (1919).

tective meaning Chafee had erroneously read into that phrase. Holmes was thus able to express his changed views while claiming that the majority in *Abrams,* which closely followed the reasoning of his own unanimous Espionage Act opinions the previous March, had deviated from precedent.

Although the *Abrams* dissent marked the transformation of Holmes and Brandeis into defenders of free speech, they developed their new approach to the First Amendment in opinions throughout the 1920s. By the end of the Warren Court in the late 1960s, the mostly dissenting positions of Holmes and Brandeis in the 1920s had become the dominant perspective of the Supreme Court majority. Tracing judicial analysis of the First Amendment since 1920 reveals the content and ramifications of the "worthy tradition" begun by the postwar civil libertarians. It also provides the historical background for understanding more recent attacks on judicial interpretation of the First Amendment by critics who believe that this "worthy tradition" has become perverted by Supreme Court decisions during the past two decades.

From Holmes's dissent in *Abrams* through Brandeis's 1927 concurrence in *Whitney v. California,*[4] Holmes and Brandeis elevated clear and present danger to constitutional significance and clung to it as the doctrinal peg for the protective interpretation of the First Amendment it did not express when Holmes first used the phrase in *Schenck.* The two justices frequently dissented together in First Amendment cases during the 1920s, but Brandeis wrote most of the opinions after *Abrams.* Unlike Holmes, Brandeis cited Chafee directly while relying on him more heavily. Building on Chafee and Holmes, Brandeis elaborated and extended the meaning of clear and present danger to provide increasing protection for speech.

Despite their joint dissents in many cases, Holmes and Brandeis developed substantially different justifications for protecting speech. Holmes invoked the economic metaphor of the free market as his model to defend the free competition of ideas unrestrained by the state. By contrast, Brandeis emphasized the role of free speech in developing the individual character traits essential to the proper operation of a democratic society. His focus on free speech as part of the mutual and potentially reinforcing relationship between the individual and society closely resembled Dewey's postwar analysis of free speech, as Dewey himself recognized. For Brandeis, as for Dewey, by protecting free speech the state liberates individuals, who in turn contribute to society.

[4] Whitney v. California, 274 U.S. 357 (1927).

Although there were important differences between the competitive market model of Holmes and the democratic citizenship model of Brandeis, both justices challenged together the traditional judicial hostility to free speech claims that the Supreme Court majority extended through the 1920s. This challenge did not rely on the major prewar approaches to the defense of free speech. Holmes and Brandeis did not invoke either the core commitment to individual autonomy of the libertarian radicals, or the more traditional individualism represented most clearly by Cooley's view that the "constitutional limitations" on government power extend to both personal and economic liberties. Using Chafee as their primary scholarly guide made it easier for Holmes and Brandeis to neglect prewar discussion of free speech.

The Supreme Court majority, without exploring the differences between Holmes and Brandeis, eventually accepted and extended many of the protections for unpopular speech they initiated in dissenting and concurring opinions in the 1920s. Many current commentators view the Warren Court's 1969 per curiam decision in *Brandenburg v. Ohio*[5] as the culmination of the "worthy tradition" begun by the postwar civil libertarians. Yet the restrictive context in which the phrase *clear and present danger* first appeared in *Schenck* proved to be a continuing constraint on emerging First Amendment theory. Civil libertarians after World War I, beginning with Chafee, may have made an understandable strategic error in promoting clear and present danger as the verbal device with which to incorporate their recently discovered free speech values into the First Amendment. It might have been wiser for them to have followed their best instincts and, like Learned Hand in *Masses,* to have attempted a clean break with a hostile judicial tradition, even if that risked challenging the country's leading jurist and entailed passing up an opportunity to reform the existing tradition from within. The libertarian radicals whose work they obscured might have helped them develop a more thorough and convincing rationale for protecting free speech.

SUPREME COURT MAJORITY DECISIONS IN THE 1920s

Throughout the 1920s, the majority of the Supreme Court remained true to the restrictive judicial tradition of free speech analysis that extended through the initial Espionage Act opinions written by Holmes. Although they cited prewar cases with some frequency, the majority opinions relied particularly on *Schenck*,

[5] 395 U.S. 444 (1969).

Frohwerk, and *Debs.* The majority opinion in *Abrams* was entirely consistent with these earlier decisions. In *Debs,* Holmes concluded that *Schenck* had "disposed of" all First Amendment issues,[6] and Justice Clarke, writing for the majority in *Abrams,* held that objections to the constitutionality of the Espionage Act were "definitely negatived" by *Schenck* and *Frohwerk.*[7] Consistent with *Goldman*[8] and with Holmes's prior decisions, Clarke treated *Abrams* as presenting only evidentiary questions; he found that there was "some evidence, competent and substantial, before the jury, fairly tending to sustain the verdict."[9]

The defendants in *Abrams* were Russian immigrants who had published and distributed leaflets in English and Yiddish. These leaflets castigated President Wilson for sending American troops into Russia after the Bolshevik Revolution and urged a general strike in protest. The defendants had been charged and convicted under the 1918 amendments to the Espionage Act for attempting to harm the prosecution of the war. Justice Clarke conceded that the "primary purpose and intent" of these "defendant alien anarchists" might have been "to aid the cause of the Russian Revolution," an activity not proscribed by any law.[10] Yet just as Holmes had held that Debs's "general program" could not protect his speech if even an "incidental" and "indirect" part tended to encourage the obstruction of recruitment,[11] Clarke determined that Abrams could be punished for the "obvious effect" of his language – "defeat of the war program of the United States."[12] Holmes had said that the use of "words tending to obstruct the recruiting service" was evidence that Debs "meant that they should have that effect."[13] According to Clarke, "[m]en must be held to have intended, and to be accountable for, the effects which their acts were likely to produce."[14]

The other majority opinions in the 1920s reiterated these familiar themes. Interlacing legal analysis with emotional outbursts, the opinions used the bad tendency doctrine as the means to punish radicals who had made a "travesty"[15] of the First Amendment by invoking its provisions "to justify the activities of anarchy or of the enemies of the United States."[16]

---

[6] United States v. Debs, 249 U.S. 211, 215 (1919).

[7] 250 U.S. at 619.

[8] Goldman v. United States, 245 U.S. 474 (1918).

[9] 250 U.S. at 619; see also id. at 624.   [10] Id at 621, 623.

[11] 249 U.S. at 214–15.   [12] 250 U.S. at 621.

[13] 249 U.S. at 216.   [14] 250 U.S. at 621.

[15] Gilbert v. Minnesota, 254 U.S. 325, 333 (1920).

[16] Schaefer v. United States, 251 U.S. 466, 477 (1920).

HOLMES'S TRANSFORMATION IN *ABRAMS*

Holmes's dissent in *Abrams* broke from this continuing restrictive tradition, yet he stressed that he had not changed his views. "I never have seen any reason to doubt," he maintained in his dissent, "that the questions of law that alone were before this Court in the cases of Schenck, Frohwerk, and Debs . . . were rightly decided."[17] He reiterated this position in his private correspondence. *Abrams,* he wrote several friends, provided the occasion for him to state the limits of the doctrine that he had already set forth in his first Espionage Act decisions.[18]

Holmes's actual language in *Abrams* belies these claims. In addition to rejecting as "absurd"[19] the doctrine of indirect intent on which he had relied in *Schenck, Frohwerk,* and *Debs,* Holmes used his dissent in *Abrams* to restate the clear and present danger standard in language that conformed to Chafee's misconstruction of its original meaning in *Schenck.*

> I do not doubt . . . that by the same reasoning that would justify punishing persuasion to murder, the United States constitutionally may punish speech that produces or is intended to produce a clear and imminent danger that it will bring about forthwith certain substantive evils that the United States constitutionally may seek to prevent. The power undoubtedly is greater in time of war than in time of peace because war opens dangers that do not exist at other times.
>
> But as against dangers peculiar to war, as against others, the principle of the right to free speech is always the same. It is only the present danger of immediate evil or an intent to bring it about that warrants Congress in setting a limit to the expression of opinion where private rights are not concerned. Congress certainly cannot forbid all effort to change the mind of the country.[20]

In the concluding paragraph of his opinion, Holmes added:

> I think that we should be eternally vigilant against attempts to check the expression of opinions that we loathe and

---

[17] 250 U.S. at 627.

[18] Letter from Oliver Wendell Holmes, Jr. to Sir Frederick Pollock (Dec. 14, 1919), reprinted in 2 Holmes-Pollock Letters 32 (M. Howe ed. 1941); letter from Oliver Wendell Holmes, Jr., to Mrs. John Chipman Gray (Dec. 10, 1919) (Oliver Wendell Holmes, Jr. Papers, Box 36, Folder 5, Harvard Law School Library) [hereinafter cited as Holmes Papers]; letter from Oliver Wendell Holmes, Jr., to Albert J. Beveridge (Dec. 8, 1919) (Holmes Papers, Box 36, Folder 5).

[19] 250 U.S. at 629.　　　　　　　　　　　　[20] Id. at 627–28.

believe to be fraught with death, unless they so imminently threaten immediate interference with the lawful and pressing purposes of the law that an immediate check is required to save the country. . . . Only the emergency that makes it immediately dangerous to leave the correction of evil counsels to time warrants making any exception to the sweeping command, "Congress shall make no law . . . abridging the freedom of speech."[21]

In *Abrams,* as in *Schenck,* Holmes still viewed speech as a category of attempt and continued to rely on his thinking about the general law of criminal attempts. The circumstances in which speech is uttered, including the proximity and seriousness of the threatened danger as well as the intent of the speaker, remained important. In *Abrams,* however, Holmes infused new elements into his restatement of clear and present danger that emphasized the importance of a very close relationship between speech and crime. He used variations of "immediate" and "imminent" with remarkable frequency throughout his dissent, and even appended "forthwith" and "pressing" for additional emphasis.

Subtle variations in language in *Abrams* also indicated that Holmes was less willing than he was in *Schenck* to defer to legislative judgments of what constitutes the "substantive evils" that justify the punishment of speech threatening their occurrence. In *Schenck,* Holmes referred to "the substantive evils that Congress has a right to prevent"[22] without anywhere indicating the limits of congressional power. By contrast, in *Abrams* Holmes rephrased this passage in words that significantly modified its meaning: "certain substantive evils that the United States constitutionally may seek to prevent."[23] By adding the word *certain,* Holmes allowed that even some admittedly substantive evils cannot be invoked to restrict freedom of expression. Holmes may also have included *constitutionally,* modifying *seek,* in order to stress that the Constitution limits the government's right to prevent evil. Moreover, by substituting *the United States* for *Congress,* Holmes suggested that these constitutional limitations apply to all branches of government, thereby insinuating a justification for judicial review of congressional legislation without announcing a new standard that would have seemed inconsistent with the great deference manifested by his prewar and Espionage Act decisions. He now stressed that "Congress certainly cannot forbid all effort to change the mind of the country,"[24] and, for the first time, referred to the First Amend-

---

[21] Id. at 630–31.

[22] 249 U.S. 47, 52 (1919).

[23] 250 U.S. at 627.

[24] Id. at 628.

ment as a "sweeping command."[25] Perhaps Holmes no longer firmly believed that the majority could legitimately exercise whatever power it deemed efficient to obtain desired results.

Holmes also appeared to identify in *Abrams* the distinction between "public" and "private" speech stressed by prewar scholarly commentary on the First Amendment. In restating the clear and present danger test, Holmes implied that "where private rights are not concerned,"[26] Congress has less power to punish speech, a point he did not make in *Schenck, Frohwerk,* or *Debs.* Holmes seems to have accepted, as he had not in the past, that speech on matters of public affairs deserves added protection and cannot be viewed in the same manner as a simple solicitation to do a private wrong. Moreover, he now rejected as historically inaccurate the government's claim that the First Amendment did not abolish the common-law crime of seditious libel,[27] a claim he had ignored the previous March.

Holmes's concluding paragraph in his *Abrams* dissent, which contains the most eloquent and best remembered passages in this famous opinion, suggests that he himself recognized the vast change in his views on free speech during the eight months since he wrote *Schenck, Frohwerk,* and *Debs.*

> Persecution for the expression of opinions seems to me perfectly logical. If you have no doubt of your premises or your power and want a certain result with all your heart you naturally express your wishes in law and sweep away all opposition. To allow opposition by speech seems to indicate that you think the speech impotent, as when a man says that he has squared the circle, or that you do not care whole-heartedly for the result, or that you doubt either your power or your premises. But when men have realized that time has upset many fighting faiths, they may come to believe even more than they believe the very foundations of their own conduct that the ultimate good desired is better reached by free trade in ideas – that the best test of truth is the power of the thought to get itself accepted in the competition of the market, and that truth is the only ground upon which their wishes safely can be carried out. That at any rate is the theory of our Constitution. It is an experiment, as all life is an experiment. Every year if not every day we have to wager our salvation upon some prophecy based upon imperfect knowledge.[28]

25 Id. at 631.   26 Id. at 628.
27 Id. at 630.   28 Id.

It is remarkable that this paragraph, which includes a stirring defense of free speech, opens with a sentence that declares, "Persecution for the expression of opinions seems to me perfectly logical." The "but" that introduces Holmes's protective language comes only in the fourth sentence. Moreover, the second and third sentences bear a remarkable similarity to the contents of Holmes's private correspondence defending his decisions in *Schenck, Frohwerk,* and *Debs,* and to *The Common Law.* The text beginning with the word *but,* the most general and least technical portion of the entire dissent, seems as much a confession of personal conversion as a statement of constitutional law. Holmes, perhaps unselfconsciously, appears to be commenting on himself and those of his contemporaries who came to a belated appreciation of the value of free speech. The phrase *fighting faith* may well refer more specifically to the American support of World War I, a faith that was "upset" in the aftermath of the war when many, including Holmes's good friends at *The New Republic,* began to doubt "the very foundations of their own conduct." Only with the disillusionment that followed the war did these men begin to believe, above all, "that the ultimate good desired is better reached by free trade in ideas." Holmes here acknowledged that "the best test of truth" is not "the majority vote of that nation that can lick all others,"[29] as he had previously written to Hand, but "the power of the thought to get itself accepted in the competition of the market."

Despite these important protective innovations, however, Holmes retained in *Abrams* significant vestiges of his lifelong beliefs. He reapplied rather than abandoned his Social Darwinism. He tested truth by the "power" of thought to prevail in the "competition of the market" of ideas, and did not specify the value of free speech to the individual or to society. He also did not conceive of the First Amendment as the legal expression of democratic political theory.[30] He still believed in the survival of the fittest, but he was now willing to let ideas battle each other rather than brute force. Holmes's dissent in *Abrams* did not constitute a complete transformation of his prior thought. In contrast to his admittedly summary treatment of the First Amendment in the initial Espionage Act cases, however, Holmes strove in *Abrams* to develop

[29] Letter from Oliver Wendell Holmes, Jr. to Learned Hand (June 24, 1918) (Learned Hand Papers, Box 103, Folder 24, Harvard Law School Library), reprinted in Gerald Gunther, Learned Hand and the Origins of Modern First Amendment Doctrine: Some Fragments of History, 27 Stan. L. Rev. 719, 756–57 (1975).

[30] See Alexander Meiklejohn, Free Speech and Its Relation to Self-Government 70–77 (1948).

meaningful protection for free speech. He even concluded his dissent, in an uncharacteristic display of modesty, by stating, "I regret that I cannot put into more impressive words my belief that in their conviction upon this indictment the defendants were deprived of their rights under the Constitution of the United States."[31]

What led Justice Holmes to change his views on free speech so dramatically between his opinions for a unanimous Supreme Court in *Schenck, Frohwerk,* and *Debs* and his dissent in *Abrams* just eight months later? This question is difficult to answer with precision, largely because there were so many factors that might have influenced him. Certain factual differences between *Abrams* and the first Espionage Act cases might have prompted Holmes to write his dissent. Current events during those eight months might have alerted Holmes, as they alerted many others, to the importance of freedom of expression. Psychological needs for approval from the postwar civil libertarians as well as his reading of books that condemned the repression of speech could have influenced Holmes. More specifically, the criticisms of his earlier Espionage Act decisions, particularly from men as prominent and respected as Chafee, Freund, and Hand, could have affected his thinking in *Abrams,* even in ways which Holmes himself might not have recognized.

As Holmes pointed out in his dissent in *Abrams,* the indictment under which the defendants were convicted alleged that they intended their publications to encourage resistance to American participation in World War I. After reviewing the texts of the defendants' leaflets, Holmes maintained that their only object was "to help Russia and stop American intervention there against the popular government – not to impede the United States in the war that it was carrying on." "An intent to prevent interference with the revolution in Russia," Holmes remarked, "might have been satisfied without any hindrance to carrying on the war in which we were engaged."[32] The fact that Alfred Bettman used similar reasoning to oppose the prosecution in *Abrams,* even while justifying the government's position in *Schenck* and *Debs,*[33] provides further evidence that the absence of a state of war with Russia was an actual basis, and not just a rationalization, for Holmes's dissent in *Abrams.*

---

[31] 250 U.S. at 631.

[32] Id. at 628–29. Holmes reiterated this point in a subsequent letter to Pollock. Letter from Oliver Wendell Holmes, Jr., to Sir Frederick Pollock (Dec. 14, 1919), reprinted in 2 Holmes-Pollock Letters, supra note 18, at 32.

[33] Letter from Alfred Bettman to Zechariah Chafee, Jr. (Oct. 27, 1919) (Chafee Papers, Box 14, Folder 3, Harvard Law School Library) [hereinafter Chafee Papers].

More generally, the opposition to the war expressed by the defendants in *Schenck, Frohwerk,* and *Debs* might have seemed much more threatening to Holmes than did the objections by the defendants in *Abrams* to American interference in the Russian Revolution. Holmes characterized the facts of *Abrams* as involving "the surreptitious publishing of a silly leaflet by an unknown man" and later described various pamphlets as "poor and puny anonymities." In such circumstances, Holmes maintained, no reasonable person could detect "any immediate danger" or "appreciable tendency" to hinder the war effort.[34] By contrast, Schenck was an important official of the Socialist Party, and Debs was the most famous socialist in the United States. Though Frohwerk, like Abrams, was an unknown, Holmes, like much of the legal community, viewed *Schenck, Frohwerk,* and *Debs* as an interconnected trilogy, which probably made it difficult for him to consider *Frohwerk* on its own facts. *Abrams,* the only Espionage Act case decided the following fall, provided a better context than *Frohwerk* for Holmes to recognize and point out that less risk existed than in *Schenck* or *Debs*. It is also possible that Holmes, writing in dissent, felt able to express his personal opinions on freedom of expression more freely than when he wrote on behalf of all the justices, many of whom had more restrictive views on the subject.[35]

Contemporary developments, many of which collectively formed part of the "Red Scare" of 1919–20, might also have made Holmes more sensitive to the value of free speech by November 1919 than he had been the previous March. The national debate over the Versailles Peace Treaty, which reached its peak in the summer and early fall of 1919, convinced many, perhaps including Holmes, that their enthusiasm for the war had been misplaced. Retrospective doubts about the wisdom of the war might have made the opposition voiced earlier by defendants in Espionage Act cases seem less threatening to the national interest. At the same time, the popular mood of repression that contributed to the convictions of the Espionage Act defendants had culminated in the hysteria of the "Red Scare" in the months between *Schenck* and *Abrams*. The creation of the Communist Third International in March 1919, designed to encourage worldwide proletarian revolutions, intensified the preexisting domestic fear of radicals and greatly assisted the efforts of

[34] 250 U.S. at 628–29.
[35] Chafee made this point to Meiklejohn, writing that Holmes's dissent in Abrams "is plainly an expression of personal faith such as he could not make when he was speaking for other men as well as for himself in the Schenck case." Letter from Zechariah Chafee, Jr., to Alexander Meiklejohn (Nov. 23, 1948) (Chafee Papers, supra note 33, Box 2, Folder 16).

American business interests and patriotic societies to identify post-war labor conflicts with communist activity.[36]

Widespread industrial unrest, which began in January 1919 with a general strike in Seattle, culminated in the Boston Police Strike in September, the nationwide steel strike, also in September, and the nationwide coal strike in November. The violence that accompanied these strikes was exaggerated and sensationally reported by the national news media. The strikes and the publicity they generated further identified labor with radicalism. A series of unsuccessful attempted bombings around May Day, 1919, an apparently coordinated effort directed at a variety of prominent Americans, including Justice Holmes, and explosions within an hour of each other in eight different cities about a month later, also encouraged popular alarm about radicals. By the fall of 1919, virtually anyone who did not succumb to the prevailing hysteria ran the risk of being labeled a radical.[37] For example, Frankfurter and Chafee were under pressure to resign from the Harvard Law School during this period.[38]

The events that made many of his friends and contemporaries more sensitive to the value of free speech probably affected Justice Holmes as well. His letters rarely referred to the hysteria, perhaps because he considered it unworthy of his interest. But when Holmes heard that Frankfurter's position at Harvard might be in jeopardy because influential people considered him too radical, he promptly wrote President Lowell praising Frankfurter for contributing to "the ferment which is more valuable than an endowment."[39] Indeed, in his own book on Holmes, Frankfurter later maintained that this "period of hysteria undoubtedly focused the attention of Mr. Justice Holmes on the practical consequences of a relaxed attitude toward" free speech.[40]

Psychological needs as well as current events may have motivated Holmes. Edmund Wilson surmised that Holmes, long lonely for intellectual companionship, found it through his friendship with the postwar liberals. These liberals "stimulated and enter-

---

[36] See William E. Leuchtenburg, The Perils of Prosperity, 1914–32, at 50–67 (1958); Robert K. Murray, Red Scare: A Study in National Hysteria, 1919–1920, at 15–18, 92–94, 121–22 (1964 ed.).

[37] See Leuchtenburg, supra note 36, at 71–76; Paul L. Murphy, The Meaning of Free Speech: First Amendment Freedoms from Wilson to FDR 65, 69–76 (1972); Murray, supra note 36, at 68–81, 122–67.

[38] See Arthur E. Sutherland, The Law at Harvard, A History of Ideas and Men, 1817–1967, at 250–258 (1967).

[39] Letter from Oliver Wendell Holmes, Jr., to A. Lawrence Lowell (June 2, 1919), reprinted in 1 Holmes-Laski Letters 211 n.2 (M. Howe ed. 1953).

[40] Felix Frankfurter, Mr. Justice Holmes and the Supreme Court 79 (2d ed. 1961).

tained him as well as gave him the admiration he craved." Wilson believed that they may have "counted for something with Holmes in his opinions after the first World War in cases in which the issue of free speech was involved."[41] G. Edward White has suggested more recently that Holmes's "unfulfilled career expectations made him more receptive to the ideas" of the influential circle who wrote in *The New Republic*.[42]

The pressure of events and psychology, however, should not obscure the intellectual influences on Holmes. As Richard Polenberg has demonstrated, Holmes's reading during the spring and summer of 1919 could have made him more sensitive to the repression of speech. Two books that Holmes read consecutively seem particularly likely to have affected his thinking about free speech. James Ford Rhodes's *History of the Civil War,* while praising Abraham Lincoln in many ways, condemned him for "the arbitrary interference with the freedom of the press in States which were not included in the theatre of the war and in which the courts remained open." Holmes next read *Authority in the Modern State* by his young friend Harold Laski, the intermediary between Chafee and Croly in 1918, and the person who introduced Chafee to Holmes in 1919. In this book, dedicated jointly to Holmes and Felix Frankfurter, Laski argued for "absolute" freedom of thought. "Where the conscience of the individual is concerned," he wrote, "the state must abate its demands, for no mind is in truth free once a penalty is attached to thought."[43] Laski added that it is "in the clash of ideas that we shall find the means of truth. There is no other safeguard of progress." Such language convinced Laski's biographers that Holmes's dissent in *Abrams* "was almost verbatim Laski's own amalgam of J. S. Mill and Charles Darwin."[44]

It also seems probable that the criticisms of his earlier Espionage Act decisions by Chafee, Freund, and Hand contributed to the more protective approach Holmes took in *Abrams*. The impact of Chafee on Holmes is easiest to trace. Harold Laski, who was well acquainted with Chafee and Holmes, invited both men to tea in late July 1919, midway between *Schenck* and *Abrams*. Laski, who had given Holmes a copy of "Freedom of Speech in War Time"

---

[41] Edmund Wilson, Patriotic Gore 770, 772 (1962).

[42] G. Edward White, Justice Oliver Wendell Holmes: Law and the Inner Self 450 (1983); G. Edward White, Holmes and Free Speech Jurisprudence, 80 Calif. L. Rev. 391, 410–11 (1992).

[43] Richard Polenberg, Fighting Faiths: The Abrams Case, the Supreme Court, and Free Speech 225 (1987) (quoting Rhodes and Laski).

[44] Isaac Kramnick and Barry Sheerman, Harold Laski: A Life on the Left 127 (1993) (quoting Laski).

before this meeting, wrote Chafee that "we must fight on it."[45] Unfortunately, no record of this meeting appears to exist. In a letter to Judge Amidon the following September, however, Chafee commented on his summer conversation with Holmes. Chafee came away from this encounter with the impression that he did not convince Holmes about several key points in his article. Although Chafee was certain that Holmes, as a juror, would have voted to acquit Debs, Chafee reported that Holmes "is inclined to allow a very wide latitude to Congressional discretion in the carrying on of the war" and "further thinks that he could not have gone behind the jury verdict in the Debs case."[46]

Holmes, although apparently not converted by his initial reading of "Freedom of Speech in War Time" or by his summer meeting with Chafee,[47] soon began to agree with him. Holmes's dissent in *Abrams,* written less than four months after this talk, provides the best evidence of Chafee's influence. It is most striking that after omitting any reference to clear and present danger in *Frohwerk* and *Debs,* Holmes reformulated this phrase in *Abrams* in ways indicating that he now interpreted these words more as Chafee had misconstrued and glorified them than as he himself had originally used them in *Schenck.*

The *Abrams* dissent incorporated other views of the First Amendment advocated by Chafee, Hand, and Freund, but missing from Holmes's own prior decisions. Holmes emphasized in *Abrams* the relationship between free speech and the search for truth, recognized its importance even during a war, and conceded that the First Amendment is inconsistent with the common law of seditious libel. Although Holmes required "specific intent" in *Debs* as well as *Abrams,* his stress in *Abrams* on a "strict" construction of intent responded to the concerns of Chafee, Hand and Freund about employing vague standards to evaluate the legality of speech. It is perhaps most impor-

---

[45] Letter from Harold Laski to Zechariah Chafee, Jr. (July 23, 1919) (Chafee Papers, supra note 33, Box 14, Folder 15).

[46] Letter from Zechariah Chafee, Jr., to Judge Charles F. Amidon (Sept. 30, 1919) (Chafee Papers, supra note 33, Box 4, Folder 1).

[47] Evidently, Holmes did not correspond about his meeting with Chafee and Laski until 1920. After receiving a copy of Chafee's book, Freedom of Speech, Holmes wrote Laski that "the preliminary extracts in (the) Harvard Law Review" were "first rate." Letter from Oliver Wendell Holmes, Jr., to Harold Laski (Dec. 17, 1920), reprinted in 1 Holmes-Laski Letters, supra note 39, at 297. In a letter earlier that year to Sir Frederick Pollock, Holmes mentioned that Chafee "is said to be a very good man" and, referring to his talk with Chafee the previous summer, described him as "unusually pleasant and intelligent." Letter from Oliver Wendell Holmes, Jr., to Sir Frederick Pollock (June 21, 1920), reprinted in 2 Holmes-Pollock Letters, supra note 18, at 45.

tant that Holmes accepted in *Abrams* the independent judicial role they all had advocated. For the first time, Holmes indicated that he had abandoned his reflexive deference to legislative or jury determinations affecting the exercise of speech. He no longer treated the Espionage Act cases as ordinary criminal appeals, and seemed instead to appreciate their constitutional dimension.

It is impossible to determine which of these plausible influences actually contributed to the protective innovations Holmes introduced in his *Abrams* dissent. Holmes himself did not help to solve this puzzle. He never directly acknowledged that he had altered his interpretation of the First Amendment between his initial Espionage Act decisions and *Abrams*. In fact, many of his statements indicate that he considered his dissent in *Abrams* to be a logical extension of *Schenck, Frohwerk,* and *Debs.* The language of the dissent, however, contradicts Holmes's claims to consistency. All or some of these factors, consciously or unconsciously, might have helped change his views. Though the reasons remain uncertain, the significant transformation in Holmes's approach to freedom of expression is evident.

THE CONTRIBUTION OF BRANDEIS

Written against an unacknowledged tradition of judicial hostility to the value of free speech, Holmes's dissent in *Abrams* constituted the most protective construction of the First Amendment in the history of the U.S. Supreme Court. For the next decade, Holmes and Brandeis dissented in almost every First Amendment case. After *Abrams,* the leadership passed to Brandeis, who wrote most of the dissenting opinions and made the major doctrinal and conceptual advances. Holmes did not retreat from the views he expressed in *Abrams* and generally went along with Brandeis, but Holmes's limited subsequent writing on the First Amendment demonstrates that he never entirely escaped from the attitudes revealed in his prior restrictive decisions. Nor did he ever again attain the eloquence that accompanied his conversion in *Abrams.*

Holmes's approach to the First Amendment in the 1920s is best revealed by his dissent in *Gitlow v. New York,* decided in 1925. Holmes repeated the immediacy requirement he imported into the clear and present danger test in *Abrams.* The publications at issue in *Gitlow,* Holmes reasoned, referred to "some indefinite time in the future" and did not constitute "an attempt to induce an uprising against government at once." He warned against punishing speech at a point "too remote from possible consequences," and he concluded that "no present danger" existed. After quoting his statement of clear and present danger in *Schenck* as "the criterion sanctioned by the full Court," he maintained, as did Chafee's scholarly writings, that the majority in *Abrams* had "departed from" its true meaning.[48]

Holmes, however, also revealed in *Gitlow* the extent to which Social Darwinism still dominated his views. "If in the long run the beliefs expressed in proletarian dictatorship are destined to be accepted by the dominant forces of the community," Holmes stated, "the only meaning of free speech is that they should be given their chance and have their way." As in *Abrams*, Holmes emphasized the defendant's relative powerlessness and his "redundant discourse."[49] In a subsequent letter to Laski, Holmes referred to his dissent in *Gitlow* as "a page of slack on the right of an ass to drool about proletarian dictatorship."[50] These comments do not reflect real appreciation of the social and individual benefits of free speech or its role in a democracy. It seems significant that it was Brandeis, not Holmes, who dissented in the only First Amendment case in the 1920s that involved a politically significant defendant, Joseph Gilbert, who was the manager of the organization department of the Nonpartisan League.[51]

Justice Brandeis, much more than Justice Holmes, developed a judicial construction of the First Amendment that emphasized the crucial function of free speech in democratic governance. In a remarkable series of opinions from 1920 through 1927, Brandeis, relying extensively on Chafee's scholarship, elaborated and expanded the protective innovations of Holmes's dissent in *Abrams* without adopting Holmes's lingering Social Darwinism. Unlike the aloof Holmes, detached from and often contemptuous of human efforts to change society, Brandeis was an activist who combined genuine humanitarianism with a firm belief in individual dignity. As often as Holmes was impressed by the acquisition and exercise of power in the struggle for existence, Brandeis was outraged by its abuse. Even when Holmes recognized that power exceeded its legitimate limits, he found it difficult to identify with its victims. As one of Holmes's law clerks summed up the difference between the

---

[48] 268 U.S. 652, 672–73 (1925).
[49] Id. at 673. Robert M. Cover, The Left, the Right, and the First Amendment, 40 Md. L. Rev. 349, 383 n.118 (1981), observed that Social Darwinism as well as the classic liberalism of John Stuart Mill provided sources for Holmes's view that "in minorities may reside the seed for future growth of society."
[50] Letter from Oliver Wendell Holmes, Jr., to Harold Laski (June 14, 1925), reprinted in 1 Holmes-Laski Letters, supra note 39, at 752.
[51] Gilbert v. Minnesota, 254 U.S. 325, 334 (Brandeis, J., dissenting).

two Justices, "Brandeis feels sympathy for the oppressed, Holmes contempt for the oppressor."[52]

Brandeis, like most postwar civil libertarians, was essentially uninvolved with free speech issues during the prewar period. His national prominence before the war as the reforming "people's lawyer" derived from his activities against banks and oil trusts, his opposition to railroad mergers, and his investigations into the corruption of government officials by big business. Yet the same values that generated Brandeis's commitment to economic reform account for his later contributions to First Amendment doctrine. In contrast to many progressive intellectuals, Brandeis had a fundamental belief in capitalism that transcended purely economic considerations. He believed that the free enterprise system has moral worth, that the struggle to make a living develops character by fostering individuality, self-reliance, personal responsibility, and an appreciation of freedom essential to a democracy.[53] According to Brandeis, economic and political liberty are inextricably connected; jeopardizing one threatens the other. He argued that economic self-sufficiency is a prerequisite to political freedom. Brandeis did not attack capitalism itself, only the centralization that, in the name of capitalism, endangered its soul and the democratic virtues it produced. The representatives of corporate capitalism, he complained, were "playing the industrial game with loaded dice."[54] Brandeis did not want to change the game, but he did want to make sure that people played by the traditional fair rules. In his opinion, the dominance of monopolies and trusts loaded the dice against the common citizen and destroyed the character of both the powerful and the dependent. The pithy titles of Brandeis's collections of

---

[52] Lockwood, Justice Holmes – Year 1928–29, at 9 (Felix Frankfurter Papers, Box 146, Library of Congress). Lockwood did not know the source of this quotation, but had heard it attributed to a foreigner. Id. at 8. "Whoever stated it," he added, "sensed something very deep in Holmes's character." Id. at 9.

[53] See, e.g., letter from Louis D. Brandeis to Winthrop Talbot (April 16, 1912), reprinted in 2 Letters of Louis D. Brandeis 586–89 (M. Urofsky & D. Levy eds. 1972) [hereinafter 2 Brandeis Letters]; letter from Louis D. Brandeis to Charles Richard Crane (Nov. 11, 1911), reprinted in 2 Brandeis Letters, at 510–11. Richard M. Abrams, Brandeis and the Ascendancy of Corporate Capitalism, Introduction to Louis D. Brandeis, Other People's Money (Harper Torchbook ed. 1967), includes an exceptionally penetrating analysis of the moral roots of Brandeis's political and economic thought. See also Richard M. Abrams, Conservativism in a Progressive Era 55–59 (1964).

[54] Letter from Louis D. Brandeis to Norman Hapgood (Feb. 27, 1911), reprinted in 2 Brandeis Letters, supra note 53, at 412.

essays, *The Curse of Bigness*[55] and *Other People's Money*,[56] conveyed the gist of his concerns.

Brandeis fought the "curse of bigness" produced by corporate conglomerations and glorified the individual struggles of entrepreneurs. He criticized bankers for relying on "other people's money" instead of their own efforts, not for wanting to get rich. Although Brandeis was confident that the dissolution of economic concentration would create "industrial efficiency," he placed greater emphasis on the anticipated personal and social benefits. Even more important than efficiency, he argued, are industrial and political liberty.[57] These views help explain both his successful striving for personal wealth and his later activities as an opponent of big business. Brandeis believed strongly that free enterprise had made the United States a great nation, but he was deeply disturbed that corporate power threatened the traditional liberties and virtues produced by free enterprise and essential to a healthy democracy.

Brandeis's almost religious commitment to individual dignity and his certainty about the connection between economic and political liberty made him much more sensitive than most of his contemporaries to the range of problems faced by people subject to the pressures of corporate capitalism. Brandeis, like most progressives, viewed the economic organization of society as the primary problem facing the country. At the same time, he was concerned about the repression of civil liberties, including free speech, in the industrial world. Brandeis protested the treatment of IWW members during a strike in Lawrence, Massachusetts. He maintained that "citizens and aliens have, under the guise of administering or enforcement of the law, been denied civil rights."[58] The use of police as strikebreakers, he added, created disrespect for law and encouraged violence.[59] Brandeis argued that the indiscriminate use of injunctions would produce unacceptable restrictions on free speech,[60] and he criticized the Massa-

---

[55] Louis D. Brandeis, The Curse of Bigness (1934).
[56] Louis D. Brandeis, Other People's Money (1914).
[57] 1 Final Report and Testimony of Commission on Industrial Relations, S. Doc. No. 415, 64th Cong., 1st Sess. 1003 (1917) (testimony of Mr. Brandeis).
[58] Letter from Louis D. Brandeis to Jocelyn Paul Yoder (Feb. 26, 1912), reprinted in 2 Brandeis Letters, supra note 53, at 563.
[59] Letter from Louis D. Brandeis to Charles Warren Clifford (July 11, 1912), reprinted in 2 Brandeis Letters, supra note 53, at 646–47.
[60] Letter from Louis D. Brandeis to Norman Hapgood (Oct. 14, 1908), reprinted in 2 Brandeis Letters, supra note 53, at 210–11.

chusetts courts for often straining the facts to interpret peaceful picketing as including illegal threats or intimidation.[61]

Even though he was concerned about these abuses, Brandeis explicitly rejected the goals of the IWW and other radical groups. He used the IWW strikes as an argument in favor of establishing the U.S. Commission on Industrial Relations.[62] He hoped that the Commission would discover the underlying causes of industrial unrest and suggest social reforms to prevent its recurrence.[63] Unlike Schroeder and Roe, who concentrated on free speech issues, Brandeis emphasized the solution of industrial problems in his testimony before the Commission.[64] Brandeis wanted to stop the growth of the IWW by bringing its members into the mainstream of society. He was afraid of the IWW and cited its successes to demonstrate that "conservative trade unionism is essential to the maintenance of law and order."[65] Brandeis helped organize a National Civic Federation, which he hoped would create "some conservative substitute for radical measures,"[66] and opposed violations of the law by the rich and the powerful because he feared that they would breed "anarchical and socialistic sentiment."[67] Brandeis emphasized his opposition to socialism. The concentration of authority in the state, in his opinion, posed the same threats to the individual as did private economic power.[68]

---

[61] Letter from Louis D. Brandeis to E. R. Thayer (May 20, 1912) (Louis D. Brandeis Papers, Box 14, Folder 11, Harvard Law School Library) [hereinafter cited as Brandeis Papers, Harvard].

[62] Letter from Brandeis to Yoder, supra note 58.

[63] Letter from Louis D. Brandeis to William Howard Taft (Dec. 30, 1911), reprinted in 2 Brandeis Letters, supra note 53, at 531–35. This letter was signed by many other prominent people. See 2 Brandeis Letters, supra note 53, at 535 n.2.

[64] Compare testimony of Louis D. Brandeis (Vol. I at 991–1011; Vol. VIII at 7657–81) with testimony of Theodore Schroeder (Vol. XI at 10,840–52, 10,866–96) and testimony of Gilbert E. Roe (Vol. XI at 10,468–93), Final Report and Testimony of Commission on Industrial Relations, S. Doc. No. 415, 64th Cong., 1st Sess. (1917).

[65] Letter from Brandeis to Talbot, supra note 53.

[66] Letter from Louis D. Brandeis to Ralph Montgomery Easley (July 16, 1907), reprinted in 2 Brandeis Letters, supra note 53, at 13.

[67] Letter from Louis D. Brandeis to William Lawrence (May 14, 1908), reprinted in 2 Brandeis Letters, supra note 53, at 152.

[68] For example, Brandeis disapproved of the German system of compulsory insurance as not being "in harmony with the American ideas of individual liberty." Instead, Brandeis argued, a worker should be able to earn sufficient wages to afford insurance "through his own efforts" and thereby develop "strength of character and self-control." Letter from Louis D. Brandeis to John Edward Pember (Feb. 4, 1908), reprinted in 2 Brandeis Letters, supra note 53, at 74.

Brandeis's background and beliefs suggested to many that he would take the lead in protecting free speech after he joined the Supreme Court in 1916. Letters to Brandeis throughout 1918 illustrate the widespread assumption that he would be sympathetic to people prosecuted for dissenting speech during the war. His friend, progressive activist Amos Pinchot, asked Brandeis to write President Wilson or Attorney General Gregory to protest the continuing prosecution of the editors of *The Masses* and enclosed his own letter to Wilson.[69] The recently organized Liberty Defense Union asked Brandeis for a contribution to a fund that would pay the legal costs of defendants charged with violating the Espionage Act and sent him literature describing the use of the law to repress free expression.[70] A personal friend of the Brandeis family, stymied by "the ban on free speech," sought advice on how "radical and liberal and not necessarily pacifist groups" could organize to support a democratic settlement of the war along the lines outlined by President Wilson.[71] A man imprisoned for making allegedly pro-German remarks, despite having frequently attempted to register for the draft, wrote Brandeis from prison "in behalf of hundreds of more or less innocent victims of war furor and hysteria."[72]

In addition, two of the few federal district court judges who tried to protect free speech during the war wrote Brandeis in 1918 about the Espionage Act prosecutions. Judge Amidon sent a copy of oral observations he had made during sentencing in an Espionage Act case,[73] and Judge Anderson mailed a copy of a letter he had written to Attorney General Gregory because he wanted to share the same thoughts with Brandeis. "The country and a good many of the Federal Courts," Anderson observed while pleading with Gregory to end the suppression of free speech, "have gone as crazy as the Federalistic party and the Federal Courts did after the Alien and Sedition Laws of 1798."[74] Brandeis also kept extensive files of clippings

---

69 Letter from Amos Pinchot to Louis D. Brandeis (May 24, 1918) (Louis D. Brandeis Papers, Box WW 3-1, University of Louisville Archives) [hereinafter cited as Brandeis Papers, Louisville].

70 Letter from Liberty Defense Union to "Dear Friend" (July 1, 1918) (Brandeis Papers, Louisville, supra note 69, Box WW 3-1).

71 Letter from Gertrude L. Winslow to Louis D. Brandeis (Oct. 3, 1918) (Brandeis Papers, Louisville, supra note 69, Box WW 3-1).

72 Letter from William K. De Blocq to Louis D. Brandeis (Nov. 19, 1918) (Brandeis Papers, Louisville, supra note 69, Box WW 3-1h).

73 Letter from Charles F. Amidon to Louis D. Brandeis (Aug. 5, 1918) (Brandeis Papers, Louisville, supra note 69, Box WW 2-1).

74 Letter from George W. Anderson to Louis D. Brandeis (Dec. 7, 1918) (Brandeis Papers, Louisville, supra note 69, Box WW 5-6); letter from George W. Anderson to T.W. Gregory (Dec. 7, 1918) (Brandeis Papers, Louisville, supra note 69, Box WW 5-6).

from the trade, labor, and general press, in which he highlighted reports of free speech violations as well as the statement in defense of conscientious objection made in open court by Roger Baldwin, the son of a former client, after being sentenced to jail.[75]

It is unclear whether Brandeis responded to most of these letters. He did write a short letter of support to his close friend, Senator La Follette, in November 1918, the day after a Senate investigating committee dropped charges that could have led to his expulsion from the Senate for his allegedly antiwar speech to the Nonpartisan League in 1917. Brandeis did not comment, however, on the merits of either the investigation or La Follette's defense.[76] In early 1919, Brandeis rejected a request that he meet with people associated with the National Civil Liberties Bureau to discuss the Espionage Act prosecutions and censorship of the press.[77] In private correspondence at the end of 1919, however, he compared contemporary events in the United States to the Spanish Inquisition. "The intensity of the frenzy," he added, "is the most hopeful feature of this disgraceful exhibition; – of hysterical, unintelligent fear – which is quite foreign to the generous American nature. It will pass like the Know-nothing days, but the sense of shame and of sin should endure."[78] In a letter to Learned Hand in January 1920, Brandeis expressed his view that "we are over the worst of the reaction, or rather, we have a counter current moving." The expulsion of elected socialists by the New York State Assembly, he observed, "was fortunate in its disgraceful excess."[79]

Despite his general concern for individual rights and the evidence he received that prosecutions under the Espionage Act, among other examples of widespread intolerance, threatened freedom of expression throughout the country, Brandeis joined the unanimous Supreme Court in the Selective Draft Law decisions and in the initial Espionage Act cases. Indeed, Brandeis

[75] See Brandeis Papers, Louisville, supra note 69, Box WW 7-1. While in private practice, Brandeis represented Baldwin's father, who owned a shoe business. When Roger Baldwin was searching for a career after college, Brandeis advised him to become a social worker, advice Baldwin followed. Roger Baldwin, Recollection of a Life in Civil Liberties – I, 2 Civ. Lib. Rev., Spring 1975, at 39–40.

[76] Letter from Louis D. Brandeis to Robert M. La Follette (Nov. 24, 1918), reprinted in 4 Letters of Louis D. Brandeis 364 (M. Urofsky & D. Levy eds. 1975) [hereinafter cited as 4 Brandeis Letters].

[77] Note by Louis D. Brandeis (Feb. 27, 1919) on letter from Elizabeth Walton to Louis D. Brandeis (Feb. 25, 1919) (Brandeis Papers, Louisville, supra note 69, Box WW 8-3b).

[78] Letter from Louis D. Brandeis to Susan Goldmark (Dec. 7, 1919), reprinted in 4 Brandeis Letters, supra note 76, at 441.

[79] Letter from Louis D. Brandeis to Learned Hand (Jan. 20, 1920), reprinted in 4 Brandeis Letters, supra note 76, at 445.

wrote for the Court in *Sugarman*,[80] the case which, together with *Schenck, Frohwerk,* and *Debs,* constituted the first group of Espionage Act opinions.

In a fascinating series of uninhibited conversations with Felix Frankfurter between 1921 and 1924,[81] Brandeis commented on many aspects of his work as a Supreme Court justice. Some of these conversations suggest reasons why he did not dissent in the initial cases. In August 1921, Brandeis told Frankfurter: "I have never been quite happy about my concurrence in [the] Debs and Schenck cases. I had not then thought the issues of freedom of speech out – I thought at the subject, not through it. Not until I came to write the Pierce and Schaefer dissents did I understand it."[82] This revealing admission, however satisfying to Brandeis as a subsequent justification, seems unconvincing as a full explanation. Brandeis may not have "thought through" free speech issues until he wrote his own dissents, but neither had he been as unsophisticated about them as his later comment to Frankfurter suggests. Brandeis had to decide to dissent before actually writing the opinions that forced him to analyze the meaning of free speech in greater detail. Why did he make this initial decision for the first time in *Abrams* rather than in *Goldman, Kramer, Sugarman, Schenck, Frohwerk,* or *Debs?*

The most probable explanation lies in Brandeis's support of the war. Brandeis was an active proponent of Woodrow Wilson's war policies. Even while sitting on the Supreme Court, he advised senior government officials, including Wilson himself, on the conduct of the war.[83] Though Brandeis may have become concerned about the evidence of repression that came to his attention during 1918, much of it from people he respected, the hostility to the war expressed by the defendants in the Supreme Court cases may have struck him as qualitatively more threatening than the examples provided by his friends and correspondents.

Even after the war, when Brandeis admitted his regrets to Frankfurter about his concurrences in Holmes's first Espionage Act decisions, he indicated that he still approved the convictions. His second thoughts were limited to the legal theory Holmes employed.

[80] Sugarman v. United States, 249 U.S. 182 (1919).
[81] Transcript of conversations between Louis D. Brandeis and Felix Frankfurter (Manuscript in Brandeis Papers, Harvard, supra note 61, Box 114, Folder 14) [hereinafter cited as Brandeis-Frankfurter Conversations]. Frankfurter took notes on these conversations. See Felix Frankfurter, A Register of His Papers in the Library of Congress 7 (1971).
[82] Brandeis-Frankfurter Conversations, supra note 81, at 23.
[83] See Alpheus T. Mason, Brandeis: A Free Man's Life 518–27 (1946).

I would have placed the Debs case on the war power – instead of taking Holmes' line about "clear and present danger." Put it frankly on the war power – like [the] Hamilton case (251 U.S.) – and then the scope of espionage legislation would be confined to war. But in peace the protection against restriction of freedom of speech would be unabated. You might as well recognize that during a war – [here Frankfurter interrupted with the words "all bets are off"]. Yes, all bets are off. But we would have a clear line to go on. I didn't know enough in the early cases to put it on that ground.[84]

Brandeis probably never "thought through" the earlier cases when he wrote his initial dissents. If he had, he probably would have found them difficult to distinguish because all of these cases involved similar language used by radicals before the end of the war. His continued acceptance of the results in the first Espionage Act cases, even after his dissents in analogous cases during the 1920s, points to his prowar views as the determining influence when the Selective Draft Law and the initial Espionage Act cases were before the Court in 1918 and 1919. Brandeis's subsequent suggestion of the war power as the doctrinal basis for affirming the convictions in *Schenck* and *Debs* underlines the importance of the war in his thinking about these cases.

By the date of the *Abrams* decision in the fall of 1919, many of the factors that led Holmes to dissent could have had a similar impact on Brandeis, who always had been more sympathetic to the value of free speech. When Brandeis first wrote his own dissents in 1920, he began to "think through" his own views about freedom of speech, with substantial assistance from Chafee's scholarly writings. In marked contrast to Holmes, Brandeis based his legal conclusions on meticulous attention to factual detail. He strengthened the transformation of the clear and present danger test begun by Holmes in *Abrams* and combined it with Hand's incitement test in a more convincing way than Chafee's conflation of the two approaches. Brandeis also supported expanded judicial review of legislation that implicated free speech. By developing the theoretical foundations of the legal standards he espoused, Brandeis made his most significant contribution. Instead of adopting Holmes's focus in *Abrams* on the "free trade in ideas" and the "competition of the market" in the search for truth, Brandeis, like

---

[84] Brandeis-Frankfurter Conversations, supra note 81, at 23. In Hamilton v. Kentucky Distilleries & Warehouse Co., 251 U.S. 146 (1919), Brandeis, writing for a unanimous Court, upheld the War-Time Prohibition Act as a valid exercise of the war power.

Dewey, emphasized free speech as an essential prerequisite to democratic citizenship.

Referring to his initial dissents in 1920, Brandeis informed Frankfurter that in the "Schaefer and Pierce cases I made up my mind I would put it all out, let the future know what we weren't allowed to say in the days of the war and following."[85] In contrast to Holmes in *Frohwerk*, who summarily rejected the claim that the law of treason limits the punishment of speech, Brandeis in *Schaefer* quoted at length from the jury charge and surmised in horror that "the jury may well have believed from the charge that the Espionage Act had in effect restored the crime of constructive treason." He asserted that the jury convicted the defendant "not merely for disloyal acts but for a disloyal heart; provided only that the disloyal heart was evidenced by some utterance."[86] In *Pierce*, Brandeis maintained that the defendants' antiwar statements, alleged by the government to be false under the Espionage Act, were expressions of opinion whose accuracy could not be determined. With typical industry, Brandeis cleverly found and quoted from *American School of Magnetic Healing*, the one prewar decision that supported his distinction between false facts and opinions. A rare case that limited the discretion of the postmaster general, *Magnetic Healing* concluded that claims by Christian Scientists are "mere matters of opinion upon subjects which are not capable of proof as to their falsity" and therefore cannot be deemed statutory frauds.[87] Brandeis observed in *Pierce* that senators and congressmen debating the war resolution disagreed with President Wilson's justification for American participation and expressed many of the same opinions for which the defendants in Espionage Act cases had been convicted. Giving a jury power to construe speech as false statements of fact rather than as expressions of opinion, he added, "would practically deny members of small political parties freedom of criticism and of discussion in times when feelings run high and the questions involved are deemed fundamental."[88]

Throughout his First Amendment opinions in the 1920s, Brandeis extended the clear and present danger test. Brandeis in *Schaefer*, like Holmes in *Abrams*, included the requirement of immediacy in his definition of clear and present danger, a requirement that was missing from Holmes's opinion for a unanimous Court in *Schenck*. Brandeis stressed that the clear and present danger test

85 Brandeis-Frankfurter Conversations, supra note 81, at 23.
86 Schaefer v. United States, 251 U.S. 466, 493 (1920).
87 Pierce v. United States, 252 U.S. 239, 267 (1920) [quoting American School of Magnetic Healing v. McAnnulty, 187 U.S., 94, 104 (1902)].
88 252 U.S. at 267–69.

precluded judging speech by its "remote or possible effect." Reflecting the actual origins of this approach, Brandeis cited Chafee's "Freedom of Speech in War Time" rather than any of Holmes's prior opinions.[89]

In *Whitney*, Brandeis observed that the Supreme Court "has not yet fixed the standard by which to determine" the meaning of clear and present danger.[90] He developed the immediacy criterion, declaring that there could be no clear and present danger "unless the incidence of the evil apprehended is so imminent that it may befall before there is opportunity for full discussion." More significantly, Brandeis added a new requirement of gravity. "Prohibition of free speech and assembly is a measure so stringent," he maintained, "that it would be inappropriate as the means of averting a relatively trivial harm to society." He found it inconceivable that a statute could constitutionally punish advocacy of trespassing as a felony even if a case presented an imminent danger of an actual trespass. For Brandeis, the likelihood that speech will cause some violence or destruction of property does not make it unlawful unless there is "probability of serious injury to the State."[91] In effect, Brandeis transformed clear and present danger into an exception to a general rule that forbade restrictions on free speech.[92]

While strengthening the clear and present danger test, Brandeis combined it with Hand's direct incitement standard. Avoiding the doctrinal confusion of Chafee's forced assimilation of *Schenck* and *Masses*, Brandeis joined Hand's analysis of the content of language and a protective version of Holmes's focus on possible consequences as alternative tests. In *Schaefer*, he examined the "nature and possible effect of a writing."[93] In *Pierce*, he similarly looked to "the nature of the words used and the circumstances under which they were used." Brandeis concluded that the language of the leaflet, "far from counseling disobedience to the law, points to the hopelessness of protest." With respect to the surrounding circumstances, he stressed that the defendants did not begin distribution until a judge in another case involving the same leaflet had directed an acquittal, and that they never circulated it to members of the armed forces.[94]

---

[89] Schaefer v. United States, 251 U.S. 466, 486 (1920).

[90] Whitney v. California, 274 U.S. 357, 373 (1927).

[91] Id. at 377–78.

[92] In their conversations, Brandeis told Frankfurter that the "right to your education and to utter speech is fundamental except clear and present danger." Brandeis-Frankfurter Conversations, supra note 81, at 21; see Cover, supra note 49, at 381.

[93] 251 U.S. at 483.

[94] 252 U.S. at 271–73.

In *Whitney*, Brandeis cemented the combination of these two standards. Citing Hand's decision in *Masses*, Chafee's book, and a decision by Amidon, Brandeis conceded that "[e]very denunciation of existing law tends in some measure to increase the probability that there will be some violation of it." But Brandeis added that "even advocacy of violation, however reprehensible morally, is not a justification for denying free speech where the advocacy falls short of incitement and there is nothing to indicate that the advocacy would be immediately acted on." To prove the existence of a clear and present danger, he required a showing "either that immediate serious violence was to be expected or was advocated, or that the past conduct furnished reason to believe that such advocacy was then contemplated."[95]

Brandeis justified the broad application of the more protective standard he developed. The majority in *Gitlow v. New York* asserted that the clear and present danger test governed only cases, such as those brought under the Espionage Act, "where the statute merely prohibits certain acts involving the danger of substantive evil, without any reference to language itself, and it is sought to apply its provisions to language used by the defendant for the purpose of bringing about the prohibited results." If the legislature itself, as in *Gitlow*, makes the determination that "utterances of a certain kind involve such danger of substantive evil that they may be punished, the question whether any specific utterances coming within the prohibited class is likely, in and of itself, to bring about the substantive evil, is not open to consideration."[96] Although Holmes did not respond to this point in his *Gitlow* dissent, Brandeis had previously criticized the state sedition statute at issue in *Gilbert v. Minnesota* because it restricted speech whatever the circumstances, rather than "in a particular emergency, in order to avert a clear and present danger."[97]

Responding to the majority's intervening opinion in *Gitlow*, Brandeis elaborated this point in *Whitney*. He admitted that a legislature may directly prohibit speech it deems dangerous, but he insisted that "the enactment of the statute cannot alone establish the facts which are essential to its validity."[98] Whenever a litigant claims a violation of free speech, Brandeis maintained, legislation, even if sustained by a lower court, "creates merely a rebuttable presumption" of legality. This presumption can be overcome if, under

[95] 274 U.S. at 376 & n.3.
[96] Gitlow v. New York, 268 U.S. 652, 670–71 (1925).
[97] Gilbert v. Minnesota, 254 U.S. 325, 334 (1920).
[98] 274 U.S. at 374.

the circumstances of a particular case, a danger is not sufficiently imminent or serious.[99]

Brandeis, who was probably prompted by Chafee, also took the lead on the postwar Supreme Court in advocating expanded federal jurisdiction over free speech issues. The lone dissenter in *Gilbert,* Brandeis relied on the supremacy of federal law to support his conclusion that the Minnesota statute violated the First Amendment. In addition, he suggested in *Gilbert,* and later declared in *Whitney,* that freedom of speech constitutes part of the substantive "liberty" protected against state deprivation by the due process clause of the Fourteenth Amendment.[100]

Brandeis's comments on these issues in *Gilbert* apparently reflected Chafee's influence. Dean Acheson, the future secretary of state who served as law clerk to Brandeis during the term in which the Supreme Court decided *Gilbert,* wrote Chafee, his former law professor, to inform him that the Court was considering this case. In a letter written less than one month before the Court released its opinion, Chafee responded by sending Acheson the relevant page proofs of *Freedom of Speech.* In an accompanying letter, Chafee complained to Acheson that, except for one dissent in a state court opinion, he had "as yet got no one to agree with my constitutional argument that the state powers over opposition to war are no stronger than state power over intrastate railroad rates, so that when Congress acts, the states must drop out." Chafee pointed out that *Gilbert* raised the additional issue of "whether the 14th Amendment guarantees freedom of speech from state action" and observed that Holmes had declined to consider this issue in the prewar case of *Fox v. Washington.* Chafee questioned the practical advantages of relying on the Fourteenth Amendment to protect speech, even assuming judicial acceptance of the state action rationale. In view of the Supreme Court's earlier Espionage Act decisions, he saw no basis for thinking that it would find any abridgment of speech by the Minnesota statute. Chafee was more optimistic that the "nationalistic" Supreme Court "would not favor the way state legislation would and to some extent did block the discussion of policy of the federal government."[101]

Despite Acheson's own "rather fundamental doubts"[102] about

---

[99] Id. at 379.

[100] 254 U.S. at 343; 274 U.S. at 373.

[101] Letter from Zechariah Chafee, Jr., to Dean Acheson (Nov. 20, 1920) (Brandeis Papers, Harvard, supra note 61, Box 5, Folder 12).

[102] Memorandum from Dean Acheson to Louis D. Brandeis (Nov. 19, 1920) (Brandeis Papers, Harvard, supra note 61, Box 5, Folder 12).

Chafee's Fourteenth Amendment and "nationalistic" approaches, Brandeis's dissent in *Gilbert* closely resembled Chafee's letter to Acheson, which is contained in Brandeis's files. Brandeis rejected the view that the First Amendment applies only to federal action. "The state law," Brandeis reasoned, "affects directly the functions of the Federal Government." He maintained that freedom of speech about these functions is a "privilege and immunity" of national citizenship, which states could not curtail even before the Fourteenth Amendment became law. Because the federal government has the "superior responsibility" for preserving government, it also has the "superior right" to determine whether the national interest requires the suppression of free speech about governmental affairs.[103] The "exclusiveness" of this federal power, Brandeis stressed, "springs from the very roots of political sovereignty." "The States may not punish treason against the United States," Brandeis pointed out while citing two early state court decisions, "although indirectly acts of treason may affect them vitally. No more may they arrogate to themselves authority to punish the teaching of pacifism which the legislature of Minnesota appears to have put into that category."[104]

Although Brandeis based his 1920 dissent in *Gilbert* on the exclusive federal power to regulate discussion of federal functions, he concluded his opinion with an impassioned plea for extending the substantive due process right of the Fourteenth Amendment beyond the "liberty to acquire and to enjoy property." Brandeis had difficulty believing that the constitutional guarantee of liberty, which the Supreme Court had repeatedly invoked to protect businessmen against restrictive legislation, "does not include liberty to teach, either in the privacy of the home or publicly, the doctrine of pacifism; so long, at least, as Congress has not declared that the public safety demands its suppression."[105] In a conversation with Frankfurter in 1924, Brandeis, reflecting his progressive background, expressed his dislike for substantive due process in any context. Brandeis also maintained, however, that substantive due process, if used at all, should apply to "fundamental rights," including speech, as well as to property.[106] In the 1925 *Gitlow* case, the full Court agreed that free speech is one of the fundamental liberties protected by the due process clause,[107] and Brandeis later reinforced this holding in *Whitney*. "The power of the courts to

---

[103] 254 U.S. at 336–38.   [104] Id. at 342–43.
[105] Id. at 343.
[106] Brandeis-Frankfurter Conversations, supra note 81, at 20–21.
[107] 268 U.S. at 666 (majority), 672 (dissent).

strike down an offending law," he concluded, "is no less when the interests involved are not property rights, but the fundamental personal rights of free speech and assembly."[108]

Throughout his First Amendment opinions in the 1920s, Brandeis harnessed his technical discussion of legal doctrine to his fundamental belief in the power of rational thought in democratic decision making. In the last of these opinions, his stirring 1927 concurrence in *Whitney v. California,* he combined analytic brilliance with emotional power to create what is probably the most effective judicial interpretation of the First Amendment ever written. Brandeis recognized individual as well as social interests in free speech and viewed them as largely reciprocal. In *Whitney,* Brandeis attributed the personal qualities he admired and considered essential in a democratic society to the people "who won our independence." He described them as "courageous self-reliant men, with confidence in the power of free and fearless reasoning applied through the processes of popular government."[109] In language that closely resembled the passage that Chafee described as "key" in his own work, Brandeis stressed their belief that "freedom to think as you will and to speak as you think are means indispensable to the discovery and spread of political truth." The founding generation, Brandeis added, was convinced that "the greatest menace to freedom is an inert people" and that "public discussion is a political duty."[110] Expressing a similar thought in *Gilbert,* Brandeis described a citizen's exercise of free speech as a duty as well as a right because it is even "more important to the Nation than it is to himself."[111]

The framers guaranteed free speech and assembly in the First Amendment, Brandeis maintained in *Whitney,* because they recognized "the occasional tyrannies of governing majorities."[112] He had made this point without invoking the framers in his initial *Schaefer* dissent, warning that "an intolerant majority, swayed by passion or by fear, may be prone in the future, as it has often been in the past, to stamp as disloyal opinions with which it disagrees."[113] Brandeis tied his concern for minority rights to his underlying emphasis on the role of speech in a democracy, where "the deliberative forces should prevail over the arbitrary."[114] "In frank expression of conflicting opinion," he asserted in *Gilbert,* "lies the greatest promise of wisdom in governmental action; and in suppression lies ordinarily the greatest peril."[115] Claiming again in *Whitney* to

[108] 274 U.S. at 374.
[110] Id. at 375.
[112] 274 U.S. at 376.
[114] Whitney, 274 U.S. at 375.

[109] Id. at 377.
[111] 254 U.S. at 338.
[113] 251 U.S. at 495.
[115] 254 U.S. at 338.

speak for the founding generation, Brandeis asserted "that it is hazardous to discourage thought, hope and imagination; that fear breeds repression; that repression breeds hate; that hate menaces stable government; that the path of safety lies in the opportunity to discuss freely supposed grievances and proposed remedies; and that the fitting remedy for evil counsels is good ones."[116]

Brandeis acknowledged that a real emergency can justify the repression of speech when there is not time to "permit reliance upon the slower conquest of error by truth."[117] But "unless the incidence of the evil apprehended is so imminent that it may befall before there is opportunity for full discussion" and so dangerous that it threatens "serious injury to the State,"[118] whether "political, economic, or moral,"[119] Brandeis maintained that the proper deterrents to crime "are education and punishment for violations of the law, not abridgement of the rights of free speech and assembly."[120] As long as there is time to expose falsehood through discussion, he insisted, "the remedy to be applied is more speech, not enforced silence."[121] Moreover, Brandeis stressed that not all perceived emergencies are serious or even rational. "Men feared witches and burnt women," he tersely observed.[122]

For all his emphasis on the contributions individual free speech makes to democratic governance, Brandeis also believed that a democratic state has obligations to promote individuality, including its expression through free speech, as an end in itself. Still invoking the founding generation but sounding more like John Dewey, Brandeis stressed that "the final end of the State was to make men free to develop their faculties." After referring to the burning of women as witches, Brandeis identified "the function of speech to free men from the bondage of irrational fears."[123] Extensive freedom of speech, Brandeis confidently maintained, would produce the reciprocal relationship between individuals and the state that fulfills the highest purposes of a democracy. By developing the human potential of its citizens, the state would enable them to participate effectively in rational public deliberation.[124]

---

[116] 274 U.S. at 375.   [117] Gilbert, 254 U.S. at 338.
[118] Whitney, 274 U.S. 337–38.   [119] Id. at 373.
[120] Id. at 378.   [121] Id. at 337.
[122] Id. at 376.   [123] Id. at 375–76.

[124] Legal scholars have used phrases such as *deliberative political process, civic virtue,* and *civic courage* to capture this aspect of Brandeis's thought. Compare Vincent Blasi, The First Amendment and the Ideal of Civic Courage: The Brandeis opinion in Whitney v. California, 29 William and Mary L. Rev. 653 (1988); Cover, supra note 49, at 380 ("deliberative political process"); Pnina Lahav, Holmes and Brandeis: Libertarian and Republican Justifications for Free Speech, 4 J. Law and Politics 451, 453 (1988) ("civic virtue").

Dewey associated his own postwar views with the First Amendment opinions by Holmes and Brandeis from *Abrams* through *Whitney*. He admired both justices "for their sturdy defense of civil liberties but even more for the fact that they based their defense on the indispensable value of free inquiry and free discussion to the normal development of public welfare, not upon anything inherent in the individual as such."[125] Yet Dewey seemed to recognize the differences between the two justices. He commended Holmes's dissent in *Abrams* for appreciating the "experimental character of life and thought" and for its "impatience with the attempt to settle matters of social policy by dialectic reasoning from fixed concepts." Dewey, however, also expressed concern that "[a]t times" Holmes's "realism seems almost to amount to a belief that whatever wins out in fair combat, in the struggle for existence, is therefore the fit, the good, and the true."[126] Dewey wrote more approvingly of Brandeis, praising him for themes that Dewey proclaimed throughout his own works. Brandeis's ideal of free individuals in a democracy, Dewey emphasized, "has to do with the development, the *making*, of individuals; it does not assume their ready-made existence." Brandeis also recognized that "many things which have been justified on the basis of 'rugged individualism' are to be condemned as hostile to the *development* of free individuals."[127] In discussing Brandeis, Dewey captured their continuing shared commitment to core themes of progressive social thought.

THE JUDICIAL TRANSFORMATION OF THE FIRST AMENDMENT

While never matching the rhetoric of Holmes in *Abrams* or Brandeis in *Whitney*, the Supreme Court majority, after a long and uneven history, has now accepted, and has in some ways moved beyond, the protective interpretations of the First Amendment advanced by scholars before World War I and by Hand, Chafee, Holmes, and Brandeis in the decade following the Espionage Act of 1917. In the process, the Court has reversed or implicitly overruled many of the restrictive prewar decisions. For example, in *Brandenburg v. Ohio*, the 1969 case considered by many current commentators to be the culmination of the "worthy tradition" begun by Holmes and Brandeis, the Court's unanimous opinion simply observed without explana-

---

[125] John Dewey, Liberalism and Civil Liberties (1936), reprinted in 11 John Dewey, The Later Works 1925–1953, at 372, 374 (Jo Ann Boydston ed., 1987).

[126] John Dewey, Justice Holmes and the Liberal Mind (1928), reprinted in 3 John Dewey, The Later Works 1925–1953, at 177, 180, 182 (Jo Ann Boydston ed., 1984).

[127] John Dewey, Book Review, Mr. Justice Brandeis, 33 Colum. L. Rev. 175, 176 (1933).

tion that "*Whitney* has been thoroughly discredited by later decisions."[128] When the Supreme Court extended the protection of the
First Amendment to movies in 1952, it announced that its contrary
1915 decision in *Mutual Film* was "out of harmony" with its new reasoning and would no longer be followed.[129] The Court in 1957 similarly rejected the longstanding *Hicklin* test of obscenity "as unconstitutionally restrictive of speech and press" because it "might well
encompass material legitimately treating with sex."[130] In a landmark
1964 decision, which dramatically transformed the constitutional
interpretation of free speech by subjecting the law of libel to First
Amendment constraints, Justice Brennan acknowledged that the
Court's new standard would have required different results in many
libel cases before World War I. But Brennan cited approvingly and
at length the atypical 1908 decision by the Supreme Court of
Kansas in *Coleman v. MacLennan* to support his view that the First
Amendment "prohibits a public official from recovering damages
for a defamatory falsehood relating to his official conduct unless he
proves that the statement was made with 'actual malice' – that is,
with knowledge that it was false or with reckless disregard of
whether it was false or not."[131]

In other cases, the Supreme Court was less explicit about its
deviations from prewar decisions. The Court asserted in 1939 that
the streets and parks "have immemorially been held in trust for
the use of the public and, time out of mind, have been used for
purposes of assembly, communicating thoughts between citizens,
and discussing public questions." The use of these public places
for speech and assembly, the Court maintained, "has from ancient
times, been a part of the privileges, immunities, rights, and liberties of citizens."[132] This statement would have surprised many
socialists, Wobblies, and members of the Salvation Army before
World War I. As Justice Butler correctly pointed out in his dissent,
the majority's assertion was precisely the claim the Supreme Court,
affirming Holmes's reasoning for the Massachusetts court,
rejected in the 1896 *Davis* case.[133] Yet the majority in *Hague,* after
unconvincingly trying to distinguish the statute in *Davis* as "not
directed solely at the exercise of speech and assembly," stated summarily that *Hague* presented "no occasion to determine" whether
Davis was correctly decided.[134] Other dissenting opinions cited

[128] 395 U.S. at 447.
[129] Joseph Burstyn, Inc. v. Wilson, 343 U.S. 495, 501–2 (1952).
[130] Roth v. United States, 354 U.S. 476, 489 (1957).
[131] New York Times Co. v. Sullivan, 376 U.S. 254, 278–82 (1964).
[132] Hague v. C.I.O., 307 U.S. 496, 515 (1939).
[133] Id. at 533.   [134] Id. at 515.

prewar cases while objecting to increased First Amendment protection. When the Supreme Court in 1948 overturned a law that prohibited the sale of publications devoted to criminal news or to stories of bloodshed and lust, Justice Frankfurter dissented, observing accurately that in 1900 the Supreme Court of Connecticut had upheld virtually identical legislation.[135]

The relatively few occasions when the Supreme Court continues to rely on prewar cases provide a useful index of the extent to which it had decided not to adopt a more protective interpretation of the First Amendment. In twice upholding the federal Hatch Act, which bars civil servants from participating in political campaigns, the Court cited comparable restrictions upheld by *Ex parte Curtis* in 1882.[136] In denying that "contemporary community standards" is too vague as the test of obscenity, the Court in 1973 cited the 1912 case, *Fox v. Washington.*[137] And in its 1972 decision sustaining the exclusion of a Belgian Marxist professor who had been invited to visit several American universities, the Court cited *Turner v. Williams,* its 1904 decision expelling a British journalist lecturing about anarchism.[138]

Given the often tortured efforts of Chafee, Holmes, and Brandeis to promote clear and present danger as the legal formula for their free speech values, it is ironic that the initial Supreme Court decisions protecting speech never mentioned this phrase. *Fiske v. Kansas,* decided the same day as *Whitney* in 1927, was the first case in which the Supreme Court majority recognized the free speech claim of a radical defendant. The Supreme Court of Kansas had reasoned that by endorsing the admittedly "equivocal language" of the preamble to the IWW constitution, an IWW organizer provided sufficient evidence for a jury to conclude that he violated the Kansas syndicalism act. The U.S. Supreme Court unanimously reversed. Inferring advocacy of criminal syndicalism from the IWW preamble, Justice Sanford's opinion concluded, was "an arbitrary and unreasonable exercise of the police power of the State, unwarrantably infringing the liberty of the defendant in violation of the due process clause of the Fourteenth Amendment."[139] Sanford asserted without elaboration that the preamble was "essen-

---

135 Winters v. New York, 333 U.S. 507, 531–32 (1948).
136 United States Civil Serv. Comm'n v. National Ass'n of Letter Carriers, 413 U.S. 548, 554–55 (1973); United Public Workers v. Mitchell, 330 U.S. 75, 96–98 (1947), citing Ex parte Curtis, 106 U.S. 371 (1882).
137 Miller v. California, 413 U.S. 15, 28 n.10 (1973), citing Fox v. Washington, 236 U.S. 273 (1915).
138 Kleindienst v. Mandel, 408 U.S. 753, 762 (1972), citing Turner v. Williams, 194 U.S. 279 (1904).

tially different"[140] from the manifesto that provided the basis for
Gitlow's conviction under the New York criminal anarchy law,
which the Supreme Court had sustained two years earlier.
Although the Supreme Court in *Gitlow* had held for the first time
that the rights protected by the First Amendment "are among the
fundamental personal rights and 'liberties' protected by the due
process clause of the Fourteenth Amendment from impairment by
the States,"[141] Justice Sanford's opinion in Fiske did not refer
explicitly to the First Amendment.

Three important decisions by Chief Justice Hughes in the 1930s
relied more directly on the incorporation of the First Amendment
into the Fourteenth while recognizing free speech claims. Writing
in 1931 for the Court majority in *Stromberg v. California,* Hughes
invalidated a California law that prohibited the display of flags or
other devices "as a sign, symbol or emblem of opposition to organized government." He identified the "maintenance of the opportunity for free political discussion" as "a fundamental principle of
our constitutional system." The California statute, Hughes concluded, unconstitutionally permitted punishment for exercising
this opportunity. Citing *Fiske* as well as *Gitlow* and *Whitney,* Hughes
reiterated that "the conception of liberty under the due process
clause of the Fourteenth Amendment embraces the right of free
speech."[142] The next month, in *Near v. Minnesota,* Hughes similarly
relied on "the liberty of the press guaranteed by the Fourteenth
Amendment"[143] to invalidate a Minnesota statute that permitted
injunctions against "malicious, scandalous, and defamatory" publications. Hughes stressed that preventing prior restraints was the
chief historical purpose behind the constitutional protection of
the press.[144] Six years later, in *De Jonge v. Oregon,*[145] Hughes wrote
for a unanimous Court that the application of the state criminal
syndicalism law to a meeting of the Communist Party violated the
rights of free speech and peaceable assembly guaranteed against
state infringement by the due process clause of the Fourteenth
Amendment. Hughes did not mention the clear and present danger test in any of these decisions, but he frequently reiterated the
distinction between legal speech and unlawful incitements that
formed the basis for Hand's analysis in *Masses.*

From the late 1930s through the early 1950s, many Supreme

---

[139] Fiske v. Kansas, 274 U.S. 380, 387 (1927).
[140] Id. at 386.
[141] Gitlow v. New York, 268 U.S. 652, 666 (1925).
[142] Stromberg v. California, 283 U.S. 359, 368–69 (1931).
[143] Near v. Minnesota, 283 U.S. 697, 723 (1931).
[144] Id. at 713.   [145] 299 U.S. 353 (1937).

Court opinions revived and expanded the scope of the clear and present danger test. *Herndon v. Lowry*, a 1937 decision reversing the conviction of a Communist Party organizer who had been attempting to recruit Southern blacks, marked the reappearance of clear and present danger. Justice Roberts's opinion for a bare majority, after unconvincingly attempting to distinguish *Gitlow*, applied a rigorous definition of the clear and present danger test to reject, for the first time in the history of Supreme Court adjudication, the bad tendency theory that had frequently provided the rationale for restrictive free speech decisions both before and after World War I. The state statute defining insurrection, the opinion observed, did not "furnish a sufficiently ascertainable standard of guilt" to enable the judge and jury to "appraise the circumstances and character of the defendant's utterances or activities as begetting a clear and present danger of forcible obstruction of a particular state function."[146] As a result, a speaker, "however peaceful his own intent," may be punished because a jury concludes that speech attacking social conditions or advocating a change in government "might, in the distant future" lead to the use of force. The Court rejected this "vague and indeterminate" standard of "dangerous tendency" as an unconstitutional "dragnet" that violates freedom of speech.[147] Without explicitly acknowledging its doctrinal innovation, the Supreme Court majority in *Herndon* accepted as a constitutional rule the protective interpretation of clear and present danger initially set forth by Chafee in "Freedom of Speech in War Time" and promoted only by Holmes and Brandeis from *Abrams* through *Whitney*. It is ironic that Chafee himself was so concerned about the potential for racial warfare in the South that he thought the Supreme Court should have denied this free speech claim.[148]

In the fifteen years following *Herndon,* the Supreme Court majority frequently invoked the phrase *clear and present danger* to sustain free speech claims, often in very different contexts from its original use in cases involving subversive advocacy. The Court used this phrase to protect speakers punished for breaching the peace,[149] contempt of court,[150] peaceful picketing,[151] solicitation of

---

[146] Herndon v. Lowry, 301 U.S. 242, 255–58 (1937).

[147] Id. at 261–64.

[148] Jonathan Prude, Portrait of a Civil Libertarian: The Faith and Fear of Zechariah Chafee, Jr., 60 J. Am. Hist. 633, 645 (1973).

[149] Terminiello v. City of Chicago, 337 U.S. 1, 4 (1949); Cantwell v. Connecticut, 310 U.S. 296, 309–11 (1940).

[150] Craig v. Harney, 331 U.S. 367, 378 (1947); Pennekamp v. Florida, 328 U.S. 331, 336, 347–50 (1946); Bridges v. California, 314 U.S. 252, 262–63, 273 (1941).

[151] Thornhill v. Alabama, 310 U.S. 88, 104–5 (1940).

union members,[152] and failure to salute the American flag.[153] Ignoring the majority's distinction in *Gitlow*, the Court applied the clear and present danger test to statutes punishing advocacy as well as to statutes punishing acts. Most strikingly, the Court twice used the clear and present danger test to reverse convictions of opponents of World War II whose appeals could easily have been denied according to the standards employed by Justice Holmes in *Schenck*, *Frohwerk*, and *Debs*.[154]

Although Supreme Court opinions after *Herndon* frequently relied on the clear and present danger test to protect speech, the test was never consistently endorsed by a clear majority of the Supreme Court. Many majority decisions throughout this period upheld free speech claims without even mentioning clear and present danger.[155] Indeed, Justice Frankfurter, a close friend and associate of Justice Holmes, stressed that Holmes never intended clear and present danger "to express a technical legal doctrine or to convey a formula for adjudicating cases." It was instead, Frankfurter emphasized, "a literary phrase not to be distorted by being taken from its context."[156] On the other hand, through the 1940s none of the Supreme Court cases that rejected free speech claims referred to clear and present danger, except in an occasional dissent.[157] The phrase had become a useful, but never a necessary, route to a protective result. Restrictive decisions used other language.

At the height of the Cold War, the Supreme Court reverted to the restrictive interpretation of clear and present danger that marked its original formulation by Holmes in *Schenck*. In its 1951 decision, *Feiner v. New York*,[158] the Supreme Court employed clear and present danger to deny a free speech claim. *Dennis v. United States*,[159] decided later the same year, dramatically highlighted this reversion. *Dennis* is particularly significant because Learned Hand, who in the years immediately following World War I viewed his own decision in *Masses* as a compelling doctrinal alternative to

---

[152] Thomas v. Collins, 323 U.S. 516, 530, 536 (1945).

[153] West Virginia State Bd. of Educ. v. Barnette, 319 U.S. 624, 633, 639 (1943); Taylor v. Mississippi, 319 U.S. 583, 589–90 (1943).

[154] Hartzel v. United States, 322 U.S. 680, 687 (1944); Taylor v. Mississippi, 319 U.S. 583, 589–90 (1943).

[155] Martin M. Shapiro, Freedom of Speech: The Supreme Court and Judicial Review 58–60 (1966); Robert B. McKay, The Preference for Freedom, 34 N.Y.U. L. Rev. 1182, 1207–8 (1959); Wallace Mendelson, Clear and Present Danger – From Schenck to Dennis, 52 Colum. L. Rev. 313, 320, 324–26 (1952).

[156] Pennekamp v. Florida, 328 U.S. 331, 353 (1946) (Frankfurter, J., concurring).

[157] Mendelson, supra note 155, at 324.   [158] 340 U.S. 315, 320–21 (1951).

[159] 341 U.S. 494 (1951).

Holmes's clear and present danger test, wrote the Second Circuit opinion in *Dennis,* which the Supreme Court affirmed.

Upholding the conviction of eleven Communist Party leaders, Hand, in language quoted verbatim by Chief Justice Vinson in his plurality opinion for the Supreme Court, rephrased the clear and present danger test. According to Hand, judges must "ask whether the gravity of the 'evil,' discounted by its improbability, justifies such invasion of free speech as is necessary to avoid the danger."[160] Unlike Brandeis in *Whitney,* who maintained that the gravity of the evil should be considered only after its imminence had been demonstrated,[161] Hand "purposely substituted 'improbability' for 'remoteness'"[162] and used gravity as a "mutually interdependent" factor to be balanced against improbability, not as an independent test.[163] Justices Frankfurter and Jackson wrote separate concurrences in *Dennis,* upholding the convictions while criticizing the clear and present danger test.[164] Justices Black and Douglas each dissented, claiming that the plurality misconstrued the meaning of clear and present danger.[165]

The *Dennis* case marked both the apex and the turning point of the Supreme Court's reliance on the clear and present danger test. The phrase could no longer bear the pressure of the inconsistent interpretations placed on it by different justices. The opinions by Hand and Vinson made painfully clear to civil libertarians that clear and present danger was no longer a guaranteed route to a protective decision. Although subsequent Supreme Court opinions occasionally cited this test, it never again recaptured the prominence it had achieved in the fifteen years between *Herndon* and *Dennis.* The Warren Court often upheld free speech claims through doctrines that did not focus directly on the dividing line between protected and unprotected speech.[166] Indeed, the Warren Court's decision not to apply the clear and present danger test, while holding that a judgment against the *New York Times* violated the First Amendment's repudiation of seditious libel, struck one astute commentator as a

---

[160] 183 F.2d 201, 212 (2d Cir. 1950), quoted in 341 U.S. at 510.

[161] 274 U.S. at 377–78.

[162] 183 F.2d at 212.

[163] Id. at 209.

[164] 341 U.S. at 570 (Jackson, J., concurring), 519, 542, 551 (Frankfurter, J., concurring).

[165] Id. at 585–90 (Douglas, J., dissenting), 579–80 (Black, J., dissenting).

[166] See Kent Greenawalt, Speech and Crime, 1980 Am. B. Found. Research J. 645, 721–22. See generally Gerald Gunther, Reflections on Robel: It's Not What the Court Did But the Way That It Did It, 20 Stan. L. Rev. 1140 (1968).

"conceptual revolution."[167] At the very least, *Dennis* and its aftermath signaled the failure of the attempt by Chafee, Holmes, and
Brandeis to make clear and present danger the constitutional
standard for a protective interpretation of the First Amendment.

Prosecutions after *Dennis* brought a renewed focus on the content of speech, the factor stressed by Hand in *Masses,* but largely
submerged in Supreme Court analysis since the opinions by Chief
Justice Hughes in the 1930s. In its 1969 decision, *Brandenburg v.
Ohio,*[168] the Warren Court seemed to join the most protective elements of the incitement and the clear and present danger standards as independent tests that must both be met before speech
can be punished.[169] The incitement standard, while protecting
advocacy short of incitement, did not preclude punishing incitements to future actions. The clear and present danger standard, as
long as it retained its immediacy requirement, protected remote
incitements but allowed the punishment of even abstract advocacy
if it produced a sufficient probability of harm. In *Whitney,* Brandeis
combined these two standards to require either the advocacy or
the likelihood of "immediate serious violence."[170] *Brandenburg*
went further by requiring both the advocacy and the likelihood of
"imminent lawless action." According to the Court in *Brandenburg,*
"the constitutional guarantees of free speech and free press do not
permit a State to forbid or proscribe advocacy of the use of force
or of law violation except where such advocacy is directed to inciting or producing imminent lawless action and is likely to incite or
produce such action."[171]

In many respects, the meaning of *Brandenburg* remains uncertain. No language in the per curiam opinion elaborated the single
sentence in which the Court announced its striking new standard.
Indeed, because this standard was neither accompanied by any
serious analysis nor necessary to the resolution of the case, one
thoughtful commentator has speculated that the Supreme Court
in *Brandenburg* might not have intended the literal meaning of its
own language.[172] In addition, the Court, even while relying on
Brandenburg, has not ever clarified its meaning. Commentators

---

[167] Harry Kalven, Jr., The New York Times Case: A Note on "The Central Meaning
Of The First Amendment," 1964 Sup. Ct. Rev. 191, 221 n.124.
[168] 395 U.S. 444 (1969) (per curiam).
[169] Gunther, supra note 29, at 754–55, was the first to stress this protective combination. See also Thomas I. Emerson, First Amendment Doctrine and the
Burger Court, 68 Calif. L. Rev. 422, 445–46 (1980); Comment, Brandenburg
v. Ohio: A Speech Test for All Seasons?, 43 U. Chi. L. Rev. 151, 159–60 (1975).
[170] 274 U.S. at 376.   [171] 395 U.S. at 447.
[172] Greenawalt, supra note 166, at 650.

question whether it can be applied outside the context of advocacy of illegal activity.[173] Even within this context, the Supreme Court has not addressed important distinctions between different kinds of advocacy. For example, there are compelling reasons rooted in First Amendment theory for affording more constitutional protection to "public ideological solicitation" than to "private nonideological solicitation." Advocating robbery or murder for private gain surely stands on a different constitutional footing than does advocating principled resistance to politically unpopular government policies.[174]

Substantial doubts can more generally be raised as to whether any constitutional standard, however protective its language, can safeguard free speech in times of crisis. The Supreme Court failed to uphold First Amendment values during the two greatest threats to free speech in the twentieth century. Restrictive Supreme Court decisions construing the Espionage Act of 1917 during the "Red Scare" following World War I and the Smith Act during the early 1950s, at the height of the virulent anticommunism personified by Senator Joseph McCarthy, promote understandable skepticism about the ability of the judiciary to withstand periods of national hysteria. This historical record makes it tempting to attribute the apparently more protective language of the *Brandenburg* standard and its subsequent reiterations to a time of greater popular acceptance of freedom of expression, perhaps produced by substantial support for or toleration of the civil rights and antiwar movements of the 1960s. It is easy to doubt the efficacy of this standard during possible future outbreaks of widespread hostility to dissenters.

The Supreme Court's failure to protect free speech during prior periods of crisis, however, can be attributed to the weaknesses of inherited legal standards as well as to judicial capitulation to national hysteria. Holmes's opinions in the first Espionage Act cases, and the majority decisions in free speech cases through-

---

[173] See, e.g., id. at 785. See generally William W. Van Alstyne, A Graphic Review of the Free Speech Clause, 70 Calif. L. Rev. 107, 110, 150 (1982). One commentator has extended the applications of the Brandenburg standard to various institutional settings, Comment, supra note 169, at 165–91, but even this limited extension has been criticized. See, e.g., Emerson, supra note 169, at 438; Greenawalt, supra note 166, at 782–83.

[174] The phrases in quotations are borrowed from Greenawalt, supra note 166, at 748–62. Greenawalt's comprehensive article contains numerous useful refinements of the Brandenburg test based on a close analysis of First Amendment principles. His analysis indicates how many important issues remain unresolved. Pages 647–53 and 783–85 provide an overview of Greenawalt's major themes and conclusions. See Van Alstyne, supra note 173, at 139–42.

out the 1920s, continued to rely on the restrictive bad tendency theory that had characterized Supreme Court decisions before World War I. The clear and present danger test, although it had been used to reach protective results, originated in Holmes's antilibertarian Social Darwinism. Its restrictive implications were noticed almost immediately by Hand and Chafee, and its weaknesses as a general analytic standard were emphasized before *Dennis* by Justice Frankfurter[175] and by eminent scholars such as Paul Freund,[176] Alexander Meiklejohn,[177] and Herbert Wechsler.[178] It is intriguing to consider whether the prior development of a more protective and less manipulable standard – the *Brandenburg* test, for example – might have produced different results in 1919 or 1951. It is also unclear whether the *Brandenburg* test, generally considered to be the most protective standard for free speech adjudication ever developed by the Supreme Court,[179] will actually shield freedom of expression against future intolerance. Only judicial construction during the next "Red Scare" or "McCarthy period" will reveal the extent to which this relatively protective test can induce judges to uphold free speech values in times of crisis.

[175] See, e.g., Pennekamp v. Florida, 328 U.S. at 353 (Frankfurter, J., concurring).
[176] Paul Freund, On Understanding the Supreme Court 27 (1949).
[177] Meiklejohn, supra note 30, at 28–50.
[178] Herbert Wechsler, Symposium on Civil Liberties, 9 Am. L. Sch. Rev. 881, 887 (1941), reprinted in Selected Essays on Constitutional Law, 1938–1962, at 628, 634 (Edward L. Barrett, Jr., 1963).
[179] See, e.g., Greenawalt, supra note 166, at 723–24; Gunther, supra note 29, at 754–55; Harry Kalven, Jr., Professor Ernst Freund and Debs v. United States, 40 U. Chi. L. Rev. 235, 236 n.6 (1973); Comment, supra note 169, at 159–60; see also Emerson, supra note 169, at 437.

9

Epilogue: Current Parallels
to Prewar Progressive Thought

Increasing skepticism about the value of broad free speech rights constitutes the most striking development in First Amendment analysis in the generation since *Brandenburg*. Some of this skepticism has come from conservative scholars, such as Walter Berns and Robert Bork, and from the probing philosophical analysis of Frederick Schauer.[1] The primary attack on recent Supreme Court decisions recognizing First Amendment claims, however, has come from the politically committed left. Much of this attack bears strong, although largely unacknowledged, parallels to arguments made by progressive intellectuals in the decade immediately preceding World War I.[2]

Irony abounds in this development. Throughout American history, the political left typically advocated greater protection for speech. Many on the left generated principled defenses of free speech, but they also had practical grounds for their theoretical views. As early as the American colonists opposing British rule, the American sympathizers with the French Revolution, and the abolitionist publicists against slavery, supporters of free speech have been advocates of social and political change seeking protected communication of their views. In the period between the Civil War and World War I, sex radicals, anarchists, socialists, and labor unions provoked a high proportion of the free speech controversies. From the opponents of World War I, whose convictions produced the famous dissents by Holmes and Brandeis, through the union organizers of the 1930s, the people accused of disloyalty

---

[1] Walter Berns, The First Amendment and the Future of American Democracy 188–228 (1976); Robert Bork, Neutral Principles and Some First Amendment Problems, 47 Ind. L.J. 1 (1971); Frederick Schauer, Free Speech: A Philosophical Enquiry (1982).

[2] Eldon J. Eisenach, The Lost Promise of Progressivism 205 (1994), observes more broadly that recent critiques of the emphasis on rights in liberal political philosophy are "conducted in happy ignorance" of the analogous attack on rights by progressives between 1885 and World War I.

and subversion during the McCarthy period of the late 1940s and 1950s, and the activists for civil rights and against American involvement in Vietnam in the 1960s, many free speech claimants were liberals or radicals who were prosecuted for unpopular speech. Unpopular free speech claimants also included Jehovah's Witnesses in the 1930s and 1940s,[3] members of the Ku Klux Klan in the 1960s,[4] and neo-Nazis in the 1970s.[5] Most people on the left, however, recognized that the legitimacy of their own theoretical and practical positions depended on their support of free speech for all viewpoints. In an attempt to demonstrate the political neutrality of its free speech principles, the liberal Supreme Court might have deliberately chosen *Brandenburg*, a case that overturned the conviction of a Ku Klux Klan leader, as the vehicle for its most protective interpretation of the First Amendment.

Since *Brandenburg*, however, scholars on the left have focused relatively little attention on its doctrinal implications or on whether its substantial constitutional protection for dissenting speech could survive another Red Scare or McCarthy Era. Instead, they have stressed that the issue of subversive advocacy, which was at the center of First Amendment analysis from the Espionage Act decisions through *Brandenburg*, no longer dominates litigation over free speech. While appreciating the "worthy tradition"[6] that culminated in *Brandenburg* as historically valuable, they have emphasized that the typical free speech claimant has changed dramatically in the past two decades. They worry that the First Amendment, rather than protecting unpopular dissenters from a repressive state, is now being invoked by rich individuals and corporations seeking to reverse laws that limit financial support of political candidates, by owners of the mass media resisting public rights of access, by racist speakers attacking the weakest members of society, and by pornographers degrading and exploiting women and children.[7]

---

[3] See Cantwell v. Connecticut, 310 U.S. 296 (1940); Lovell v. City of Griffin, 303 U.S. 444 (1938).

[4] See Brandenburg v. Ohio, 395 U.S. 444 (1969).

[5] See Collin v. Smith, 578 F.2d 1197 (7th Cir.), cert. denied, 439 U.S. 916 (1978).

[6] Harry Kalven, Jr., A Worthy Tradition: Freedom of Speech in America (Jamie Kalven ed., 1988).

[7] See Mark A. Graber, Transforming Free Speech: The Ambiguous Legacy of Civil Libertarianism 187–215 (1991); Cass R. Sunstein, Democracy and the Problem of Free Speech 2–3 (1993); J. M. Balkin, Some Realism About Pluralism: Legal Realist Approaches to the First Amendment, 1990 Duke L.J. 375, 387; Owen M. Fiss, Free Speech and Social Structure, 71 Iowa L. Rev. 1405, 1410–11 (1986); Morton J. Horwitz, Forward: The Constitution of Change: Legal Fundamentality Without Fundamentalism, 107 Harv. L. Rev. 32, 109–16 (1993).

In response to these developments, scholars of the First Amendment have joined a broader challenge to contemporary liberal theory and to its manifestations in constitutional law. These critics object to the liberal claim that autonomous individuals have antecedent rights against the state. They emphasize instead that individuals are interdependent and that social interests should define and limit individual rights. They are confident that benevolent government action can create a better and more harmonious society. First Amendment scholars have extended the general critique of liberal autonomy to the specific issue of free speech. The Supreme Court's current recognition of the First Amendment as a right of individuals to speak without interference from the state, these scholars observe, resembles its discredited reliance before the New Deal on individual economic rights under the Fourteenth Amendment as a barrier to progressive social legislation. They protest that the formal equality of individual constitutional rights has in both situations produced substantive inequality in practice.

These scholars, however, seem essentially unaware that progressive intellectuals before World War I had already expressed many similar criticisms of liberal thought. Neglecting the past has produced several unfortunate consequences. Instead of building on the work of prior eminent thinkers, scholars are reinventing earlier arguments in formulations that often lack the intellectual depth and subtlety of their predecessors. The connection between comprehensive social theory and legal analysis, revealed most clearly in Roscoe Pound's derivation of sociological jurisprudence from philosophical pragmatism, seems largely absent from current critiques of First Amendment doctrine. For example, these critiques contain no counterpart to the ways in which progressive intellectuals analyzed the social construction of individual rights as part of their general theory about the relationship between the individual and society.

It is perhaps more significant that historical insensitivity has prevented current scholars from appreciating the impact of World War I on progressive social thought. Government repression of civil liberties during and after the war forced many progressives to reevaluate their prewar confidence in benevolent state action and to emphasize both the individual and the social value of the constitutional right to free speech. While retaining their essential objections to liberal individualism, progressives after the war integrated more realism about the dangers of an activist state and about the importance of constitutionally protected rights into their thought. Current scholars urging new interpretations of the First Amendment, although more explicit about these dangers than the prewar progressives, minimize them to an extent that was impossible for most intellectuals who lived through World War I. Uninfluenced by either the social thought or the transformative experiences of the progressive intellectuals, current scholars seem more unsophisticated in their assumptions and more conclusory in their reasoning even as they raise legitimate doubts about modern First Amendment doctrine.

The book published by Michael J. Sandel in 1982, *Liberalism and the Limits of Justice,* may be the first and most important recent philosophical attack on contemporary liberalism. Sandel challenges "a version of liberalism prominent in the moral and legal and political philosophy of the day: a liberalism in which the notions of justice, fairness, and individual rights play a central role." This liberalism "asserts the priority of the right over the good."[8] It claims that "'the rights secured by justice are not subject to the calculus of social interests', but instead 'function as trump cards held by individuals' against policies that would impose some particular vision of the good on society as a whole."[9] It also claims that individuals are "always antecedent to any conditions." The conception of an "antecedently individual subject, the bounds of whose self are fixed prior to experience," rejects the possibility that visions of common purposes and goods within a broader community could constitute one's individual identity.[10]

By contrast, Sandel believes that individuals "conceive their identity . . . as defined to some extent by the community of which they are a part." "To imagine a person incapable of constitutive attachments" based on family, community, nation, or people, Sandel asserts, "is not to conceive an ideally free and rational agent, but to imagine a person wholly without character, without moral depth." According to Sandel, an individual cannot exist outside of history, a history one shares with others. He closes his book by invoking "the possibility that when politics goes well, we can know a good in common that we cannot know alone."[11]

In a book written for a more popular audience, Mary Ann Glendon raises similar concerns about liberal individualism while focusing on how "rights talk" has led to "the impoverishment of political discourse" in the United States. Acknowledging her debt to Sandel, Glendon objects that American constitutional law, reflecting liberal theory, pays "extraordinary homage to independence and self-suffi-

---

[8] Michael J. Sandel, Liberalism and the Limits of Justice 1 (1982).

[9] Id. at 9 [quoting John Rawls, A Theory of Justice 4 (1971) and Ronald Dworkin, Liberalism, in Public and Private Morality 113, 136 (Stuart Hampshire ed., 1978)].

[10] Id. at 10, 55, 62–65.   [11] Id. at 150, 179, 181, 183.

ciency, based on an image of the rights-bearer as a self-determin-
ing, unencumbered individual, a being connected to others only by
choice." This image, she observes, entails a "corresponding neglect
of the social dimensions of human personality." Glendon complains that American "rights talk," in contrast to conceptions of
rights in other countries, is characterized by "its legalistic character,
its exaggerated absoluteness, its hyperindividualism, its insularity,
and its silence with respect to personal, civic, and collective responsibilities." American rhetoric about rights, she believes, "heightens
social conflict, and inhibits dialogue that might lead to consensus,
accommodation, or at least the discovery of common ground."
Although Glendon contends that the distinctive form of "rights
talk" to which she objects has become dominant in the United
States only in the last thirty years,[12] Chafee used similar language in
his 1919 article while complaining about "the great evil of all this
talk about rights."[13] Glendon's themes echo the prewar progressives who asserted that the exaggerated place of individual rights in
traditional American social thought posed barriers to the welfare
and harmony of the entire community. She even writes, as did
Dewey, about the value of heterogeneity and the importance of
education in producing democratic character.[14]

Neither Sandel nor Glendon focuses on the issue of free
speech. Several important books and articles written in the last
decade, however, criticize the Supreme Court's current protection
of free speech rights in ways that resemble the attacks made by
prewar progressives on the Court's protection of economic rights.
Some of these authors, who generally write from the perspective of
the political left, felt compelled to explain in personal terms their
own departures from the traditional leftist support of constitutional free speech. Owen Fiss reports that he first realized in the
1970s how thoroughly economic power corrupted politics. He was
"startled" to discover that in Supreme Court cases involving the
relationship between economic and political power, "[c]apitalism
almost always won." He eventually became convinced that judicial
precedents protecting free speech rights were largely responsible
for these unfortunate results and concluded that existing doctrinal
interpretations were inadequate.[15] Jack Balkin similarly describes
the discomfort he felt in the 1980s when, at the request of the

[12] Mary A. Glendon, Rights Talk: The Impoverishment of Political Discourse x, 14,
   48, 109, 191 n.4 (1991).
[13] Zechariah Chafee, Jr., Freedom of Speech in War Time, 32 Harv. L. Rev. 932,
   957 (1919).
[14] Glendon, supra note 12, at xii, 126–27, 176.
[15] Fiss, supra note 7, at 1406–8.

ACLU, he defended the First Amendment right of the Ku Klux Klan to show racist propaganda on a local public access station. In contrast to the typical ACLU case, his opponent was a liberal city councilman who was a leader of the black community. Although Balkin initially identified content neutrality as the key issue, he ultimately saw the dispute as posing a conflict between "the need to ensure effective access to the means of communication for all points of view, including unpopular ones," and "the important state interest in eliminating racial discrimination and protecting racial minorities from harassment and abuse."[16]

The change in the paradigmatic free speech claimant since 1970, current scholars on the left assert, indicates parallels between free speech under the First Amendment today and property and liberty rights under the Fourteenth Amendment during the Progressive Era. Just as business interests then attempted to stretch as far as possible the definition of property and liberty entitled to substantive due process under the Fourteenth Amendment, their successors are now trying to bring more and more of their activities under the rubric of the First Amendment.[17] And just as Roscoe Pound observed in 1908 that "liberty of contract" under the Fourteenth Amendment "has given rise to rules and decisions which, tested by their practical operation, defeat liberty,"[18] current critics complain that the First Amendment doctrine of content neutrality has in many cases undermined the free speech of people who lack the economic power to purchase effective communication.[19] "The notion that protection of formal equality of economic liberty can lead to unacceptable degrees of substantive inequality," Balkin writes, "has been understood for many years; it should hardly be surprising, then, that a similar analysis applies to the liberty of expression."[20] Balkin and Morton Horwitz observe that liberty of contract and free speech, which both began as liberating doctrines, became coopted by conservatives and enforced by the Supreme Court to support inequality.[21] Horwitz appropriately quotes Dewey to capture this process,[22] and could easily have quoted Pound.

Critics of current First Amendment law more specifically high-

---

[16] Balkin, supra note 7, at 375–76, 428.
[17] See Balkin, supra note 7, at 384; Fiss, supra note 7, at 1408.
[18] Roscoe Pound, Mechanical Jurisprudence, 8 Colum. L. Rev. 605, 616 (1908).
[19] E.g., Sunstein, supra note 7, at 50, 178–79; Balkin, supra note 7, at 394–404; Fiss, supra note 7, at 1406–1408.
[20] Balkin, supra note 7, at 397–98.
[21] See id. at 392–93; Horwitz, supra note 7, at 109–10.
[22] Horwitz, supra note 7, at 110 & n.390.

light its parallels to the Supreme Court's 1905 landmark decision in *Lochner v. New York*.[23] *Lochner* relied on liberty of contract to invalidate a law that limited working hours and produced the memorable comment by Justice Holmes in dissent that "the Fourteenth Amendment does not enact Mr. Herbert Spencer's Social Statics."[24] Cass Sunstein views the Supreme Court's 1976 decision in *Buckley v. Valeo*,[25] which relied on the First Amendment to invalidate a law restricting campaign contributions, as "the modern-day analogue of the infamous and discredited" *Lochner* case. "Both cases," Sunstein observes, "accepted existing distributions of resources as prepolitical and just, and both cases invalidated democratic efforts at reform." The equal right of rich and poor to express themselves by spending money on political campaigns, Sunstein suggests, has as little meaning as the equal liberty of employers and employees to contract over working conditions.[26] Horwitz similarly perceives "the Lochnerization of the First Amendment" in the Supreme Court's application of content neutrality to hate speech, an "approach that substitutes the manipulation of neutral abstractions for making concrete value judgments."[27] The Court in *R.A.V. v. City of St. Paul*,[28] Horwitz complains, used a "mega-theory of 'content neutrality'" to ignore the social consequences of expression and shield "a rather concrete terrorist act of cross-burning on the lawn of a black family."[29]

The parallels between the "discredited" judicial analysis of the Fourteenth Amendment during the "*Lochner* era" and current judicial analysis of the First Amendment have prompted pleas for what Sunstein aptly calls "a New Deal for speech." The New Deal, Sunstein emphasizes, self-consciously rejected the laissez-faire ideology that stood as a barrier to government regulation of the economy. Supreme Court decisions upholding New Deal legislation produced a dramatic transformation of constitutional law.[30] As Fiss concisely observes, the Supreme Court legitimated the New Deal largely by overruling *Lochner*.[31] Commenting on the "obvious" parallel between the laissez-faire of the past and current legal analysis of free speech, Sunstein claims that in its First Amendment jurisprudence the Supreme Court "has failed precisely to the

---

[23] 198 U.S. 45 (1905).

[24] Id. at 75 (Holmes, J., dissenting).

[25] 424 U.S. 1 (1976).

[26] Sunstein, supra note 7, at 97–98.

[27] Horwitz, supra note 7, at 111, 112–13.

[28] 505 U.S. 377 (1992).

[29] Horwitz, supra note 7, at 114–15. Balkin and Fiss also observe analogies between the substantive due process of Lochner and current free speech doctrine. Balkin, supra note 7, at 419–20; Owen M. Fiss, Why the State?, 100 Harv. L. Rev. 781, 782 (1987).

[30] Sunstein, supra note 7, at xix, 17, 29.

[31] Fiss, supra note 29, at 782.

extent that it has not taken the New Deal reformation seriously enough."[32] Fiss similarly complains that the Supreme Court's interpretation of the First Amendment is hobbled by "the tenets of classical liberalism and its plea for limited government." Responding to free market theorists who "have confronted New Deal liberals with the free speech tradition in order to remind them of the virtues of laissez faire and to build a case against state intervention in economic matters," Fiss, like Sunstein and other critics of the First Amendment from the left, assumes the benefits of state regulation of the economy and argues as well for similar state regulation of speech.[33] Suggested areas for benevolent government regulation include public broadcasting, campaign financing, hate speech, and pornography.[34]

In attacking the invocation of First Amendment rights to protect actual inequality against legislation in the public interest and in viewing state regulation as a force for social good, current critics of First Amendment law employ the same arguments that progressives used against the liberal individualism that supported constitutional interpretation during the *Lochner* era. Fiss and Sunstein, exhibiting the hostility to claims of personal autonomy and individual rights previously expressed by progressive intellectuals, reject arguments for free speech based on these justifications and, like Pound before World War I, maintain that expression must be regulated in the democratic social interest.[35] Dewey's pragmatic skepticism about truth claims, faith in democratic participation within an activist state, and emphasis on education as the laboratory of democracy are all echoed in the assertion by Fiss that the state must "preserve the integrity of public debate – in much the same way as a great teacher – not to indoctrinate, not to advance the 'Truth,' but to safeguard the conditions for true and free collective self-determination."[36] Frank Michelman exceeds even Dewey at his most optimistic by "modestly proposing" that the "American aspiration to the ideal of deliberating democracy . . . is true in practice." Michelman defends state regulation of pornogra-

---

[32] Sunstein, supra note 7, at 29, 34.

[33] Fiss, supra note 7, at 1424; Fiss, supra note 29, at 783.

[34] Sunstein, supra note 7, at 88, 95, 193, 198, 225; Graber, supra note 7, at 233; Balkin, supra note 7, at 386, 429; Fiss, supra note 7, at 1415; Frank I. Michelman, Conceptions of Democracy in American Constitutional Argument: The Case of Pornography Regulation, 56 Tenn. L. Rev. 291 (1989).

[35] See, e.g., Sunstein, supra note 7, at xviii, 21, 142, 252; Fiss, supra note 7, at 1411, 1415.

[36] Fiss, supra note 7, at 1416.

phy by assuming that it can be based on "*deliberative* politics," a process by which citizens committed to equal authority and respect voluntarily accept social choices.[37]

Moreover, the frequent argument that changing social conditions require the revision of free speech doctrine[38] parallels Dewey's position that "ideas once true" may become "unfit, and therefore wrong."[39] Just as Dewey bemoaned the anachronistic survival of the individualistic spirit from the pioneer society of the distant past,[40] Fiss objects that current judicial interpretation of the First Amendment, which is based upon potential threats to individual autonomy, "presupposes a world that no longer exists and that is beyond our capacity to recall."[41] Graber similarly protests that First Amendment theorists continue to focus on the issue of subversive advocacy "in a world where the major threat to meaningful debate on matters of public importance in not that many are prevented from speaking but that many do not have the resources necessary to be heard."[42]

Sunstein is the contemporary First Amendment theorist who most closely resembles Dewey. The very title of his book, *Democracy and the Problem of Free Speech*, evokes Dewey's emphasis on the relationship between legal rules and democratic life. And just as Dewey believed that judicial interpretation of individual constitutional rights undermined meaningful democracy in an industrial society, Sunstein opens his book by asserting that "in light of astonishing economic and technological changes, we must now doubt whether, as interpreted, the constitutional guarantee of free speech is adequately serving democratic goals." Constantly invoking James Madison but thinking more like John Dewey, Sunstein emphasizes the dependence of deliberative democracy on education, discussion of public issues, and diversity of viewpoints. Although Sunstein claims to be a pragmatist, he only once associates pragmatism with Dewey, and even then links Dewey's version of pragmatism to "the Madisonian conception of free speech" that Sunstein unconvincingly cites throughout his book as the foundation of his own approach to the

---

[37] Michelman, supra note 34, at 293, 318–19.

[38] See, e.g., Sunstein, supra note 7, at 252; Balkin, supra note 7, at 430.

[39] John Dewey & James H. Tufts, Ethics (1908), reprinted in 10 John Dewey, The Middle Works 1899–1924, at 291 (Jo Ann Boydston ed., 1980).

[40] John Dewey, Schools of To-Morrow (1915), reprinted in 8 The Middle Works, at 314 (1979).

[41] Fiss, supra note 7, at 1425.

[42] Graber, supra note 7, at 200, 215.

First Amendment.[43] Other contemporary critics of the First Amendment seem not to recognize the many parallels between their own
views and progressive social thought.

Leftist critics of current First Amendment law, despite their
many affinities with the progressives before World War I, differ
from their predecessors in two important respects. They challenge
the individual right of free speech more directly, and they are
more explicit about the dangers posed by the activist state they
desire. Both of these differences are easily explicable. During the
Progressive Era, liberal individualism expressed itself primarily
through economic rights, such as property and contract. These
were the individual constitutional rights that the Supreme Court
protected through the Fourteenth Amendment and that stood as
a barrier to progressive social legislation. Progressive opposition to
individual rights extended to free speech, a conclusion best illustrated by Pound's application of his general analysis of social interests to speech and by Dewey's ridicule of radical dissenters during
World War I for relying on "platitudes" about "the sanctity of individual rights and constitutional guaranties."[44] Progressive thinkers,
however, understandably focused their attacks on the economic
rights they properly viewed as primarily responsible for the actual
inequalities produced by liberal individualism. The Supreme
Court weakened rights based on property and contract during the
New Deal. In subsequent decades, the Court has elevated free
speech to a "preferred position"[45] among constitutional rights
while extending First Amendment protection to the interests of
the rich and powerful. It is not surprising that critics of liberal
individualism in the late twentieth century have shifted their atten-

---

[43] Sunstein, supra note 7, at xi, 19, 22, 108, 112, 248. Despite his constant reitera-
tion of "the Madisonian conception" of free speech and the First Amendment,
Sunstein does not intensively analyze Madison's own writings or explore secondary literature about Madison. I fully agree with Jack Balkin's witty comment
that "Sunstein's 'Madisonian' theory of the First Amendment is about as Madisonian as Madison, Wisconsin: It is a tribute to a great man and his achievements, but bears only a limited connection to his actual views." J. M. Balkin,
Populism and Progressivism as Constitutional Categories, 104 Yale L.J. 1935,
1955 (1995). I also agree with Balkin that Sunstein probably invokes Madison
so frequently in an effort to rely on the authority of the Framers. Id. at 1954.

[44] John Dewey, Conscription of Thought (1917), reprinted in 10 John Dewey,
The Middle Works, supra note 39, at 276, 278–79.

[45] Justice Frankfurter's concurring opinion in Kovacs v. Cooper, 336 U.S. 77, 89,
96 (1949), usefully reviewed the development of the phrase *preferred position*
while objecting that "it expresses a complicated process of constitutional adjudication by a deceptive formula."

tion to the First Amendment in attacking the perversion of individual constitutional rights to support inequality.

Current critics of the First Amendment are also more self-conscious than the progressives were about the potential abuses of state power, even though they share the progressive belief that government can act benevolently by regulating individual rights in the social interest. The progressives opposed socialism and other forms of collectivism as threats to individuality, but they were extraordinarily optimistic that dramatically increased government regulation of individual rights would produce greater actual freedom and equality in a more harmonious society. They were largely oblivious to government repression of the speech of anarchists, workers, and sex radicals in the early years of the twentieth century. World War I and its repressive aftermath prompted disillusioned progressives to temper their confidence in the state and to recognize the importance of free speech and other civil liberties.

By contrast, current scholars are well aware of government threats to free speech during the McCarthy Era, the civil rights movement, and the Vietnam War. They recognize that the First Amendment jurisprudence they now criticize provided political dissenters, mostly on the left, with meaningful protection against the state. As a result, they acknowledge the "severe" and even "alarming"[46] risks in government regulation of speech, concessions that the progressives did not make before World War I about government regulation of individual rights. For example, Fiss admits that "the state does have some unique resources at its disposal, including a monopoly over the lawful means of violence." He realizes that under his proposals for increased government regulation of speech the judiciary is likely to have an "excruciating" burden in protecting legitimate First Amendment values against wrongful action by the state. Sunstein maintains that the judiciary must be particularly alert to the danger of abuse when government regulates "speech that might harm its own interests." Balkin admits that he "can't imagine a social context that would change so radically that the left would find it in its best interests to abandon completely its commitment to protecting the speech of unpopular groups." In fact, he concludes his article by reporting that even after he became concerned about the manipulation of the First Amendment to reinforce inequality, he still thought

---

[46] Sunstein, supra note 7, at 35; Fiss, supra note 7, at 1415.

the denial of public access to the Ku Klux Klan was "probably unconstitutional."[47]

The greater sensitivity of current scholars to the dangers of an activist state, however, has not prevented them from using progressive arguments to advocate increased government regulation of speech in the public interest. Fiss is most explicit in maintaining that the risks of state regulation, while real, are justified. The "hidden costs of an unrestricted regime of autonomy," he warns, may be significantly greater than the danger of government repression. According to Fiss, state restrictions on autonomy through regulations on the content of speech, "however elemental and repressive they might at first seem," can actually enrich public debate when the speaker is a television network or a wealthy political activist. The state, he repeatedly observes, can be a friend as well as an enemy of free speech.[48]

Current critics of First Amendment law further minimize the dangers of an activist state by emphasizing that the paradigmatic First Amendment claimant is now more likely to be a rich corporation or a powerful individual than a political dissenter. They often seem to suggest that state repression of speech was a legitimate historical concern, but is now an anachronistic diversion from the contemporary abuse of free speech rights to sustain inequality and subvert the public welfare. They treat the Supreme Court's doctrinal safeguards for unpopular speech, achieved after a long and uneven course from its first Espionage Act cases through its 1969 decision in *Brandenburg v. Ohio*,[49] much as the progressives regarded the Constitution: deserving of historical respect as a "worthy tradition," but irrelevant or even an obstacle to dealing with more pressing current concerns.[50]

I agree that the formal protection of abstract individual rights, when wrenched from social context, frequently yields results that reinforce inequality while preventing desirable social change. Just as the "liberty of contract" between an employer and an employee is significantly different from the "liberty of contract" of two farmers negotiating about the price of a horse,[51] the "freedom of speech" of a wealthy contributor to a political candidate is signifi-

---

[47] Fiss, supra note 29, at 787; Fiss, supra note 7, at 1420; Sunstein, supra note 7, at 134; Balkin, supra note 7, at 384, 428.

[48] Fiss, supra note 7, at 1415; Fiss, supra note 29, at 787.

[49] 395 U.S. 444 (1969).

[50] See, e.g., Graber, supra note 7, at 200–1; Fiss, supra note 7, at 1405–6.

[51] Roscoe Pound, Liberty of Contract, 18 Yale L.J. 454 (1909).

cantly different from the "freedom of speech" of an unpopular speaker criticizing government policy. Government regulations limiting the "right" to contract over maximum hours, like government regulations limiting the "right" to contribute more than maximum monetary sums, understandably have considerable appeal to people concerned about public welfare in a democracy.

As the progressives learned so painfully during and after World War I, however, even a democratic state may not act in the public interest, and individual rights, especially the right to free speech, may provide necessary safeguards against government power. It may be, as Sandel maintains, "that when politics goes well, we can know a good in common that we cannot know alone."[52] But when politics does not go well, and produces a Red Scare or a McCarthy Era or some other state enforcement of "political correctness," the right to free speech may serve important purposes for society as well as for individuals. Just as the prewar progressives seemed to assume that dissent would not be a problem in the harmonious participatory democracy they were confidently creating, many current critics of First Amendment law seem to assume that the protection of political dissenters is not a problem today. Yet even if the unpopular dissenter is no longer the paradigmatic free speech claimant, a proposition that many advocates would challenge, the explanation might be found in the protection afforded by some of the First Amendment theories and doctrines critics now attack.

We should be open to doctrinal innovation in the areas of concern to current critics of First Amendment law. But it is useful to remember that Dewey, chastened by the repression of speech during and after World War I, worried that political as well as economic power threatened people who criticized the status quo and advocated social change. Dewey and Brandeis were able to retain their critique of individualism and their insights into the social construction of individual rights even as they realized the importance of protecting free speech from an activist state. A commitment to an interdependent society devoted to equality – as the progressives who became postwar libertarians learned through bitter experience – can include an appreciation for the insights of Holmes in *Abrams* and especially Brandeis in *Whitney*. The experience of the progressives should at least make us wary of disparaging "rights talk" about freedom of speech and abandoning the "worthy" yet fragile First Amendment tradition that may be able to protect dissent in a democracy.

---

[52] Sandel, supra note 8, at 183.

Index